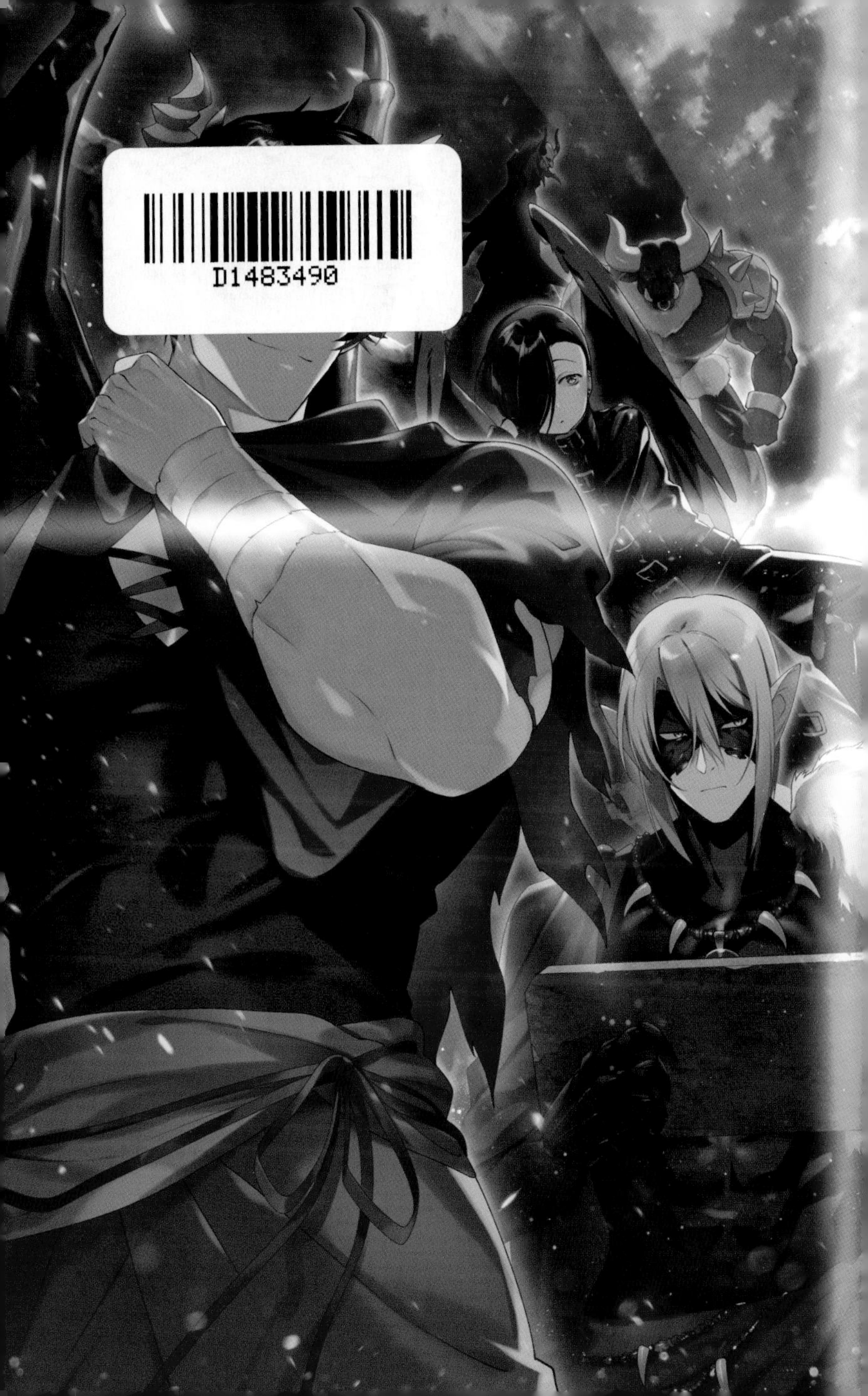

THE DEVIL IS A PART-TIMER! 17

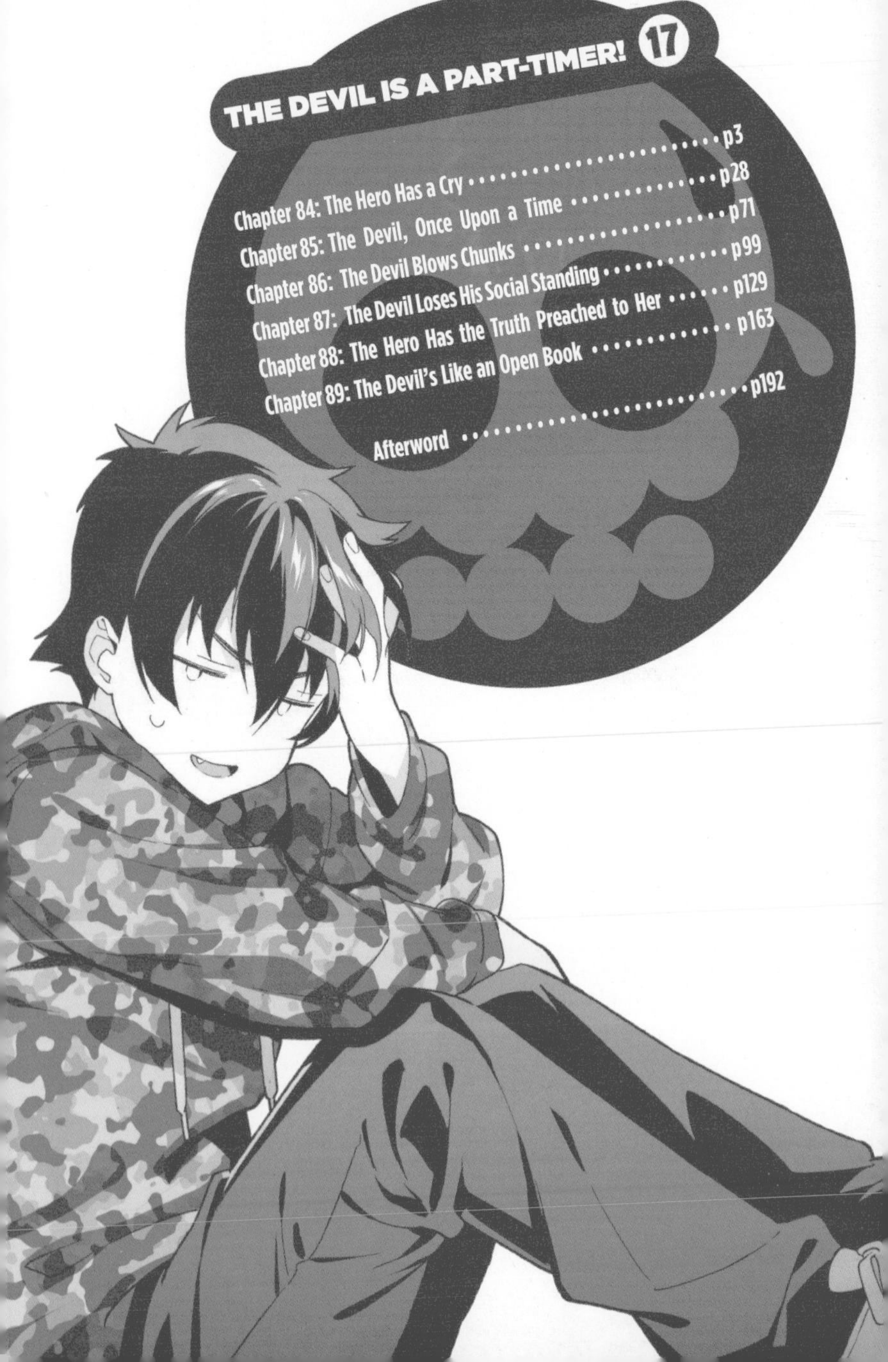

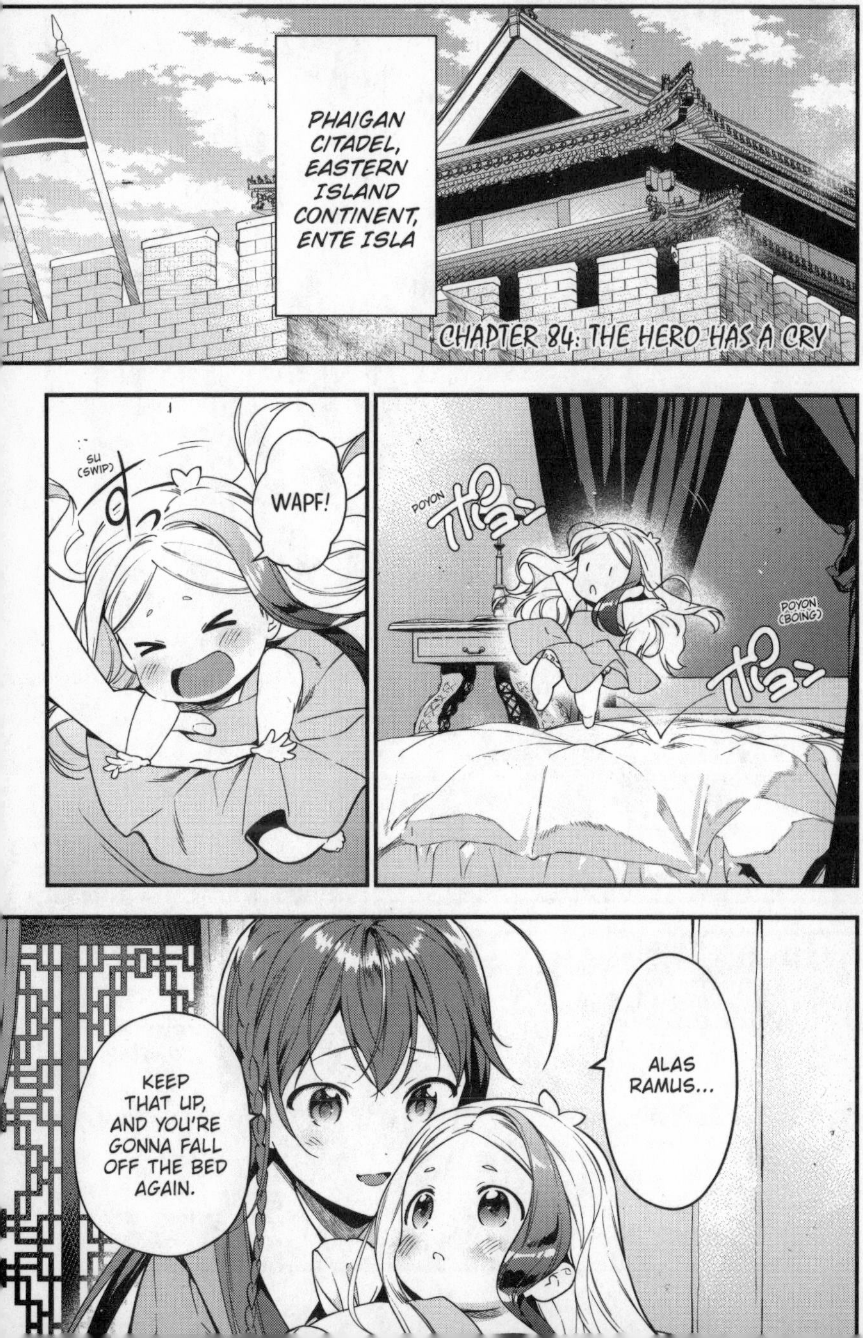
PHAIGAN CITADEL, EASTERN ISLAND CONTINENT, ENTE ISLA
CHAPTER 84: THE HERO HAS A CRY
POYON
POYON (BOING)
SU (SWIP)
WAPF!
ALAS RAMUS...
KEEP THAT UP, AND YOU'RE GONNA FALL OFF THE BED AGAIN.

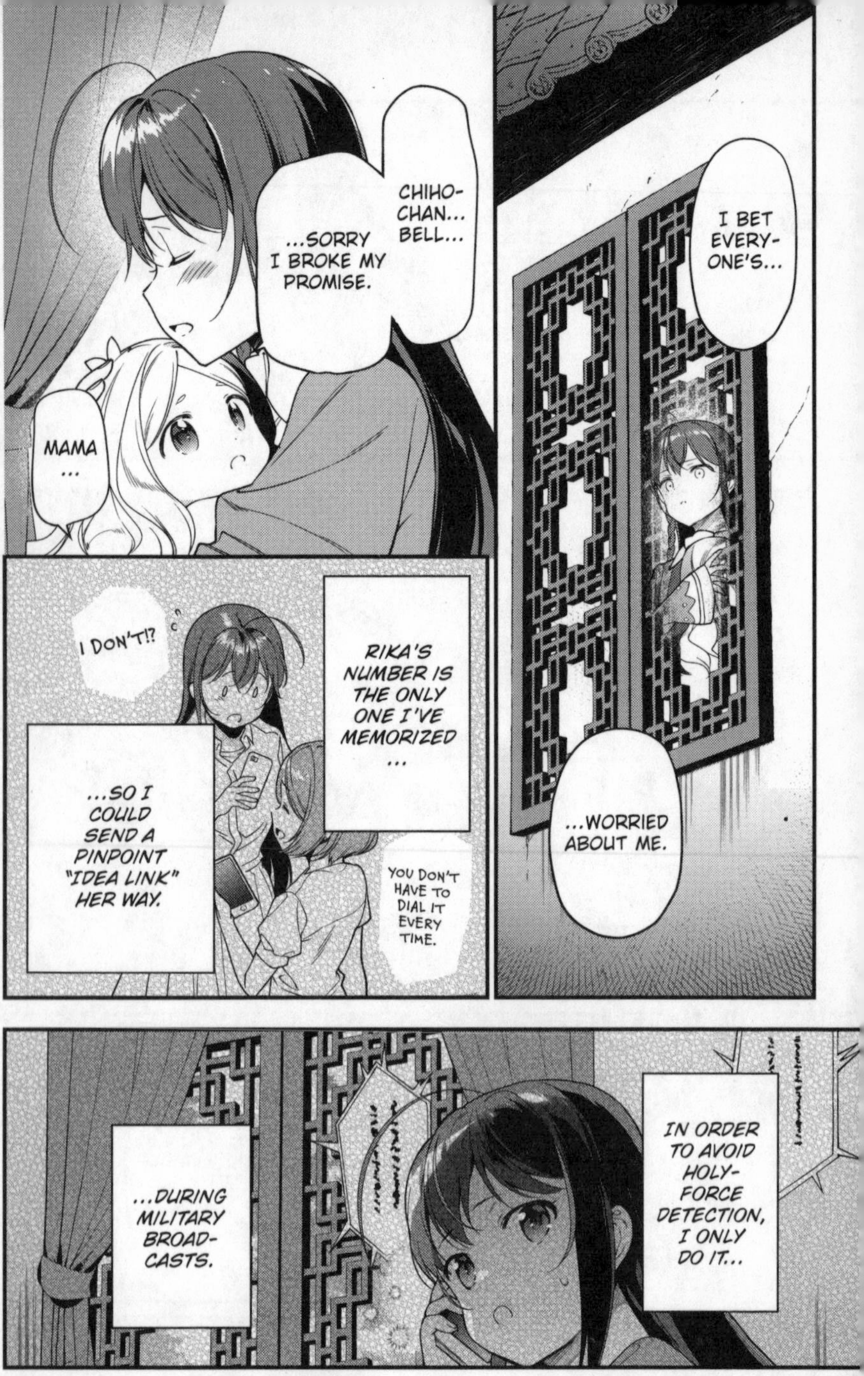
I BET EVERY-ONE'S...
...WORRIED ABOUT ME.
CHIHO-CHAN... BELL...
...SORRY I BROKE MY PROMISE.
MAMA ...
RIKA'S NUMBER IS THE ONLY ONE I'VE MEMORIZED ...
I DON'T!?
...SO I COULD SEND A PINPOINT "IDEA LINK" HER WAY.
YOU DON'T HAVE TO DIAL IT EVERY TIME.
IN ORDER TO AVOID HOLY-FORCE DETECTION, I ONLY DO IT...
...DURING MILITARY BROAD-CASTS.

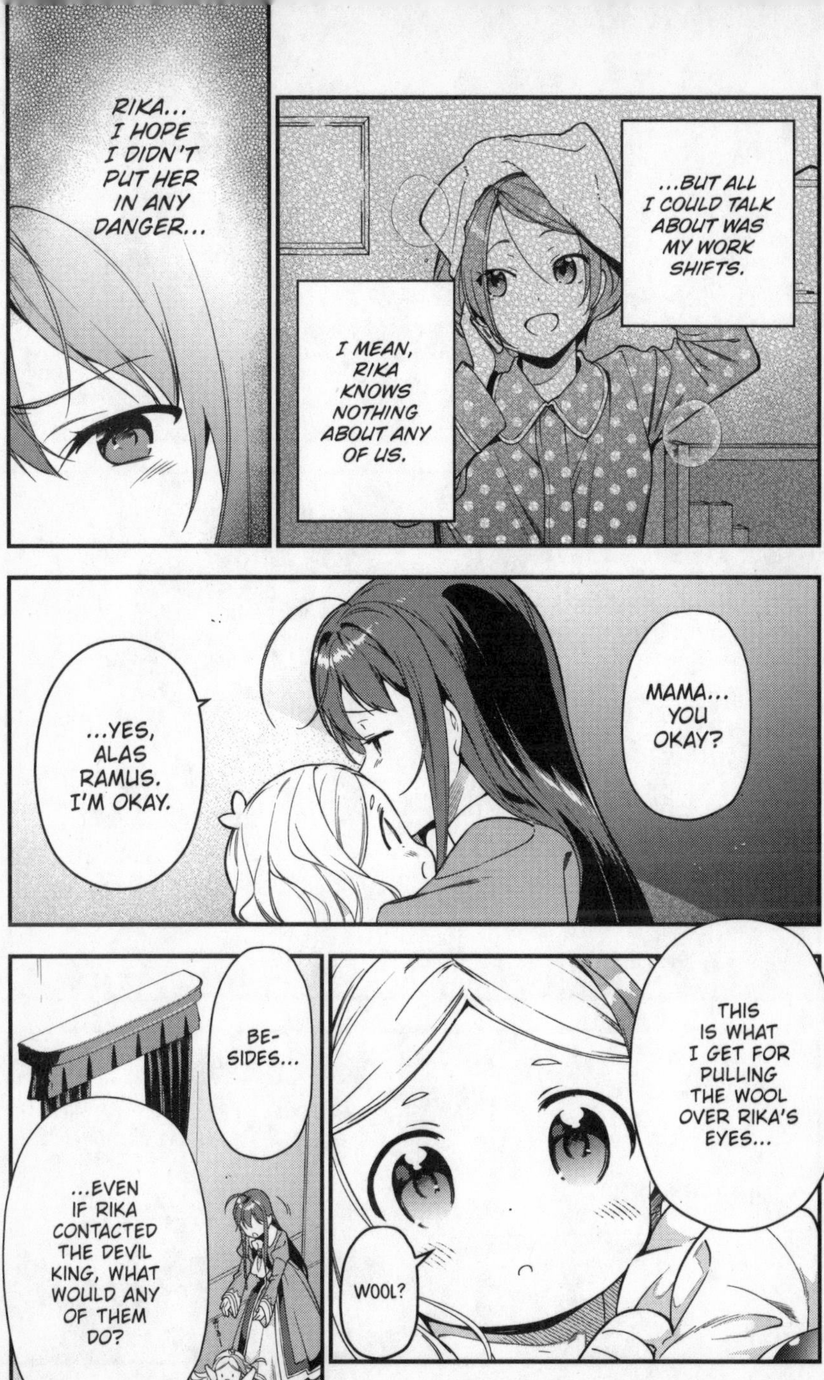
...BUT ALL I COULD TALK ABOUT WAS MY WORK SHIFTS.
I MEAN, RIKA KNOWS NOTHING ABOUT ANY OF US.
RIKA... I HOPE I DIDN'T PUT HER IN ANY DANGER...
MAMA... YOU OKAY?
...YES, ALAS RAMUS. I'M OKAY.
THIS IS WHAT I GET FOR PULLING THE WOOL OVER RIKA'S EYES...
WOOL?
BE-SIDES...
...EVEN IF RIKA CONTACTED THE DEVIL KING, WHAT WOULD ANY OF THEM DO?

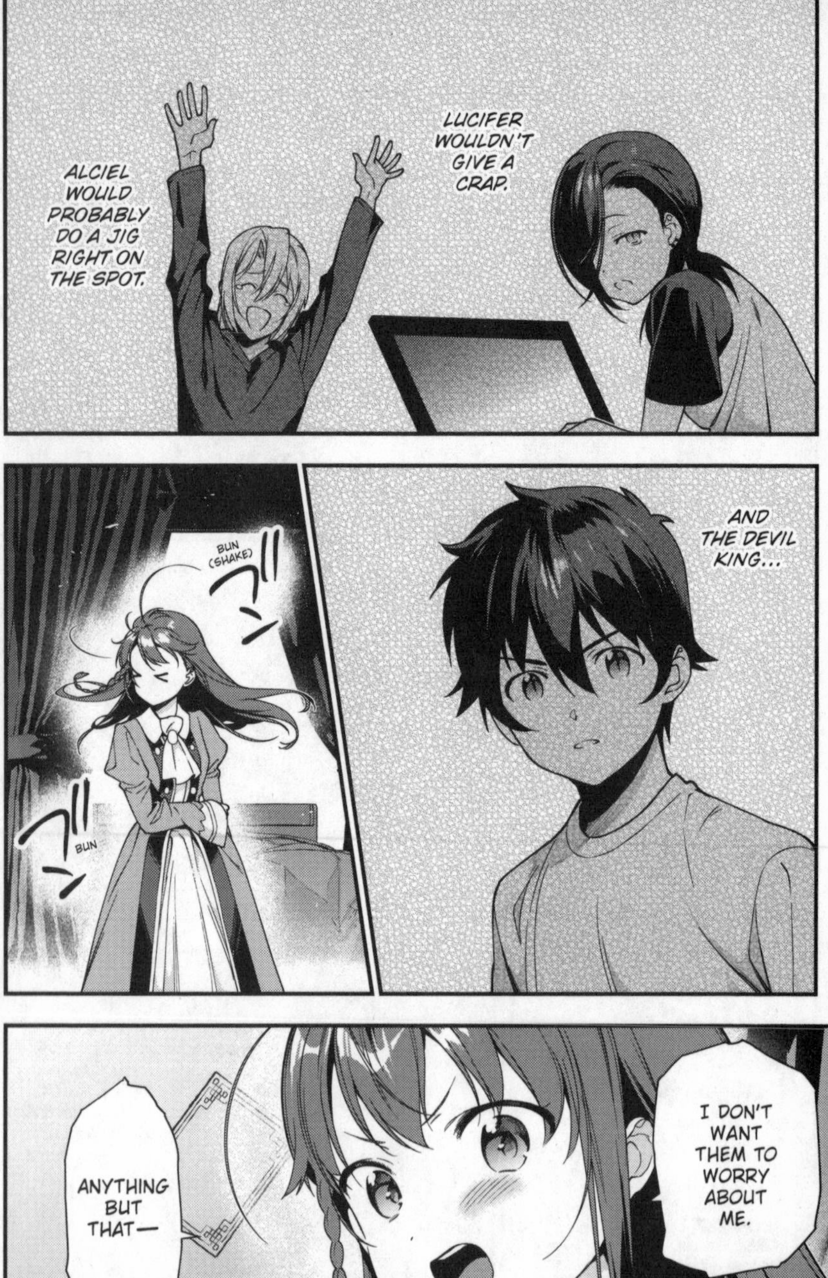
LUCIFER WOULDN'T GIVE A CRAP.
ALCIEL WOULD PROBABLY DO A JIG RIGHT ON THE SPOT.
AND THE DEVIL KING...
BUN (SHAKE)
BUN
I DON'T WANT THEM TO WORRY ABOUT ME.
ANYTHING BUT THAT—

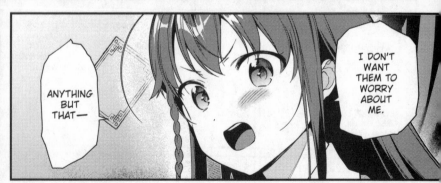

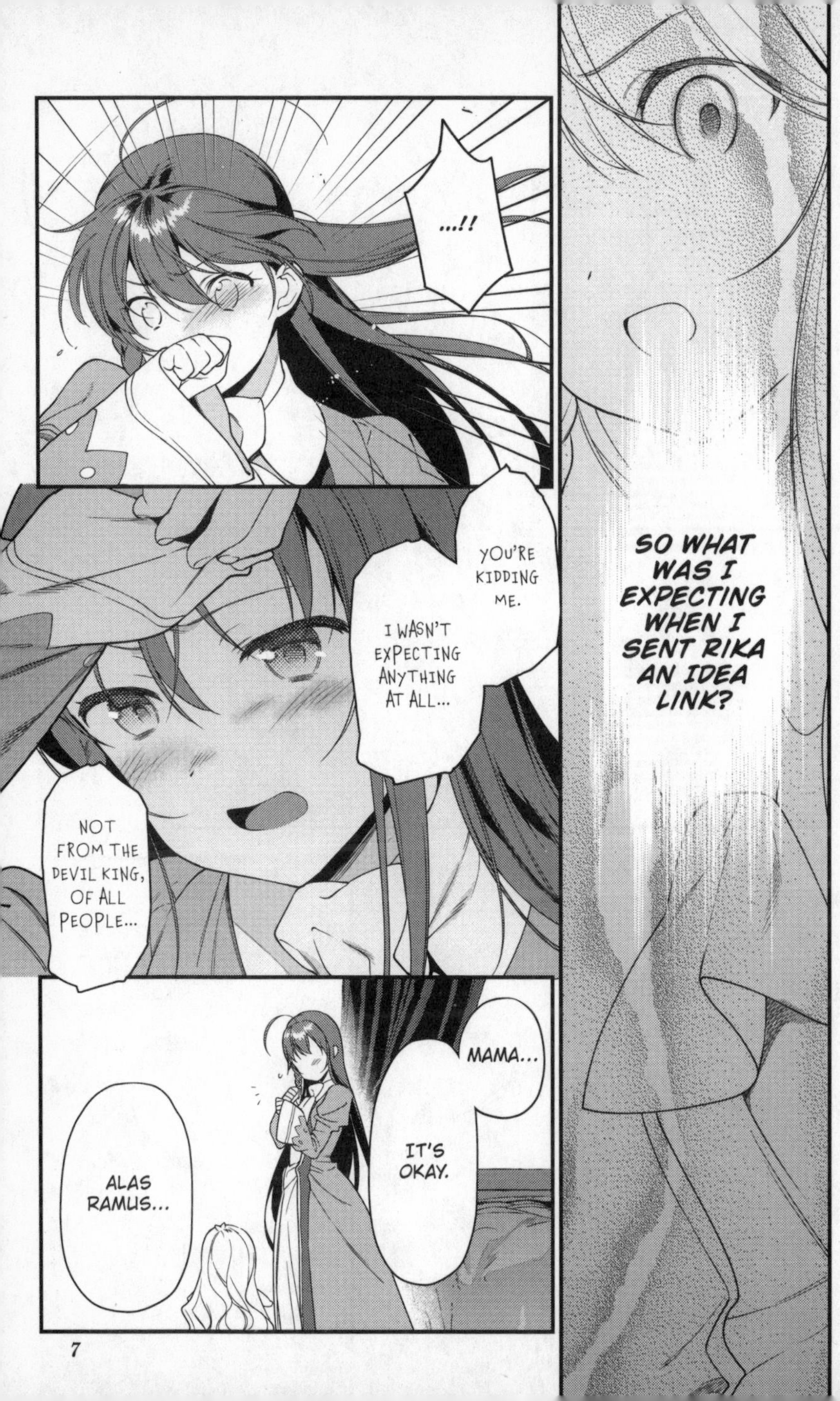
SO WHAT WAS I EXPECTING WHEN I SENT RIKA AN IDEA LINK?
...!!
YOU'RE KIDDING ME.
I WASN'T EXPECTING ANYTHING AT ALL...
NOT FROM THE DEVIL KING, OF ALL PEOPLE...
MAMA...
IT'S OKAY.
ALAS RAMUS...

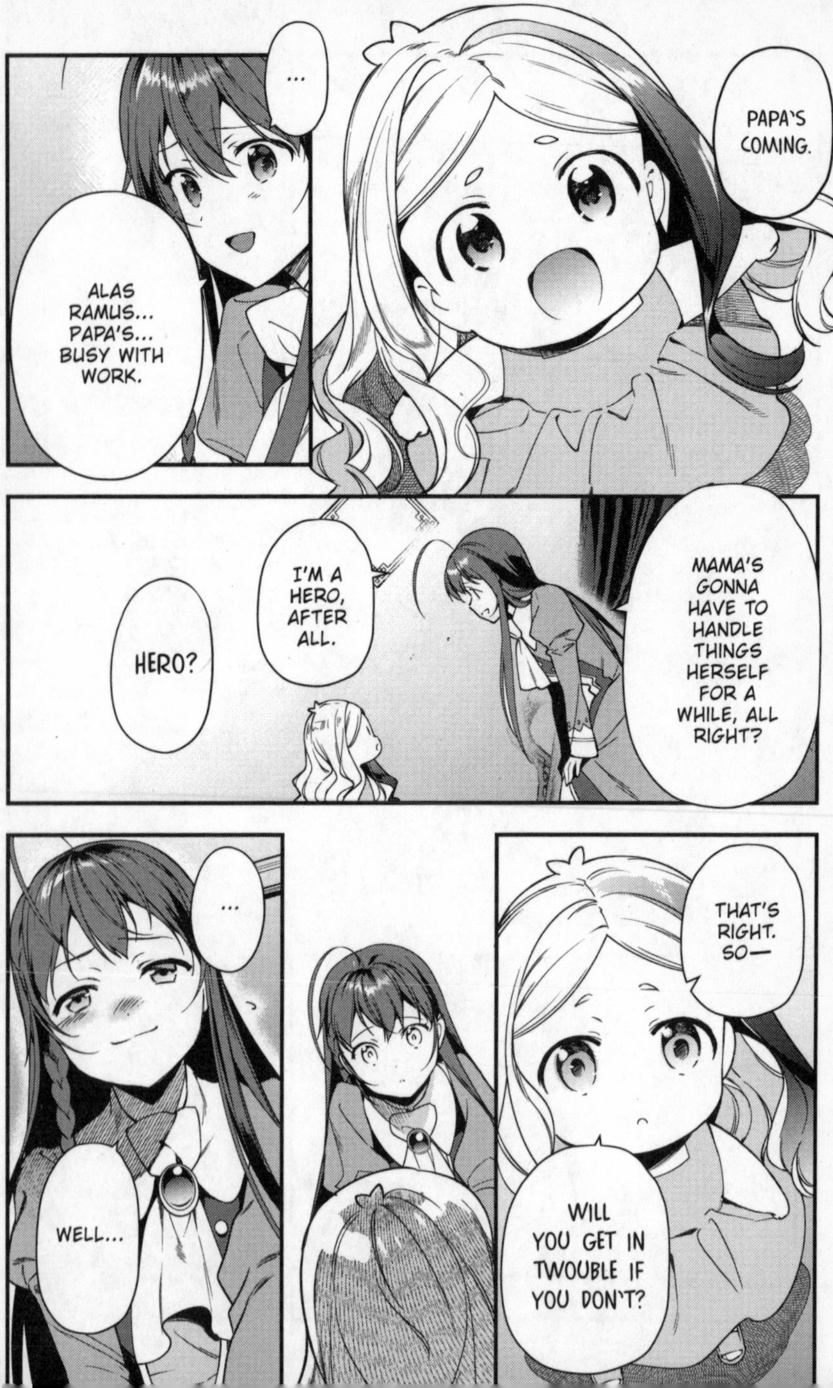
PAPA'S COMING.
...
ALAS RAMUS... PAPA'S... BUSY WITH WORK.
MAMA'S GONNA HAVE TO HANDLE THINGS HERSELF FOR A WHILE, ALL RIGHT?
I'M A HERO, AFTER ALL.
HERO?
THAT'S RIGHT. SO—
WILL YOU GET IN TWOUBLE IF YOU DON'T?
...
WELL...

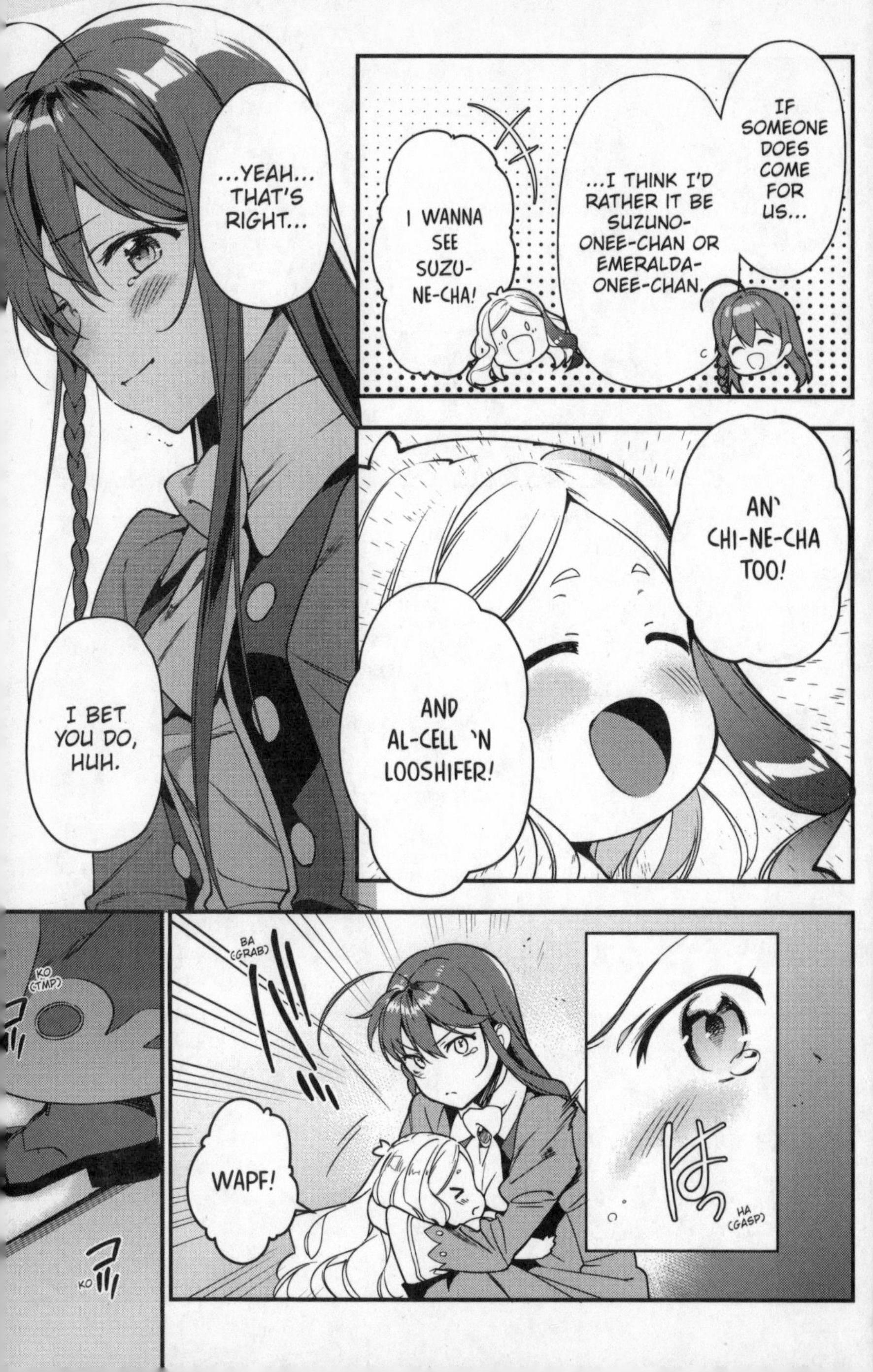
IF SOMEONE DOES COME FOR US...
...I THINK I'D RATHER IT BE SUZUNO-ONEE-CHAN OR EMERALDA-ONEE-CHAN.
I WANNA SEE SUZU-NE-CHA!
AN` CHI-NE-CHA TOO!
AND AL-CELL `N LOOSHIFER!
...YEAH... THAT'S RIGHT...
I BET YOU DO, HUH.
HA (GASP)
BA (GRAB)
WAPF!
KO (TMP)
KO

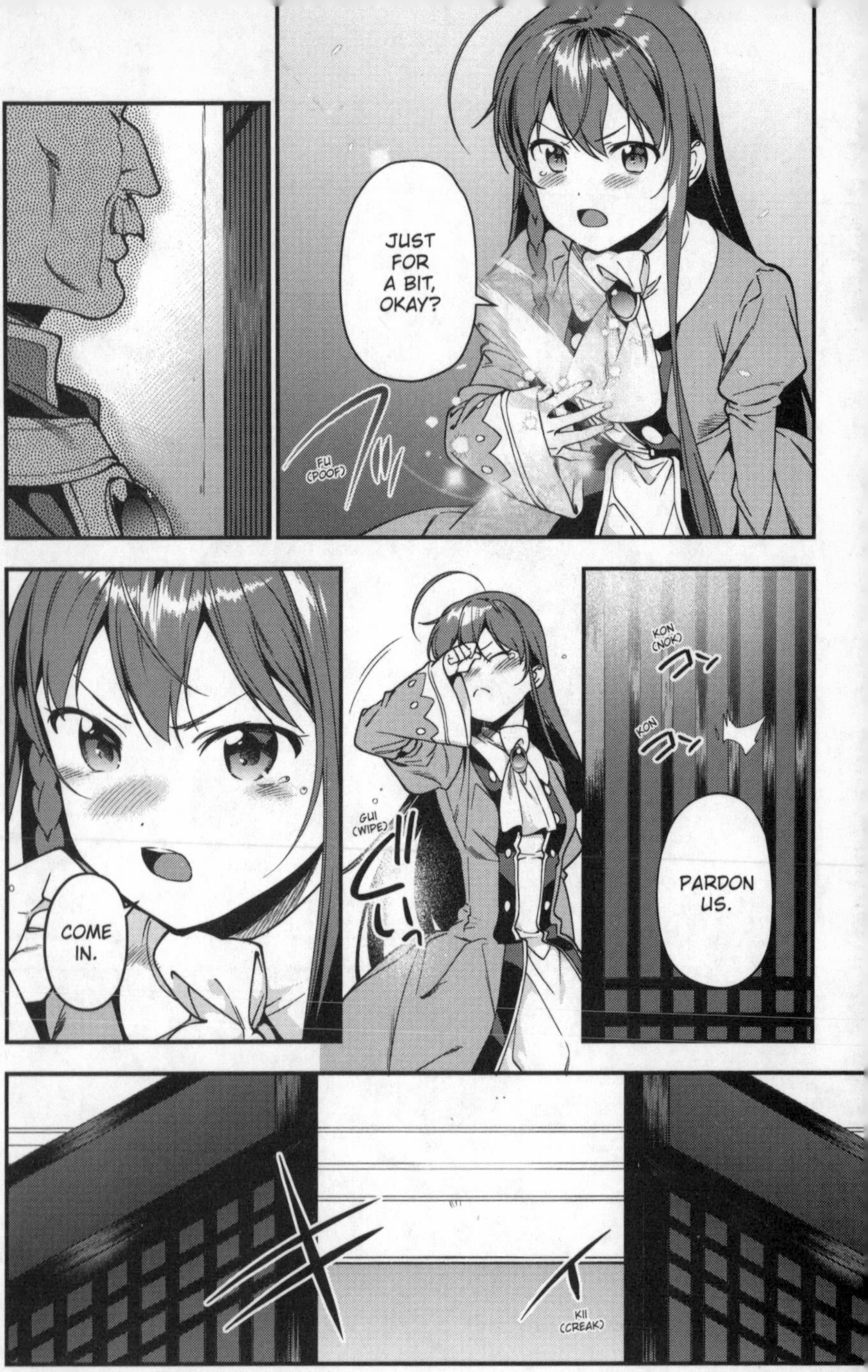
JUST FOR A BIT, OKAY?
FU (POOF)
KON (NOK)
KON
PARDON US.
GUI (WIPE)
COME IN.
KII (CREAK)

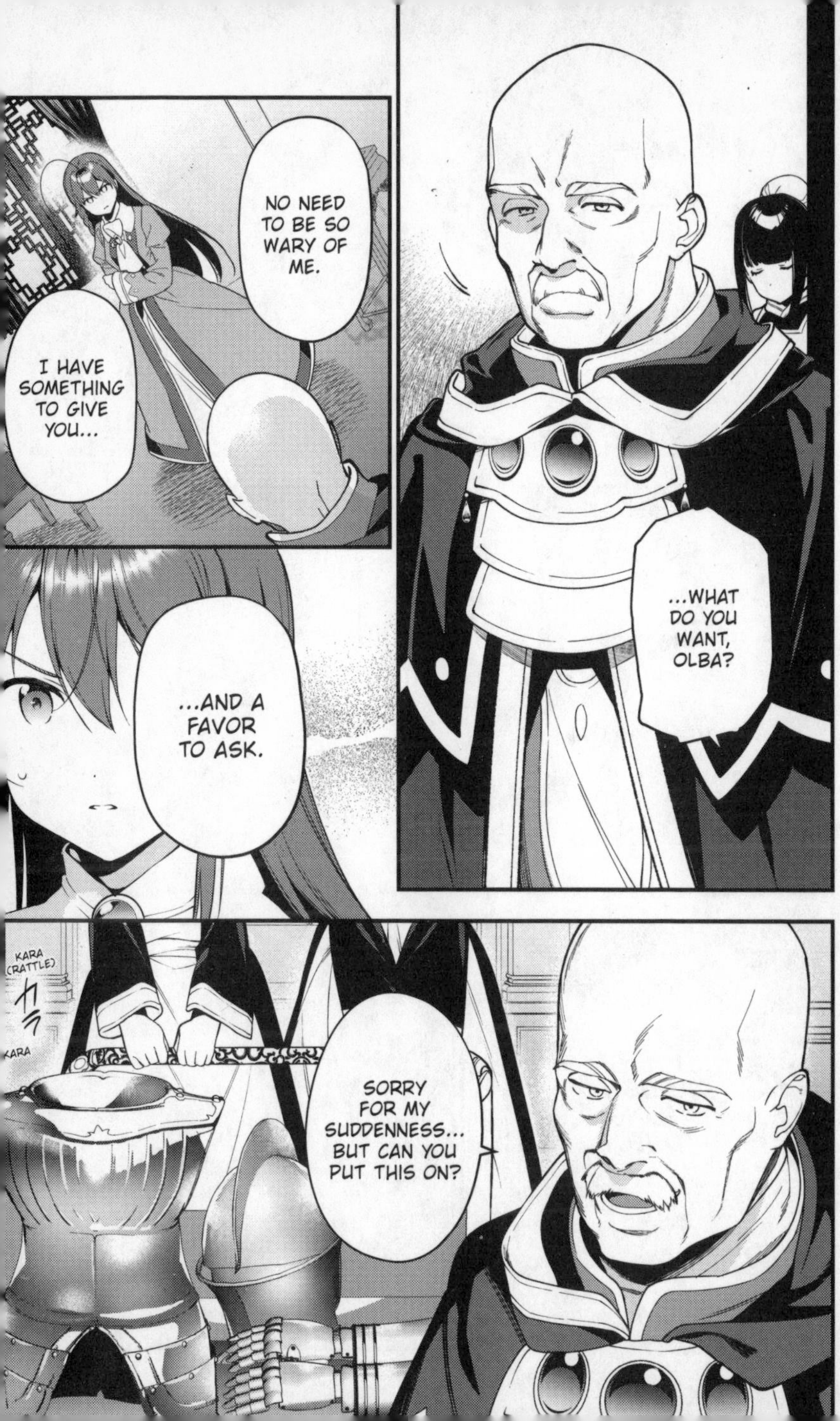
...WHAT DO YOU WANT, OLBA?
NO NEED TO BE SO WARY OF ME.
I HAVE SOMETHING TO GIVE YOU...
...AND A FAVOR TO ASK.
SORRY FOR MY SUDDENNESS... BUT CAN YOU PUT THIS ON?
KARA (RATTLE)
カラ
KARA

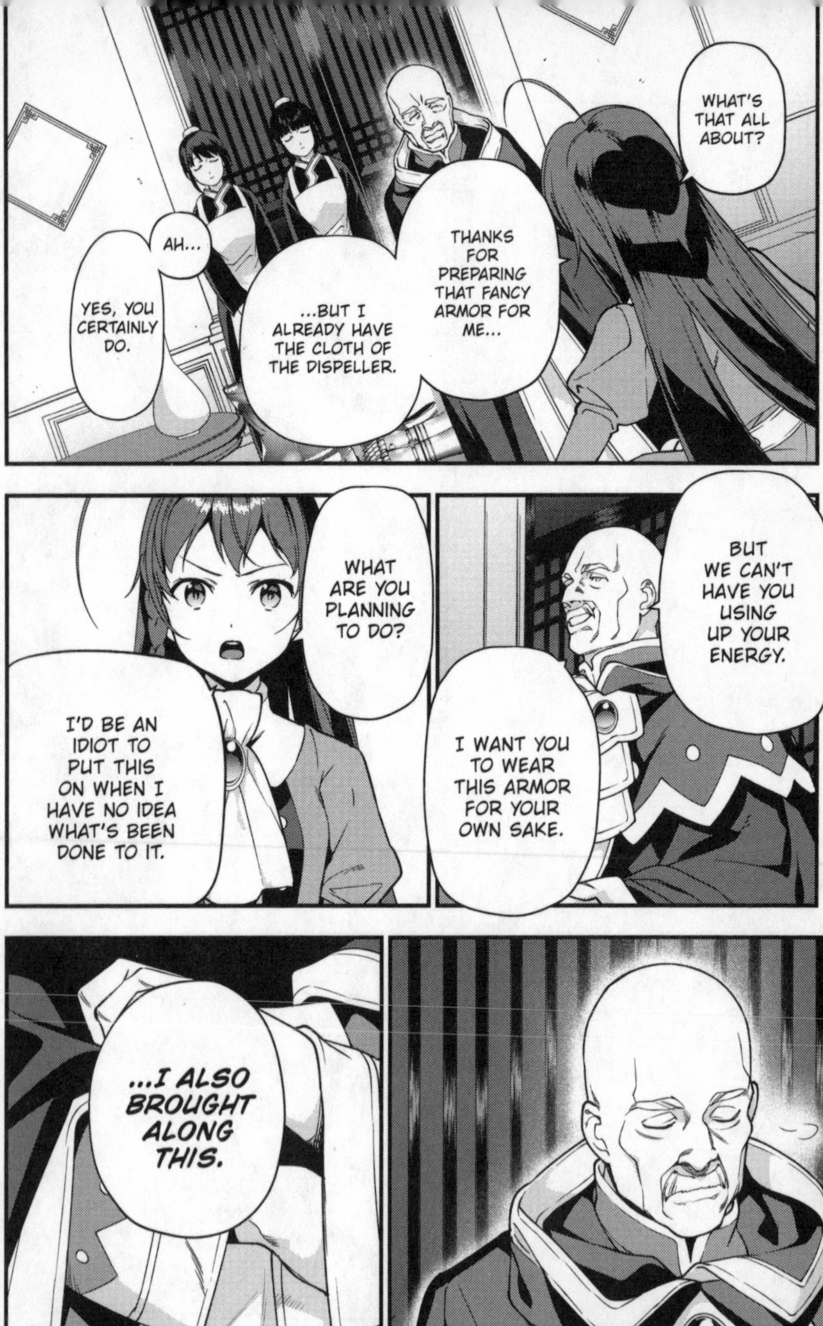
WHAT'S THAT ALL ABOUT?
THANKS FOR PREPARING THAT FANCY ARMOR FOR ME...
...BUT I ALREADY HAVE THE CLOTH OF THE DISPELLER.
AH...
YES, YOU CERTAINLY DO.
BUT WE CAN'T HAVE YOU USING UP YOUR ENERGY.
I WANT YOU TO WEAR THIS ARMOR FOR YOUR OWN SAKE.
WHAT ARE YOU PLANNING TO DO?
I'D BE AN IDIOT TO PUT THIS ON WHEN I HAVE NO IDEA WHAT'S BEEN DONE TO IT.
...I ALSO BROUGHT ALONG THIS.

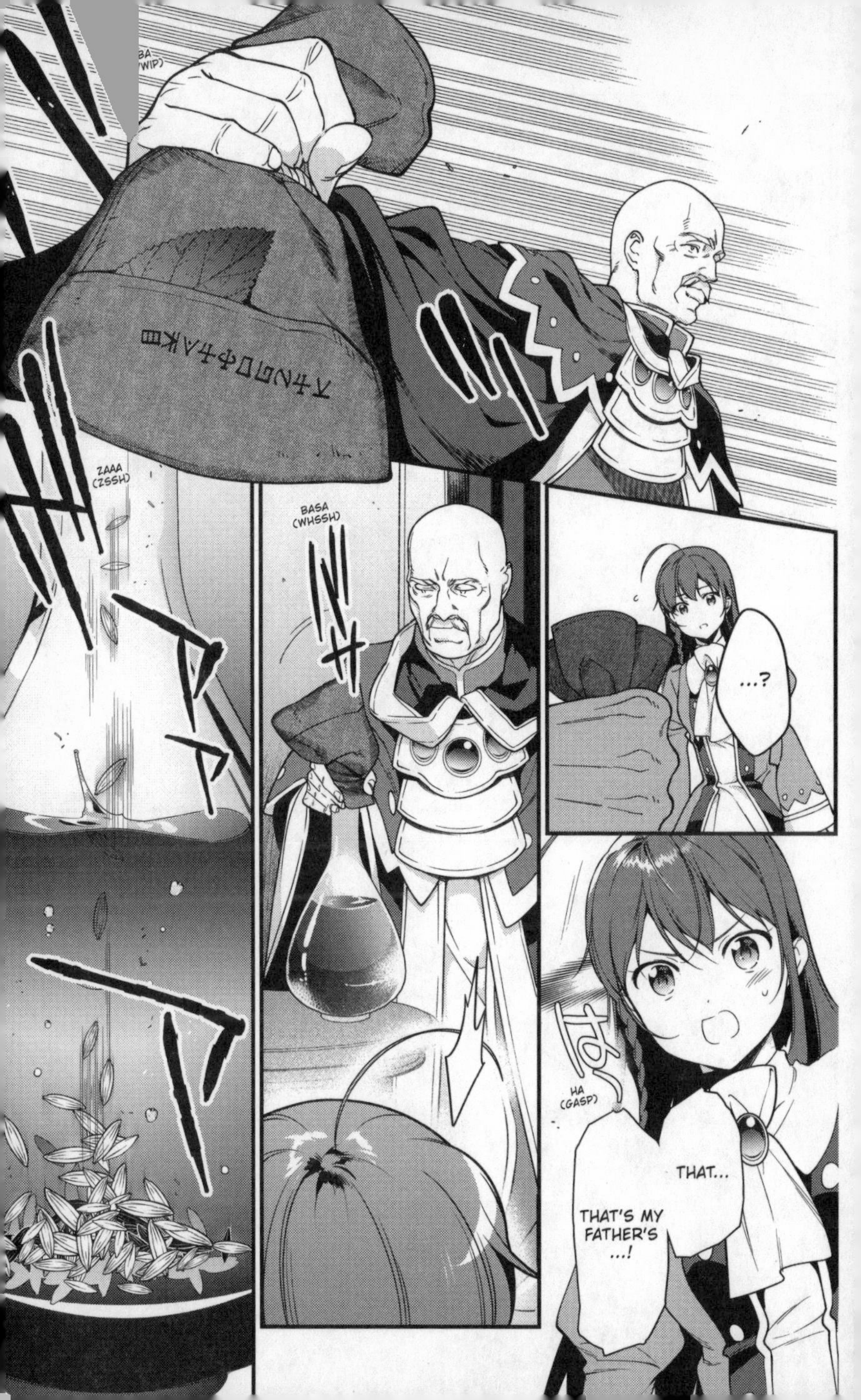
BA
WIP)
...?
HA (GASP)
THAT...
THAT'S MY FATHER'S ...!
BASA (WHSSH)
ZAAA (ZSSH)

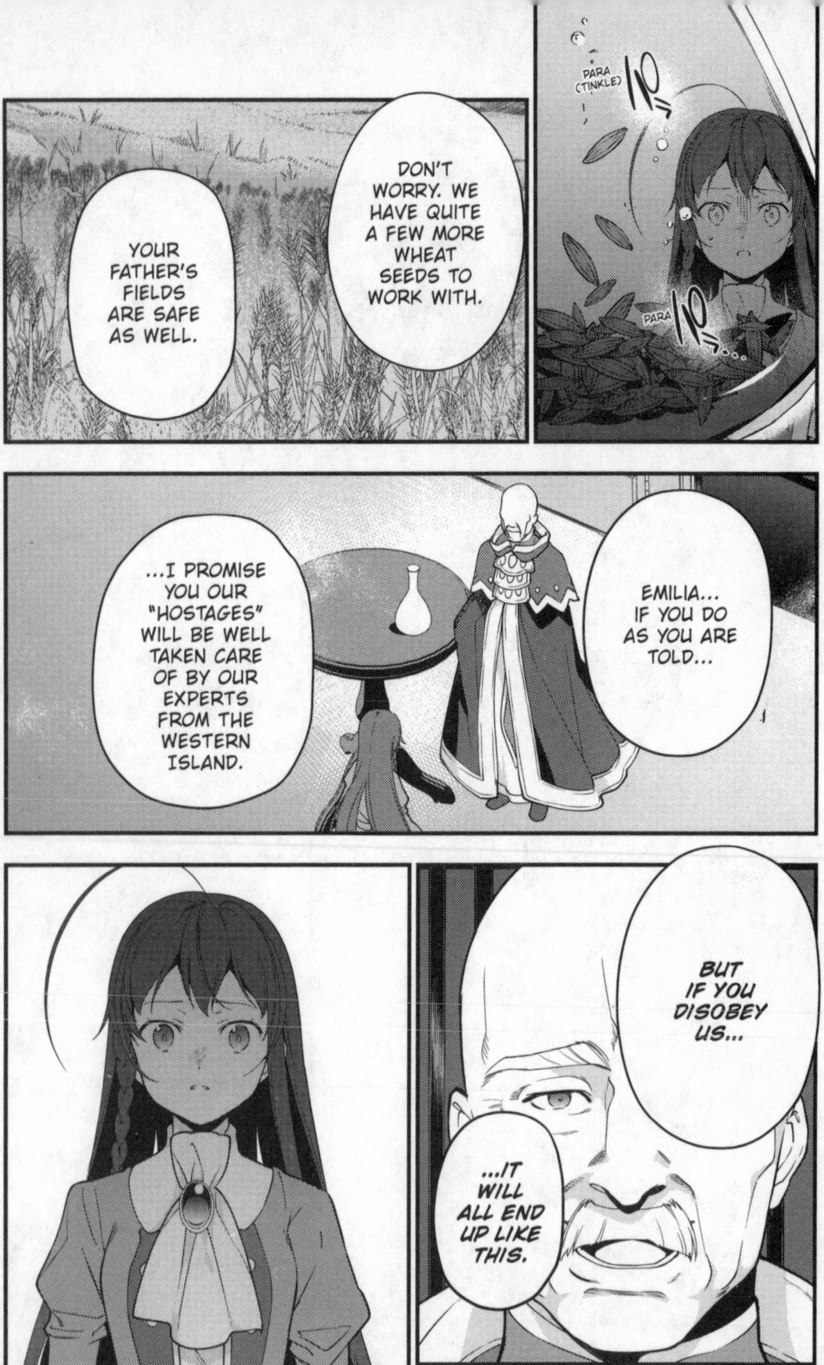
PARA (TINKLE)
PARA
DON'T WORRY. WE HAVE QUITE A FEW MORE WHEAT SEEDS TO WORK WITH.
YOUR FATHER'S FIELDS ARE SAFE AS WELL.
EMILIA... IF YOU DO AS YOU ARE TOLD...
...I PROMISE YOU OUR "HOSTAGES" WILL BE WELL TAKEN CARE OF BY OUR EXPERTS FROM THE WESTERN ISLAND.
BUT IF YOU DISOBEY US...
...IT WILL ALL END UP LIKE THIS.

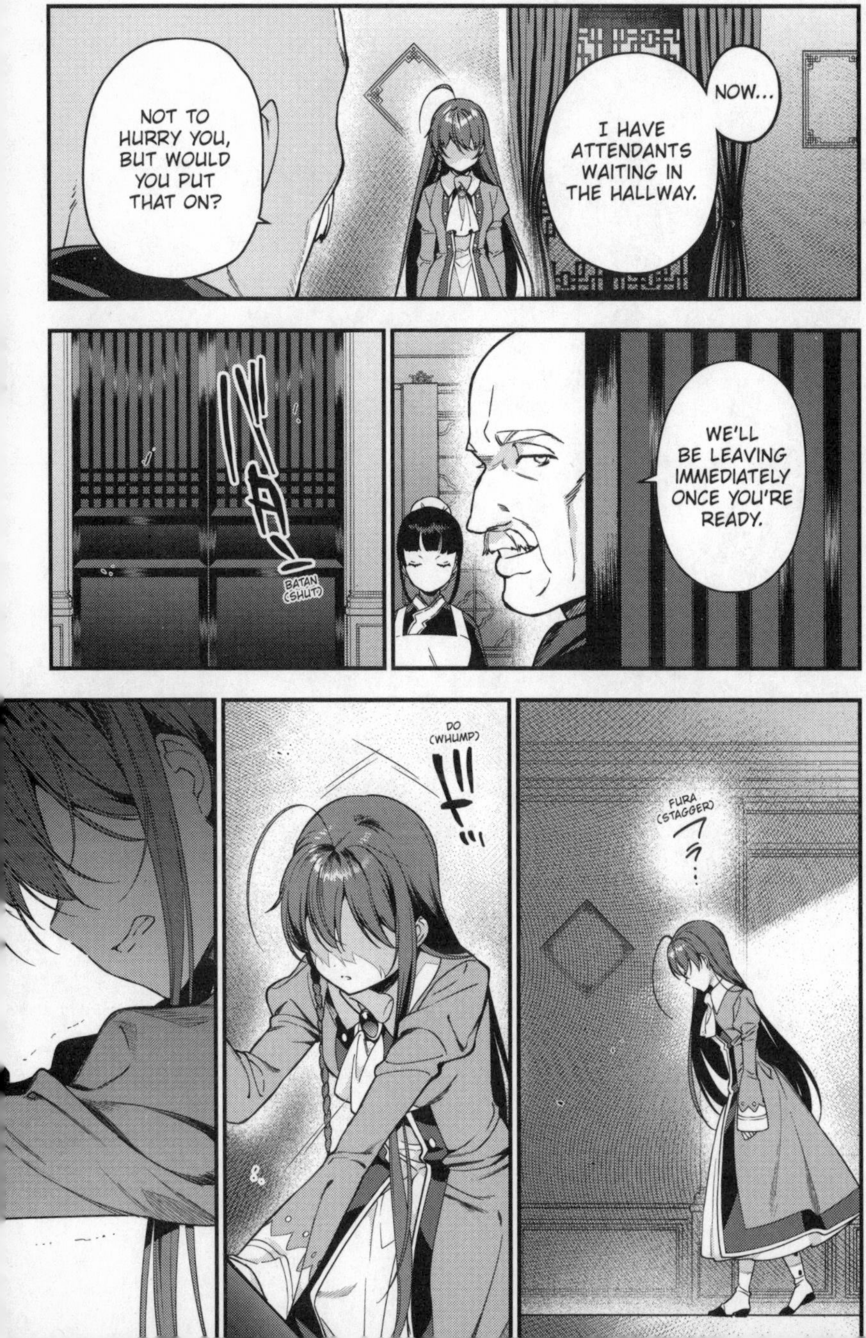
NOW...
I HAVE ATTENDANTS WAITING IN THE HALLWAY.
NOT TO HURRY YOU, BUT WOULD YOU PUT THAT ON?
WE'LL BE LEAVING IMMEDIATELY ONCE YOU'RE READY.
BATAN (SHUT)
FURA (STAGGER)
DO (WHUMP)

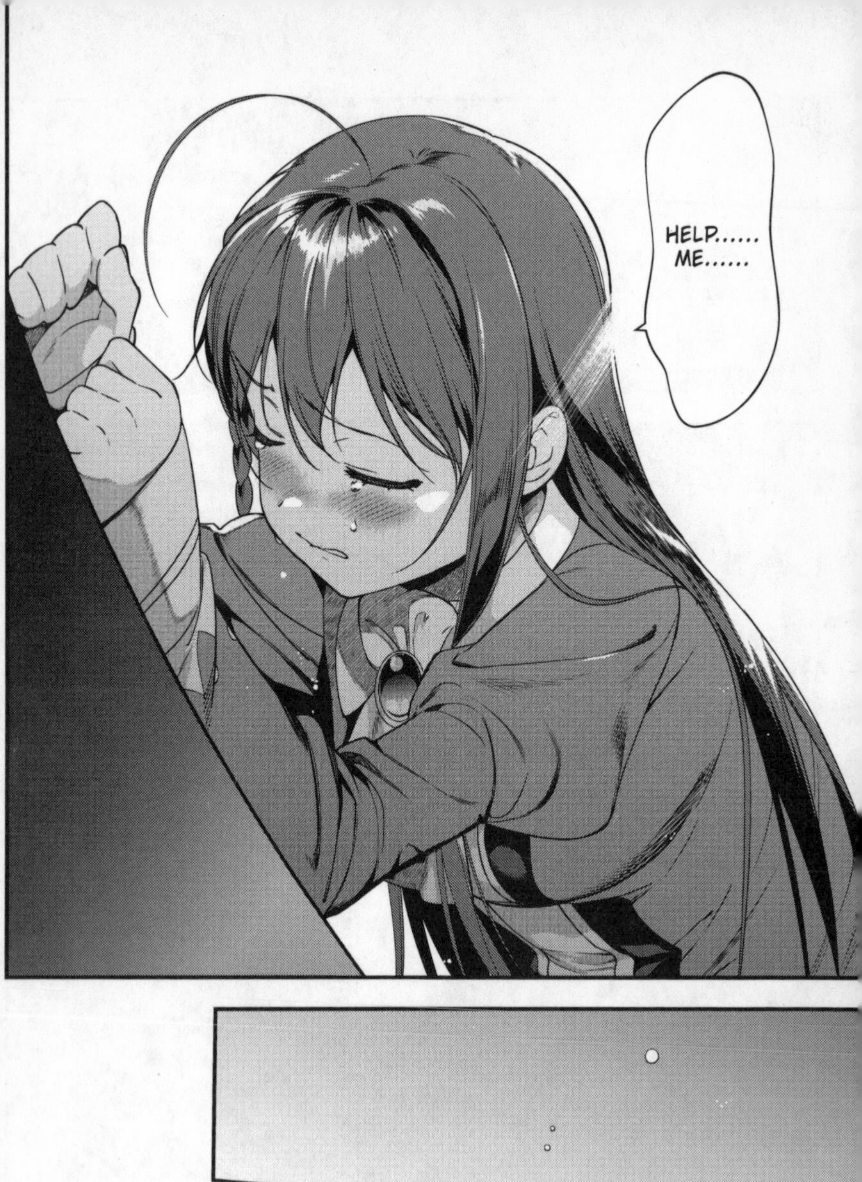
HELP...... ME......

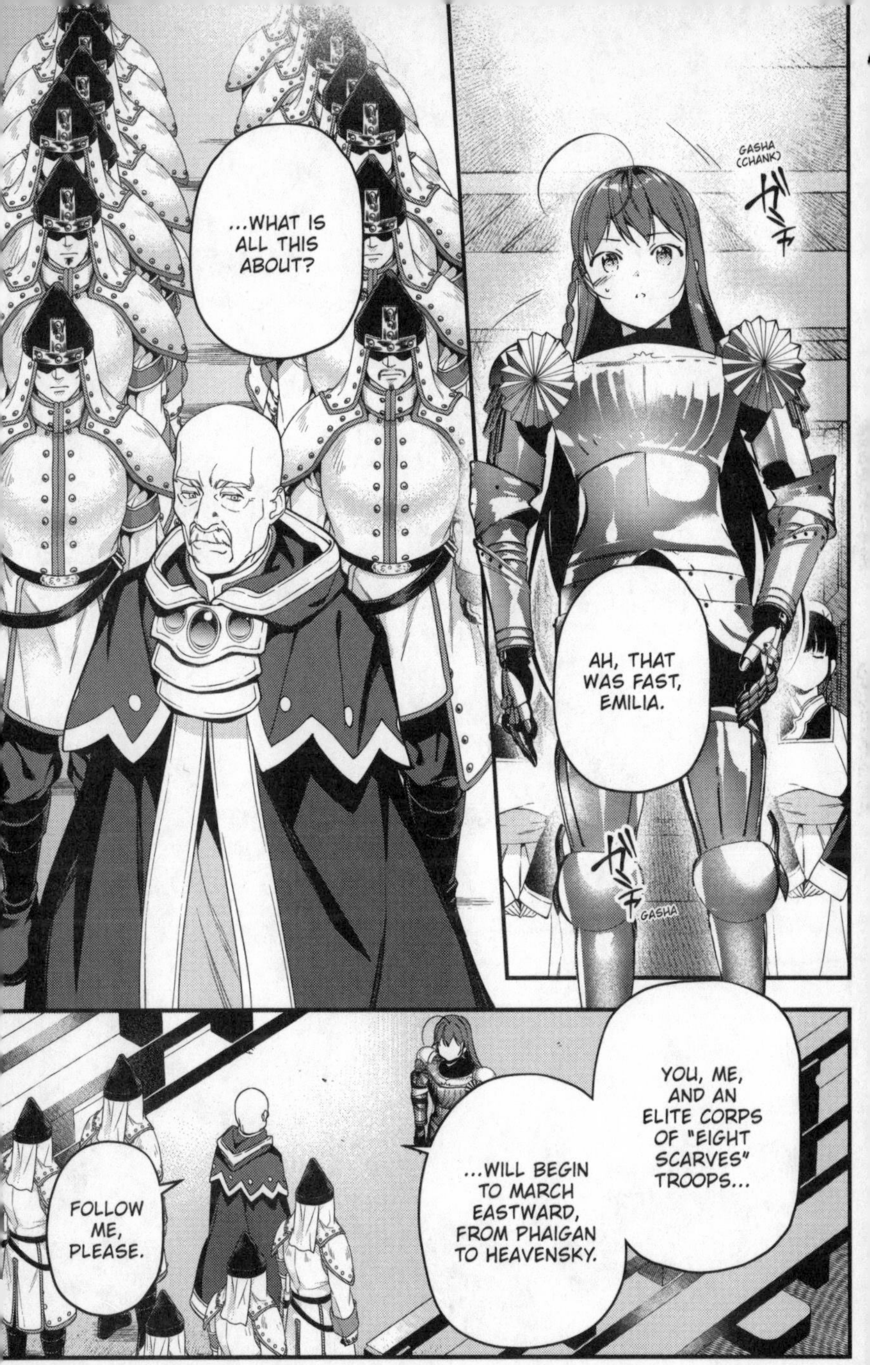
GASHA (CHANK)
AH, THAT WAS FAST, EMILIA.
GASHA
...WHAT IS ALL THIS ABOUT?
YOU, ME, AND AN ELITE CORPS OF "EIGHT SCARVES" TROOPS...
...WILL BEGIN TO MARCH EASTWARD, FROM PHAIGAN TO HEAVENSKY.
FOLLOW ME, PLEASE.

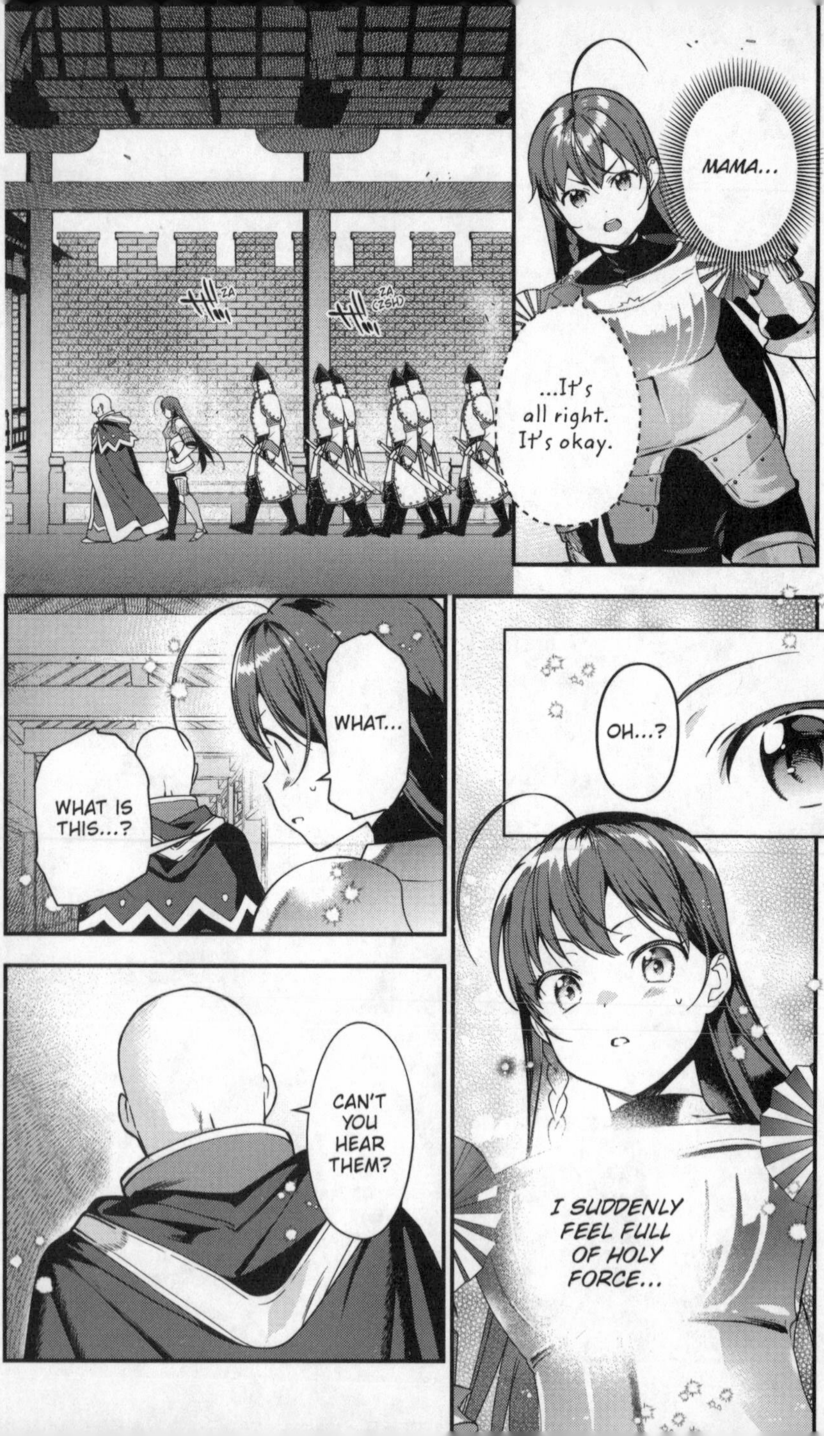
MAMA...
...It's all right. It's okay.
ZA
ZA (ZSH)
OH...?
I SUDDENLY FEEL FULL OF HOLY FORCE...
WHAT...
WHAT IS THIS...?
CAN'T YOU HEAR THEM?

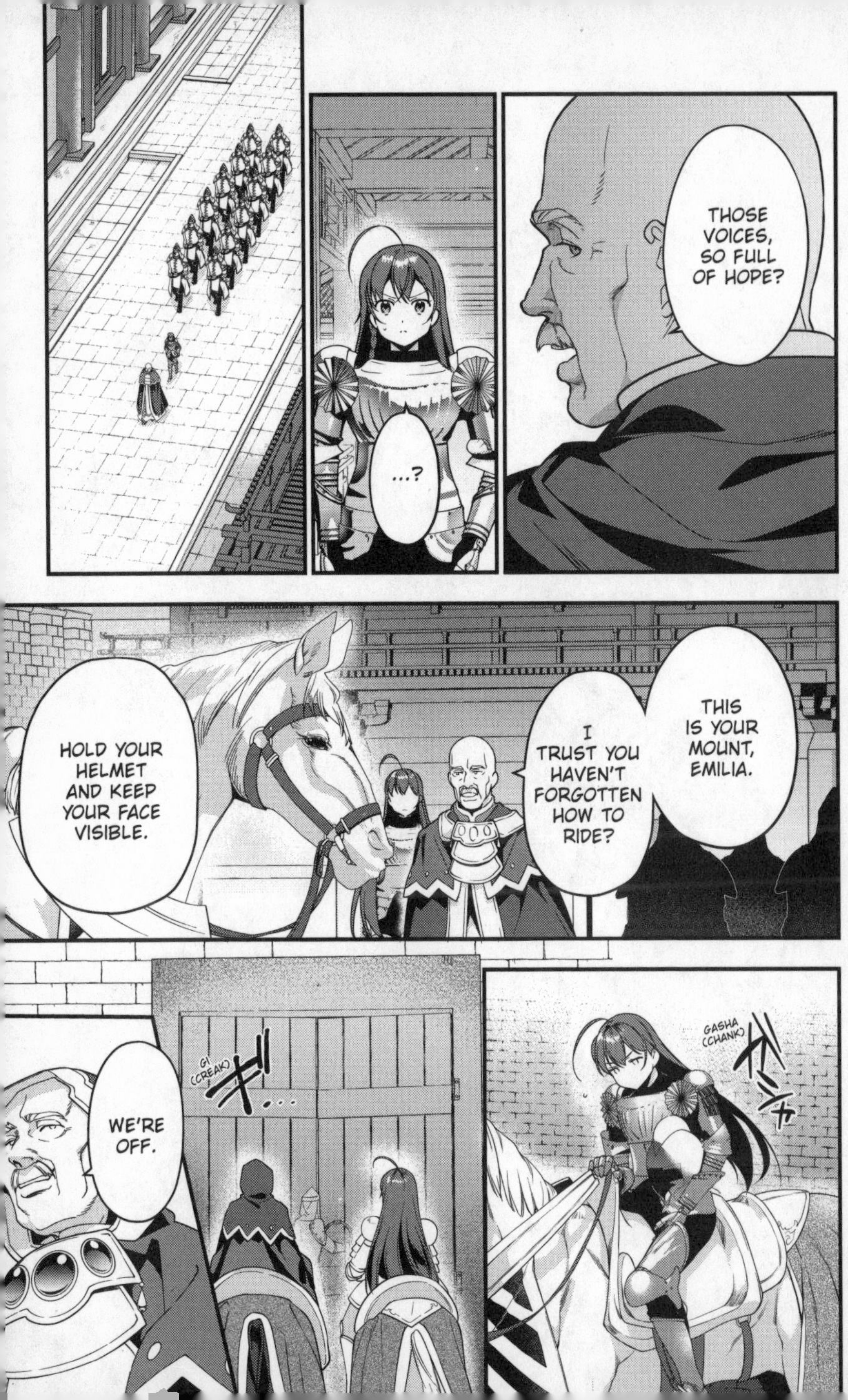
THOSE VOICES, SO FULL OF HOPE?
...?
THIS IS YOUR MOUNT, EMILIA.
I TRUST YOU HAVEN'T FORGOTTEN HOW TO RIDE?
HOLD YOUR HELMET AND KEEP YOUR FACE VISIBLE.
GASHA (CHANK)
GI (CREAK)...
WE'RE OFF.

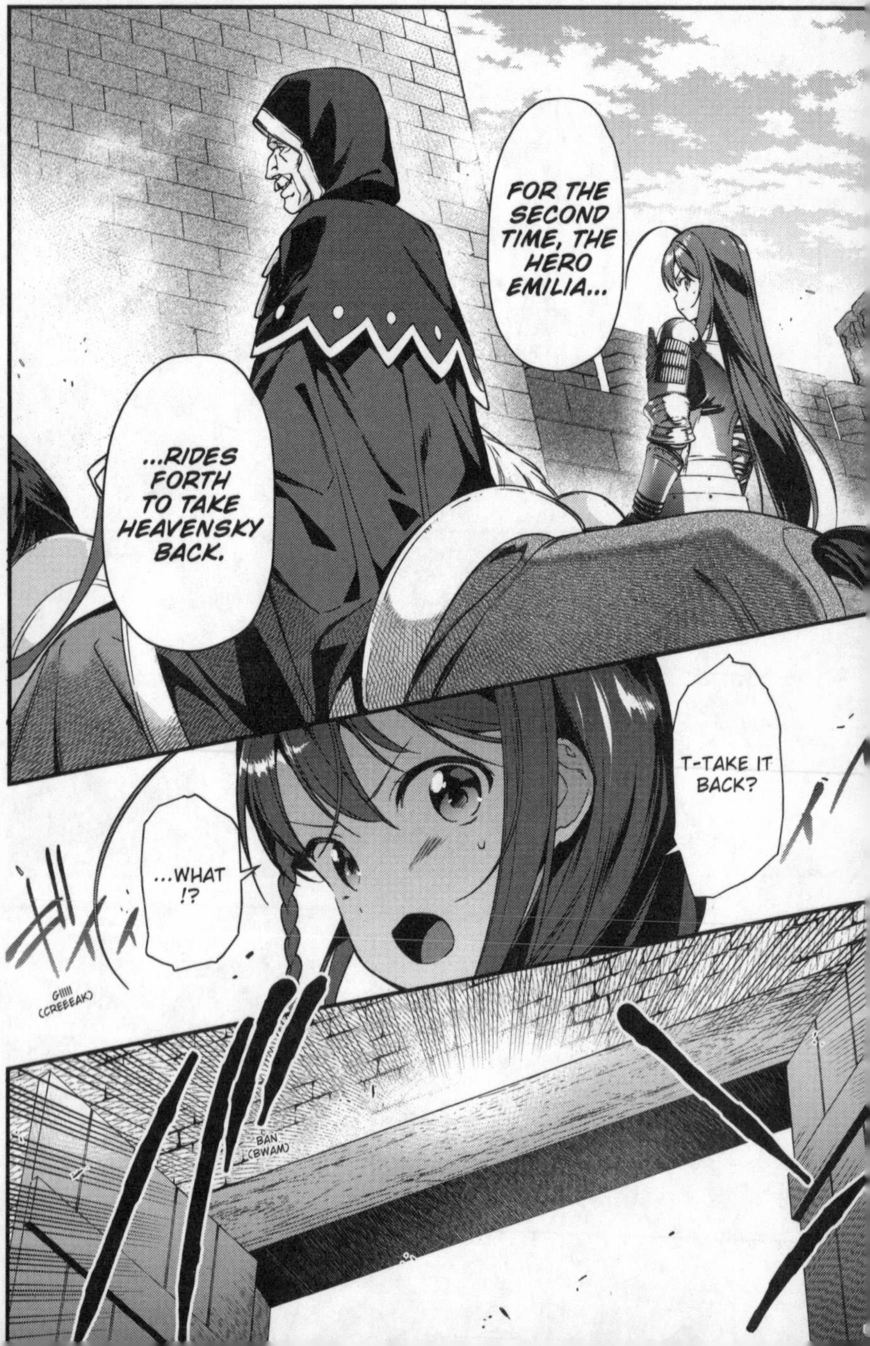
FOR THE SECOND TIME, THE HERO EMILIA...
...RIDES FORTH TO TAKE HEAVENSKY BACK.
T-TAKE IT BACK?
...WHAT !?
GIIII (CREEEAK)
BAN (BWAM)

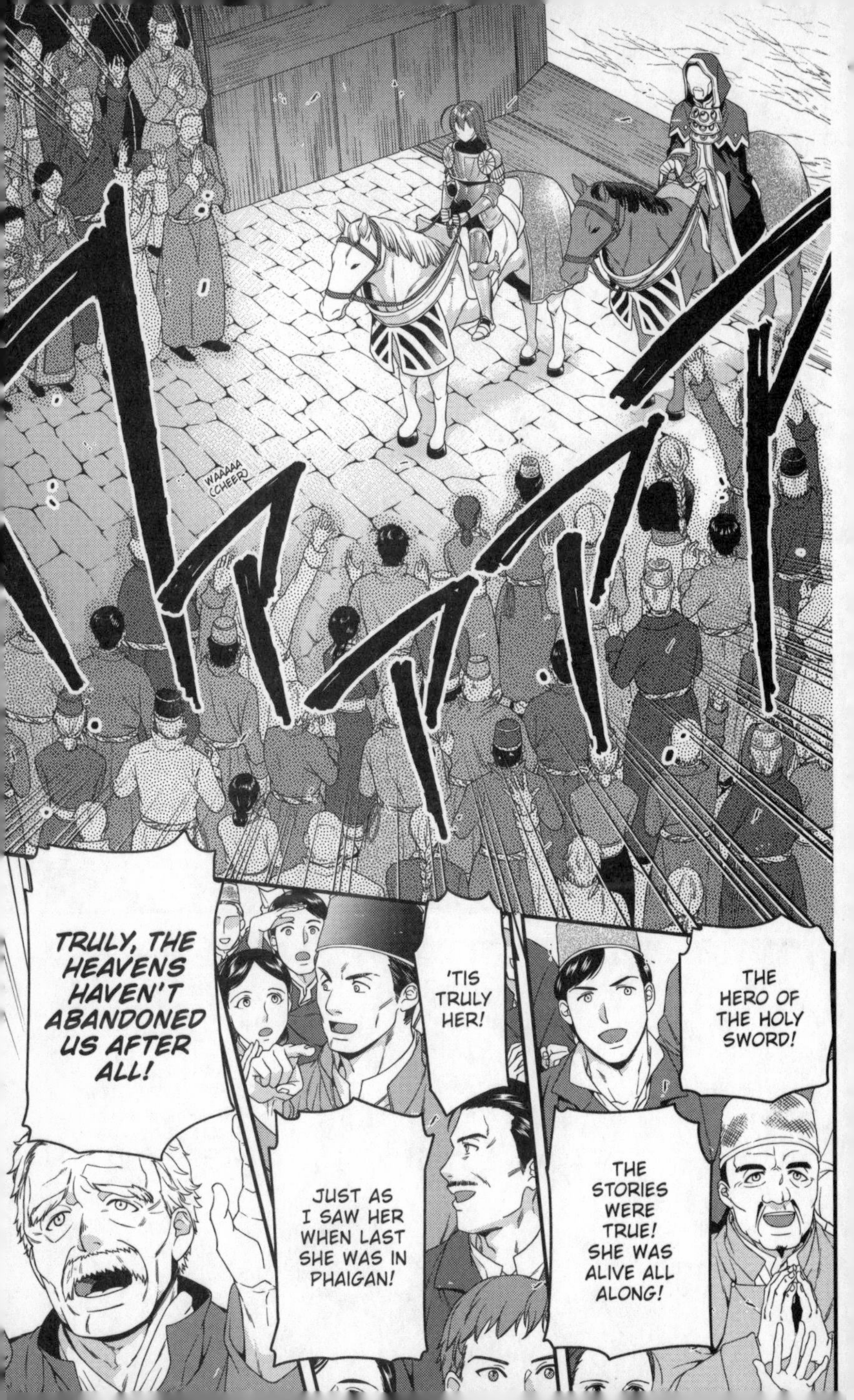
WAAAAA (CHEER)
THE HERO OF THE HOLY SWORD!
'TIS TRULY HER!
TRULY, THE HEAVENS HAVEN'T ABANDONED US AFTER ALL!
THE STORIES WERE TRUE! SHE WAS ALIVE ALL ALONG!
JUST AS I SAW HER WHEN LAST SHE WAS IN PHAIGAN!

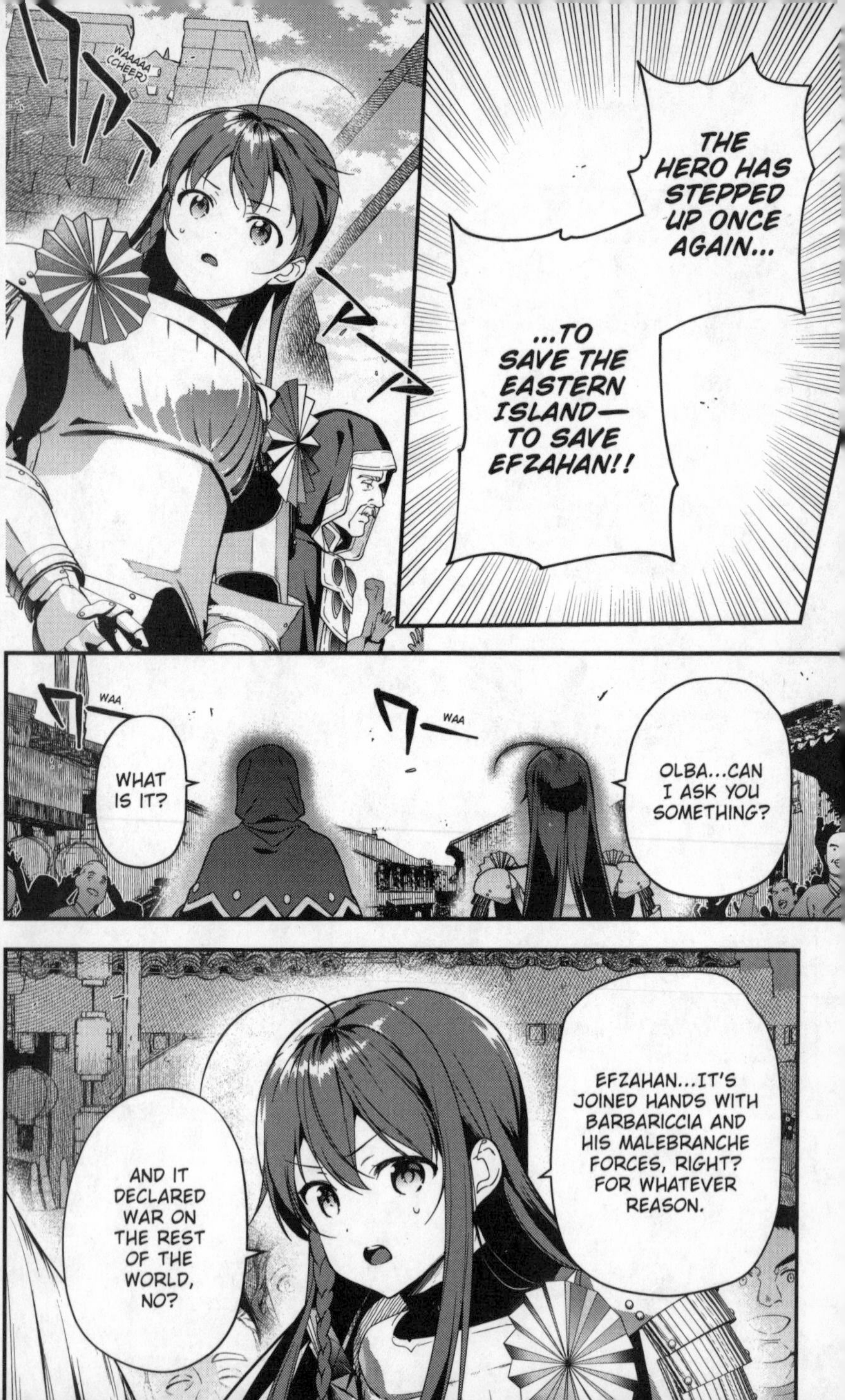
THE HERO HAS STEPPED UP ONCE AGAIN...
...TO SAVE THE EASTERN ISLAND— TO SAVE EFZAHAN!!
WAAAAA (CHEER)
OLBA...CAN I ASK YOU SOMETHING?
WAA
WHAT IS IT?
WAA
EFZAHAN...IT'S JOINED HANDS WITH BARBARICCIA AND HIS MALEBRANCHE FORCES, RIGHT? FOR WHATEVER REASON.
AND IT DECLARED WAR ON THE REST OF THE WORLD, NO?

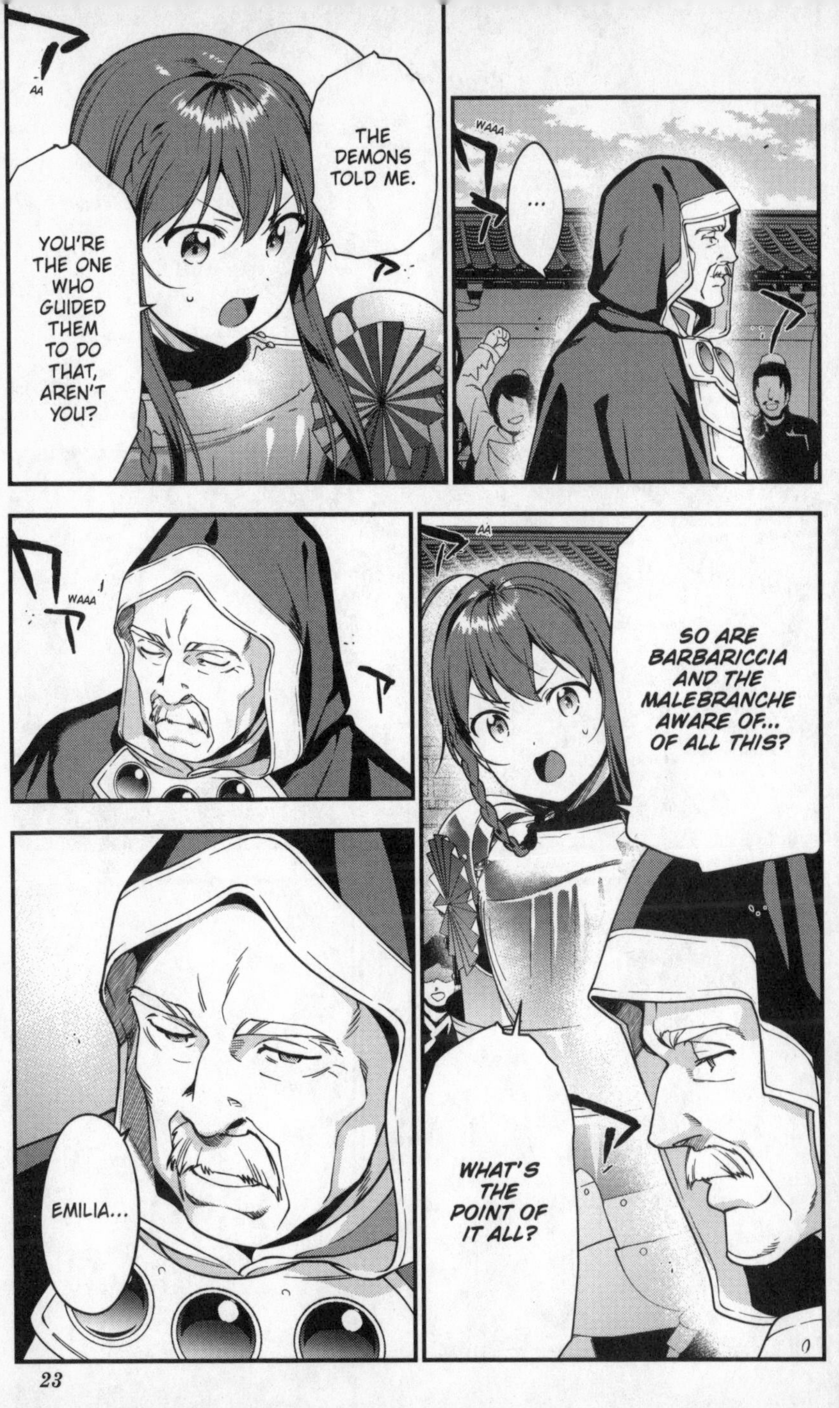
WAAA
...
AA
THE DEMONS TOLD ME.
YOU'RE THE ONE WHO GUIDED THEM TO DO THAT, AREN'T YOU?
AA
SO ARE BARBARICCIA AND THE MALEBRANCHE AWARE OF... OF ALL THIS?
WHAT'S THE POINT OF IT ALL?
WAAA
EMILIA...

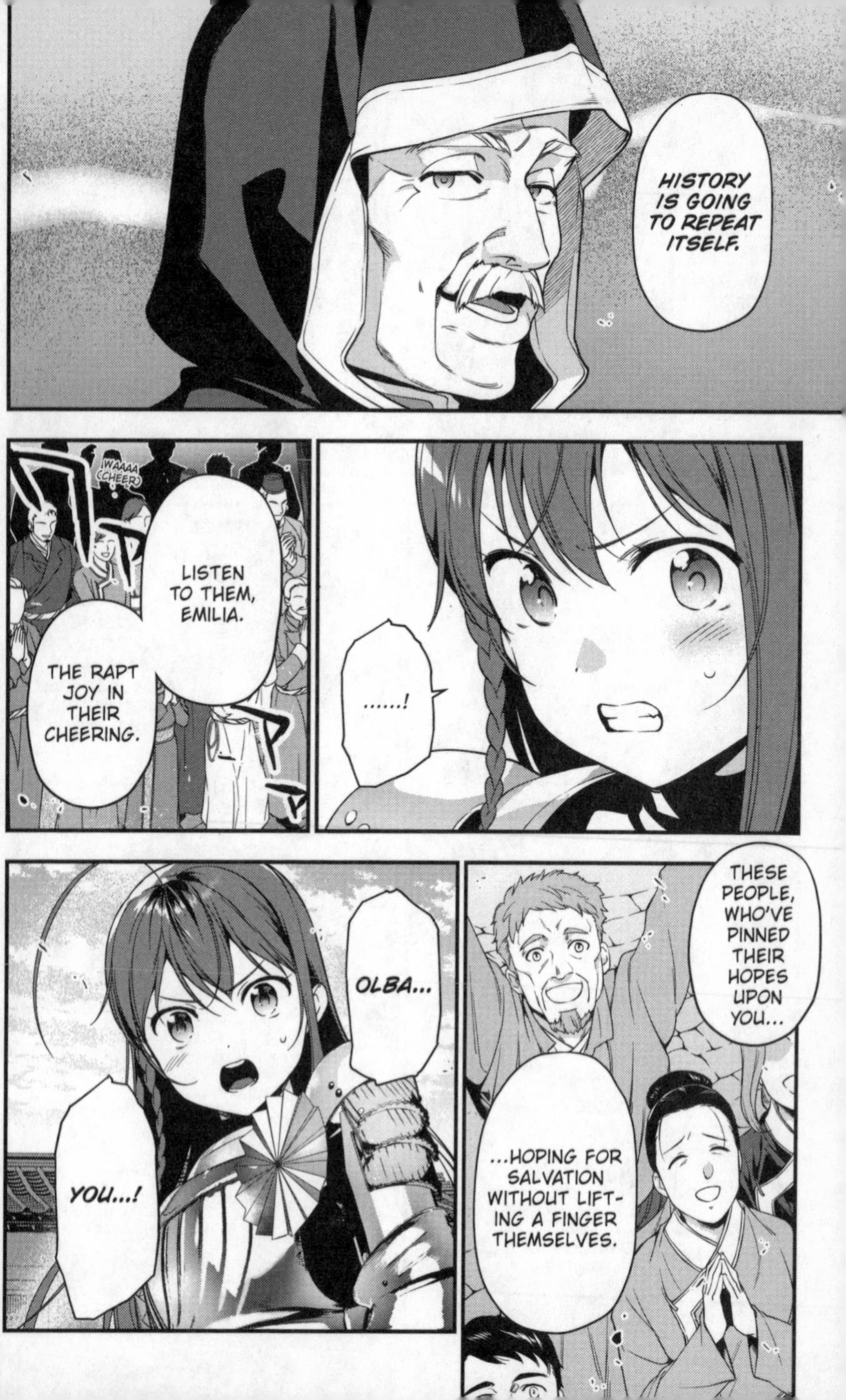
HISTORY IS GOING TO REPEAT ITSELF.
......!
WAAAA (CHEER)
LISTEN TO THEM, EMILIA.
THE RAPT JOY IN THEIR CHEERING.
THESE PEOPLE, WHO'VE PINNED THEIR HOPES UPON YOU...
...HOPING FOR SALVATION WITHOUT LIFT-ING A FINGER THEMSELVES.
OLBA...
YOU...!

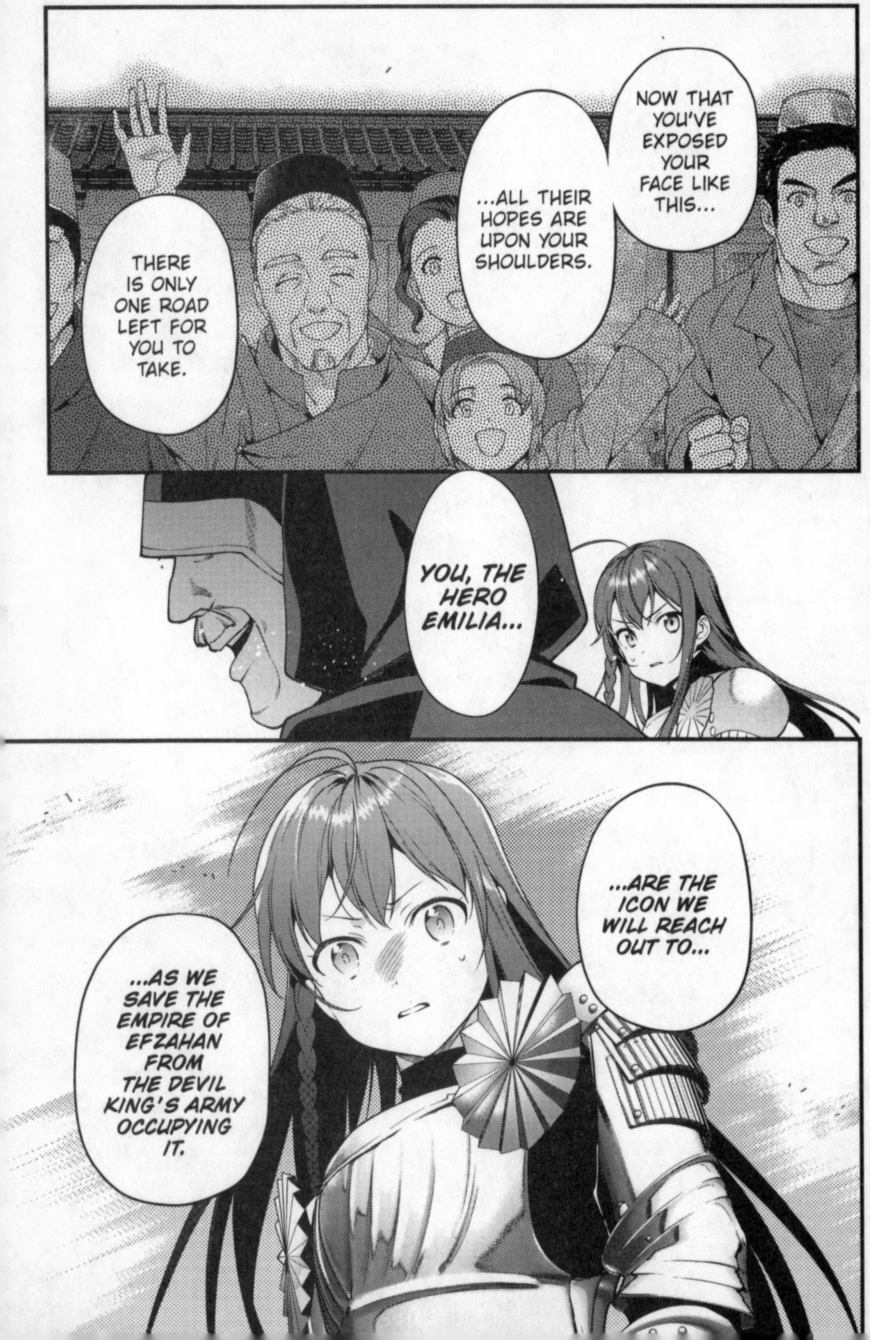
NOW THAT YOU'VE EXPOSED YOUR FACE LIKE THIS...
...ALL THEIR HOPES ARE UPON YOUR SHOULDERS.
THERE IS ONLY ONE ROAD LEFT FOR YOU TO TAKE.
YOU, THE HERO EMILIA...
...ARE THE ICON WE WILL REACH OUT TO...
...AS WE SAVE THE EMPIRE OF EFZAHAN FROM THE DEVIL KING'S ARMY OCCUPYING IT.

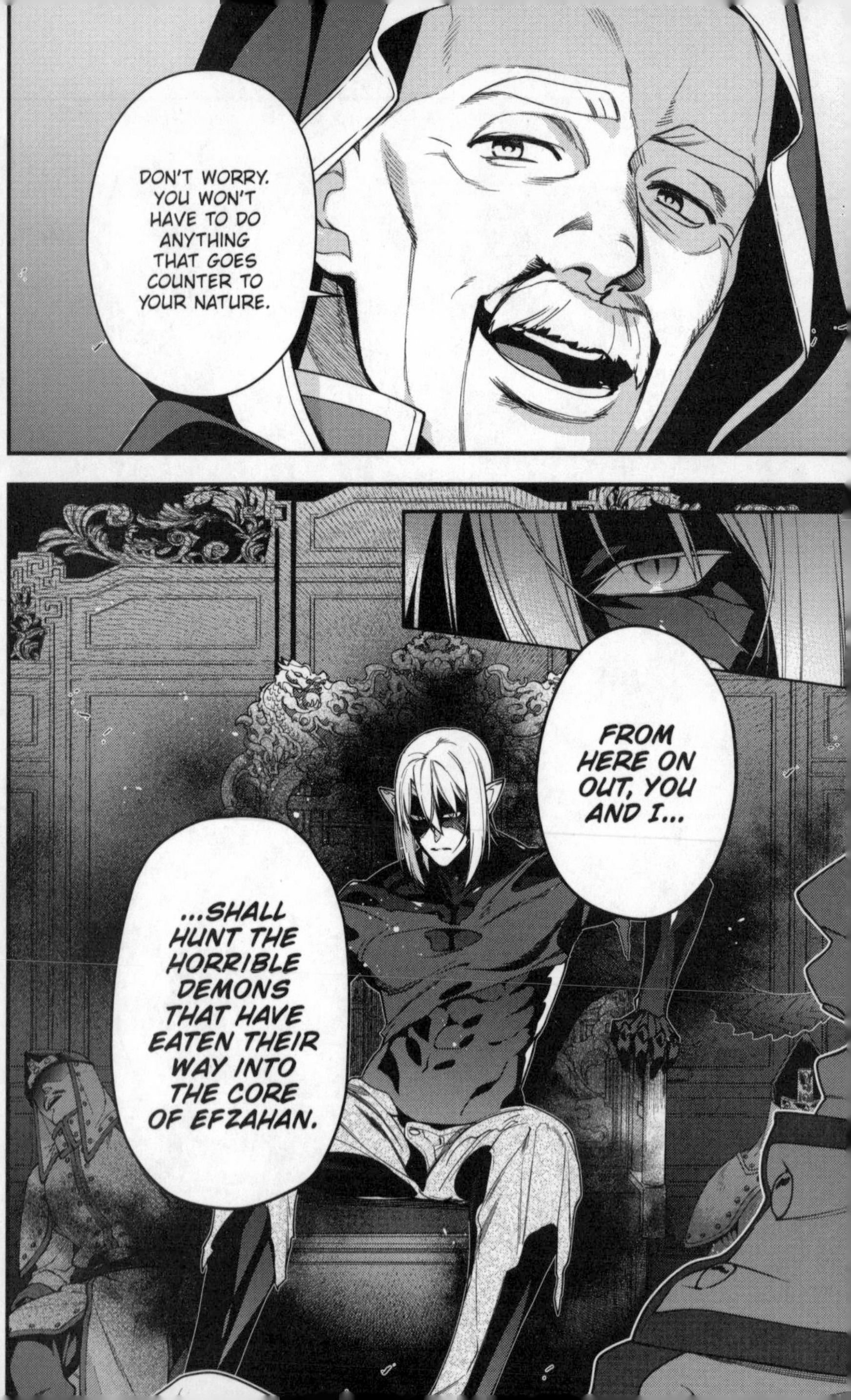
DON'T WORRY. YOU WON'T HAVE TO DO ANYTHING THAT GOES COUNTER TO YOUR NATURE.
FROM HERE ON OUT, YOU AND I...
...SHALL HUNT THE HORRIBLE DEMONS THAT HAVE EATEN THEIR WAY INTO THE CORE OF EFZAHAN.

Olba Meiyer

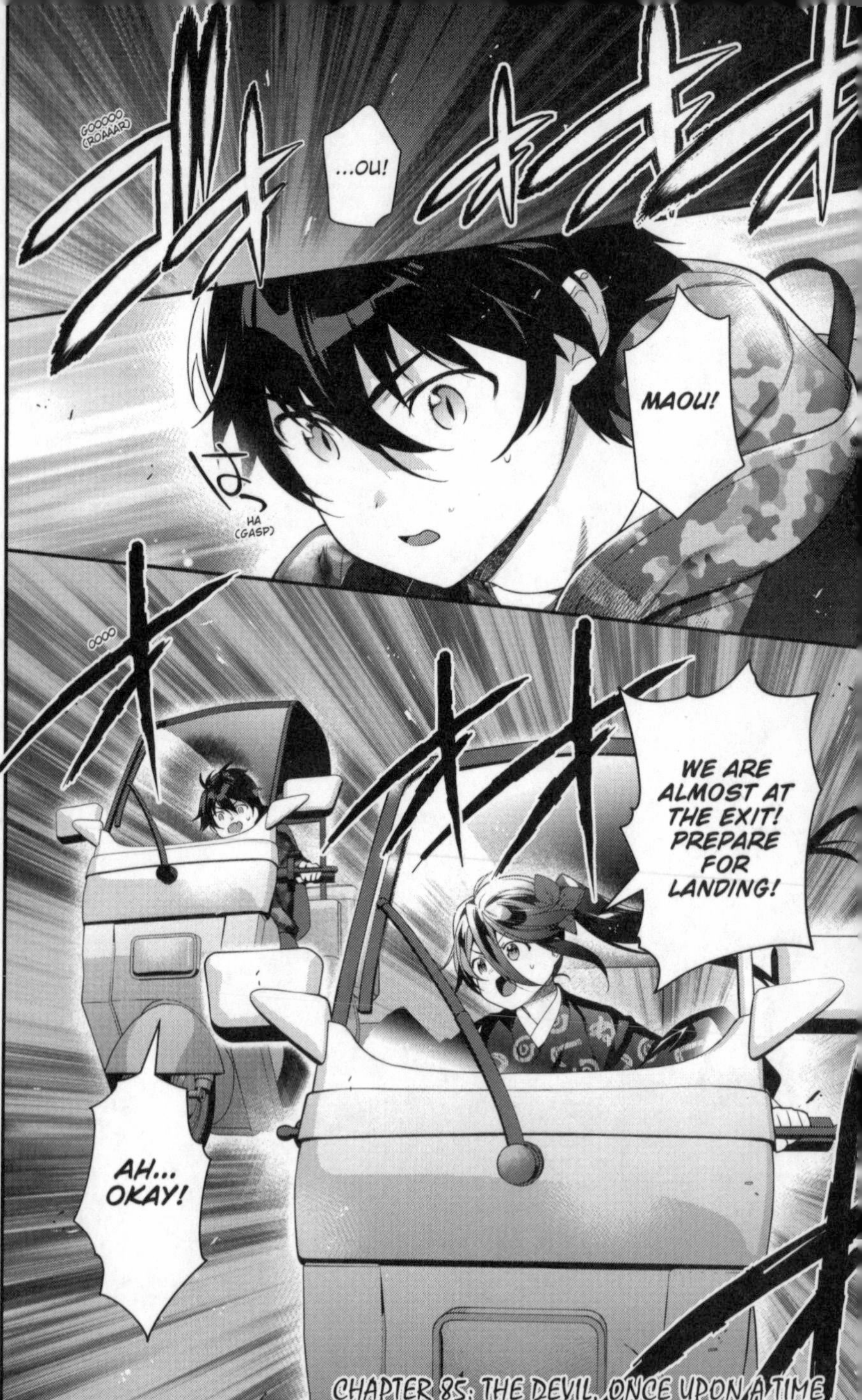
...OU!
GOOOOO (ROAAAR)
MAOU!
HA (GASP)
OOOO
WE ARE ALMOST AT THE EXIT! PREPARE FOR LANDING!
AH... OKAY!

CHAPTER 85: THE DEVIL, ONCE UPON A TIME

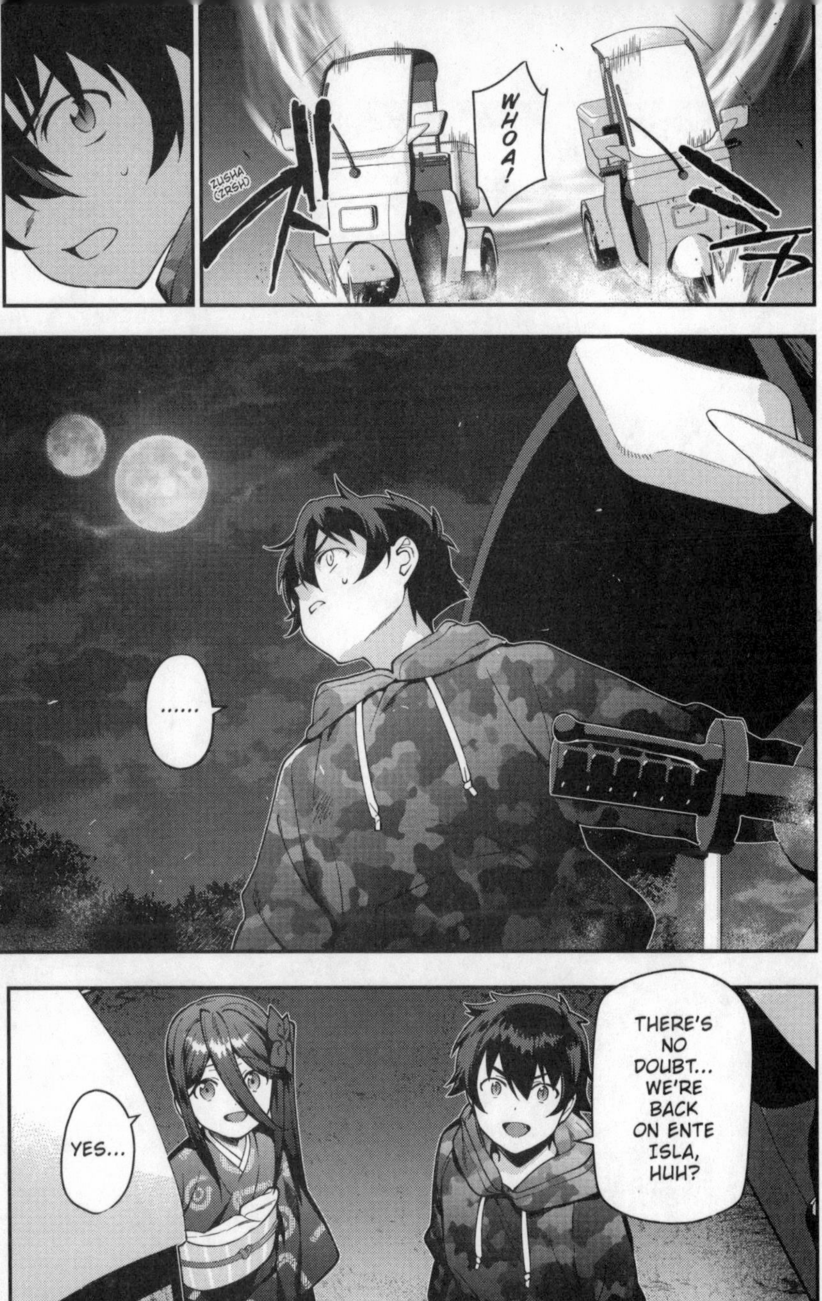
WHOA!
ZUSHA (ZRSH)
......
THERE'S NO DOUBT... WE'RE BACK ON ENTE ISLA, HUH?
YES...

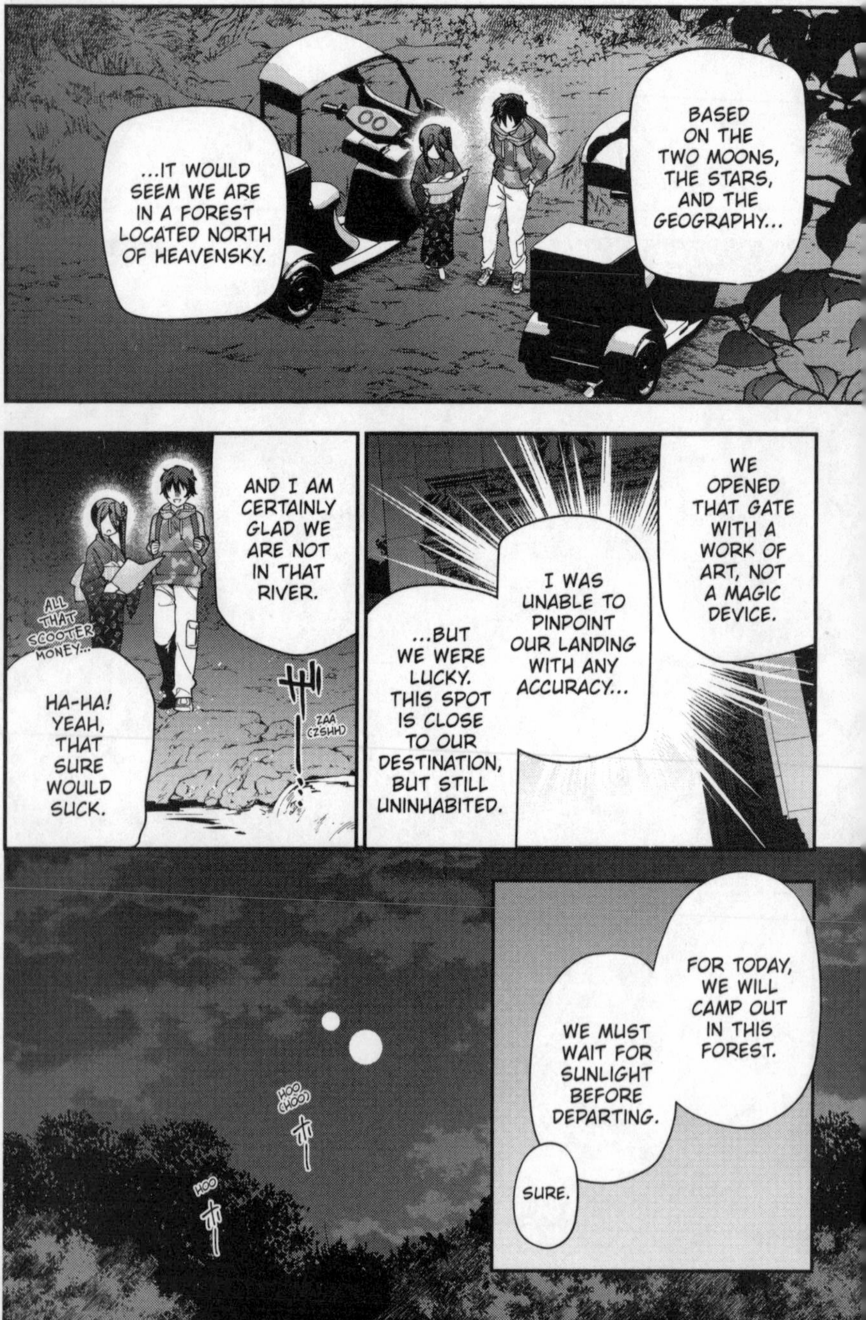
BASED ON THE TWO MOONS, THE STARS, AND THE GEOGRAPHY...
...IT WOULD SEEM WE ARE IN A FOREST LOCATED NORTH OF HEAVENSKY.
WE OPENED THAT GATE WITH A WORK OF ART, NOT A MAGIC DEVICE.
I WAS UNABLE TO PINPOINT OUR LANDING WITH ANY ACCURACY...
...BUT WE WERE LUCKY. THIS SPOT IS CLOSE TO OUR DESTINATION, BUT STILL UNINHABITED.
AND I AM CERTAINLY GLAD WE ARE NOT IN THAT RIVER.
ALL THAT SCOOTER MONEY...
HA-HA! YEAH, THAT SURE WOULD SUCK.
ZAA (ZSHH)
FOR TODAY, WE WILL CAMP OUT IN THIS FOREST.
WE MUST WAIT FOR SUNLIGHT BEFORE DEPARTING.
SURE.
HOO (HOO)
HOO

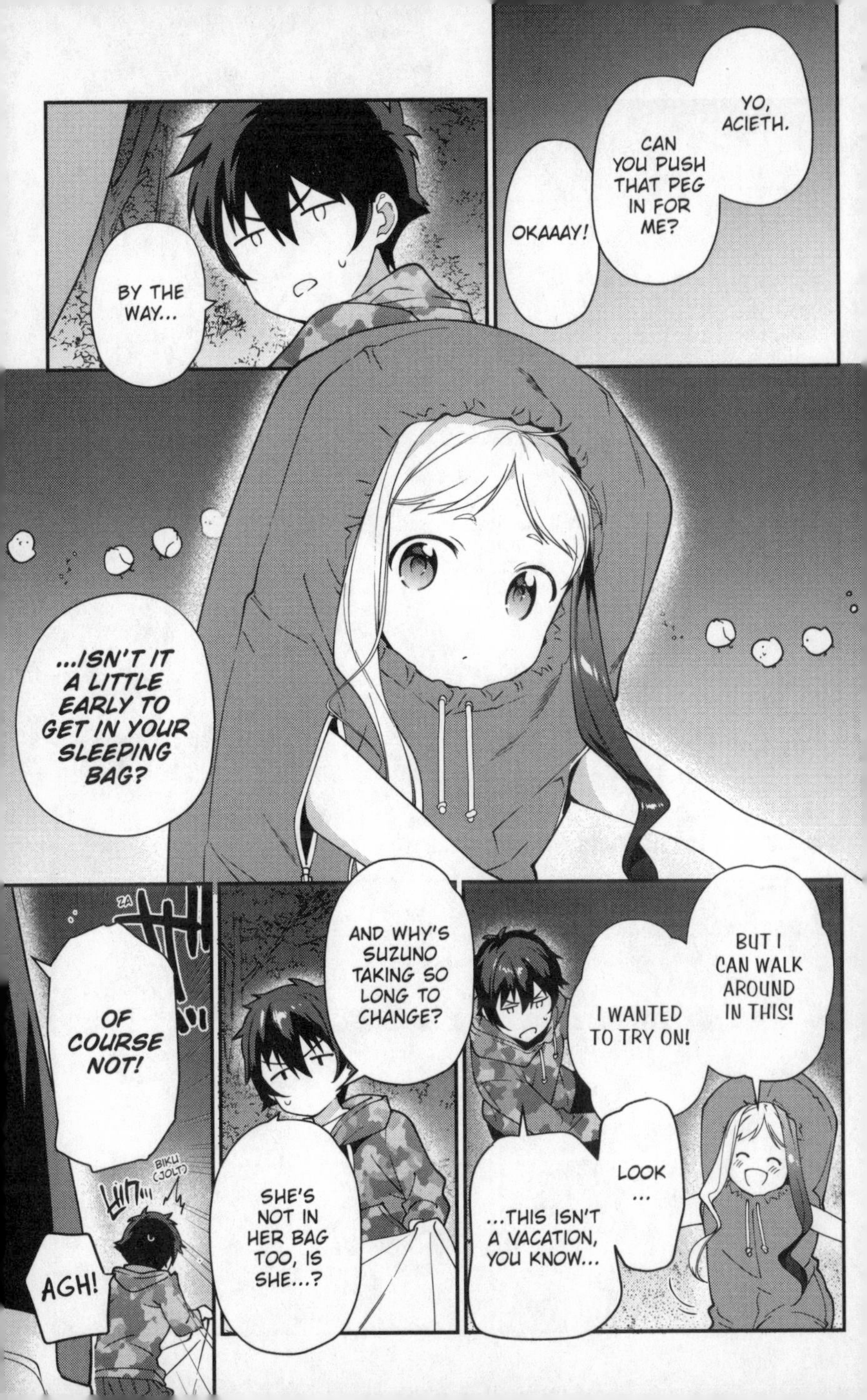
YO, ACIETH.
CAN YOU PUSH THAT PEG IN FOR ME?
OKAAAY!
BY THE WAY...
...ISN'T IT A LITTLE EARLY TO GET IN YOUR SLEEPING BAG?
BUT I CAN WALK AROUND IN THIS!
I WANTED TO TRY ON!
LOOK ...
...THIS ISN'T A VACATION, YOU KNOW...
AND WHY'S SUZUNO TAKING SO LONG TO CHANGE?
SHE'S NOT IN HER BAG TOO, IS SHE...?
ZA
OF COURSE NOT!
BIKU (JOLT)
AGH!

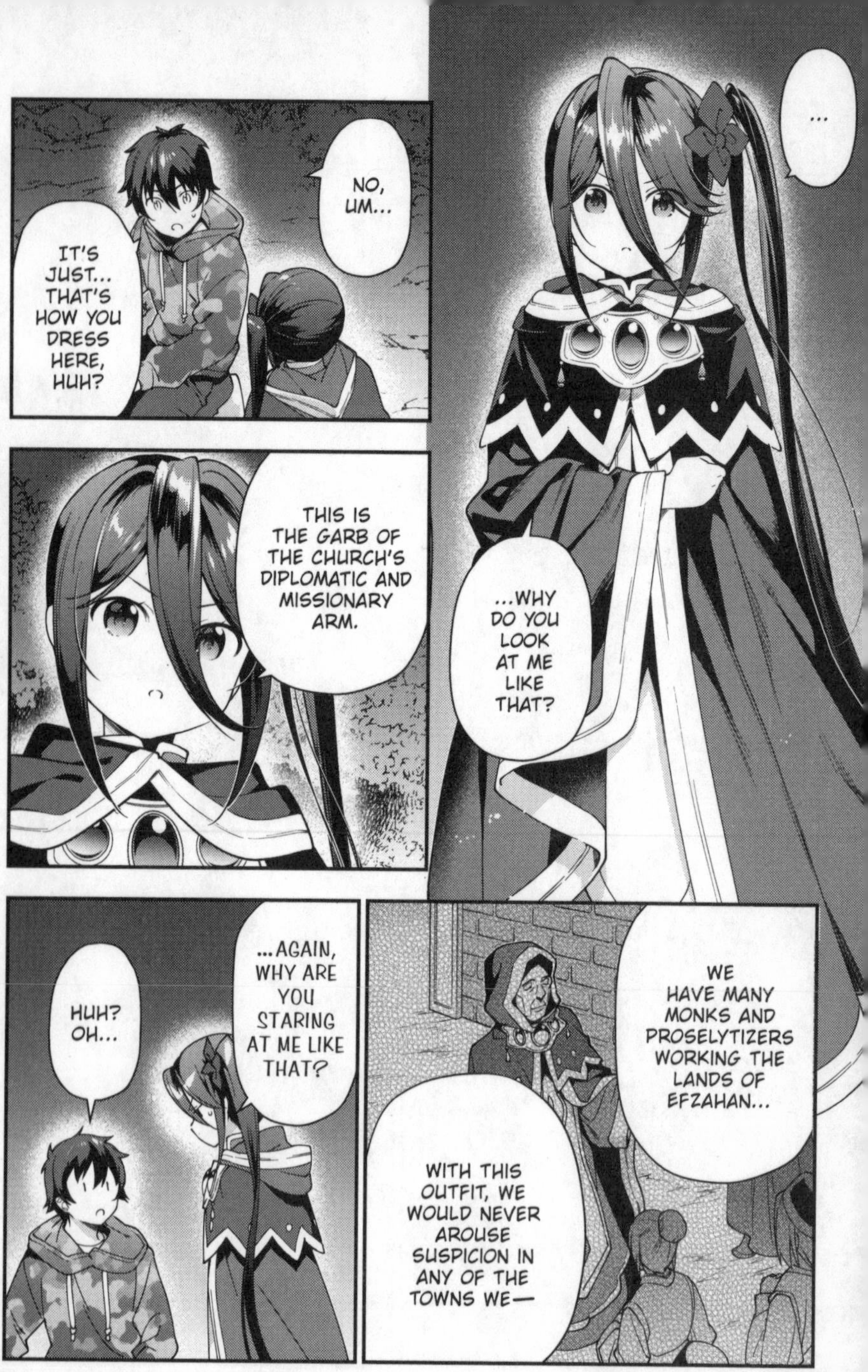
...
...WHY DO YOU LOOK AT ME LIKE THAT?
NO, UM...
IT'S JUST... THAT'S HOW YOU DRESS HERE, HUH?
THIS IS THE GARB OF THE CHURCH'S DIPLOMATIC AND MISSIONARY ARM.
WE HAVE MANY MONKS AND PROSELYTIZERS WORKING THE LANDS OF EFZAHAN...
WITH THIS OUTFIT, WE WOULD NEVER AROUSE SUSPICION IN ANY OF THE TOWNS WE—
...AGAIN, WHY ARE YOU STARING AT ME LIKE THAT?
HUH? OH...

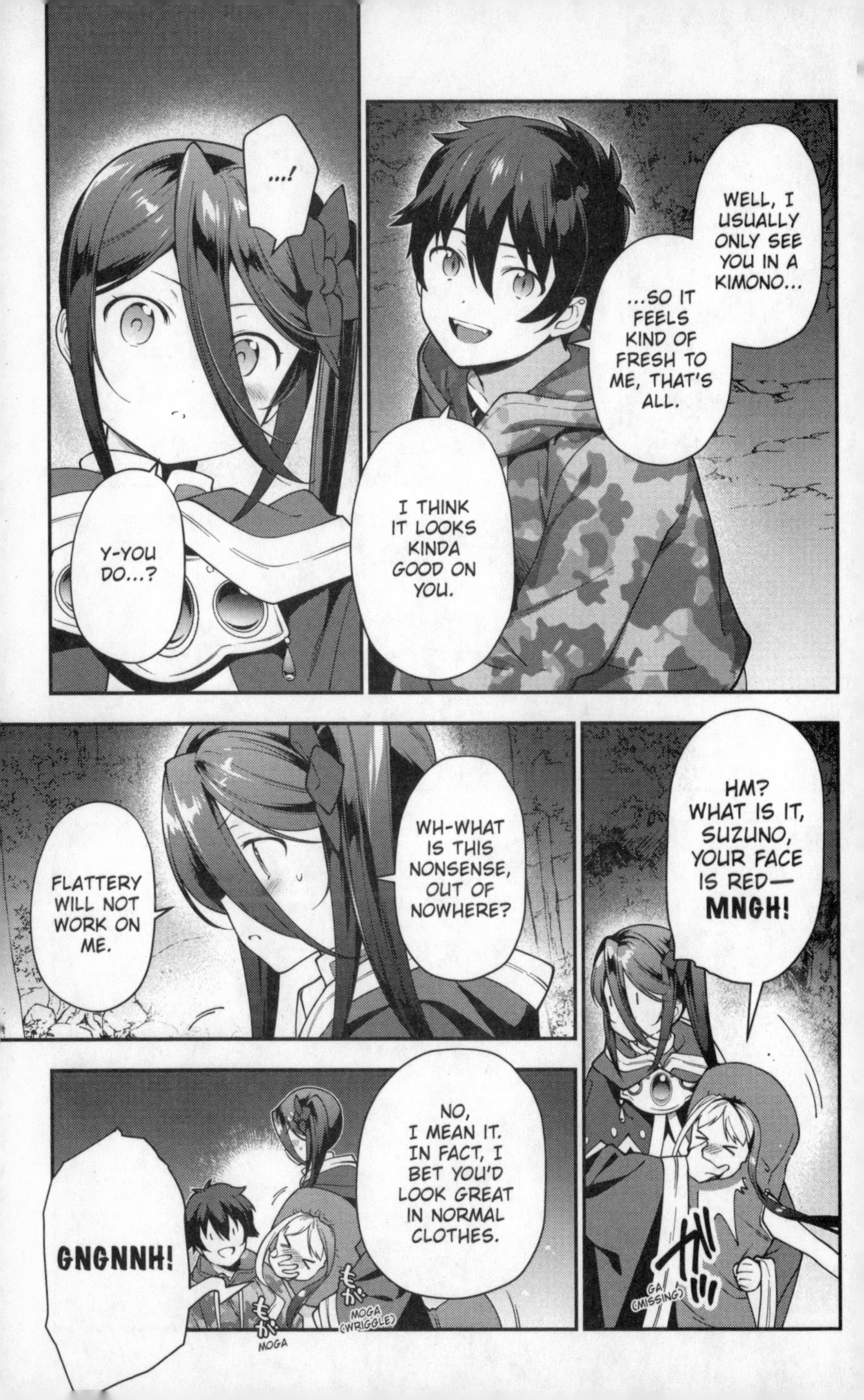

WELL, I USUALLY ONLY SEE YOU IN A KIMONO...
...SO IT FEELS KIND OF FRESH TO ME, THAT'S ALL.
I THINK IT LOOKS KINDA GOOD ON YOU.
...!
Y-YOU DO...?
HM? WHAT IS IT, SUZUNO, YOUR FACE IS RED—MNGH!
GA (MISSING)
WH-WHAT IS THIS NONSENSE, OUT OF NOWHERE?
FLATTERY WILL NOT WORK ON ME.
NO, I MEAN IT. IN FACT, I BET YOU'D LOOK GREAT IN NORMAL CLOTHES.
MOGA (WRIGGLE)
MOGA
GNGNNH!

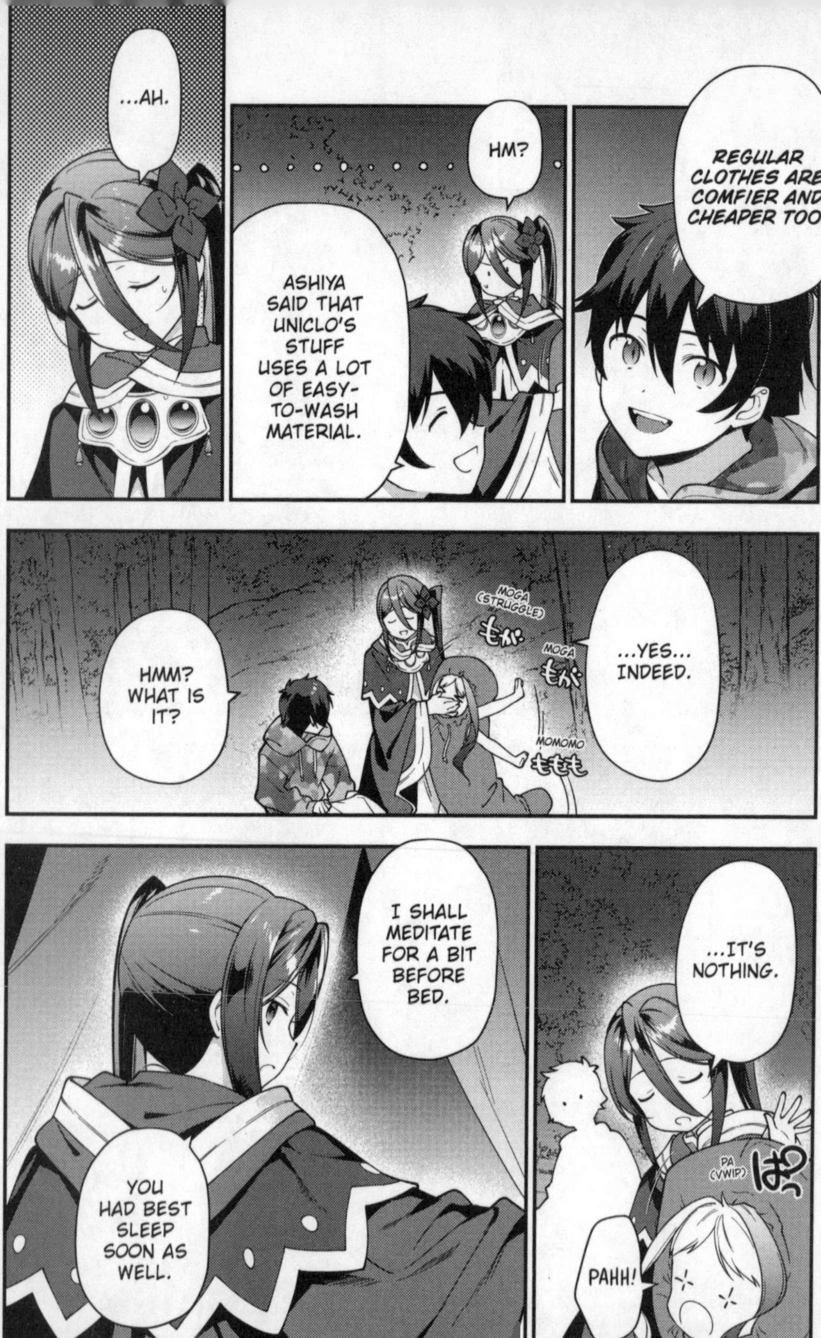
REGULAR CLOTHES ARE COMFIER AND CHEAPER TOO.
HM?
ASHIYA SAID THAT UNICLO'S STUFF USES A LOT OF EASY-TO-WASH MATERIAL.
...AH.
...YES... INDEED.
MOGA (STRUGGLE) もが
MOGA もが
MOMOMO ももも
HMM? WHAT IS IT?
...IT'S NOTHING.
PA (VWIP) はっ
PAHH!
I SHALL MEDITATE FOR A BIT BEFORE BED.
YOU HAD BEST SLEEP SOON AS WELL.

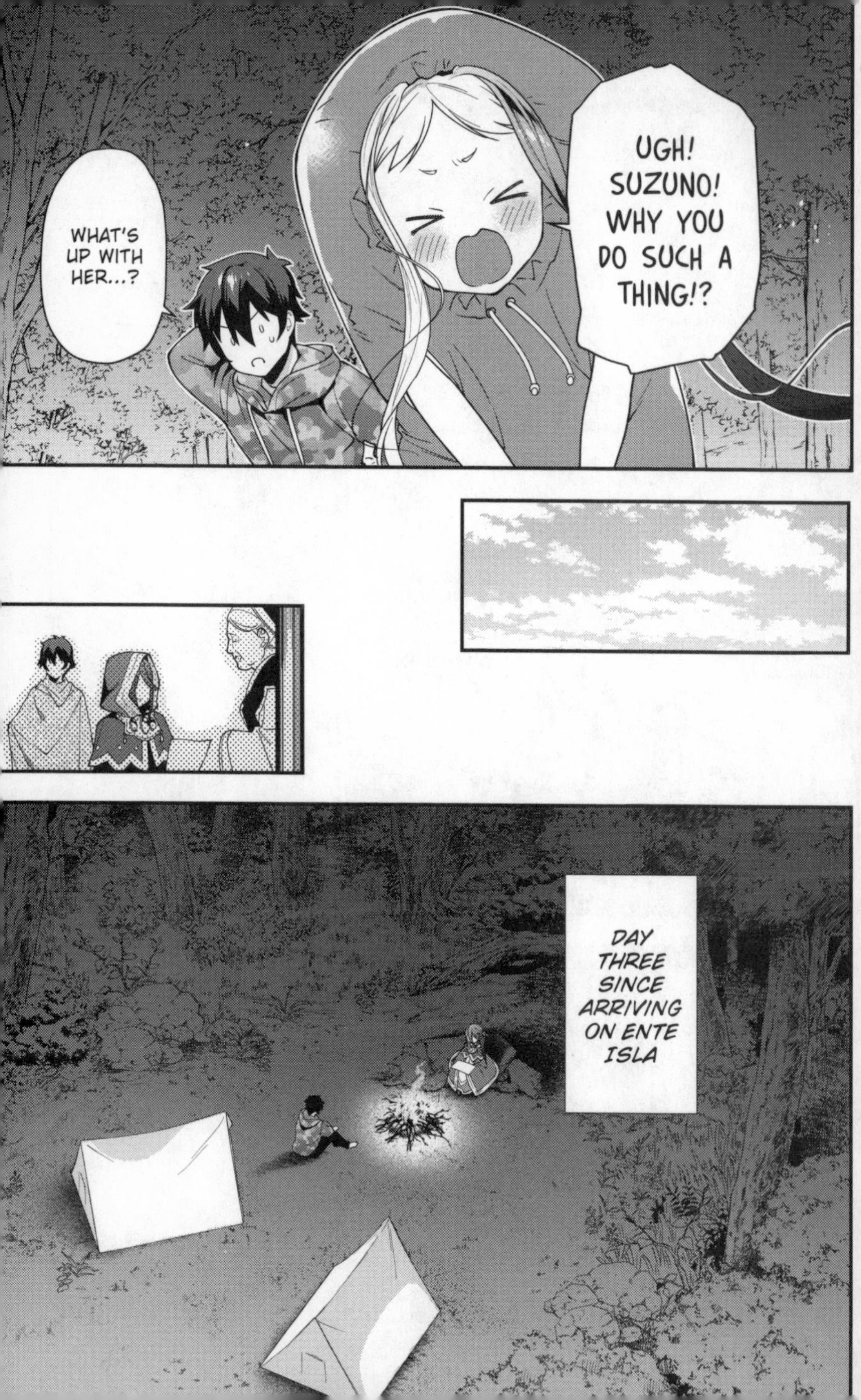
UGH! SUZUNO! WHY YOU DO SUCH A THING!?
WHAT'S UP WITH HER...?
DAY THREE SINCE ARRIVING ON ENTE ISLA

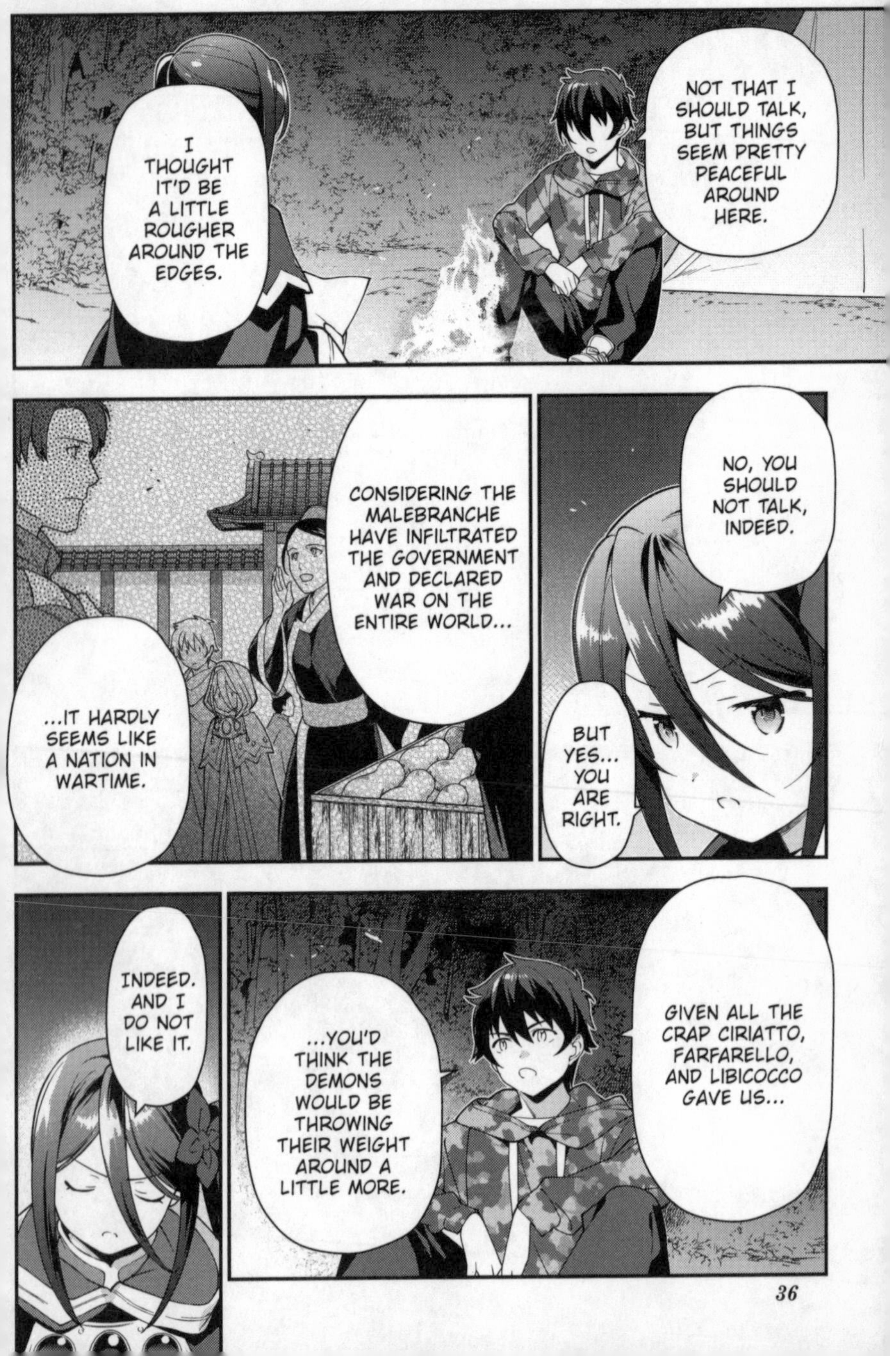
NOT THAT I SHOULD TALK, BUT THINGS SEEM PRETTY PEACEFUL AROUND HERE.
I THOUGHT IT'D BE A LITTLE ROUGHER AROUND THE EDGES.
NO, YOU SHOULD NOT TALK, INDEED.
BUT YES... YOU ARE RIGHT.
CONSIDERING THE MALEBRANCHE HAVE INFILTRATED THE GOVERNMENT AND DECLARED WAR ON THE ENTIRE WORLD...
...IT HARDLY SEEMS LIKE A NATION IN WARTIME.
GIVEN ALL THE CRAP CIRIATTO, FARFARELLO, AND LIBICOCCO GAVE US...
...YOU'D THINK THE DEMONS WOULD BE THROWING THEIR WEIGHT AROUND A LITTLE MORE.
INDEED. AND I DO NOT LIKE IT.

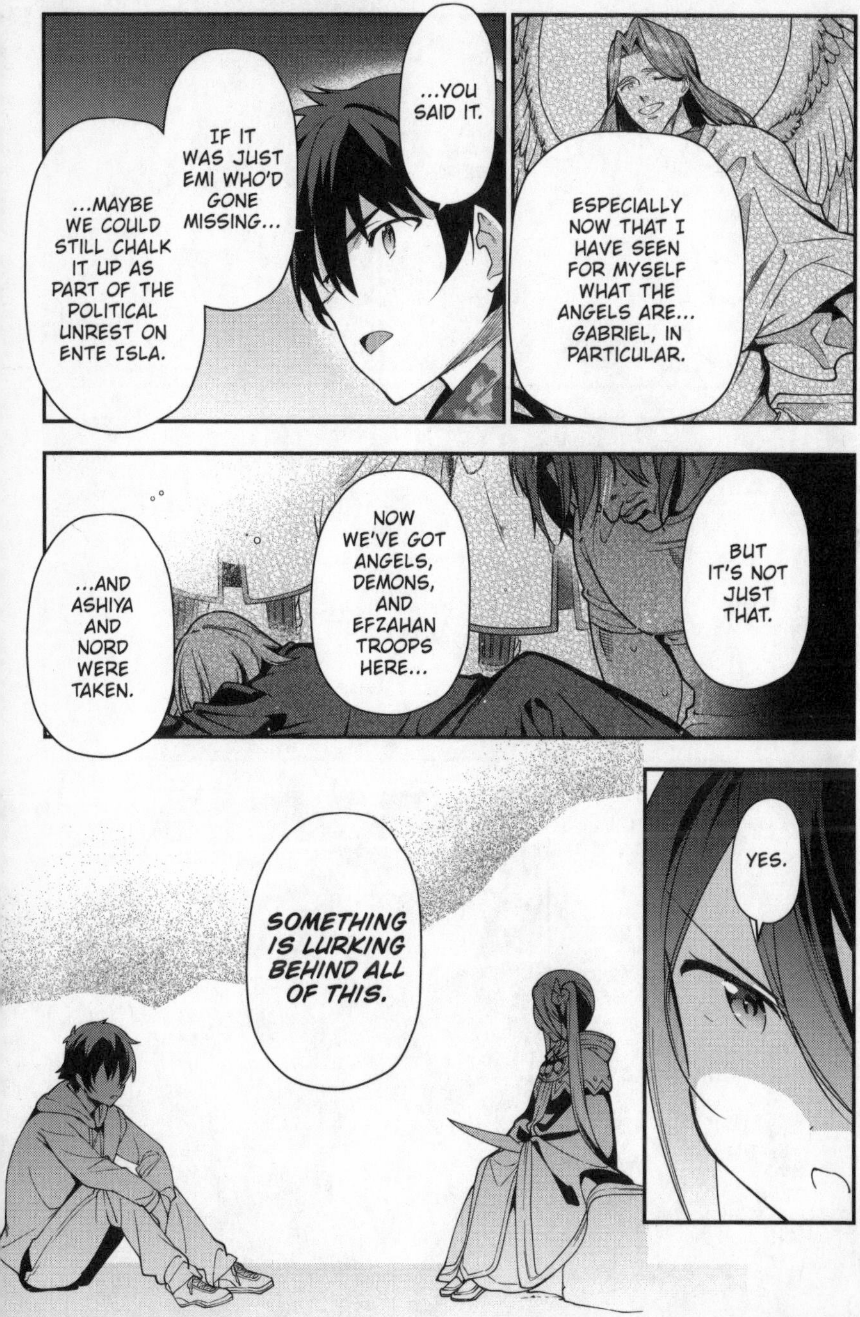
ESPECIALLY NOW THAT I HAVE SEEN FOR MYSELF WHAT THE ANGELS ARE... GABRIEL, IN PARTICULAR.
...YOU SAID IT.
IF IT WAS JUST EMI WHO'D GONE MISSING...
...MAYBE WE COULD STILL CHALK IT UP AS PART OF THE POLITICAL UNREST ON ENTE ISLA.
BUT IT'S NOT JUST THAT.
NOW WE'VE GOT ANGELS, DEMONS, AND EFZAHAN TROOPS HERE...
...AND ASHIYA AND NORD WERE TAKEN.
YES.
SOMETHING IS LURKING BEHIND ALL OF THIS.

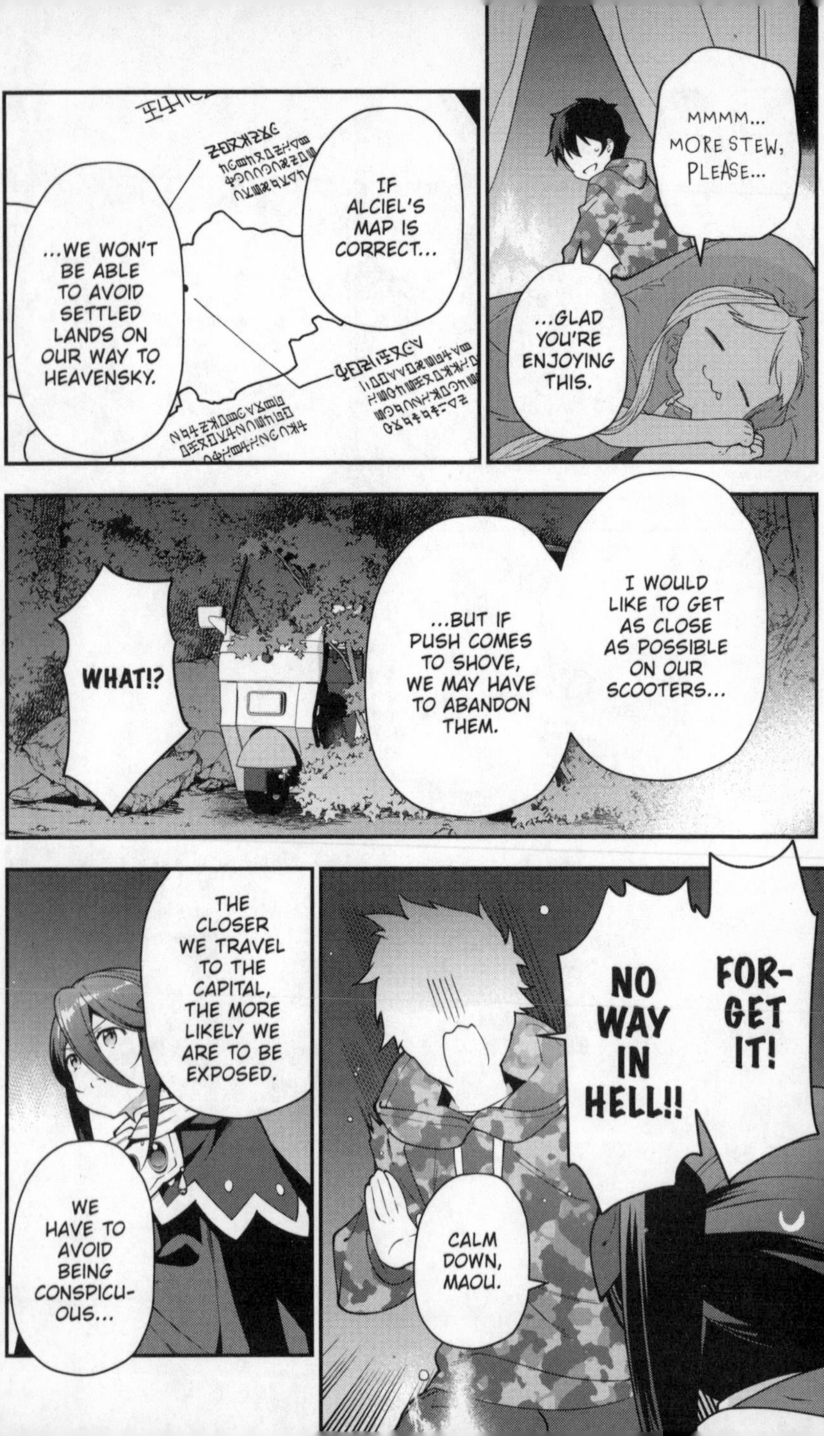
MMMM... MORE STEW, PLEASE...
...GLAD YOU'RE ENJOYING THIS.
IF ALCIEL'S MAP IS CORRECT...
...WE WON'T BE ABLE TO AVOID SETTLED LANDS ON OUR WAY TO HEAVENSKY.
I WOULD LIKE TO GET AS CLOSE AS POSSIBLE ON OUR SCOOTERS...
...BUT IF PUSH COMES TO SHOVE, WE MAY HAVE TO ABANDON THEM.
WHAT!?
FOR-GET IT!
NO WAY IN HELL!!
CALM DOWN, MAOU.
THE CLOSER WE TRAVEL TO THE CAPITAL, THE MORE LIKELY WE ARE TO BE EXPOSED.
WE HAVE TO AVOID BEING CONSPICU-OUS...

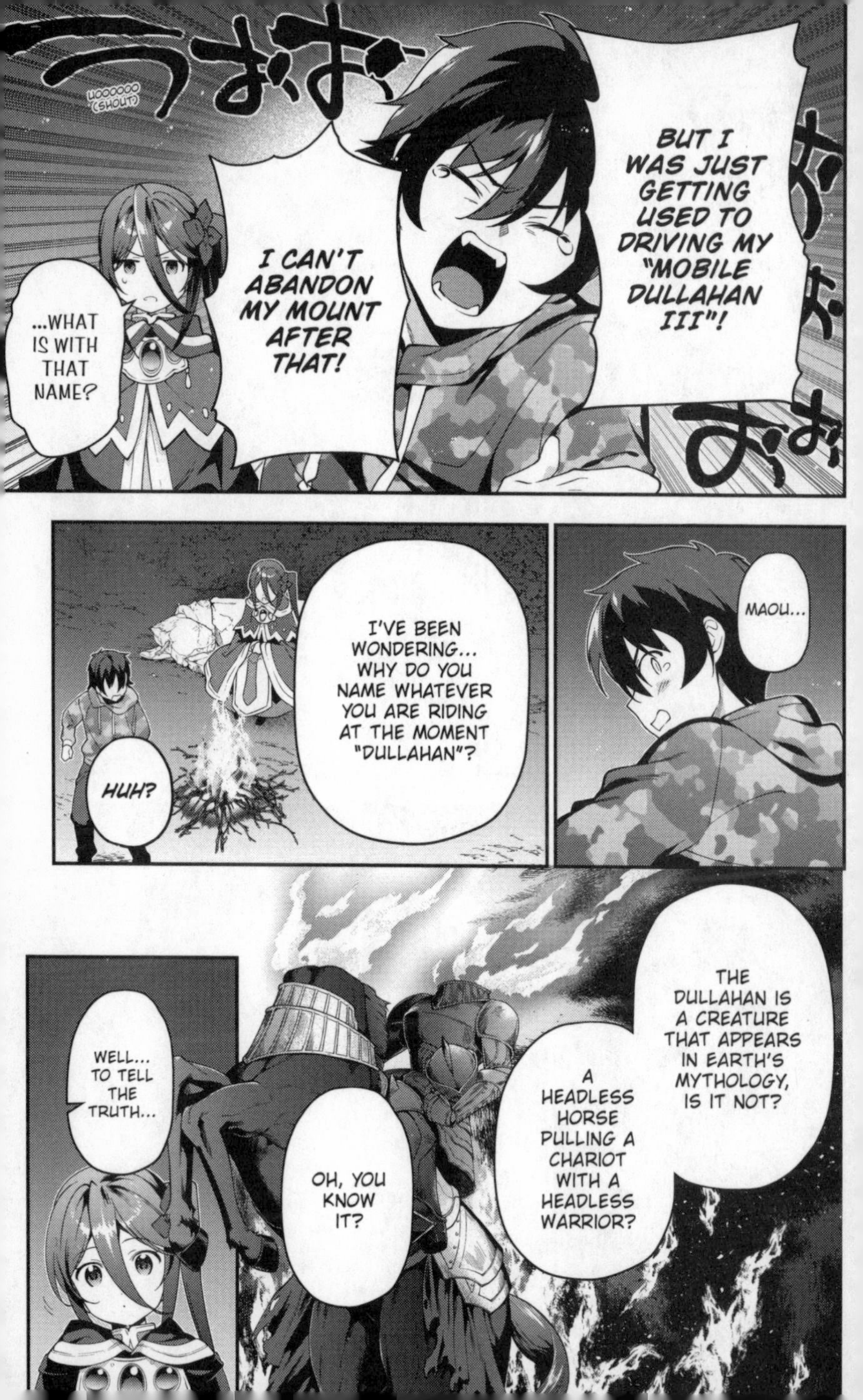
BUT I WAS JUST GETTING USED TO DRIVING MY "MOBILE DULLAHAN III"!
I CAN'T ABANDON MY MOUNT AFTER THAT!
UOOOOOO (SHOUT)
...WHAT IS WITH THAT NAME?
MAOU...
I'VE BEEN WONDERING... WHY DO YOU NAME WHATEVER YOU ARE RIDING AT THE MOMENT "DULLAHAN"?
HUH?
THE DULLAHAN IS A CREATURE THAT APPEARS IN EARTH'S MYTHOLOGY, IS IT NOT?
A HEADLESS HORSE PULLING A CHARIOT WITH A HEADLESS WARRIOR?
OH, YOU KNOW IT?
WELL... TO TELL THE TRUTH...

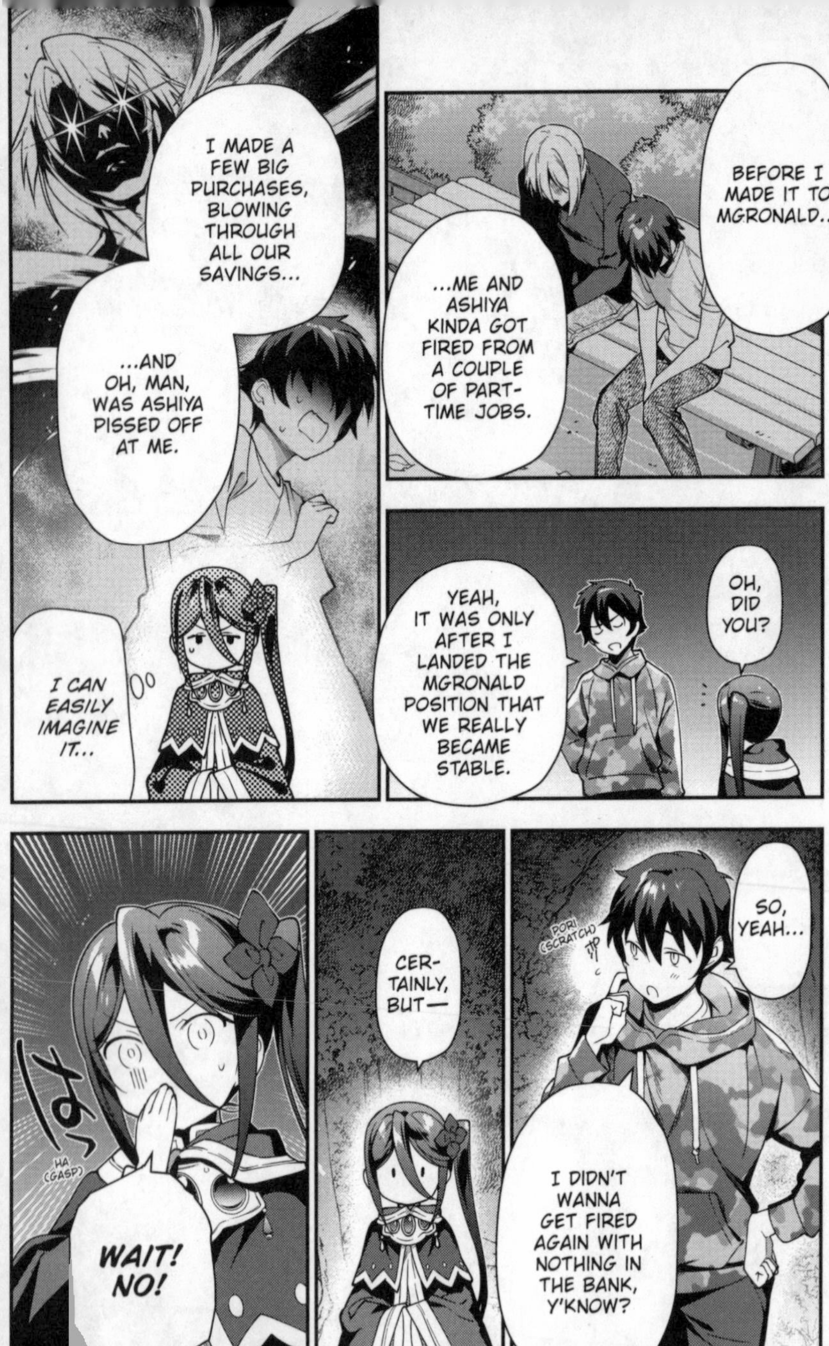
BEFORE I MADE IT TO MGRONALD...
...ME AND ASHIYA KINDA GOT FIRED FROM A COUPLE OF PART-TIME JOBS.
OH, DID YOU?
YEAH, IT WAS ONLY AFTER I LANDED THE MGRONALD POSITION THAT WE REALLY BECAME STABLE.
I MADE A FEW BIG PURCHASES, BLOWING THROUGH ALL OUR SAVINGS...
...AND OH, MAN, WAS ASHIYA PISSED OFF AT ME.
I CAN EASILY IMAGINE IT...
SO, YEAH...
PORI (SCRATCH)
I DIDN'T WANNA GET FIRED AGAIN WITH NOTHING IN THE BANK, Y'KNOW?
CER-TAINLY, BUT—
HA (GASP)
WAIT! NO!

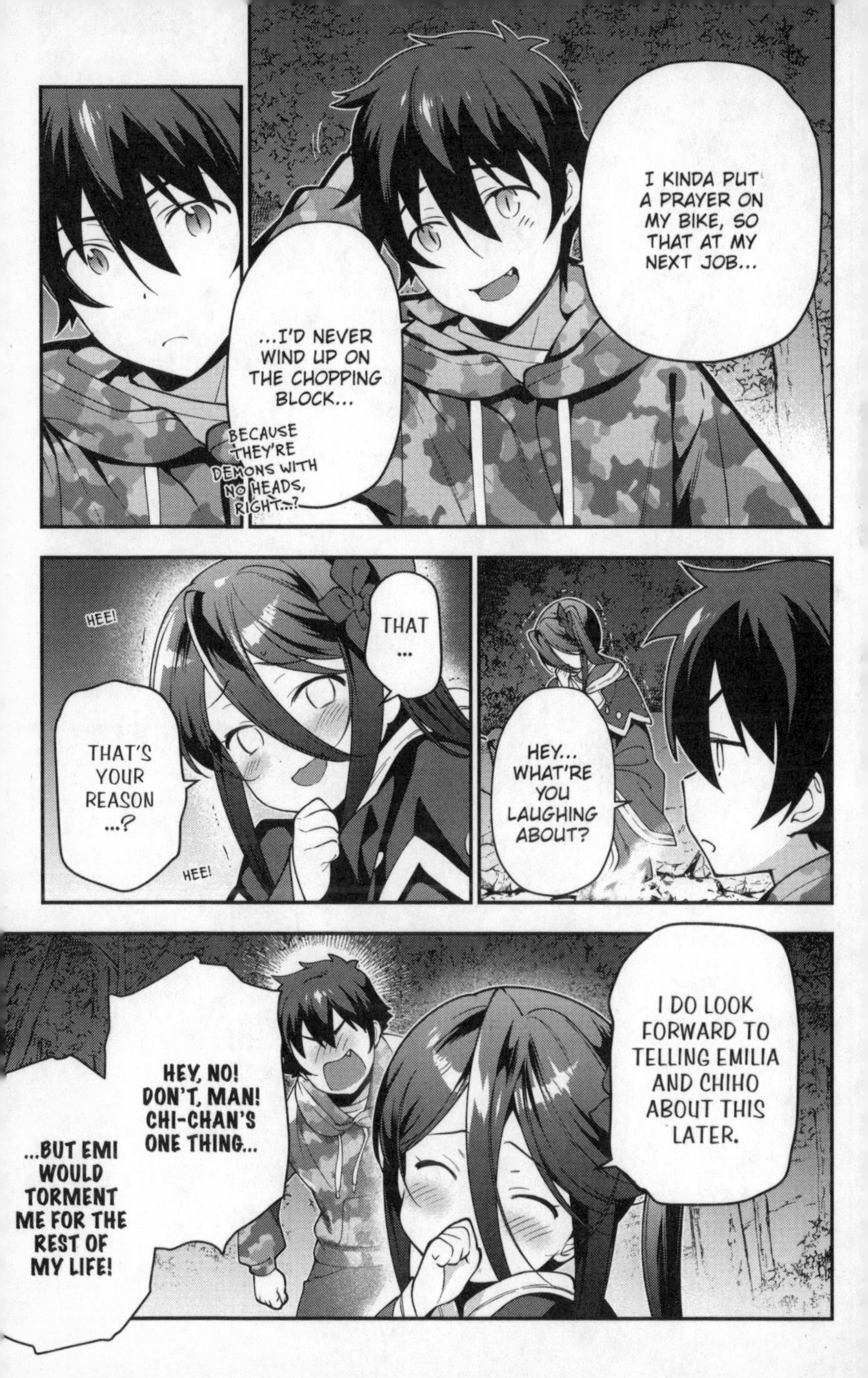
I KINDA PUT A PRAYER ON MY BIKE, SO THAT AT MY NEXT JOB...
...I'D NEVER WIND UP ON THE CHOPPING BLOCK...
BECAUSE THEY'RE DEMONS WITH NO HEADS, RIGHT...?
HEY... WHAT'RE YOU LAUGHING ABOUT?
THAT ...
HEE!
THAT'S YOUR REASON ...?
HEE!
I DO LOOK FORWARD TO TELLING EMILIA AND CHIHO ABOUT THIS LATER.
HEY, NO! DON'T, MAN! CHI-CHAN'S ONE THING...
...BUT EMI WOULD TORMENT ME FOR THE REST OF MY LIFE!

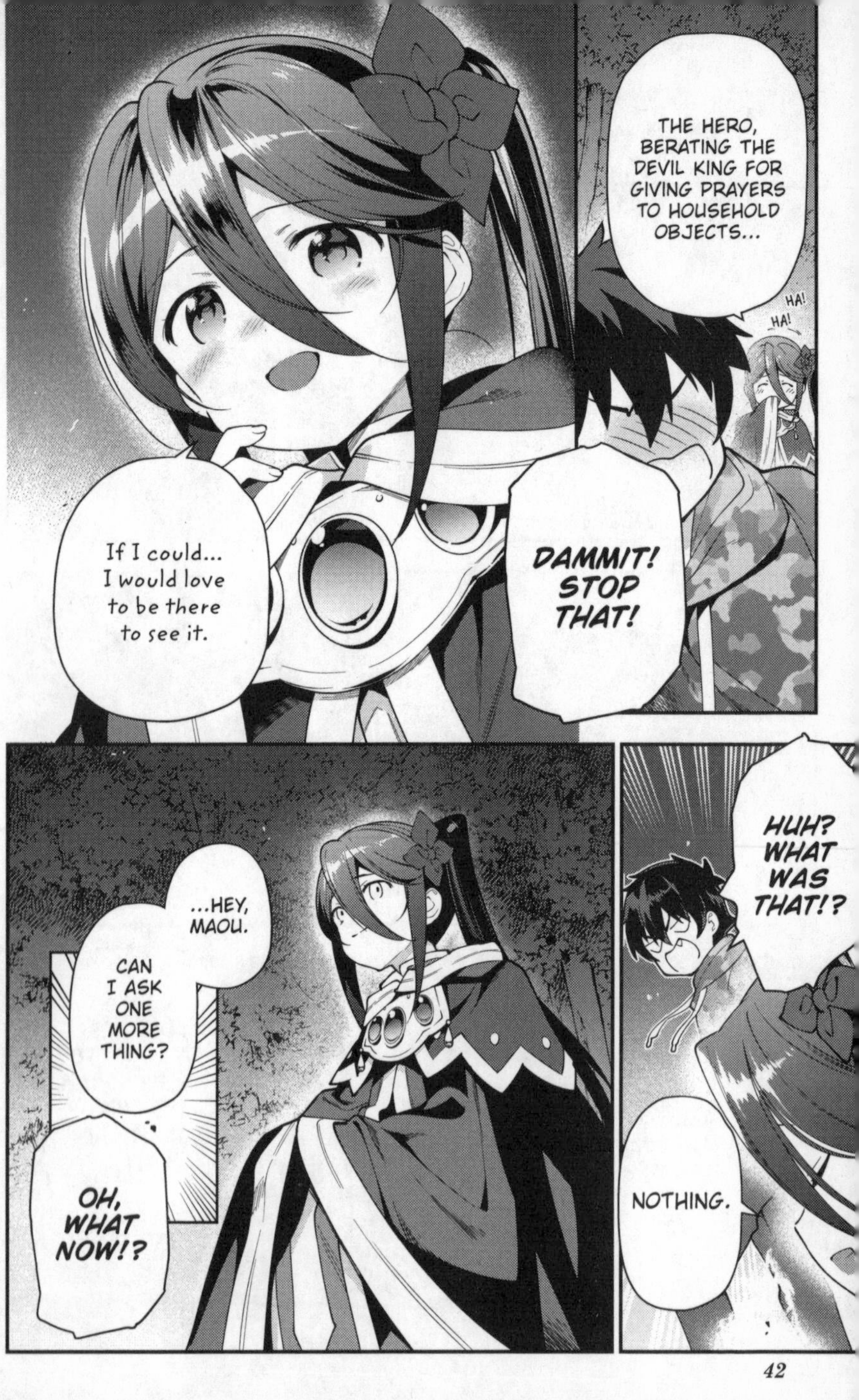
THE HERO, BERATING THE DEVIL KING FOR GIVING PRAYERS TO HOUSEHOLD OBJECTS...
HA! HA!
DAMMIT! STOP THAT!
If I could... I would love to be there to see it.
HUH? WHAT WAS THAT!?
NOTHING.
...HEY, MAOU.
CAN I ASK ONE MORE THING?
OH, WHAT NOW!?

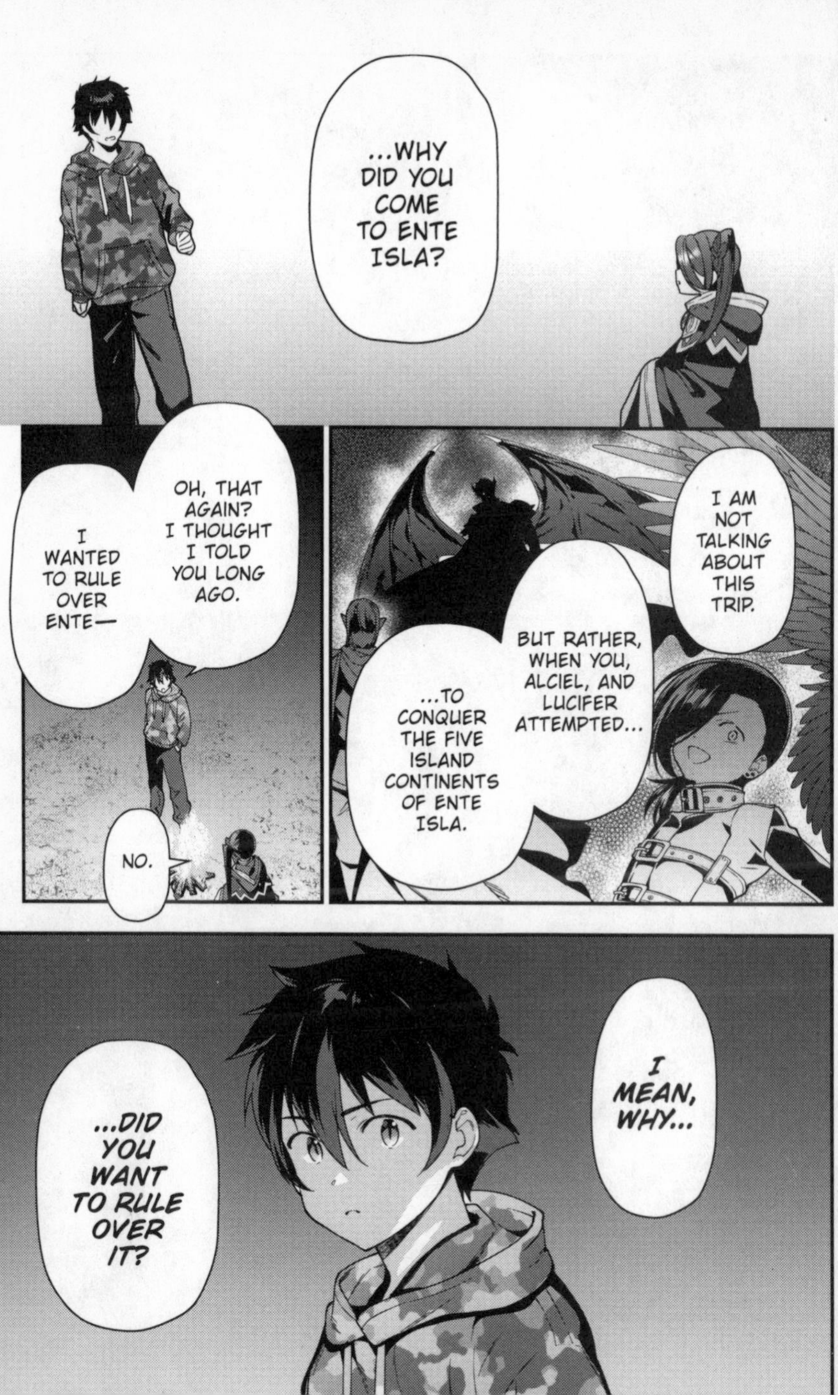
...WHY DID YOU COME TO ENTE ISLA?
OH, THAT AGAIN? I THOUGHT I TOLD YOU LONG AGO.
I WANTED TO RULE OVER ENTE—
NO.
I AM NOT TALKING ABOUT THIS TRIP.
BUT RATHER, WHEN YOU, ALCIEL, AND LUCIFER ATTEMPTED...
...TO CONQUER THE FIVE ISLAND CONTINENTS OF ENTE ISLA.
I MEAN, WHY...
...DID YOU WANT TO RULE OVER IT?

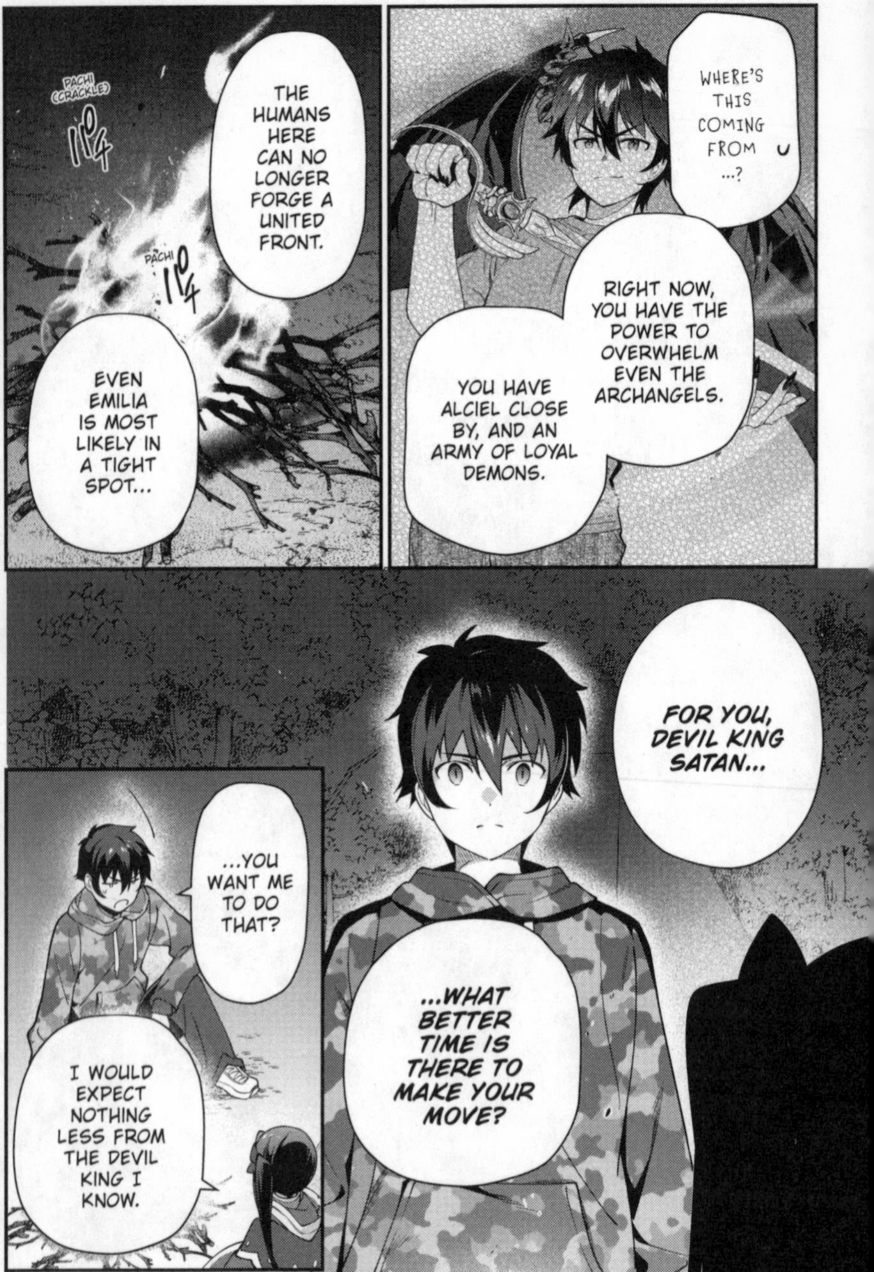
WHERE'S THIS COMING FROM ...?
RIGHT NOW, YOU HAVE THE POWER TO OVERWHELM EVEN THE ARCHANGELS.
YOU HAVE ALCIEL CLOSE BY, AND AN ARMY OF LOYAL DEMONS.
PACHI (CRACKLE)
THE HUMANS HERE CAN NO LONGER FORGE A UNITED FRONT.
PACHI
EVEN EMILIA IS MOST LIKELY IN A TIGHT SPOT...
FOR YOU, DEVIL KING SATAN...
...WHAT BETTER TIME IS THERE TO MAKE YOUR MOVE?
...YOU WANT ME TO DO THAT?
I WOULD EXPECT NOTHING LESS FROM THE DEVIL KING I KNOW.

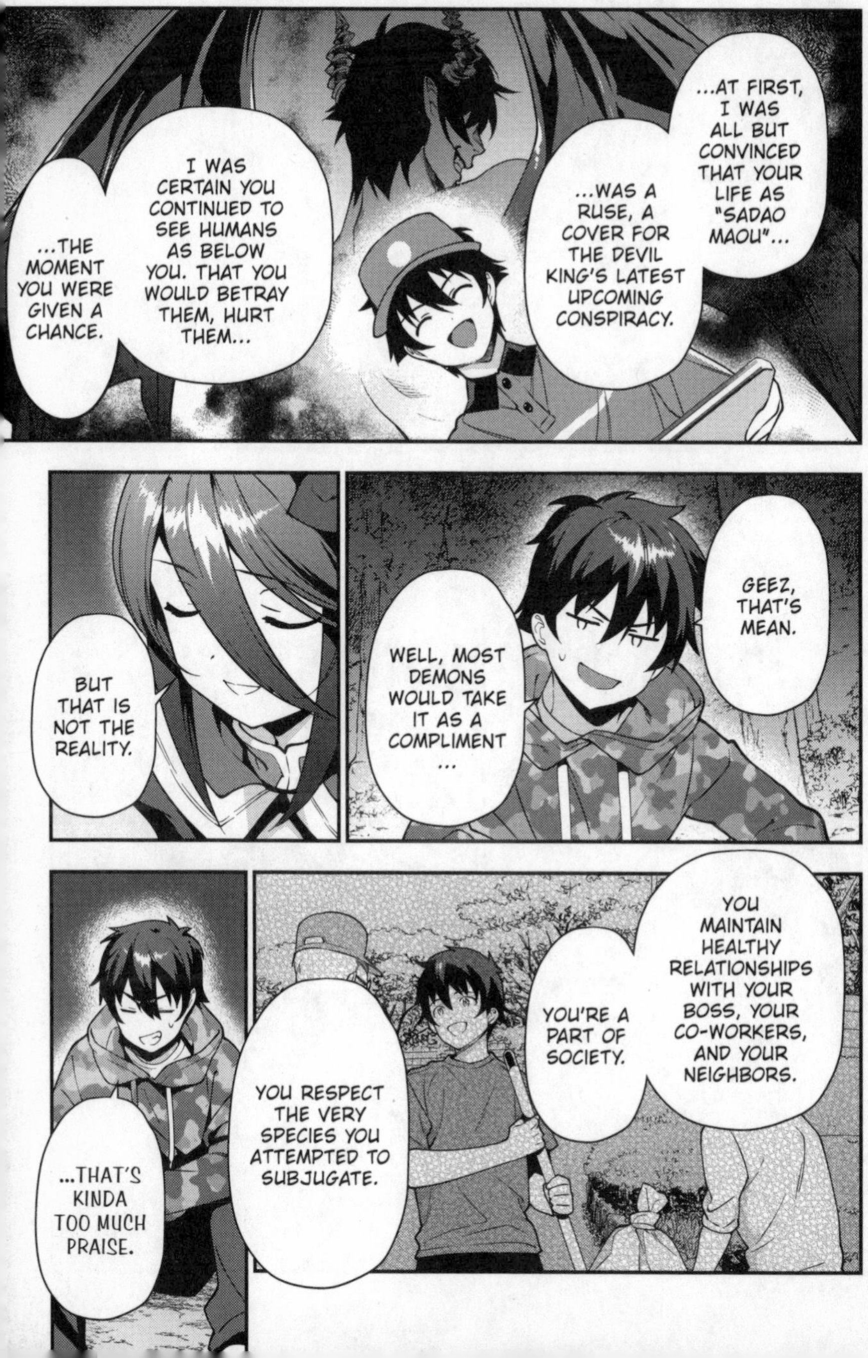
...AT FIRST, I WAS ALL BUT CONVINCED THAT YOUR LIFE AS "SADAO MAOU"...
...WAS A RUSE, A COVER FOR THE DEVIL KING'S LATEST UPCOMING CONSPIRACY.
I WAS CERTAIN YOU CONTINUED TO SEE HUMANS AS BELOW YOU. THAT YOU WOULD BETRAY THEM, HURT THEM...
...THE MOMENT YOU WERE GIVEN A CHANCE.
GEEZ, THAT'S MEAN.
WELL, MOST DEMONS WOULD TAKE IT AS A COMPLIMENT...
BUT THAT IS NOT THE REALITY.
YOU MAINTAIN HEALTHY RELATIONSHIPS WITH YOUR BOSS, YOUR CO-WORKERS, AND YOUR NEIGHBORS.
YOU'RE A PART OF SOCIETY.
YOU RESPECT THE VERY SPECIES YOU ATTEMPTED TO SUBJUGATE.
...THAT'S KINDA TOO MUCH PRAISE.

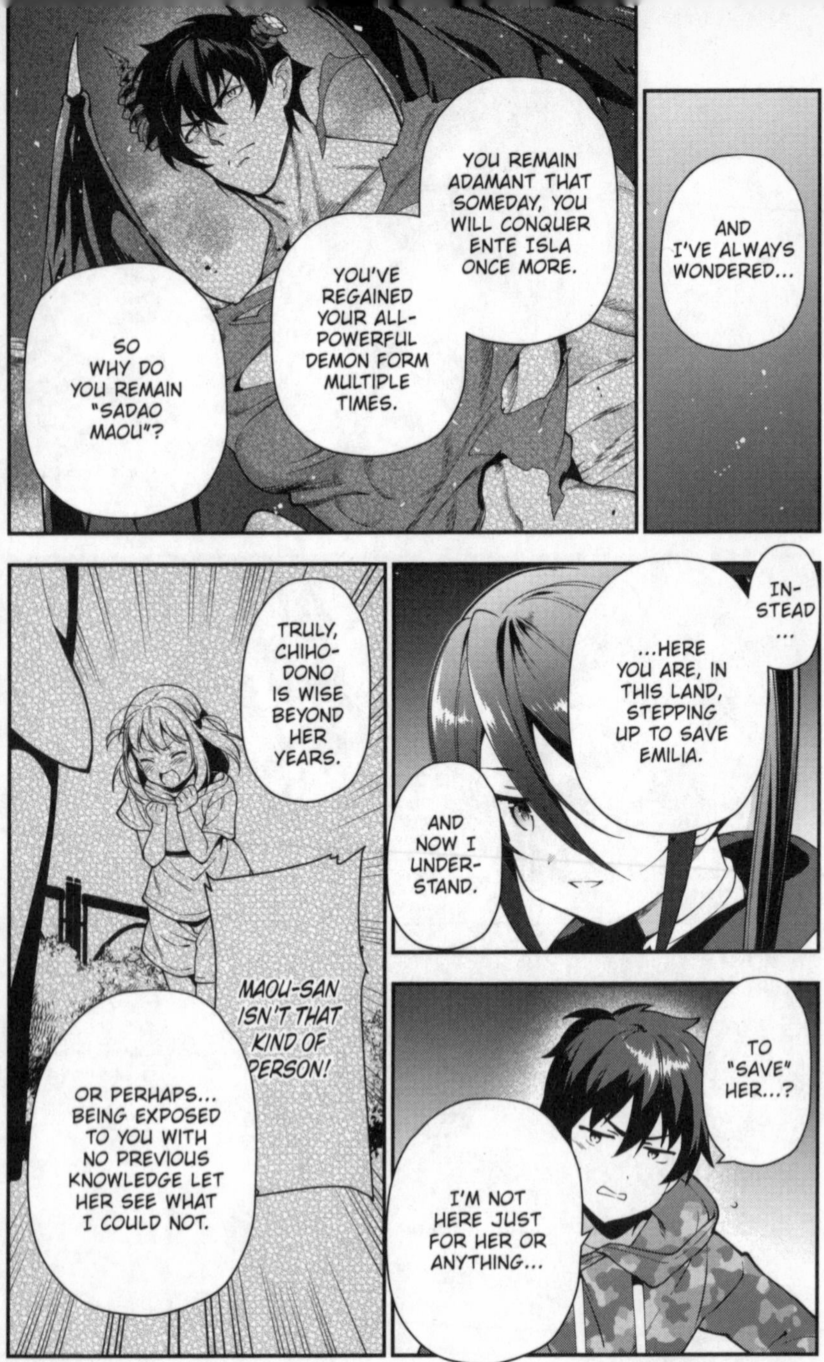
AND I'VE ALWAYS WONDERED...
YOU REMAIN ADAMANT THAT SOMEDAY, YOU WILL CONQUER ENTE ISLA ONCE MORE.
YOU'VE REGAINED YOUR ALL-POWERFUL DEMON FORM MULTIPLE TIMES.
SO WHY DO YOU REMAIN "SADAO MAOU"?
IN-STEAD...
...HERE YOU ARE, IN THIS LAND, STEPPING UP TO SAVE EMILIA.
AND NOW I UNDER-STAND.
TO "SAVE" HER...?
I'M NOT HERE JUST FOR HER OR ANYTHING...
TRULY, CHIHO-DONO IS WISE BEYOND HER YEARS.
MAOU-SAN ISN'T THAT KIND OF PERSON!
OR PERHAPS... BEING EXPOSED TO YOU WITH NO PREVIOUS KNOWLEDGE LET HER SEE WHAT I COULD NOT.

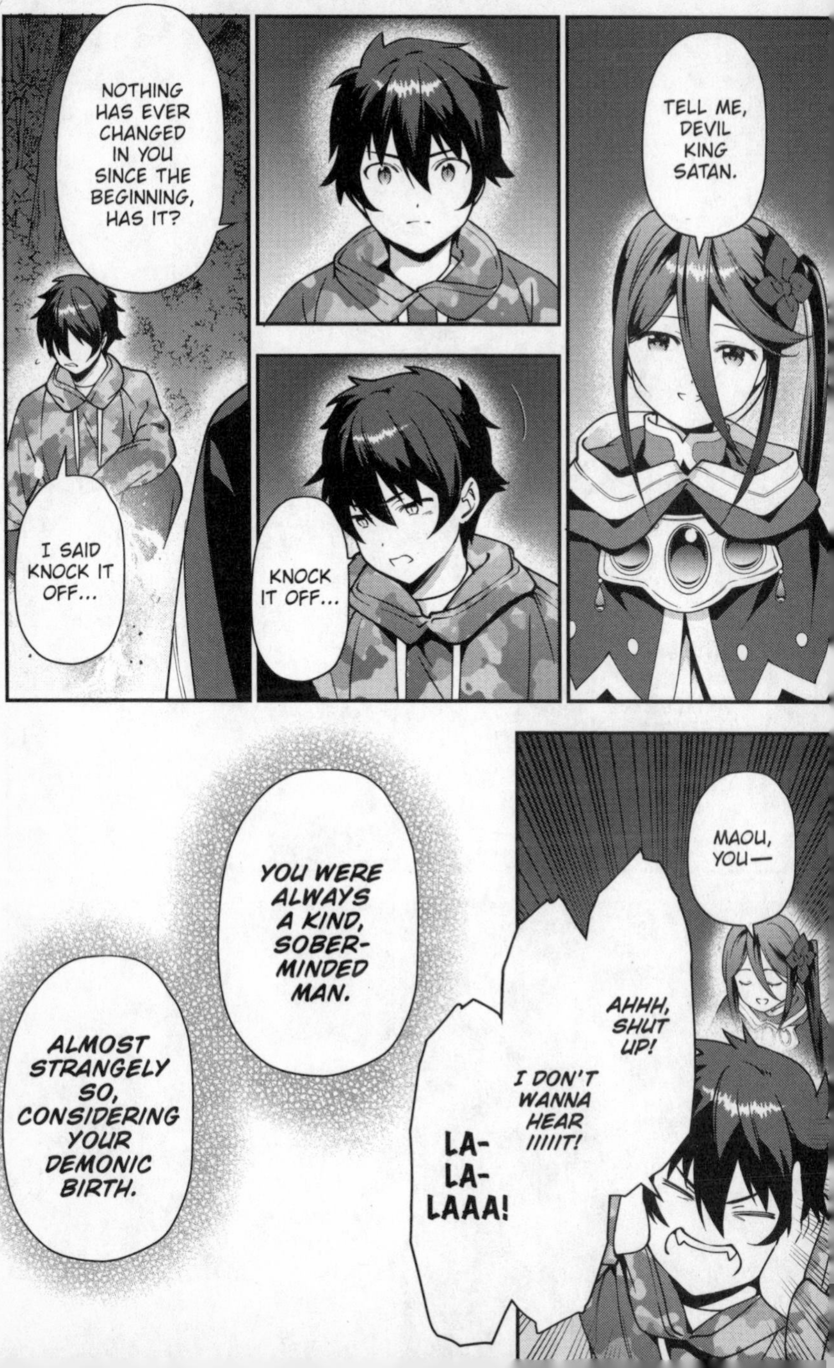
TELL ME, DEVIL KING SATAN.
KNOCK IT OFF...
NOTHING HAS EVER CHANGED IN YOU SINCE THE BEGINNING, HAS IT?
I SAID KNOCK IT OFF...
MAOU, YOU—
AHHH, SHUT UP!
I DON'T WANNA HEAR IIIIIT!
LA-LA-LAAA!
YOU WERE ALWAYS A KIND, SOBER-MINDED MAN.
ALMOST STRANGELY SO, CONSIDERING YOUR DEMONIC BIRTH.

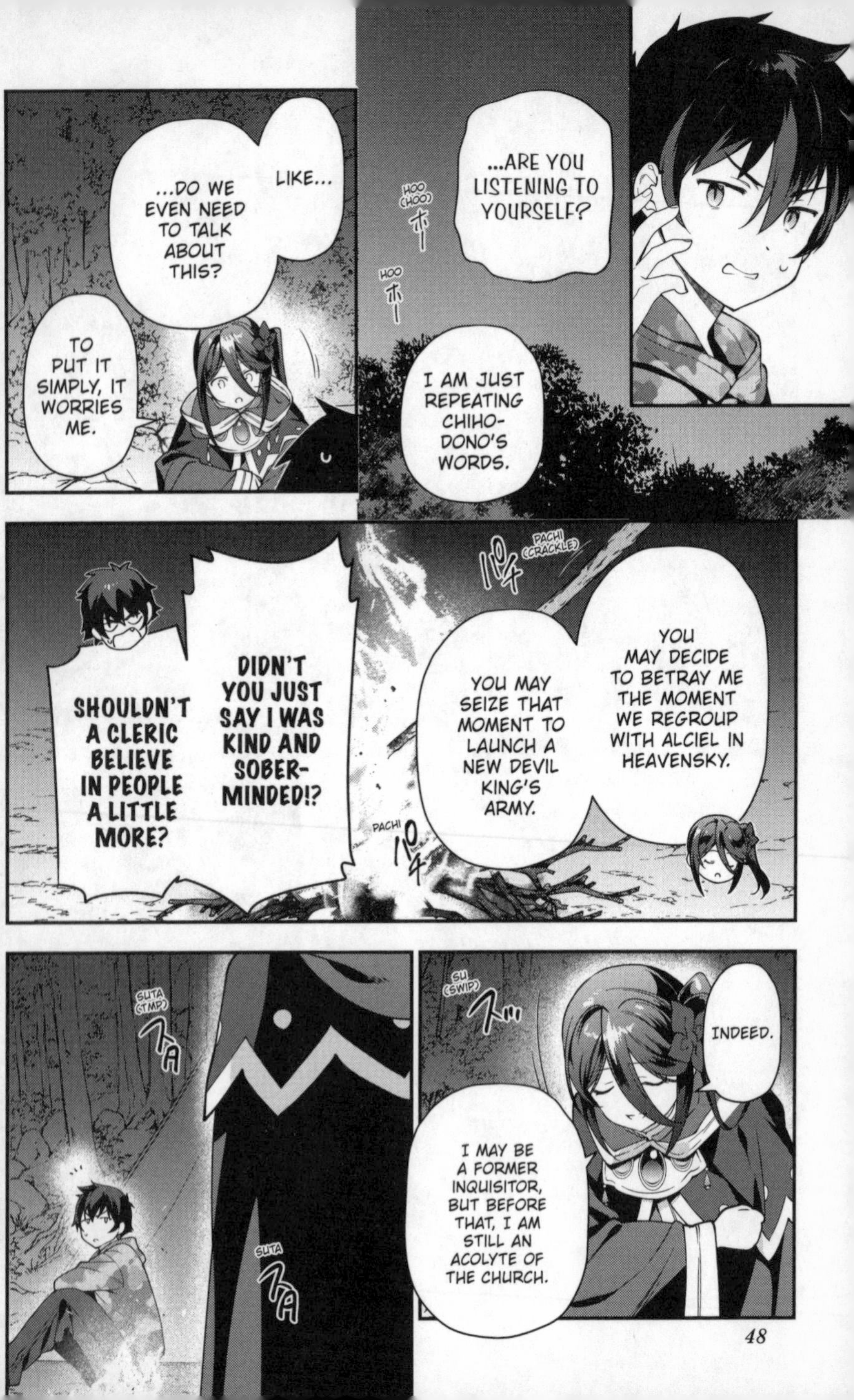
...ARE YOU LISTENING TO YOURSELF?
HOO (CHOO) ホー
HOO ホー
I AM JUST REPEATING CHIHO-DONO'S WORDS.
LIKE...
...DO WE EVEN NEED TO TALK ABOUT THIS?
TO PUT IT SIMPLY, IT WORRIES ME.
PACHI (CRACKLE) パチ
YOU MAY DECIDE TO BETRAY ME THE MOMENT WE REGROUP WITH ALCIEL IN HEAVENSKY.
YOU MAY SEIZE THAT MOMENT TO LAUNCH A NEW DEVIL KING'S ARMY.
PACHI パチ
DIDN'T YOU JUST SAY I WAS KIND AND SOBER-MINDED!?
SHOULDN'T A CLERIC BELIEVE IN PEOPLE A LITTLE MORE?
SU (SWIP) スッ
INDEED.
I MAY BE A FORMER INQUISITOR, BUT BEFORE THAT, I AM STILL AN ACOLYTE OF THE CHURCH.
SUTA (TMP) スタ
SUTA スタ

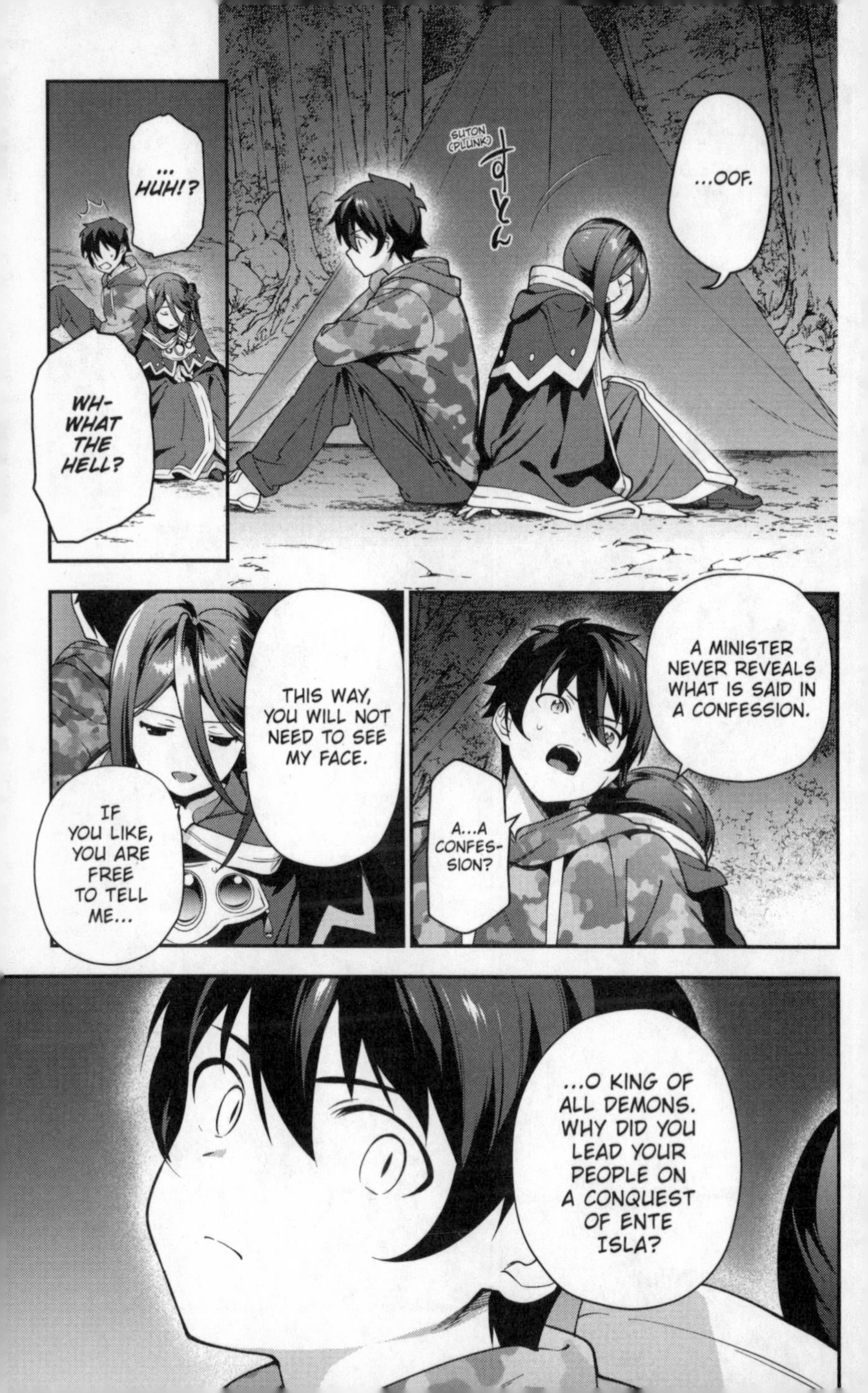
SUTON (PLUNK)
すとん
...OOF.
...HUH!?
WH- WHAT THE HELL?
A MINISTER NEVER REVEALS WHAT IS SAID IN A CONFESSION.
A...A CONFESSION?
THIS WAY, YOU WILL NOT NEED TO SEE MY FACE.
IF YOU LIKE, YOU ARE FREE TO TELL ME...
...O KING OF ALL DEMONS. WHY DID YOU LEAD YOUR PEOPLE ON A CONQUEST OF ENTE ISLA?

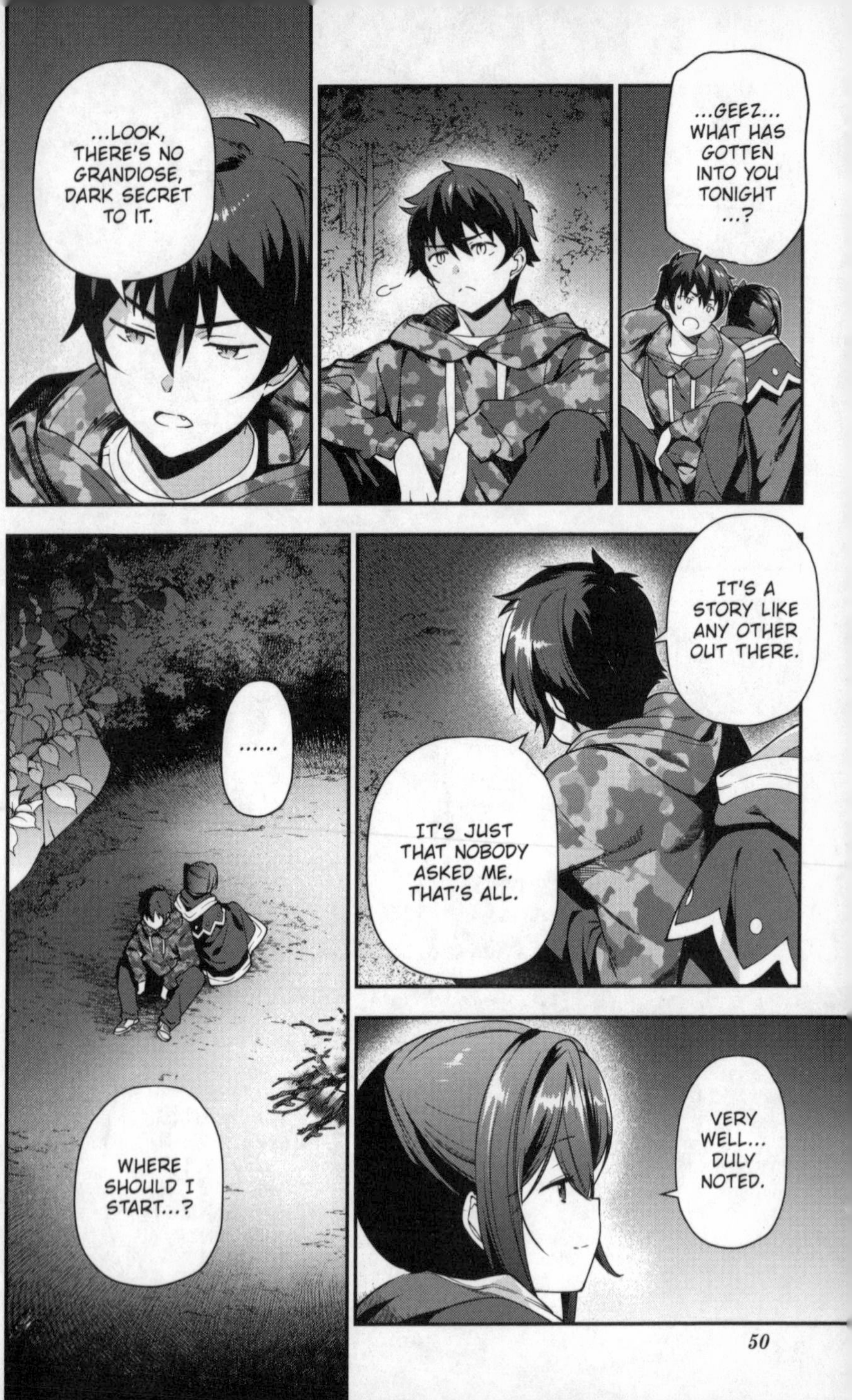
...GEEZ... WHAT HAS GOTTEN INTO YOU TONIGHT ...?
...LOOK, THERE'S NO GRANDIOSE, DARK SECRET TO IT.
IT'S A STORY LIKE ANY OTHER OUT THERE.
IT'S JUST THAT NOBODY ASKED ME. THAT'S ALL.
VERY WELL... DULY NOTED.
......
WHERE SHOULD I START...?

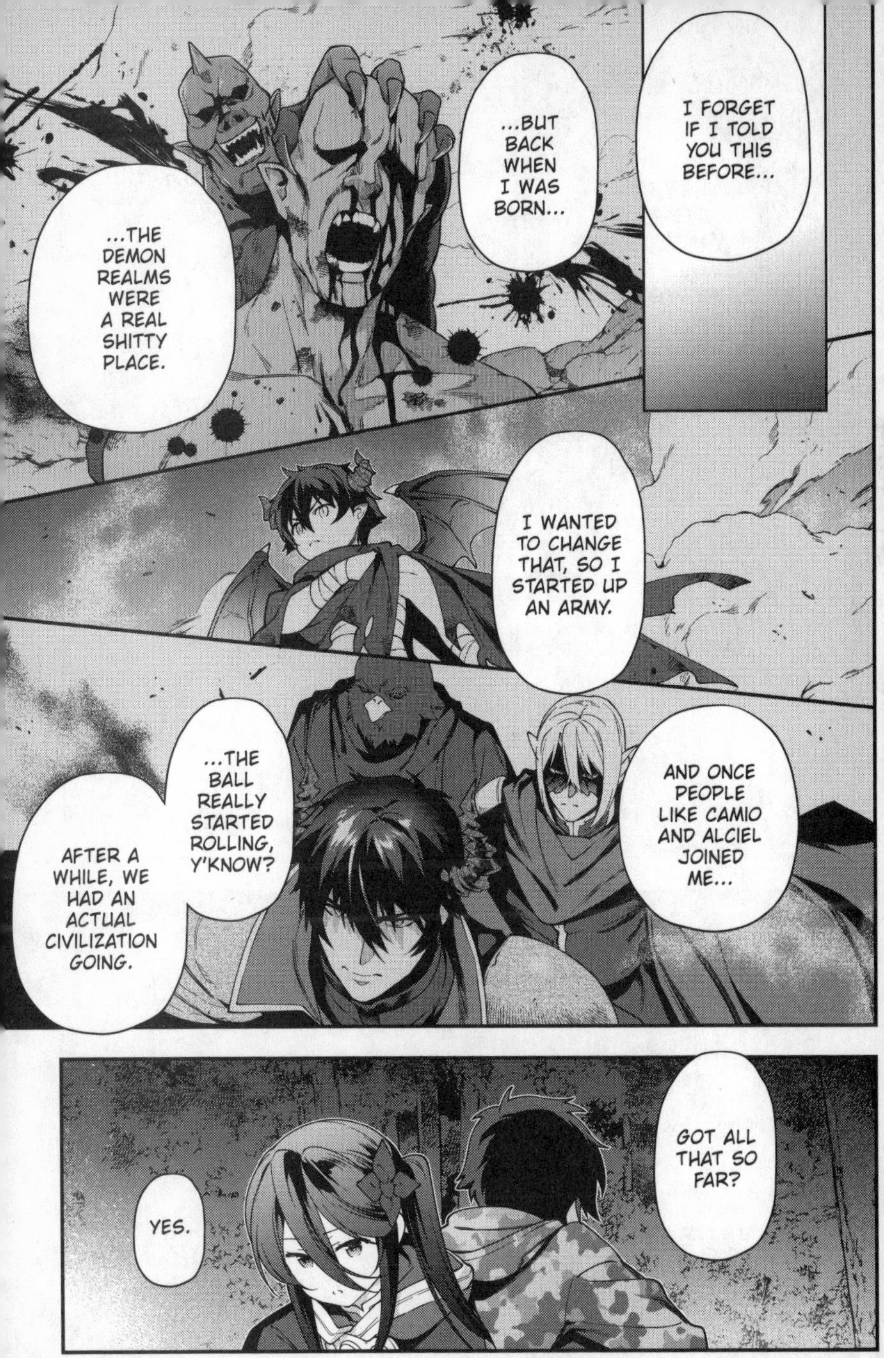
I FORGET IF I TOLD YOU THIS BEFORE...
...BUT BACK WHEN I WAS BORN...
...THE DEMON REALMS WERE A REAL SHITTY PLACE.
I WANTED TO CHANGE THAT, SO I STARTED UP AN ARMY.
AND ONCE PEOPLE LIKE CAMIO AND ALCIEL JOINED ME...
...THE BALL REALLY STARTED ROLLING, Y'KNOW?
AFTER A WHILE, WE HAD AN ACTUAL CIVILIZATION GOING.
GOT ALL THAT SO FAR?
YES.

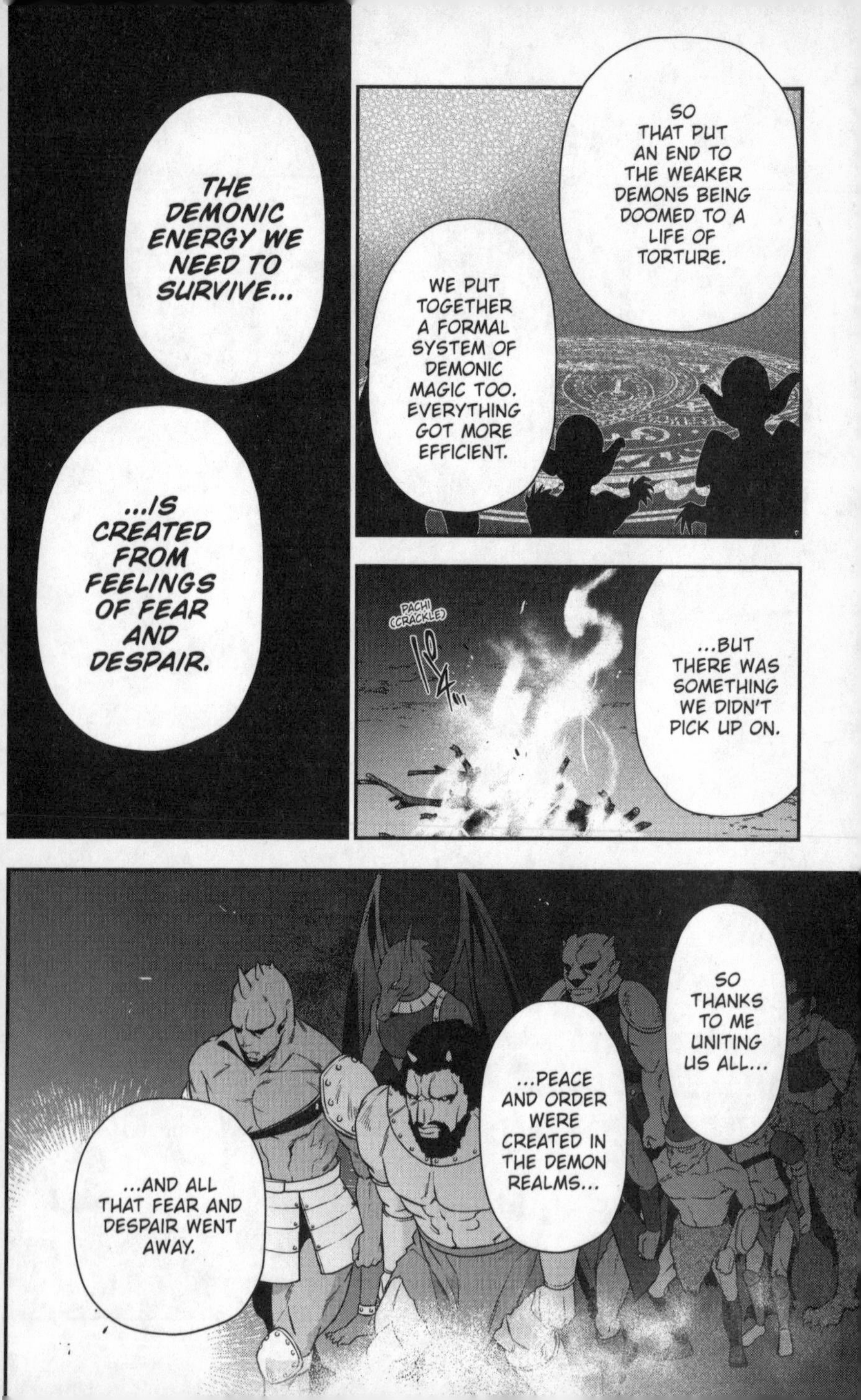
SO THAT PUT AN END TO THE WEAKER DEMONS BEING DOOMED TO A LIFE OF TORTURE.
WE PUT TOGETHER A FORMAL SYSTEM OF DEMONIC MAGIC TOO. EVERYTHING GOT MORE EFFICIENT.
...BUT THERE WAS SOMETHING WE DIDN'T PICK UP ON.
PACHI (CRACKLE)
THE DEMONIC ENERGY WE NEED TO SURVIVE...
...IS CREATED FROM FEELINGS OF FEAR AND DESPAIR.
SO THANKS TO ME UNITING US ALL...
...PEACE AND ORDER WERE CREATED IN THE DEMON REALMS...
...AND ALL THAT FEAR AND DESPAIR WENT AWAY.

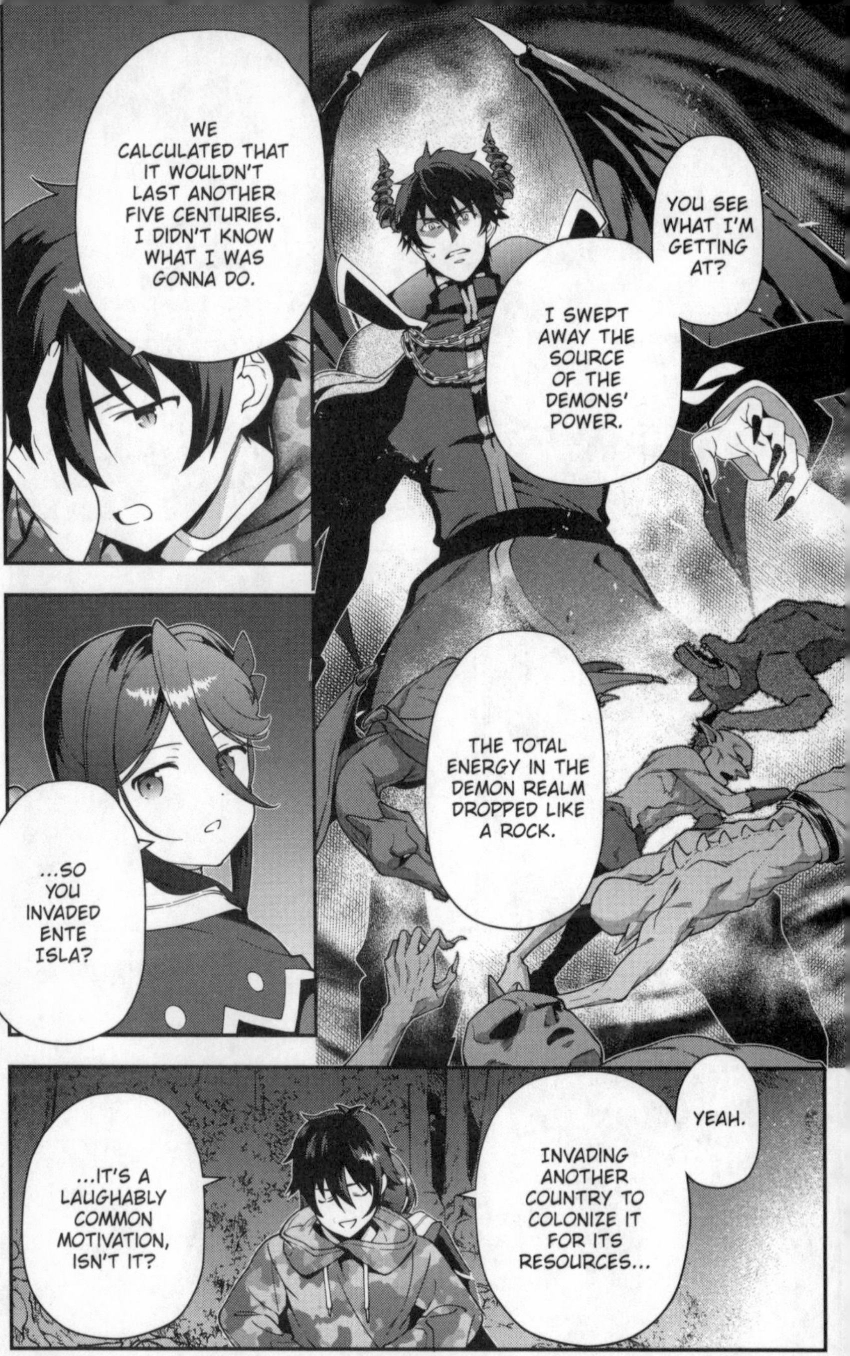
YOU SEE WHAT I'M GETTING AT?
I SWEPT AWAY THE SOURCE OF THE DEMONS' POWER.
THE TOTAL ENERGY IN THE DEMON REALM DROPPED LIKE A ROCK.
WE CALCULATED THAT IT WOULDN'T LAST ANOTHER FIVE CENTURIES. I DIDN'T KNOW WHAT I WAS GONNA DO.
...SO YOU INVADED ENTE ISLA?
YEAH.
INVADING ANOTHER COUNTRY TO COLONIZE IT FOR ITS RESOURCES...
...IT'S A LAUGHABLY COMMON MOTIVATION, ISN'T IT?

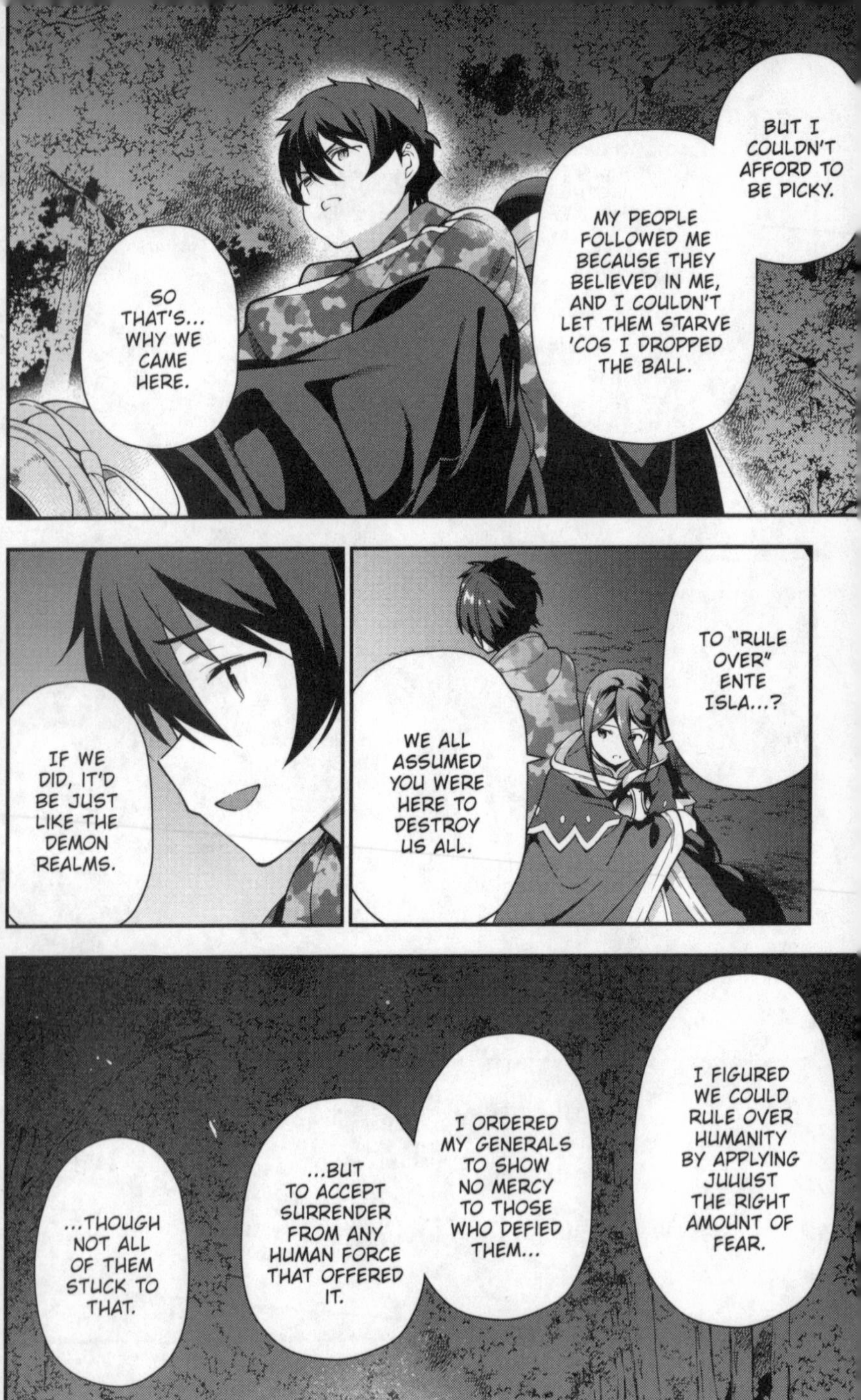
BUT I COULDN'T AFFORD TO BE PICKY.
MY PEOPLE FOLLOWED ME BECAUSE THEY BELIEVED IN ME, AND I COULDN'T LET THEM STARVE 'COS I DROPPED THE BALL.
SO THAT'S... WHY WE CAME HERE.
TO "RULE OVER" ENTE ISLA...?
WE ALL ASSUMED YOU WERE HERE TO DESTROY US ALL.
IF WE DID, IT'D BE JUST LIKE THE DEMON REALMS.
I FIGURED WE COULD RULE OVER HUMANITY BY APPLYING JUUUST THE RIGHT AMOUNT OF FEAR.
I ORDERED MY GENERALS TO SHOW NO MERCY TO THOSE WHO DEFIED THEM...
...BUT TO ACCEPT SURRENDER FROM ANY HUMAN FORCE THAT OFFERED IT.
...THOUGH NOT ALL OF THEM STUCK TO THAT.

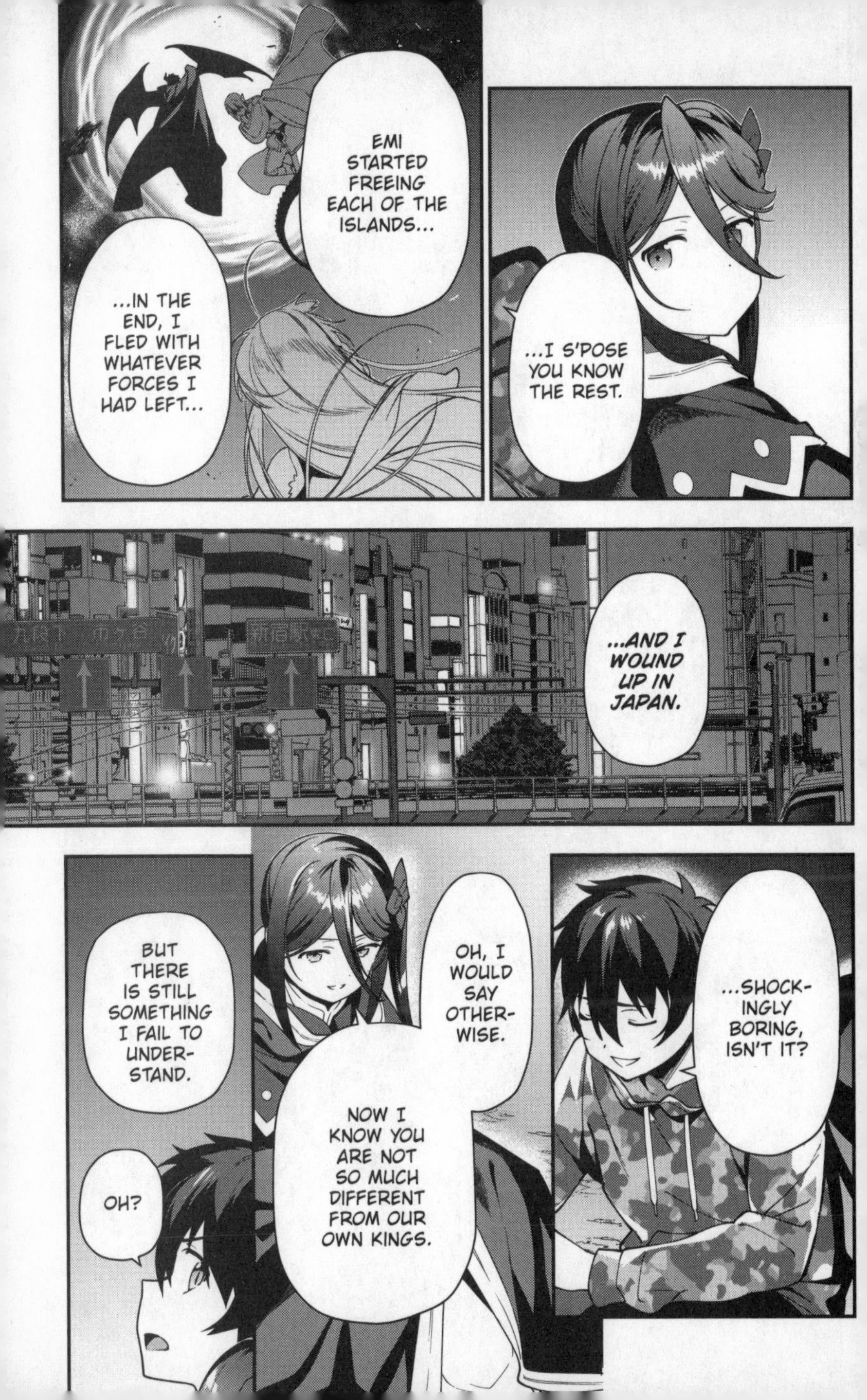
...I S'POSE YOU KNOW THE REST.
EMI STARTED FREEING EACH OF THE ISLANDS...
...IN THE END, I FLED WITH WHATEVER FORCES I HAD LEFT...
...AND I WOUND UP IN JAPAN.
...SHOCKINGLY BORING, ISN'T IT?
OH, I WOULD SAY OTHERWISE.
NOW I KNOW YOU ARE NOT SO MUCH DIFFERENT FROM OUR OWN KINGS.
BUT THERE IS STILL SOMETHING I FAIL TO UNDERSTAND.
OH?

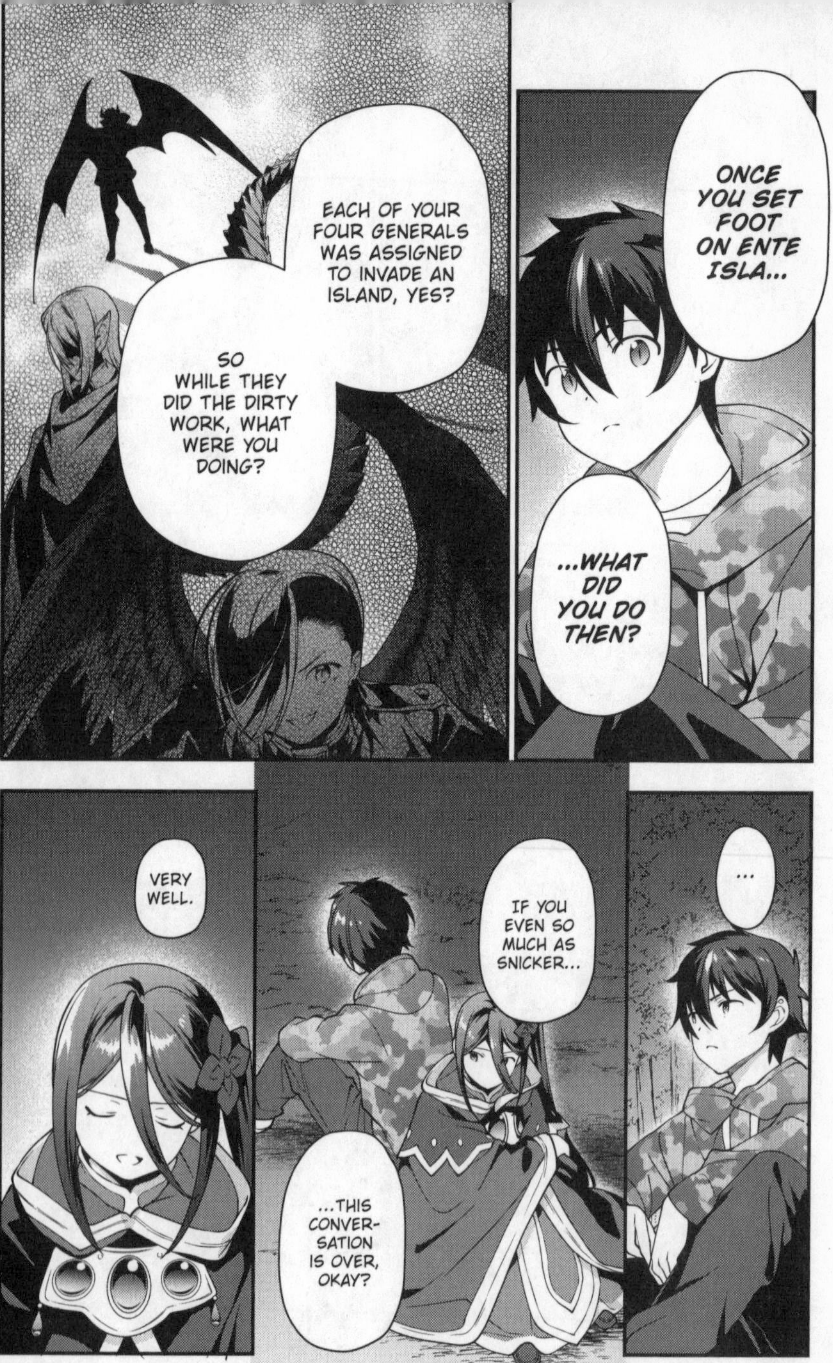
ONCE YOU SET FOOT ON ENTE ISLA...
...WHAT DID YOU DO THEN?
EACH OF YOUR FOUR GENERALS WAS ASSIGNED TO INVADE AN ISLAND, YES?
SO WHILE THEY DID THE DIRTY WORK, WHAT WERE YOU DOING?
...
IF YOU EVEN SO MUCH AS SNICKER...
...THIS CONVER-SATION IS OVER, OKAY?
VERY WELL.

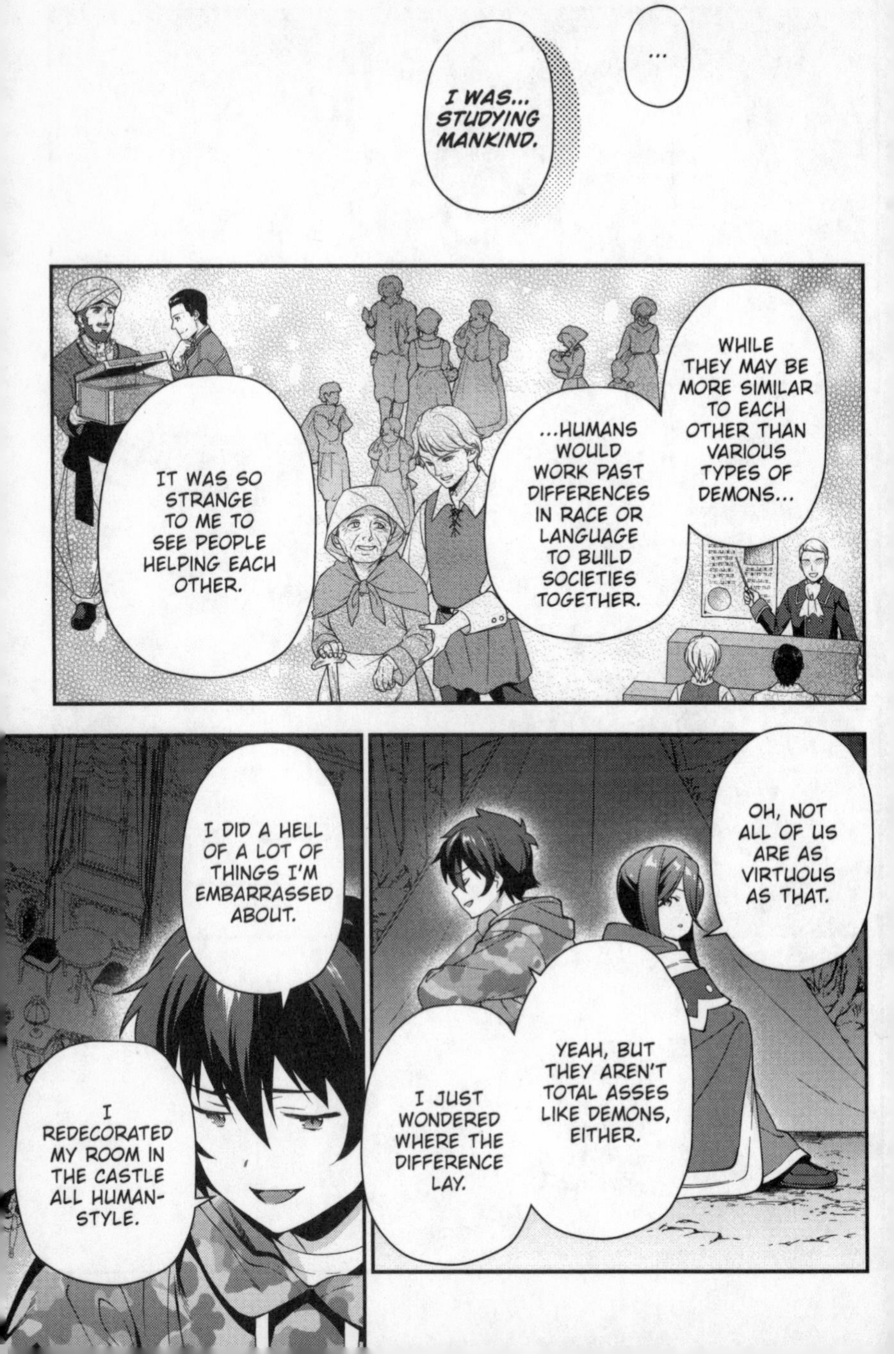
...
I WAS... STUDYING MANKIND.
WHILE THEY MAY BE MORE SIMILAR TO EACH OTHER THAN VARIOUS TYPES OF DEMONS...
...HUMANS WOULD WORK PAST DIFFERENCES IN RACE OR LANGUAGE TO BUILD SOCIETIES TOGETHER.
IT WAS SO STRANGE TO ME TO SEE PEOPLE HELPING EACH OTHER.
OH, NOT ALL OF US ARE AS VIRTUOUS AS THAT.
YEAH, BUT THEY AREN'T TOTAL ASSES LIKE DEMONS, EITHER.
I JUST WONDERED WHERE THE DIFFERENCE LAY.
I DID A HELL OF A LOT OF THINGS I'M EMBARRASSED ABOUT.
I REDECORATED MY ROOM IN THE CASTLE ALL HUMAN-STYLE.

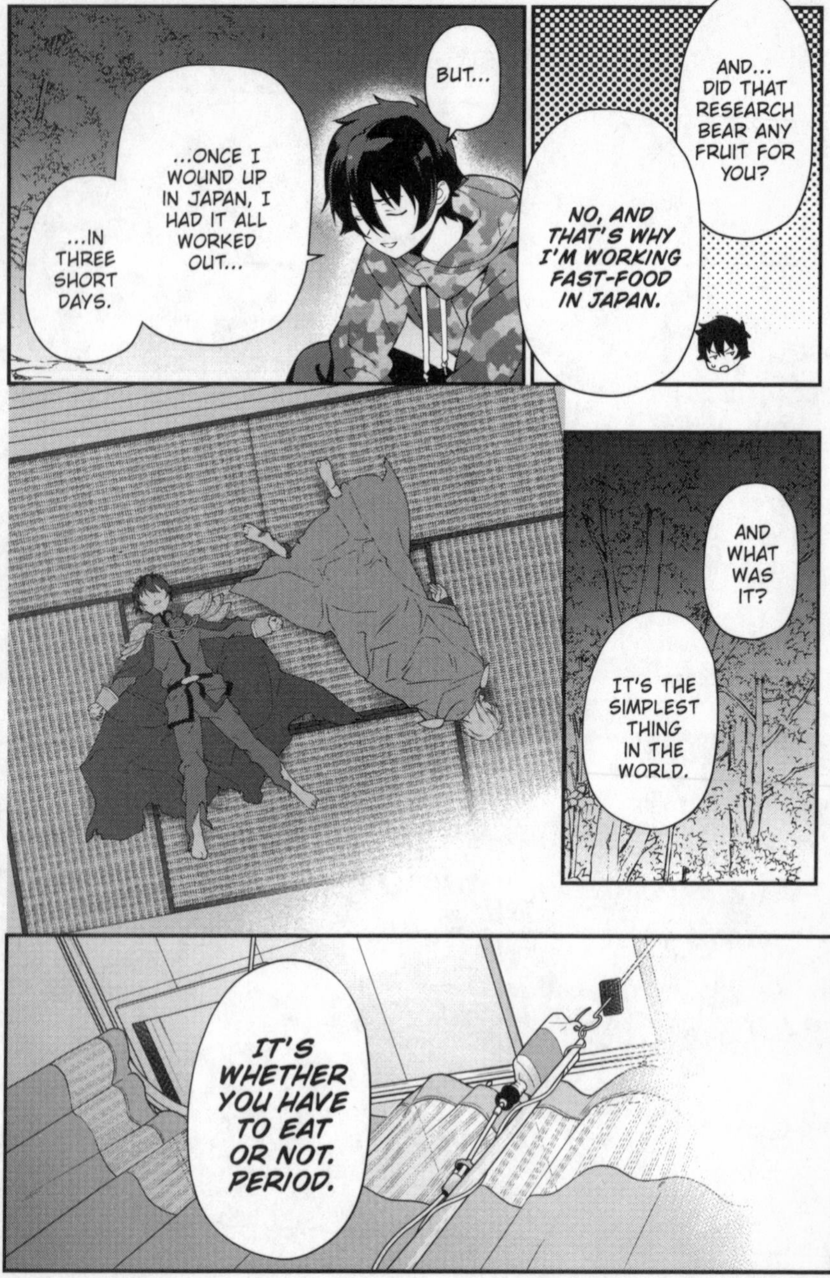
AND... DID THAT RESEARCH BEAR ANY FRUIT FOR YOU?
NO, AND THAT'S WHY I'M WORKING FAST-FOOD IN JAPAN.
BUT...
...ONCE I WOUND UP IN JAPAN, I HAD IT ALL WORKED OUT...
...IN THREE SHORT DAYS.
AND WHAT WAS IT?
IT'S THE SIMPLEST THING IN THE WORLD.
IT'S WHETHER YOU HAVE TO EAT OR NOT. PERIOD.

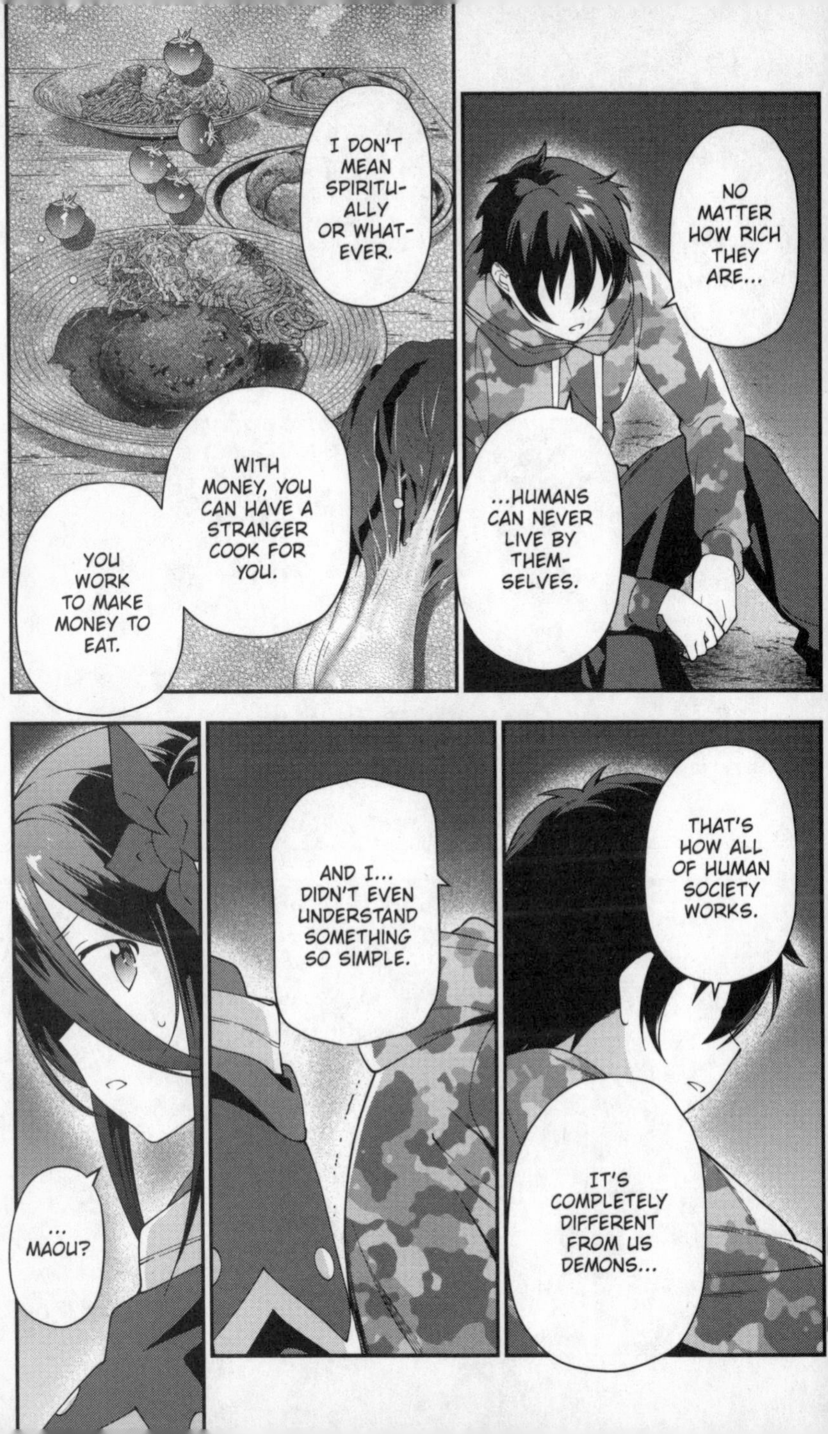
NO MATTER HOW RICH THEY ARE...
...HUMANS CAN NEVER LIVE BY THEM-SELVES.
I DON'T MEAN SPIRITU-ALLY OR WHAT-EVER.
WITH MONEY, YOU CAN HAVE A STRANGER COOK FOR YOU.
YOU WORK TO MAKE MONEY TO EAT.
THAT'S HOW ALL OF HUMAN SOCIETY WORKS.
IT'S COMPLETELY DIFFERENT FROM US DEMONS...
AND I... DIDN'T EVEN UNDERSTAND SOMETHING SO SIMPLE.
...MAOU?

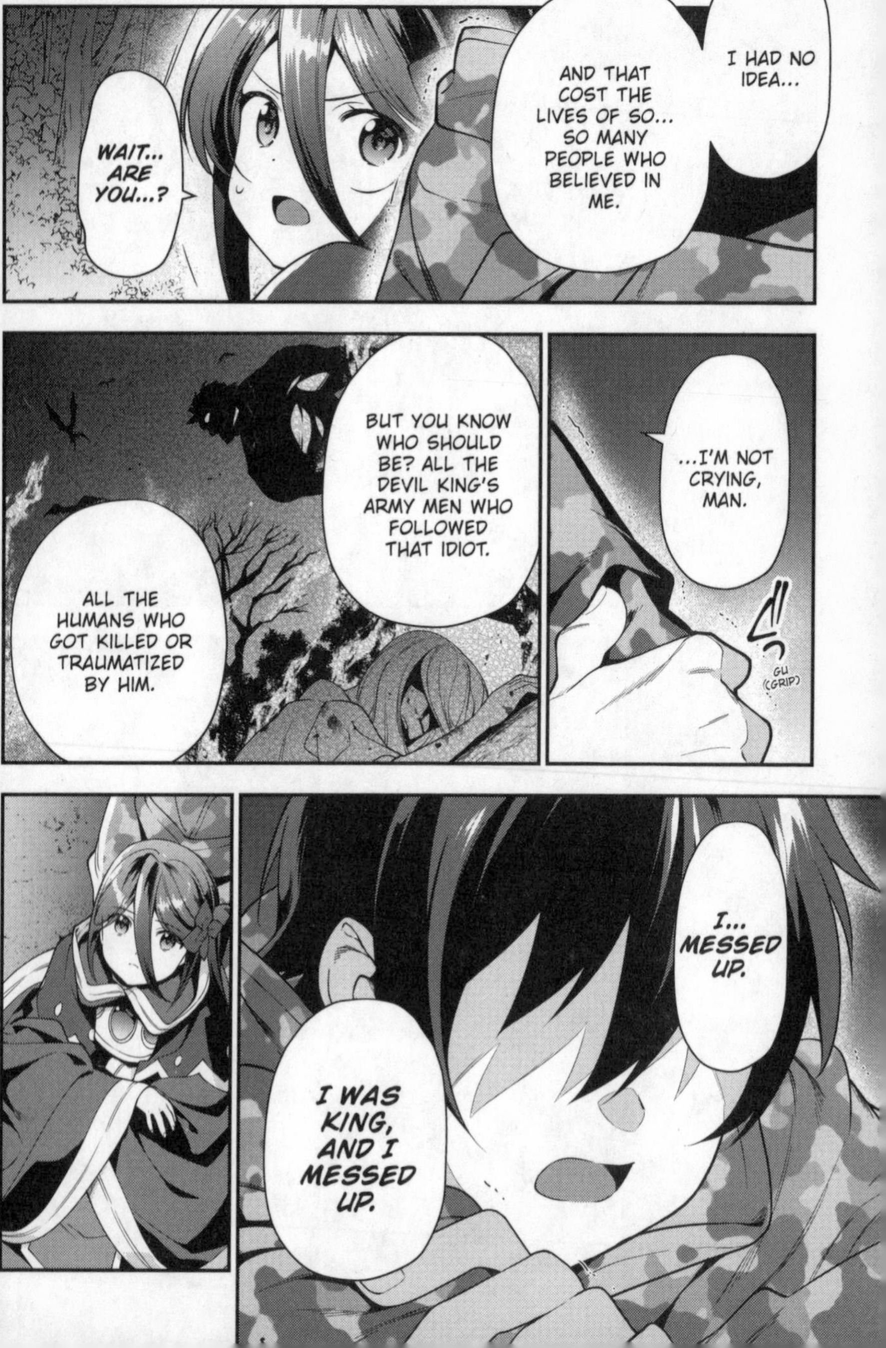
I HAD NO IDEA...
AND THAT COST THE LIVES OF SO... SO MANY PEOPLE WHO BELIEVED IN ME.
WAIT... ARE YOU...?
...I'M NOT CRYING, MAN.
GU (GRIP)
BUT YOU KNOW WHO SHOULD BE? ALL THE DEVIL KING'S ARMY MEN WHO FOLLOWED THAT IDIOT.
ALL THE HUMANS WHO GOT KILLED OR TRAUMATIZED BY HIM.
I... MESSED UP.
I WAS KING, AND I MESSED UP.

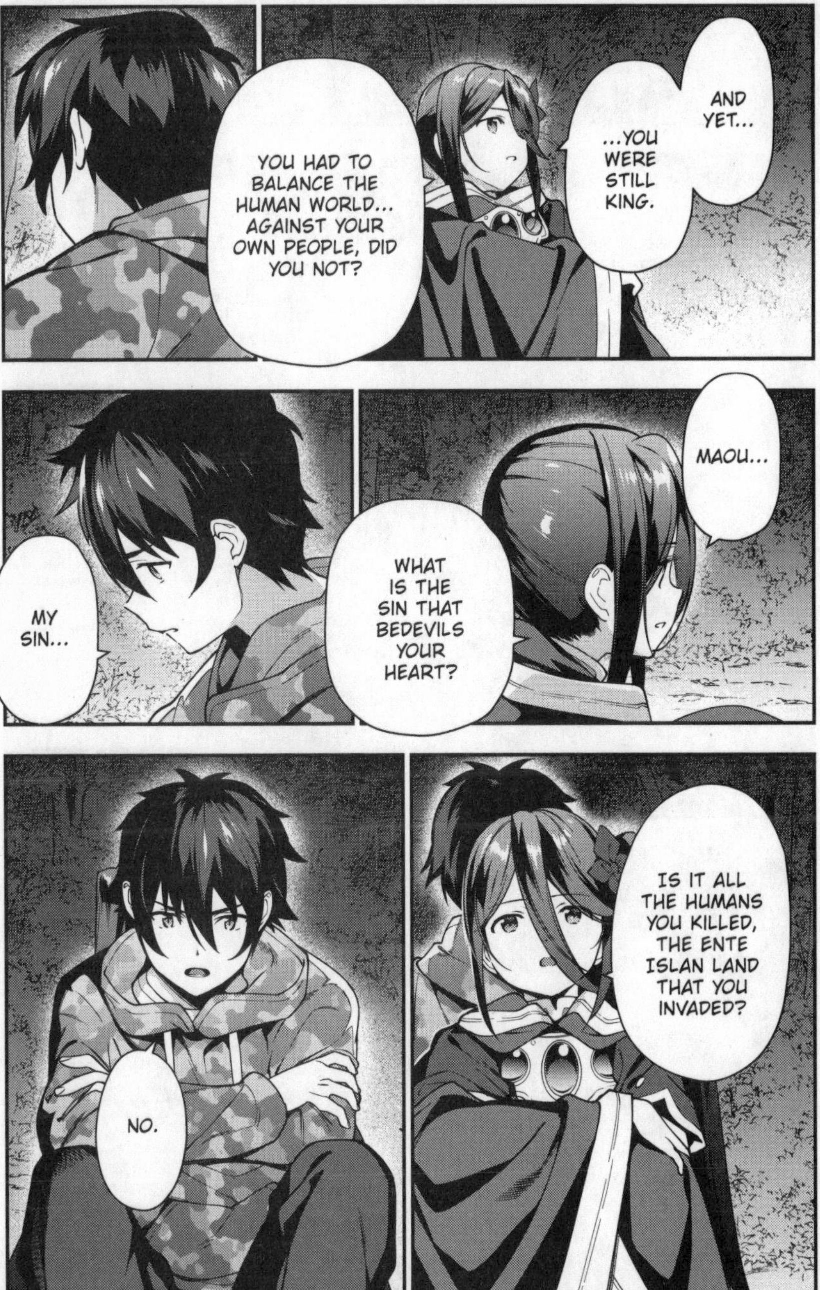
AND YET...
...YOU WERE STILL KING.
YOU HAD TO BALANCE THE HUMAN WORLD... AGAINST YOUR OWN PEOPLE, DID YOU NOT?
MAOU...
WHAT IS THE SIN THAT BEDEVILS YOUR HEART?
MY SIN...
IS IT ALL THE HUMANS YOU KILLED, THE ENTE ISLAN LAND THAT YOU INVADED?
NO.

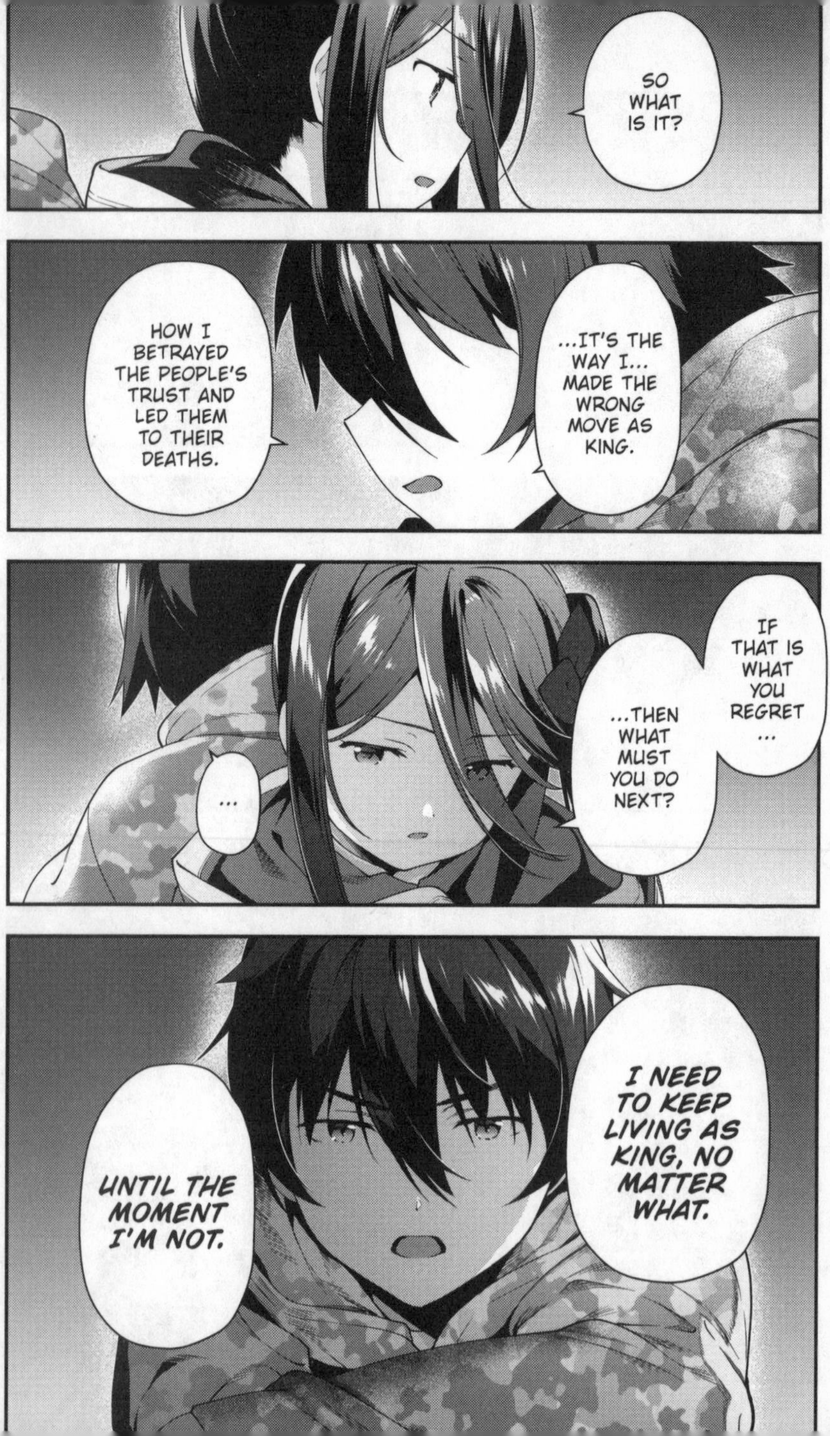
SO WHAT IS IT?
...IT'S THE WAY I... MADE THE WRONG MOVE AS KING.
HOW I BETRAYED THE PEOPLE'S TRUST AND LED THEM TO THEIR DEATHS.
IF THAT IS WHAT YOU REGRET...
...THEN WHAT MUST YOU DO NEXT?
...
I NEED TO KEEP LIVING AS KING, NO MATTER WHAT.
UNTIL THE MOMENT I'M NOT.

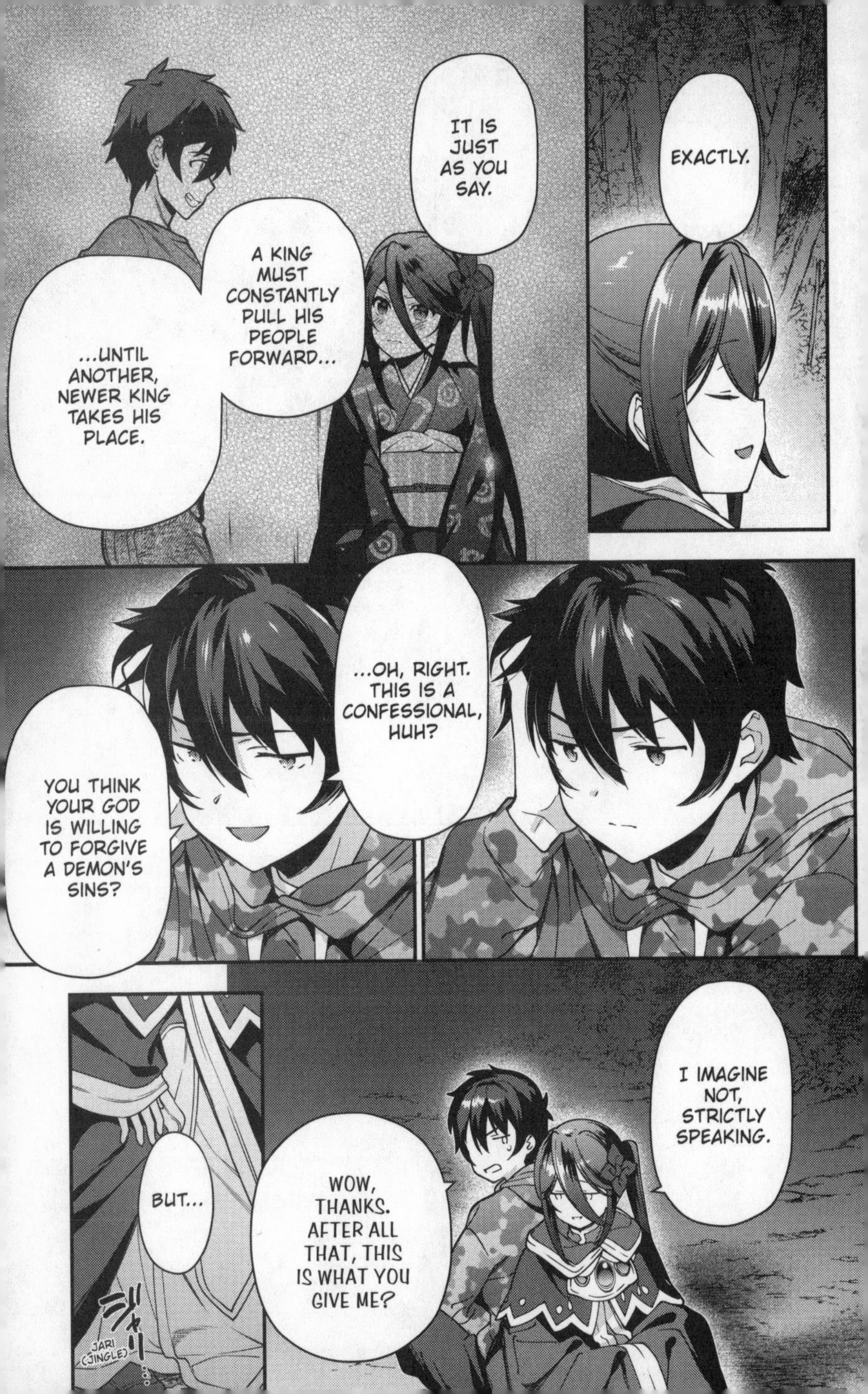
EXACTLY.
IT IS JUST AS YOU SAY.
A KING MUST CONSTANTLY PULL HIS PEOPLE FORWARD...
...UNTIL ANOTHER, NEWER KING TAKES HIS PLACE.
...OH, RIGHT. THIS IS A CONFESSIONAL, HUH?
YOU THINK YOUR GOD IS WILLING TO FORGIVE A DEMON'S SINS?
I IMAGINE NOT, STRICTLY SPEAKING.
WOW, THANKS. AFTER ALL THAT, THIS IS WHAT YOU GIVE ME?
BUT...
JARI (JINGLE)

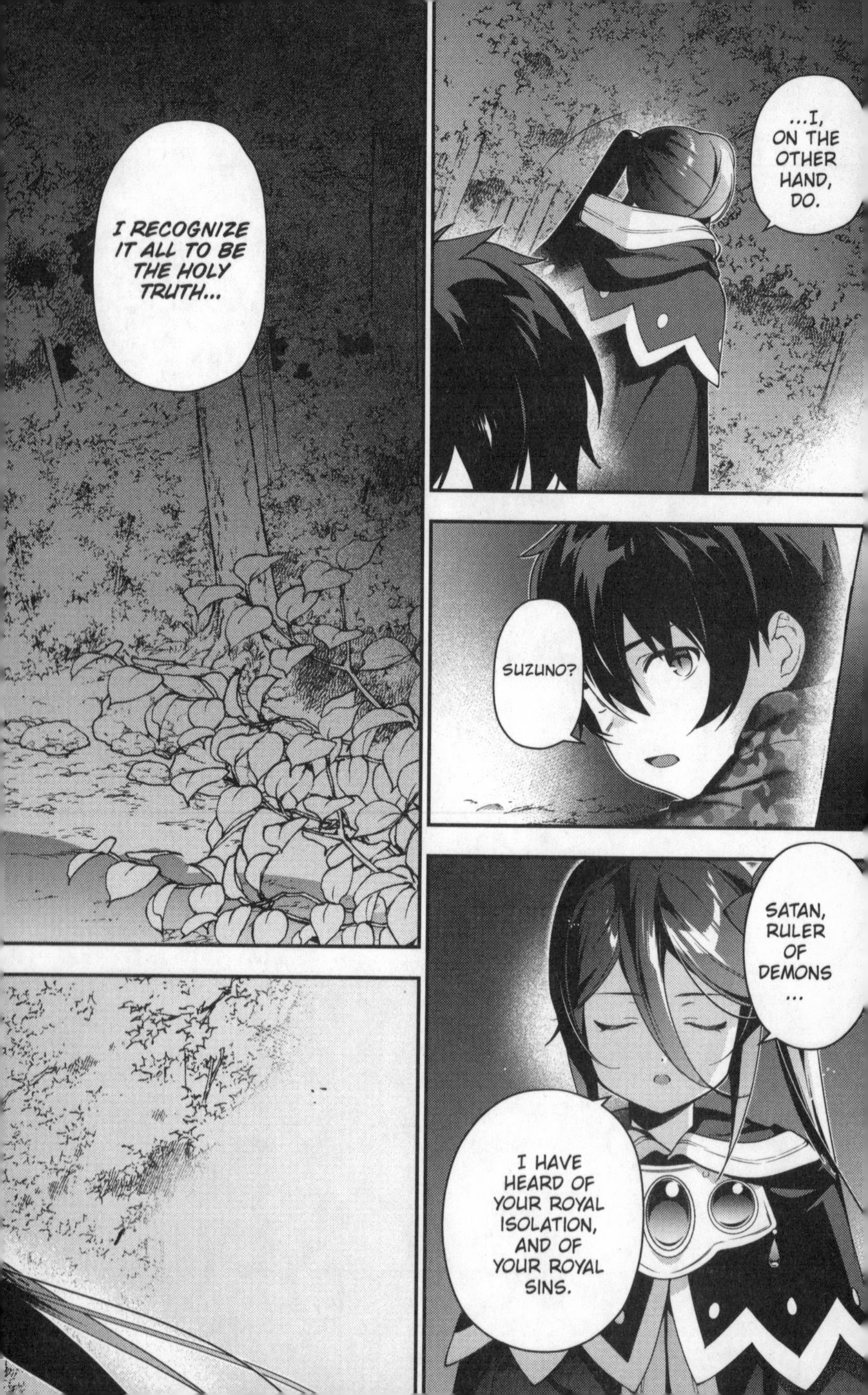
...I, ON THE OTHER HAND, DO.
I RECOGNIZE IT ALL TO BE THE HOLY TRUTH...
SUZUNO?
SATAN, RULER OF DEMONS ...
I HAVE HEARD OF YOUR ROYAL ISOLATION, AND OF YOUR ROYAL SINS.

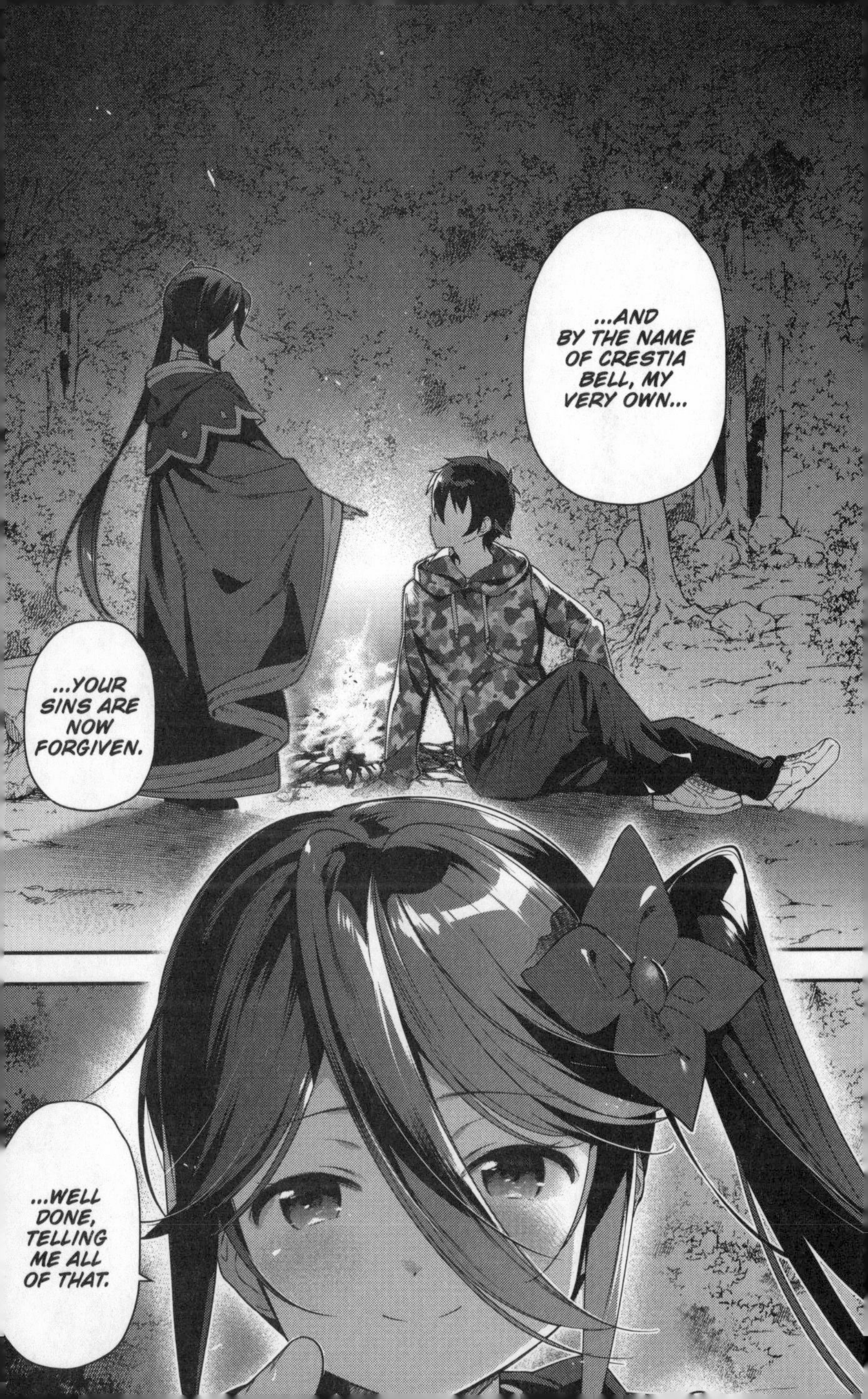
...AND BY THE NAME OF CRESTIA BELL, MY VERY OWN...
...YOUR SINS ARE NOW FORGIVEN.
...WELL DONE, TELLING ME ALL OF THAT.

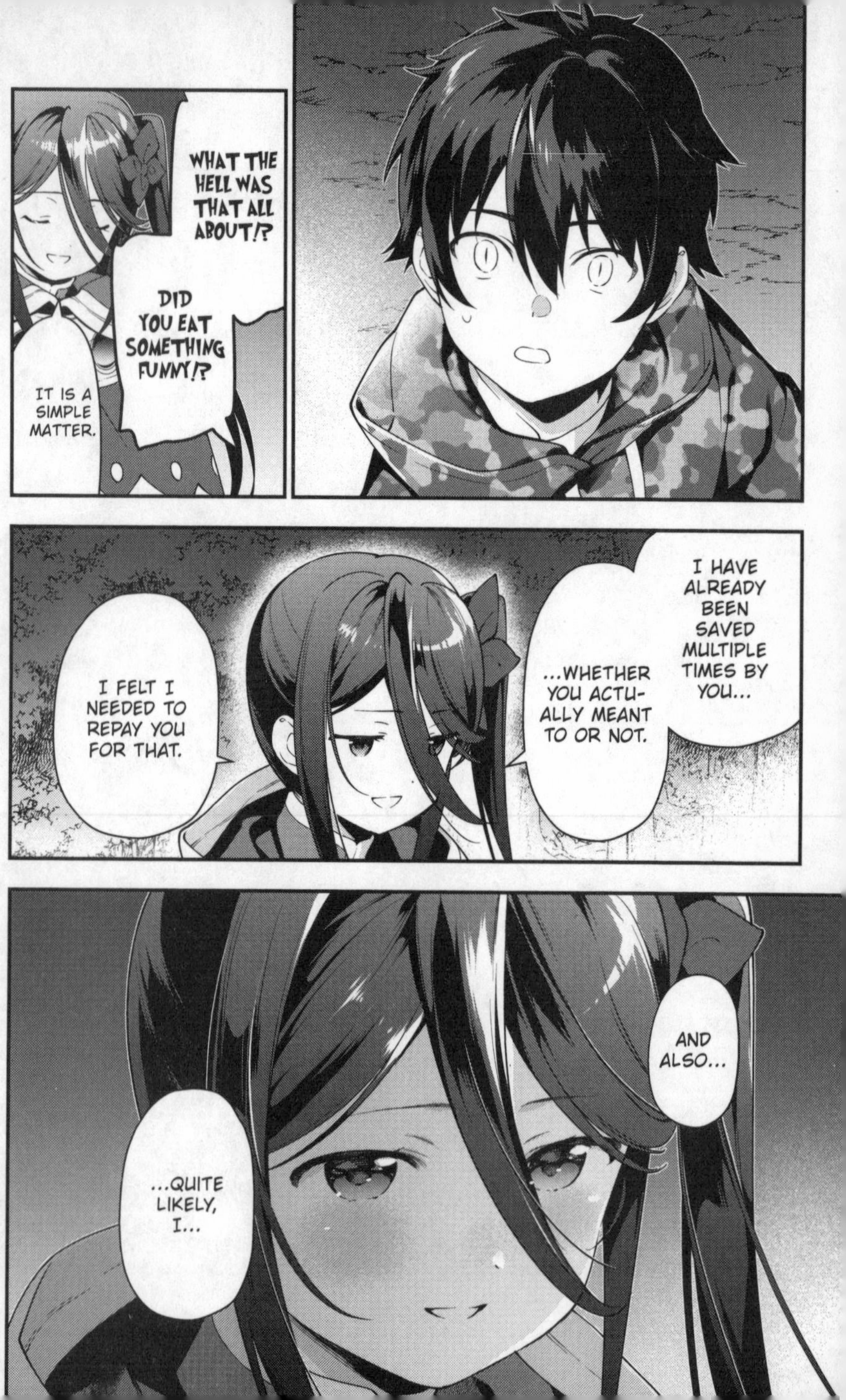
WHAT THE HELL WAS THAT ALL ABOUT!?
DID YOU EAT SOMETHING FUNNY!?
IT IS A SIMPLE MATTER.
I HAVE ALREADY BEEN SAVED MULTIPLE TIMES BY YOU...
...WHETHER YOU ACTU-ALLY MEANT TO OR NOT.
I FELT I NEEDED TO REPAY YOU FOR THAT.
AND ALSO...
...QUITE LIKELY, I...

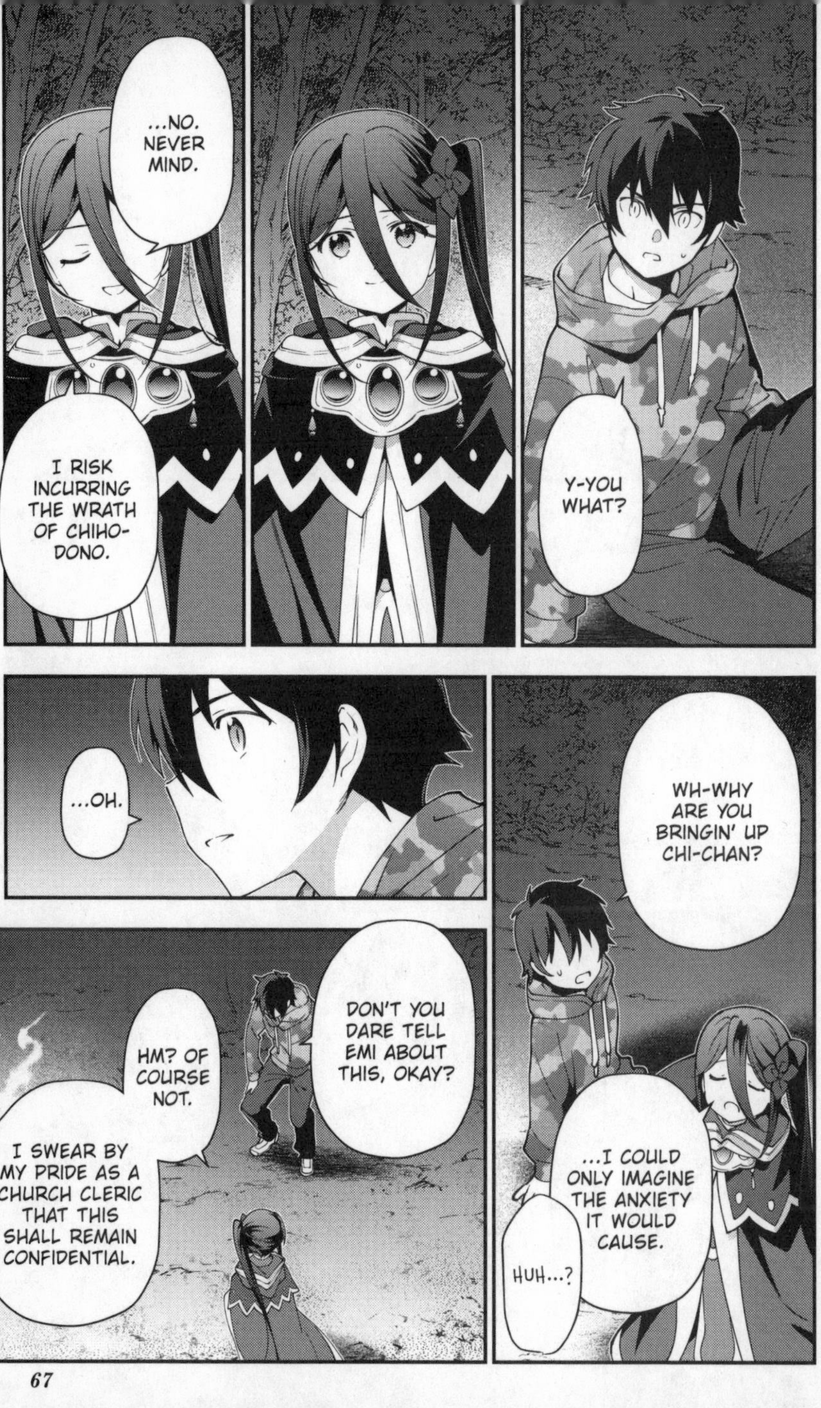
Y-YOU WHAT?
...NO. NEVER MIND.
I RISK INCURRING THE WRATH OF CHIHO-DONO.
WH-WHY ARE YOU BRINGIN' UP CHI-CHAN?
...I COULD ONLY IMAGINE THE ANXIETY IT WOULD CAUSE.
HUH...?
...OH.
DON'T YOU DARE TELL EMI ABOUT THIS, OKAY?
HM? OF COURSE NOT.
I SWEAR BY MY PRIDE AS A CHURCH CLERIC THAT THIS SHALL REMAIN CONFIDENTIAL.

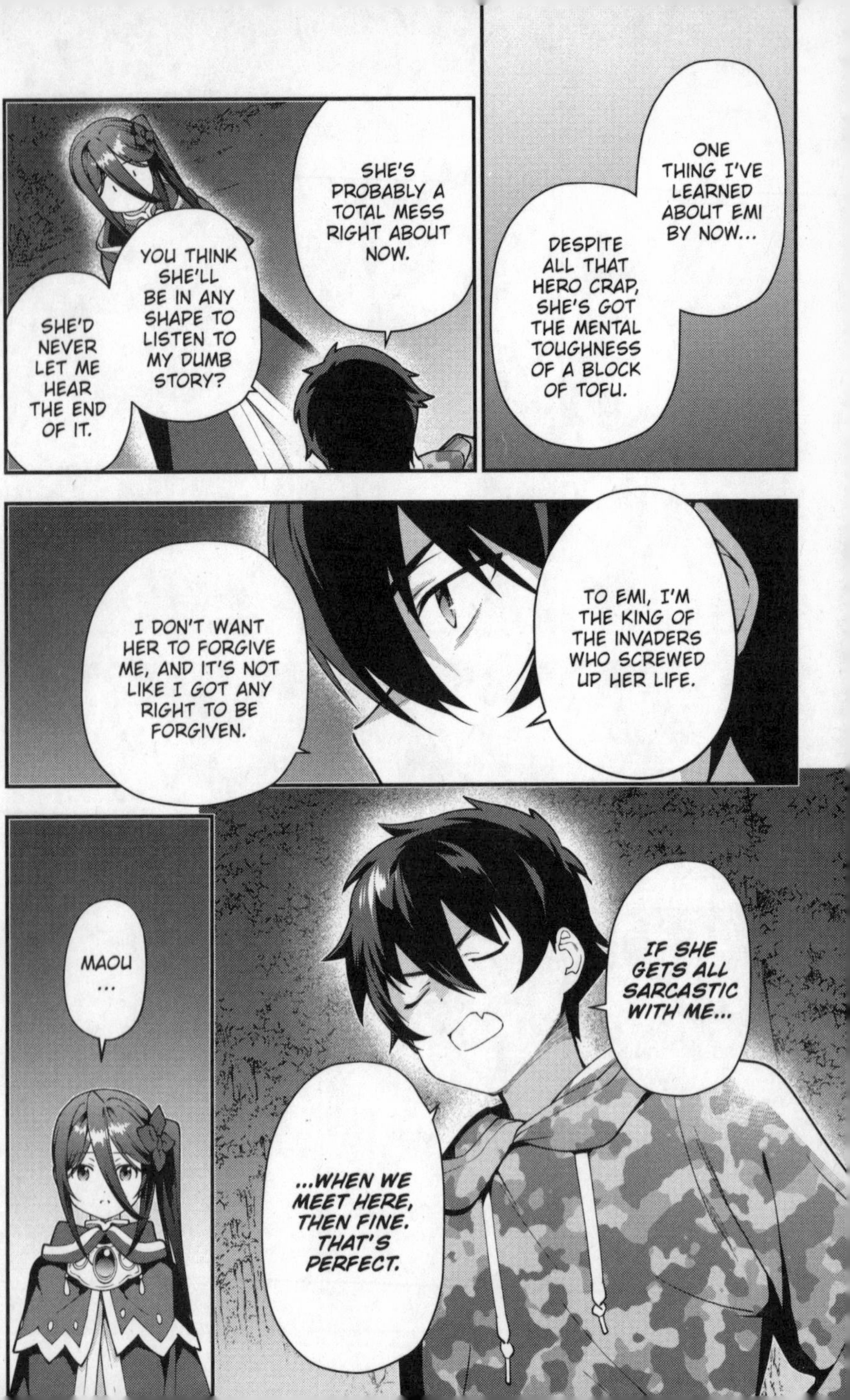
ONE THING I'VE LEARNED ABOUT EMI BY NOW...
DESPITE ALL THAT HERO CRAP, SHE'S GOT THE MENTAL TOUGHNESS OF A BLOCK OF TOFU.
SHE'S PROBABLY A TOTAL MESS RIGHT ABOUT NOW.
YOU THINK SHE'LL BE IN ANY SHAPE TO LISTEN TO MY DUMB STORY?
SHE'D NEVER LET ME HEAR THE END OF IT.
TO EMI, I'M THE KING OF THE INVADERS WHO SCREWED UP HER LIFE.
I DON'T WANT HER TO FORGIVE ME, AND IT'S NOT LIKE I GOT ANY RIGHT TO BE FORGIVEN.
IF SHE GETS ALL SARCASTIC WITH ME...
...WHEN WE MEET HERE, THEN FINE. THAT'S PERFECT.
MAOU ...

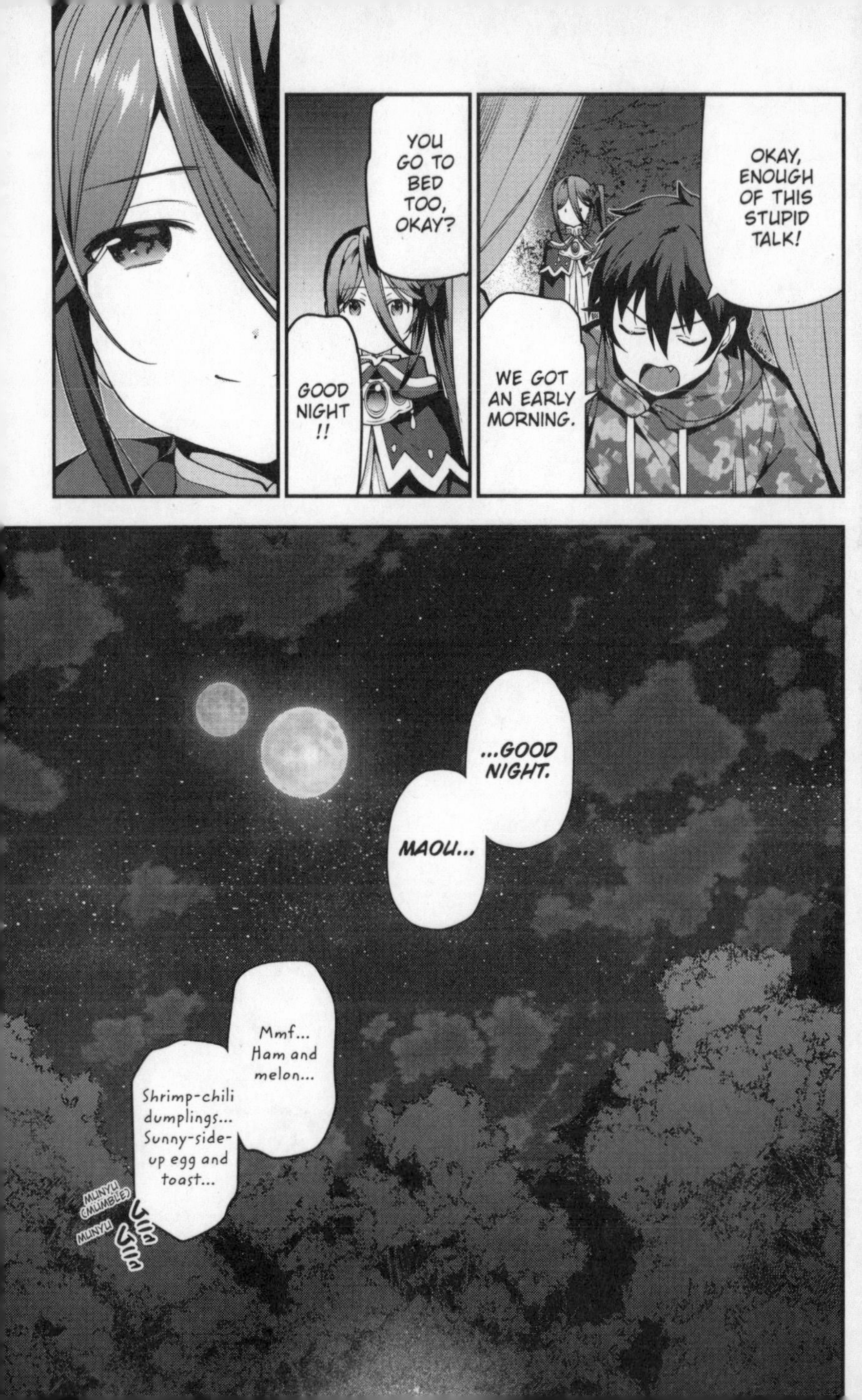
OKAY, ENOUGH OF THIS STUPID TALK!
WE GOT AN EARLY MORNING.
YOU GO TO BED TOO, OKAY?
GOOD NIGHT !!
...GOOD NIGHT.
MAOU...
Mmf... Ham and melon...
Shrimp-chili dumplings... Sunny-side-up egg and toast...
MUNYU (MUMBLE)
MUNYU

THE DEVIL IS A PART-TIMER!

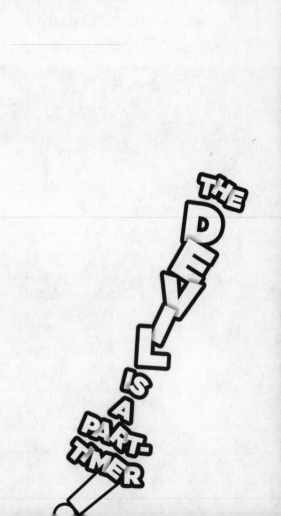

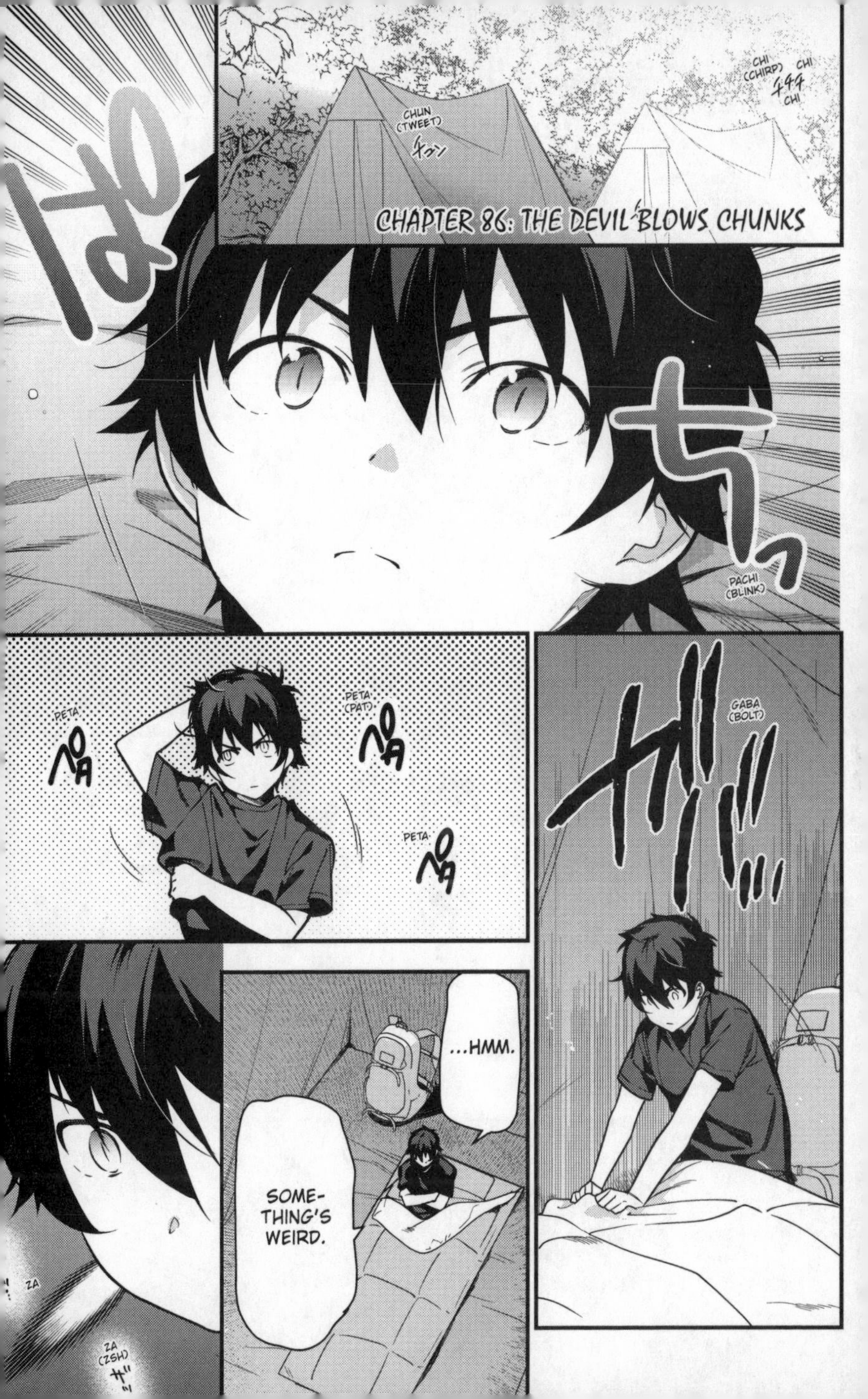
CHI (CHIRP) CHI
チチチ
CHUN (TWEET)
チュン
CHAPTER 86: THE DEVIL BLOWS CHUNKS
ぱちっ
PACHI (BLINK)
ガバ
GABA (BOLT)
PETA (PAT)
ペタ
PETA
ペタ
PETA
ペタ
...HMM.
SOME-THING'S WEIRD.
ZA
ZA (ZSH)
ザ

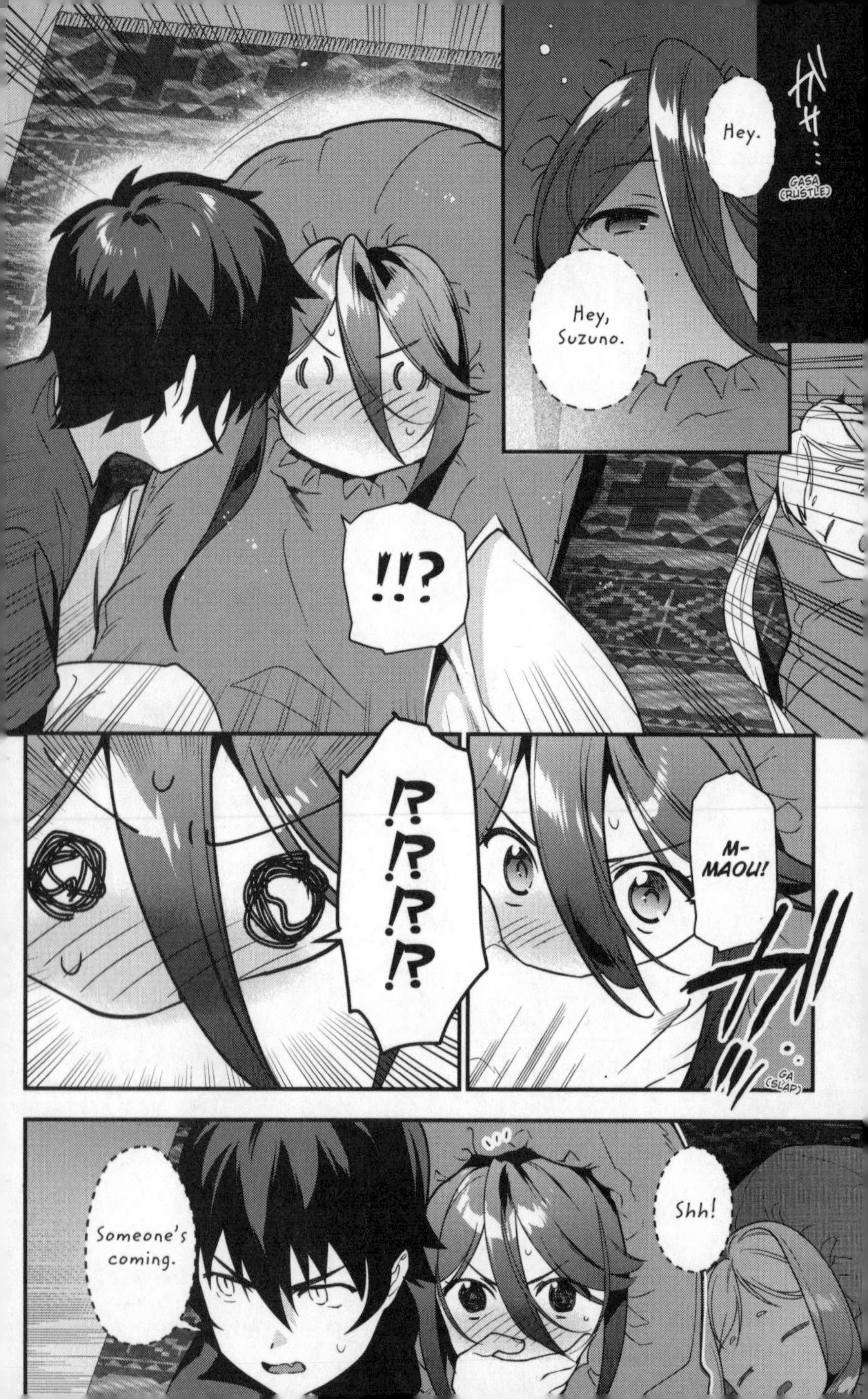
GASA (RUSTLE)
Hey.
Hey, Suzuno.
!!?
M-MAOU!
GA (SLAP)
!?!?!?
Shh!
Someone's coming.

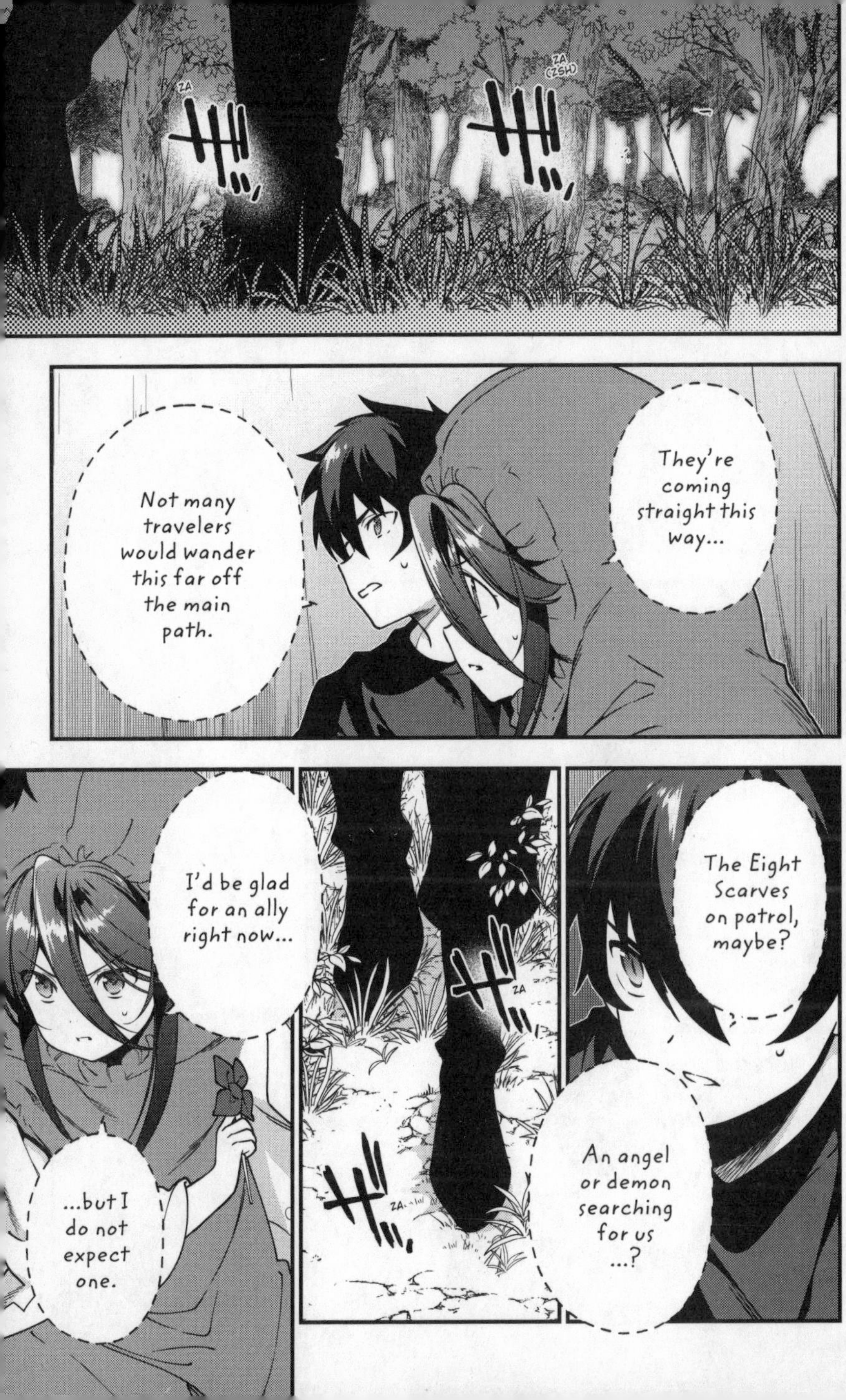
ZA (ZSH)
ZA
They're coming straight this way...
Not many travelers would wander this far off the main path.
The Eight Scarves on patrol, maybe?
An angel or demon searching for us ...?
ZA
ZA
I'd be glad for an ally right now...
...but I do not expect one.

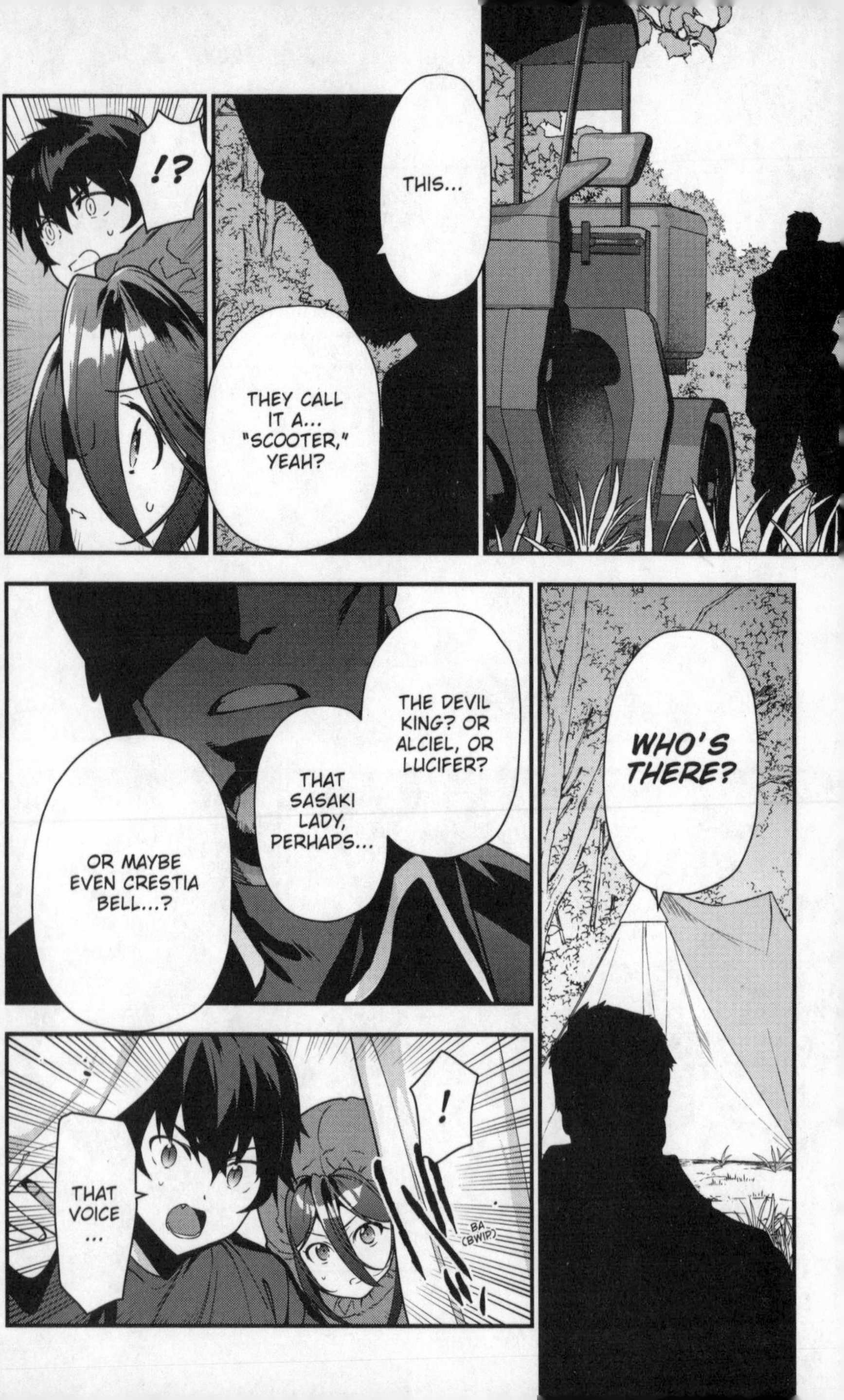
THIS...
THEY CALL IT A... "SCOOTER," YEAH?
!?
WHO'S THERE?
THE DEVIL KING? OR ALCIEL, OR LUCIFER?
THAT SASAKI LADY, PERHAPS...
OR MAYBE EVEN CRESTIA BELL...?
!
BA (BWIP)
THAT VOICE ...

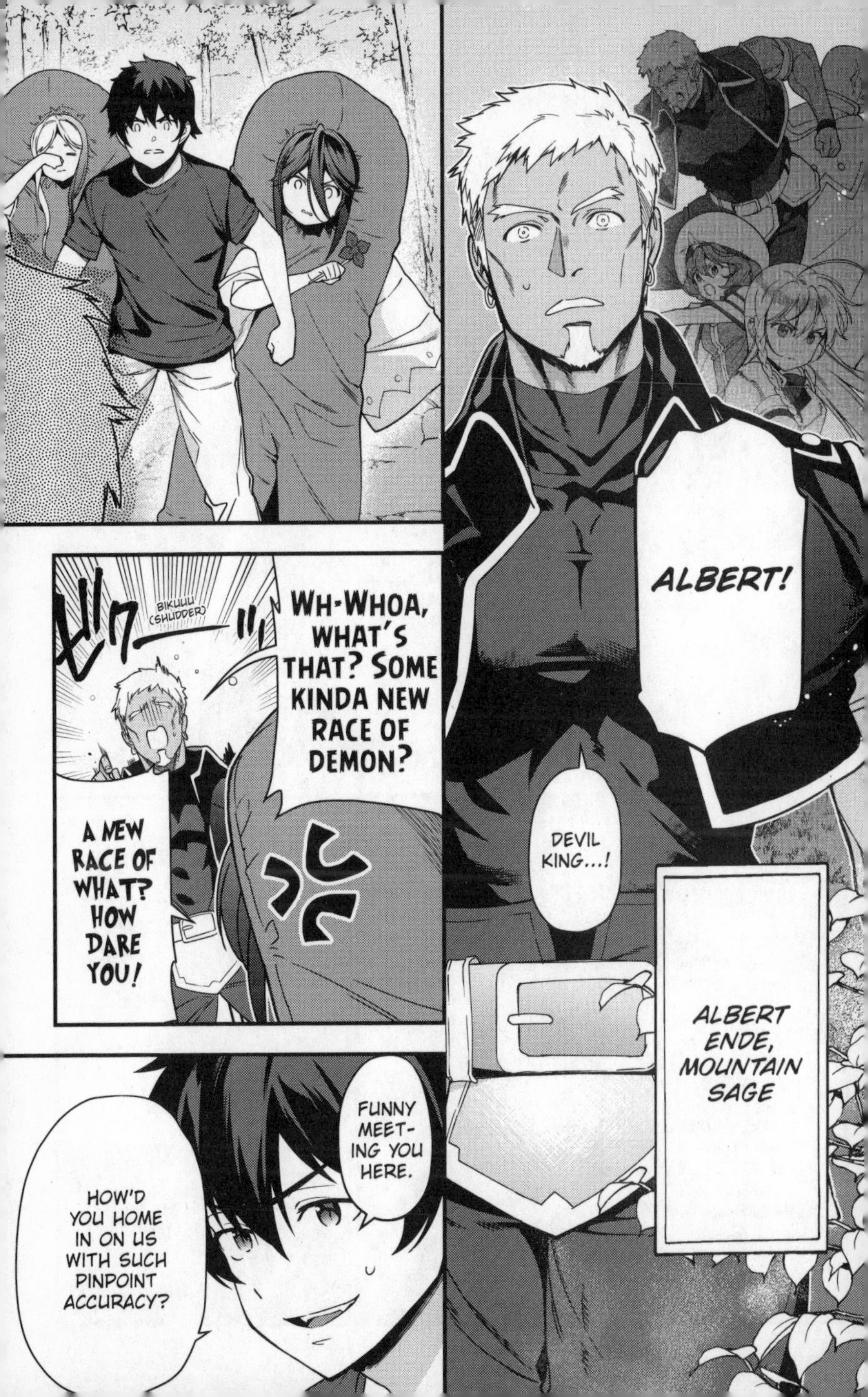
ALBERT!
DEVIL KING...!
ALBERT ENDE, MOUNTAIN SAGE
BIKUUU (SHUDDER)
WH-WHOA, WHAT'S THAT? SOME KINDA NEW RACE OF DEMON?
A NEW RACE OF WHAT? HOW DARE YOU!
FUNNY MEET-ING YOU HERE.
HOW'D YOU HOME IN ON US WITH SUCH PINPOINT ACCURACY?

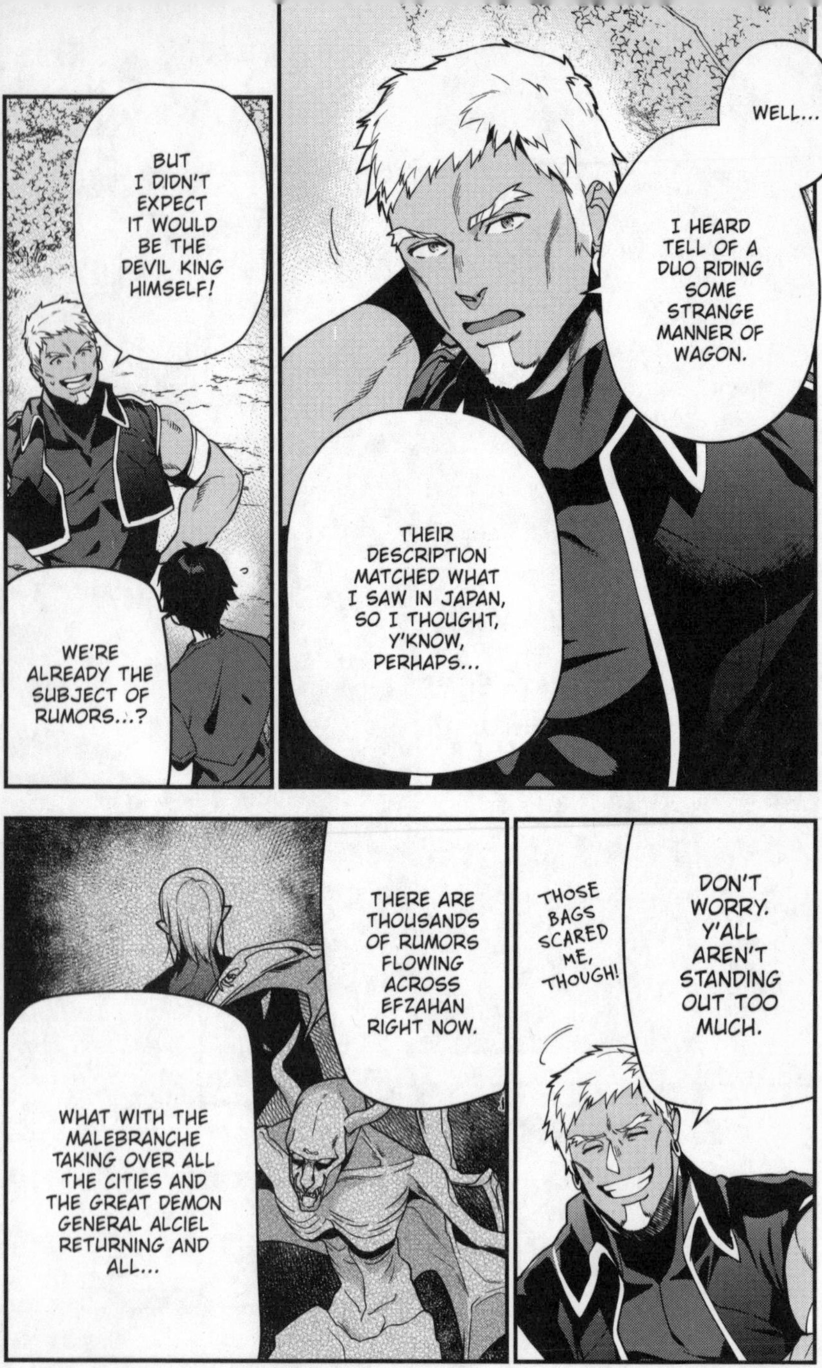
WELL...
I HEARD TELL OF A DUO RIDING SOME STRANGE MANNER OF WAGON.
THEIR DESCRIPTION MATCHED WHAT I SAW IN JAPAN, SO I THOUGHT, Y'KNOW, PERHAPS...
BUT I DIDN'T EXPECT IT WOULD BE THE DEVIL KING HIMSELF!
WE'RE ALREADY THE SUBJECT OF RUMORS...?
DON'T WORRY. Y'ALL AREN'T STANDING OUT TOO MUCH.
THOSE BAGS SCARED ME, THOUGH!
THERE ARE THOUSANDS OF RUMORS FLOWING ACROSS EFZAHAN RIGHT NOW.
WHAT WITH THE MALEBRANCHE TAKING OVER ALL THE CITIES AND THE GREAT DEMON GENERAL ALCIEL RETURNING AND ALL...

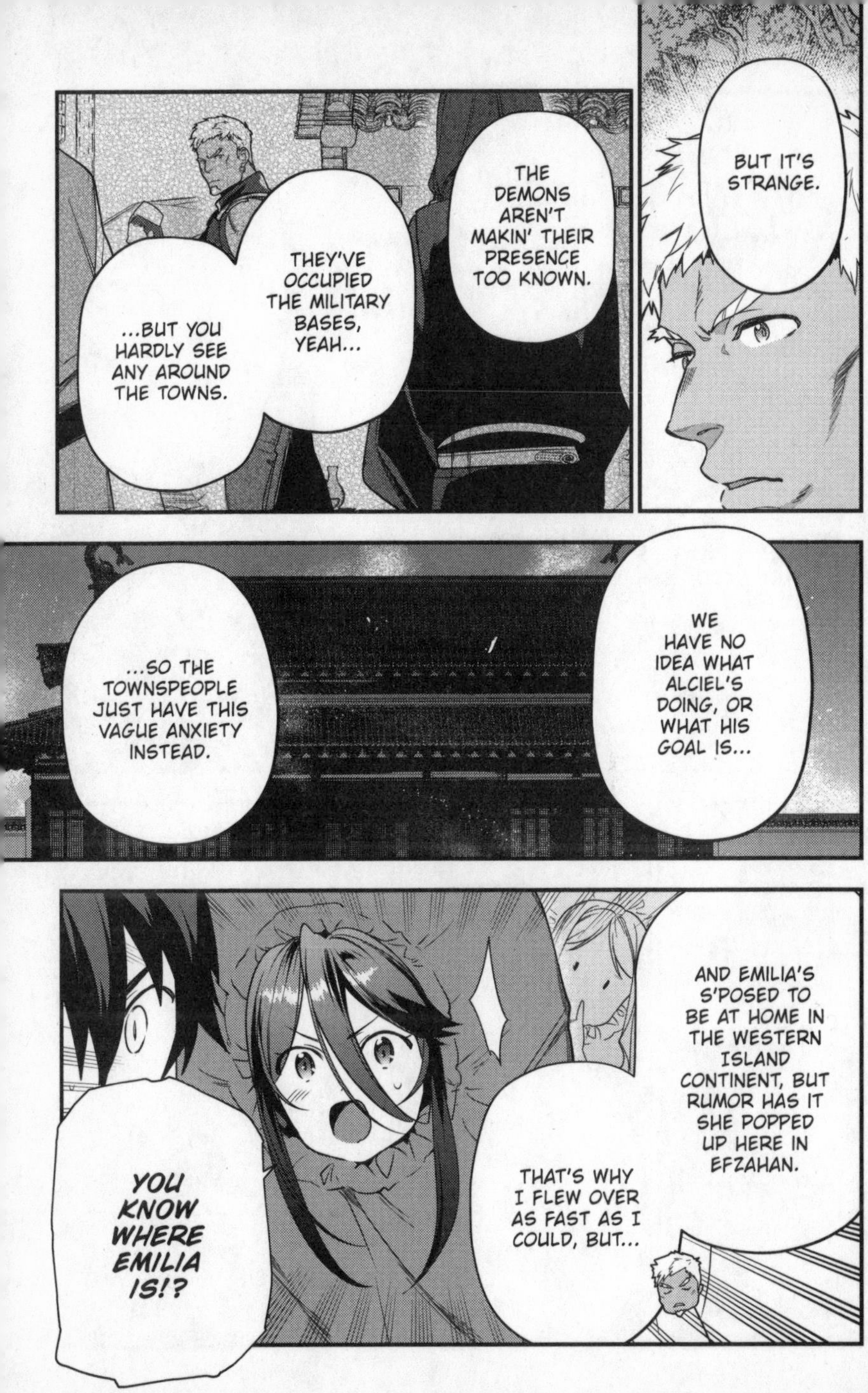
BUT IT'S STRANGE.
THE DEMONS AREN'T MAKIN' THEIR PRESENCE TOO KNOWN.
THEY'VE OCCUPIED THE MILITARY BASES, YEAH...
...BUT YOU HARDLY SEE ANY AROUND THE TOWNS.
WE HAVE NO IDEA WHAT ALCIEL'S DOING, OR WHAT HIS GOAL IS...
...SO THE TOWNSPEOPLE JUST HAVE THIS VAGUE ANXIETY INSTEAD.
AND EMILIA'S S'POSED TO BE AT HOME IN THE WESTERN ISLAND CONTINENT, BUT RUMOR HAS IT SHE POPPED UP HERE IN EFZAHAN.
THAT'S WHY I FLEW OVER AS FAST AS I COULD, BUT...
YOU KNOW WHERE EMILIA IS!?

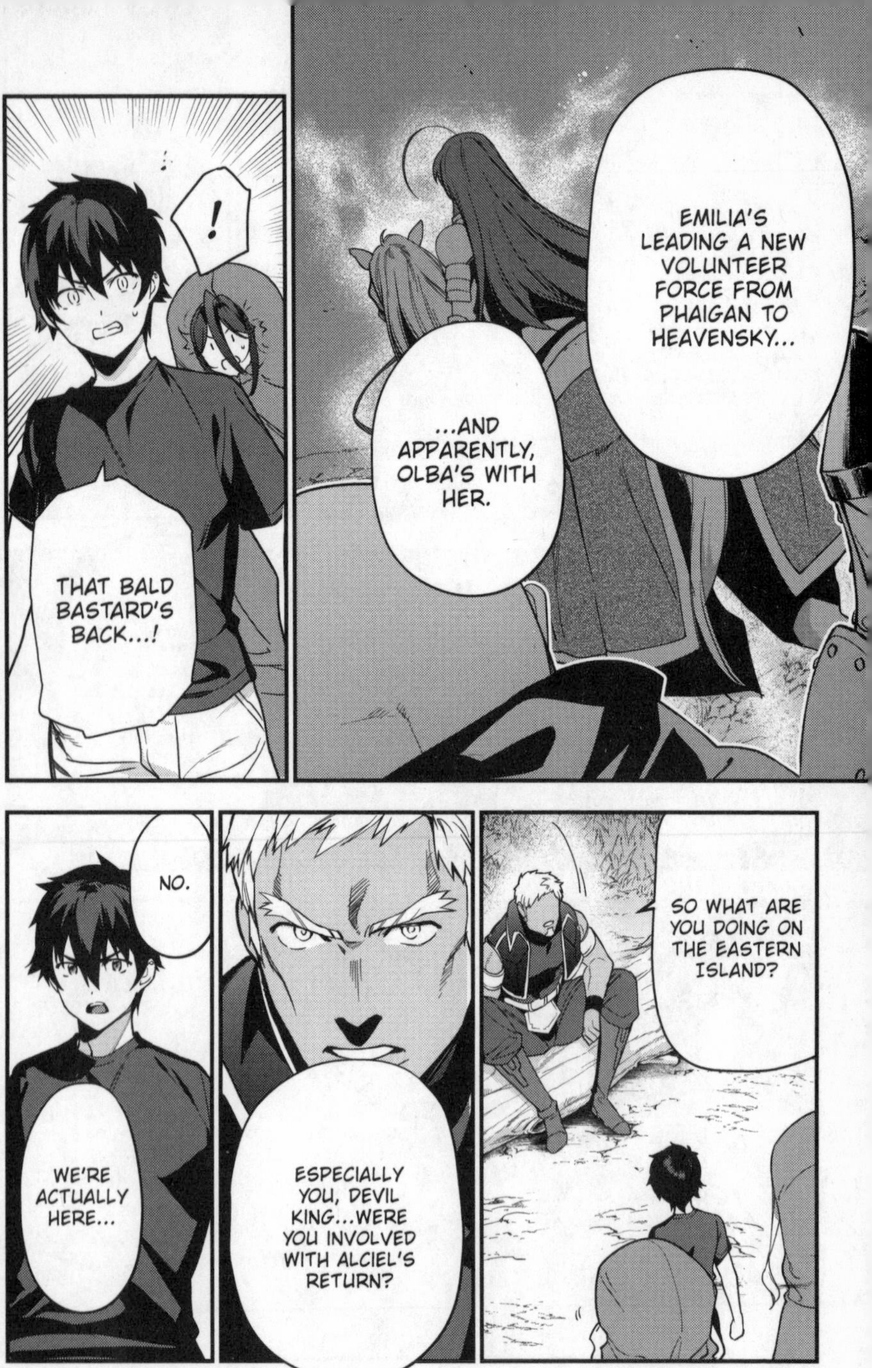
EMILIA'S LEADING A NEW VOLUNTEER FORCE FROM PHAIGAN TO HEAVENSKY...
...AND APPARENTLY, OLBA'S WITH HER.
!
THAT BALD BASTARD'S BACK...!
SO WHAT ARE YOU DOING ON THE EASTERN ISLAND?
ESPECIALLY YOU, DEVIL KING...WERE YOU INVOLVED WITH ALCIEL'S RETURN?
NO.
WE'RE ACTUALLY HERE...

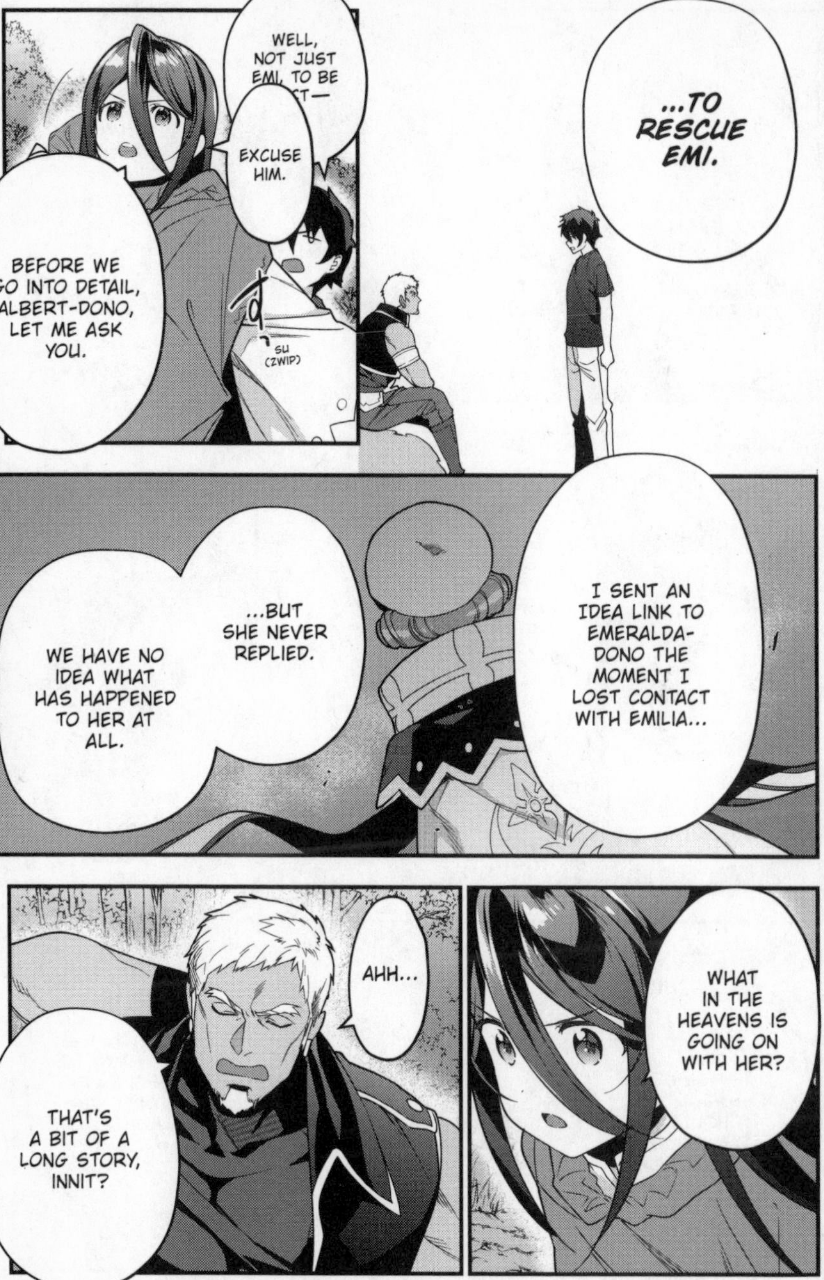
...TO RESCUE EMI.
WELL, NOT JUST EMI, TO BE
EXCUSE HIM.
SU (ZWIP)
BEFORE WE GO INTO DETAIL, ALBERT-DONO, LET ME ASK YOU.
I SENT AN IDEA LINK TO EMERALDA-DONO THE MOMENT I LOST CONTACT WITH EMILIA...
...BUT SHE NEVER REPLIED.
WE HAVE NO IDEA WHAT HAS HAPPENED TO HER AT ALL.
WHAT IN THE HEAVENS IS GOING ON WITH HER?
AHH...
THAT'S A BIT OF A LONG STORY, INNIT?

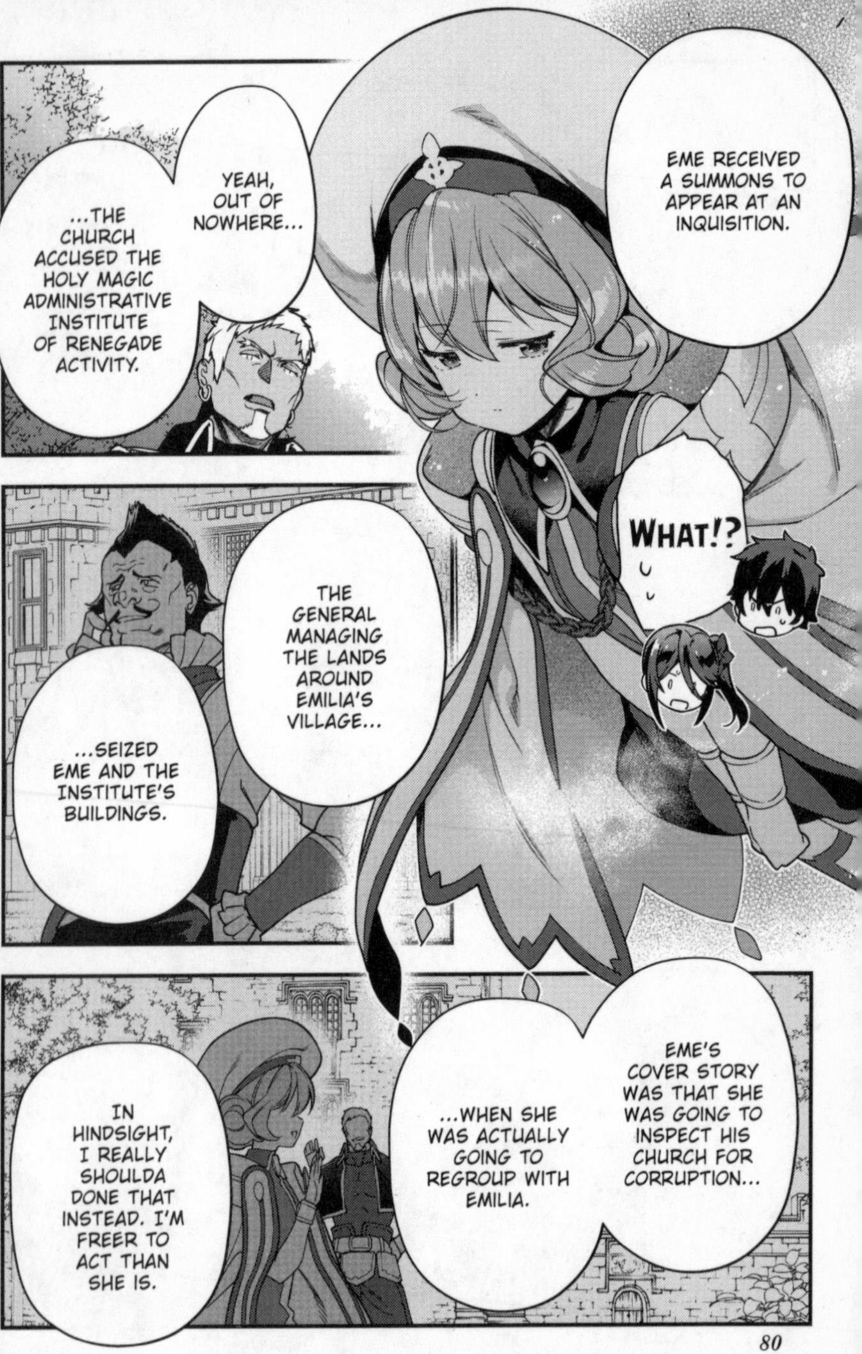
EME RECEIVED A SUMMONS TO APPEAR AT AN INQUISITION.
YEAH, OUT OF NOWHERE...
...THE CHURCH ACCUSED THE HOLY MAGIC ADMINISTRATIVE INSTITUTE OF RENEGADE ACTIVITY.
WHAT!?
THE GENERAL MANAGING THE LANDS AROUND EMILIA'S VILLAGE...
...SEIZED EME AND THE INSTITUTE'S BUILDINGS.
EME'S COVER STORY WAS THAT SHE WAS GOING TO INSPECT HIS CHURCH FOR CORRUPTION...
...WHEN SHE WAS ACTUALLY GOING TO REGROUP WITH EMILIA.
IN HINDSIGHT, I REALLY SHOULDA DONE THAT INSTEAD. I'M FREER TO ACT THAN SHE IS.

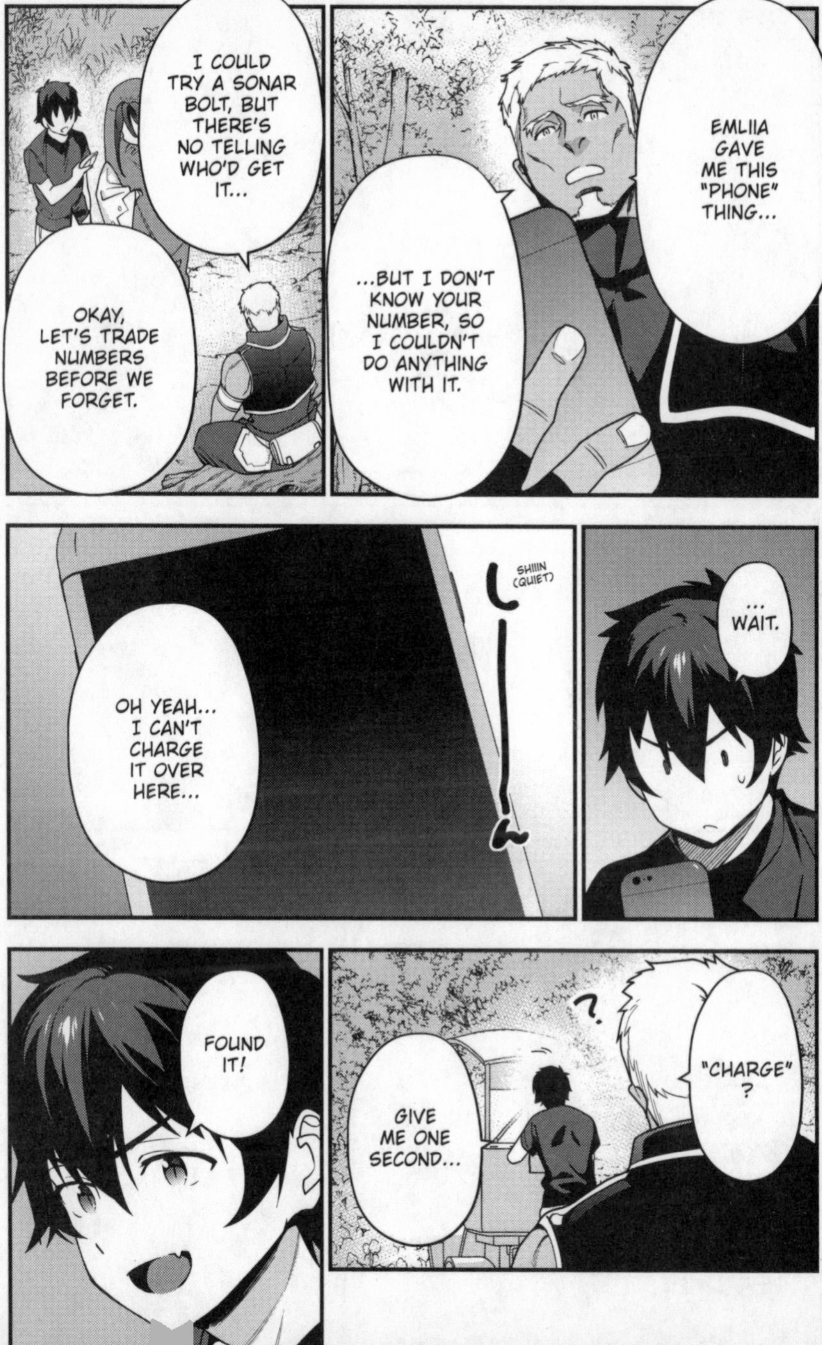
EMLIIA GAVE ME THIS "PHONE" THING...
...BUT I DON'T KNOW YOUR NUMBER, SO I COULDN'T DO ANYTHING WITH IT.
I COULD TRY A SONAR BOLT, BUT THERE'S NO TELLING WHO'D GET IT...
OKAY, LET'S TRADE NUMBERS BEFORE WE FORGET.
... WAIT.
SHIIIN (QUIET)
OH YEAH... I CAN'T CHARGE IT OVER HERE...
"CHARGE"?
?
GIVE ME ONE SECOND...
FOUND IT!

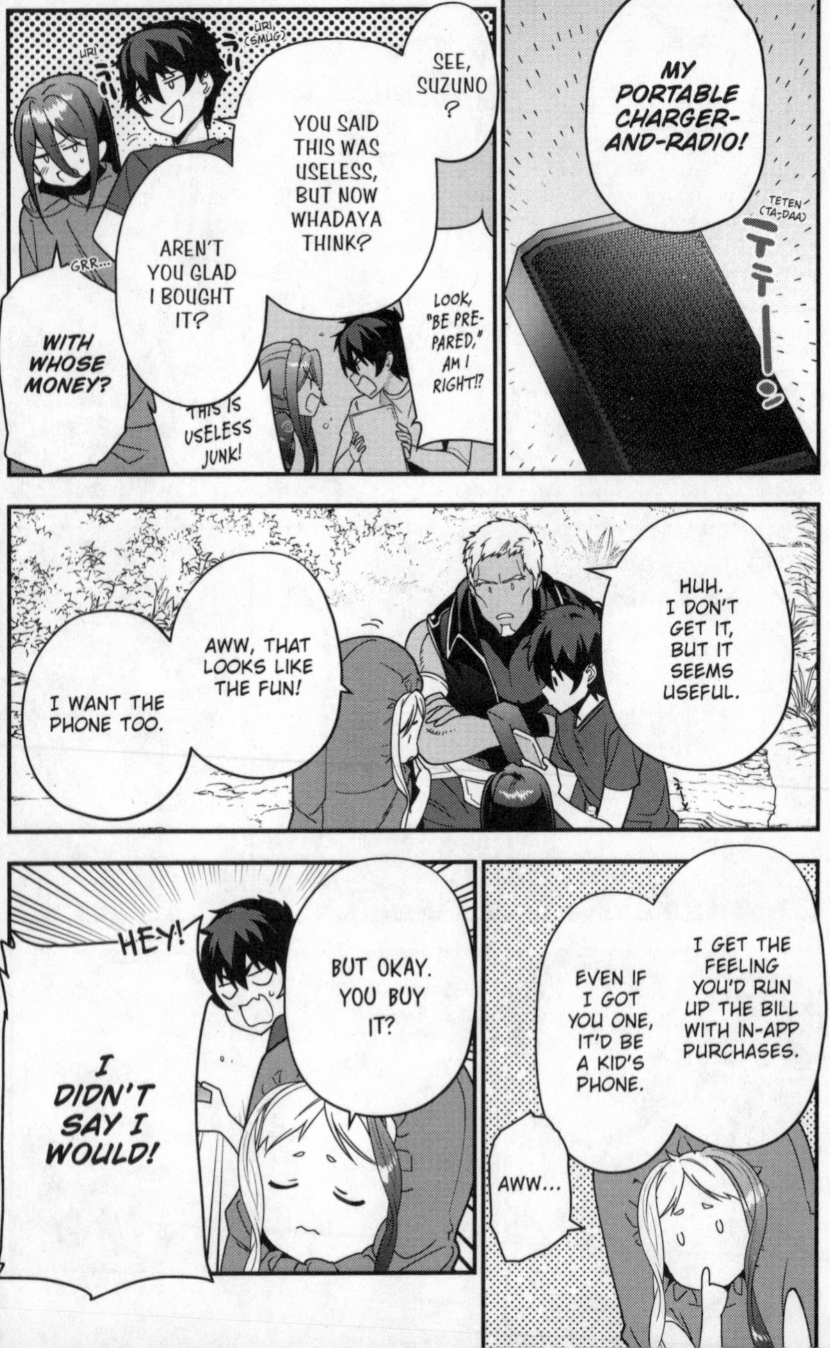
MY PORTABLE CHARGER-AND-RADIO!
TETEN (TA-DAA)
SEE, SUZUNO?
URI, (SMUG)
URI
YOU SAID THIS WAS USELESS, BUT NOW WHADAYA THINK?
LOOK, "BE PRE-PARED," AM I RIGHT!?
AREN'T YOU GLAD I BOUGHT IT?
THIS IS USELESS JUNK!
GRR...
WITH WHOSE MONEY?
HUH. I DON'T GET IT, BUT IT SEEMS USEFUL.
AWW, THAT LOOKS LIKE THE FUN!
I WANT THE PHONE TOO.
I GET THE FEELING YOU'D RUN UP THE BILL WITH IN-APP PURCHASES.
EVEN IF I GOT YOU ONE, IT'D BE A KID'S PHONE.
AWW...
BUT OKAY. YOU BUY IT?
HEY!
I DIDN'T SAY I WOULD!

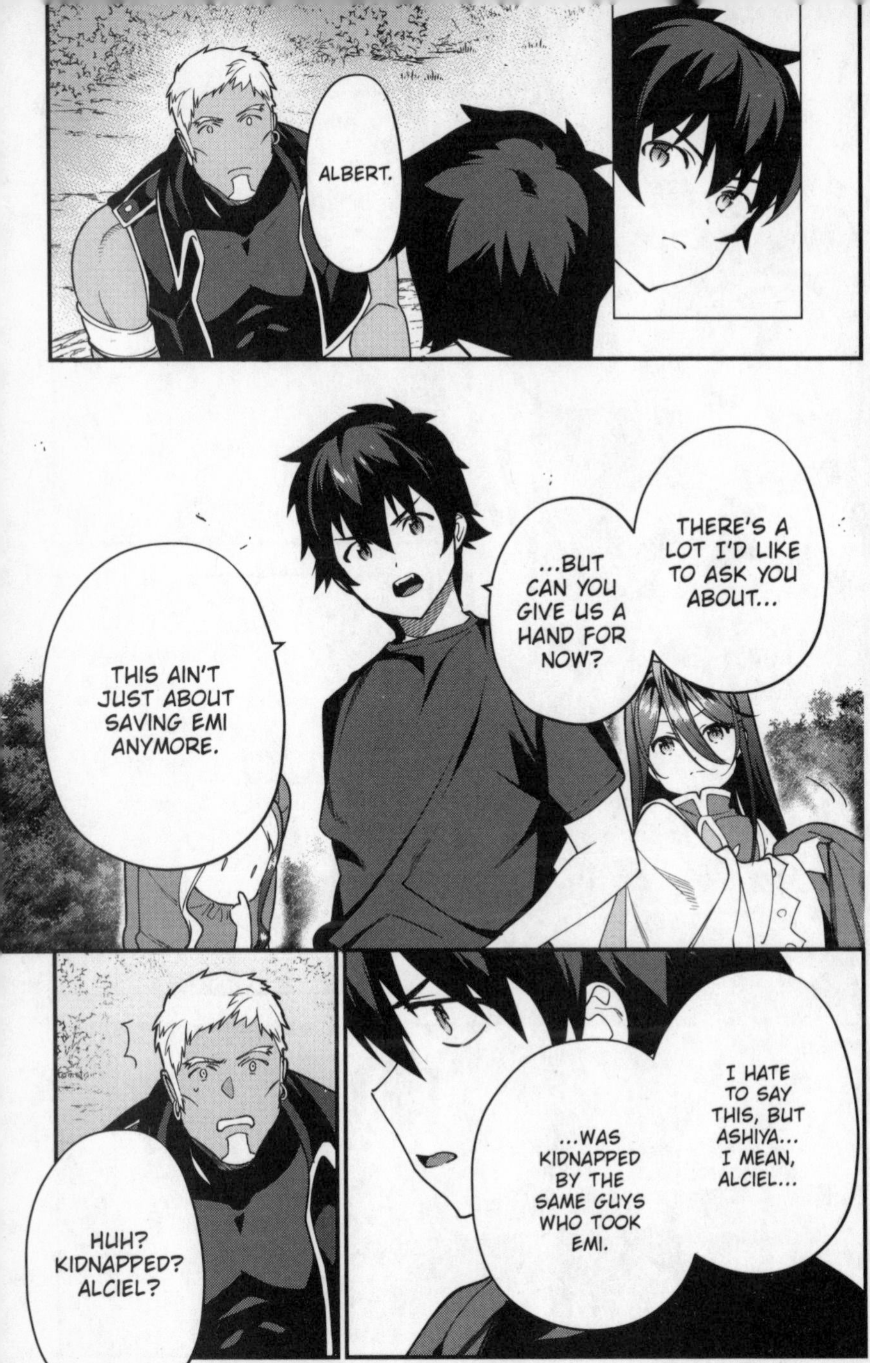
ALBERT.
THERE'S A LOT I'D LIKE TO ASK YOU ABOUT...
...BUT CAN YOU GIVE US A HAND FOR NOW?
THIS AIN'T JUST ABOUT SAVING EMI ANYMORE.
I HATE TO SAY THIS, BUT ASHIYA... I MEAN, ALCIEL...
...WAS KIDNAPPED BY THE SAME GUYS WHO TOOK EMI.
HUH? KIDNAPPED? ALCIEL?

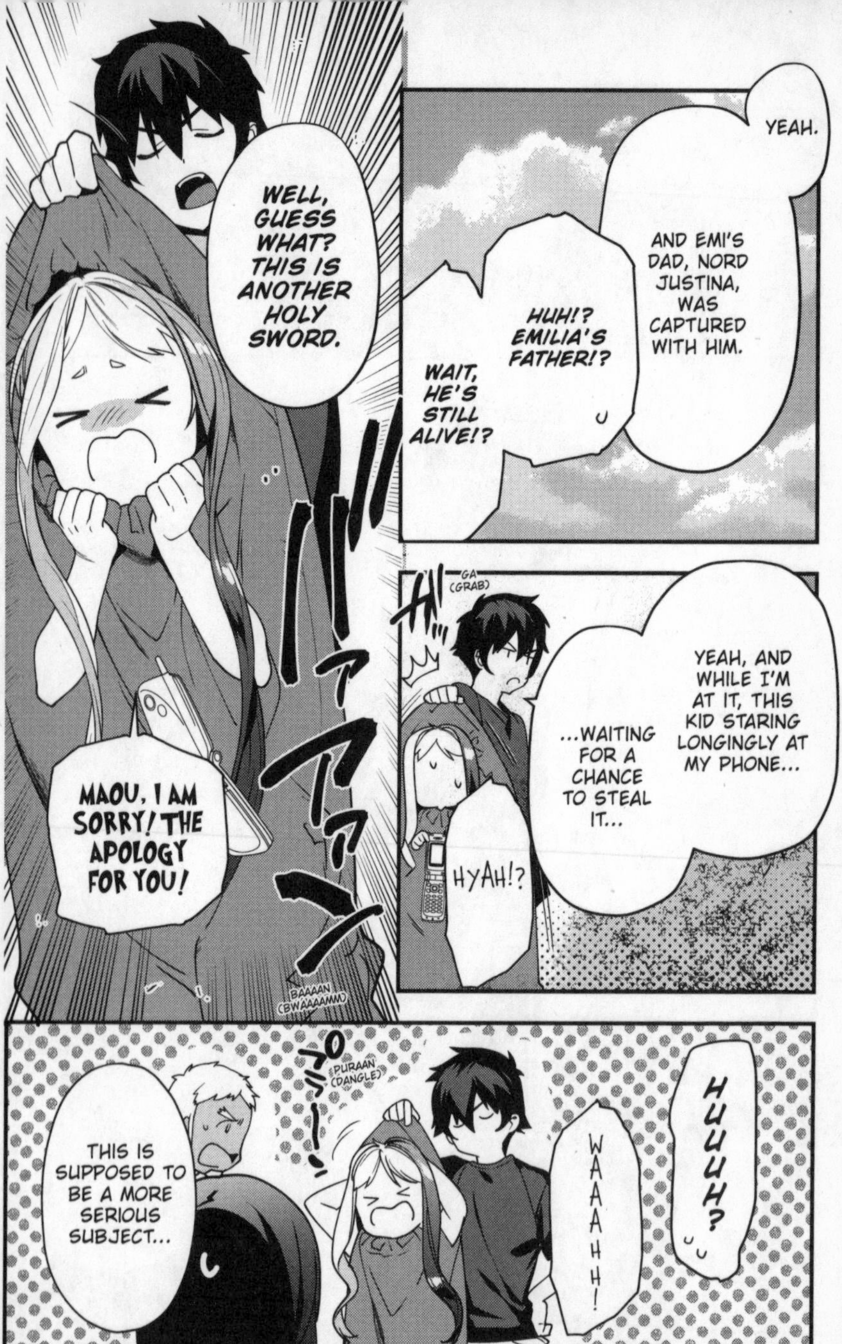
YEAH.
AND EMI'S DAD, NORD JUSTINA, WAS CAPTURED WITH HIM.
HUH!? EMILIA'S FATHER!?
WAIT, HE'S STILL ALIVE!?
GA (GRAB)
YEAH, AND WHILE I'M AT IT, THIS KID STARING LONGINGLY AT MY PHONE...
...WAITING FOR A CHANCE TO STEAL IT...
HYAH!?
WELL, GUESS WHAT? THIS IS ANOTHER HOLY SWORD.
BAAAAN (BWAAAAMM)
MAOU, I AM SORRY! THE APOLOGY FOR YOU!
HUUUH?
WAAAAHH!
PURAAN (DANGLE)
THIS IS SUPPOSED TO BE A MORE SERIOUS SUBJECT...

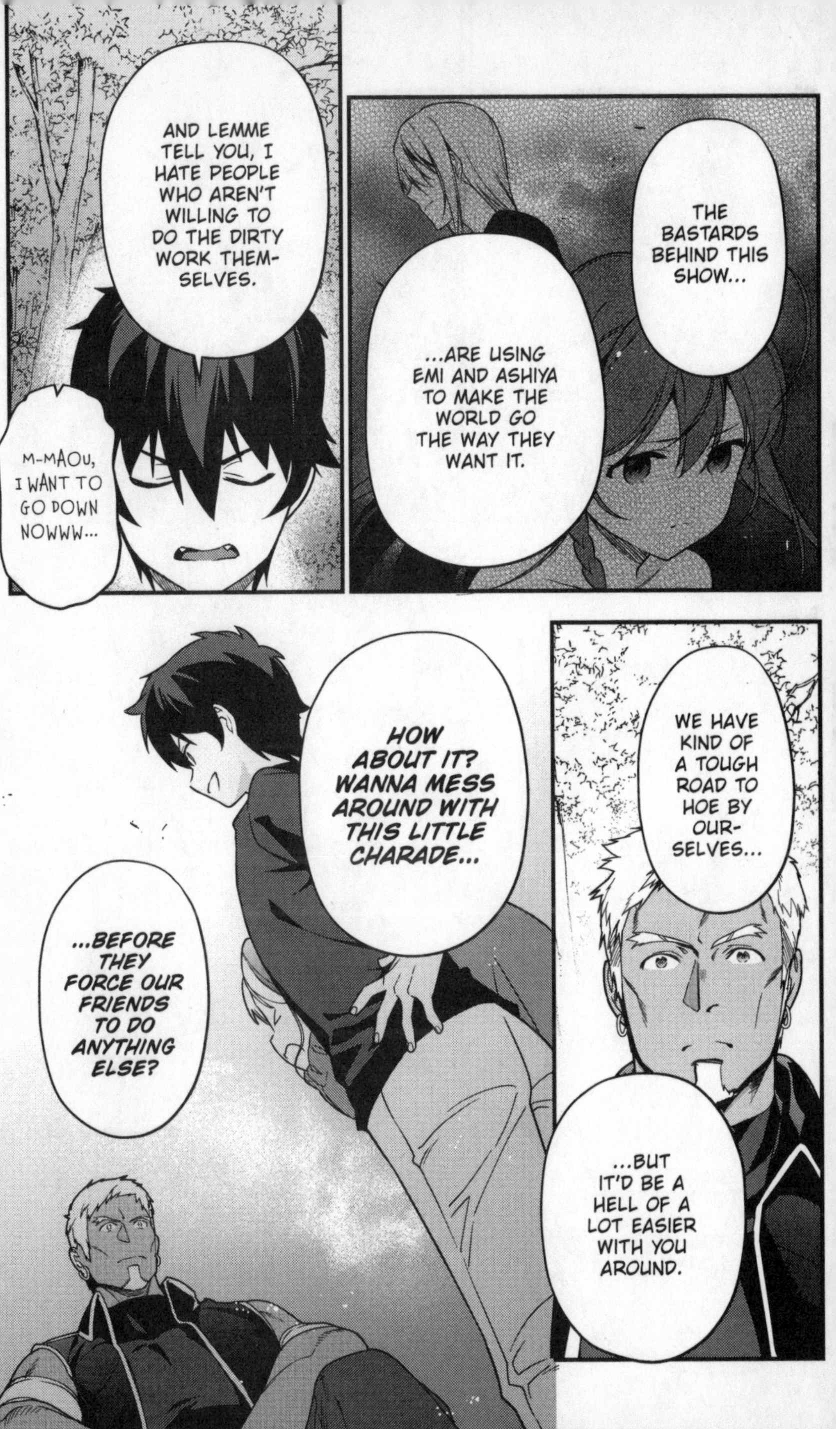
THE BASTARDS BEHIND THIS SHOW...
...ARE USING EMI AND ASHIYA TO MAKE THE WORLD GO THE WAY THEY WANT IT.
AND LEMME TELL YOU, I HATE PEOPLE WHO AREN'T WILLING TO DO THE DIRTY WORK THEM-SELVES.
M-MAOU, I WANT TO GO DOWN NOWWW...
WE HAVE KIND OF A TOUGH ROAD TO HOE BY OUR-SELVES...
...BUT IT'D BE A HELL OF A LOT EASIER WITH YOU AROUND.
HOW ABOUT IT? WANNA MESS AROUND WITH THIS LITTLE CHARADE...
...BEFORE THEY FORCE OUR FRIENDS TO DO ANYTHING ELSE?

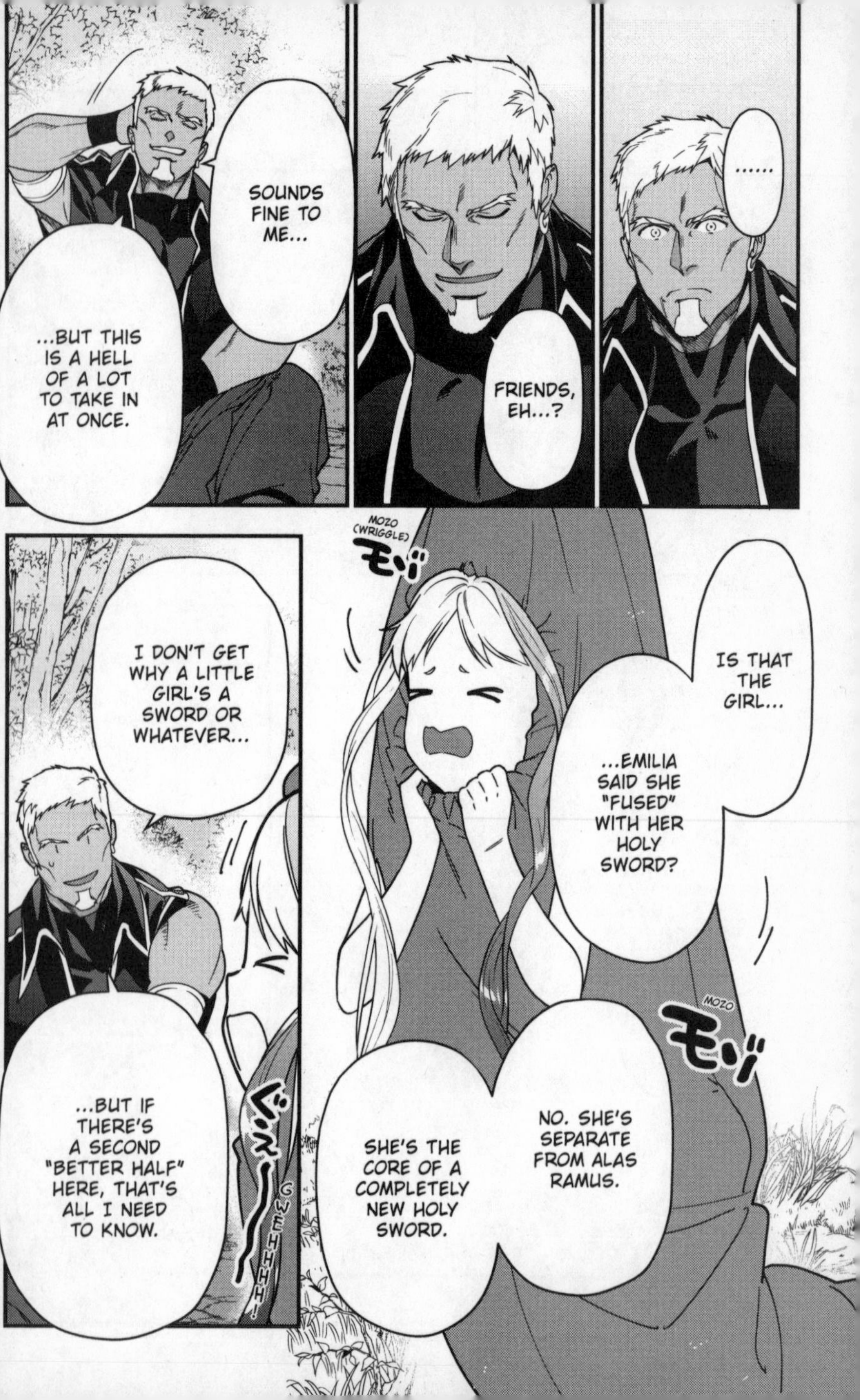
......
FRIENDS, EH...?
SOUNDS FINE TO ME...
...BUT THIS IS A HELL OF A LOT TO TAKE IN AT ONCE.
MOZO (WRIGGLE)
モゾ
IS THAT THE GIRL...
...EMILIA SAID SHE "FUSED" WITH HER HOLY SWORD?
MOZO
モゾ
NO. SHE'S SEPARATE FROM ALAS RAMUS.
SHE'S THE CORE OF A COMPLETELY NEW HOLY SWORD.
GWEHHHH!
I DON'T GET WHY A LITTLE GIRL'S A SWORD OR WHATEVER...
...BUT IF THERE'S A SECOND "BETTER HALF" HERE, THAT'S ALL I NEED TO KNOW.

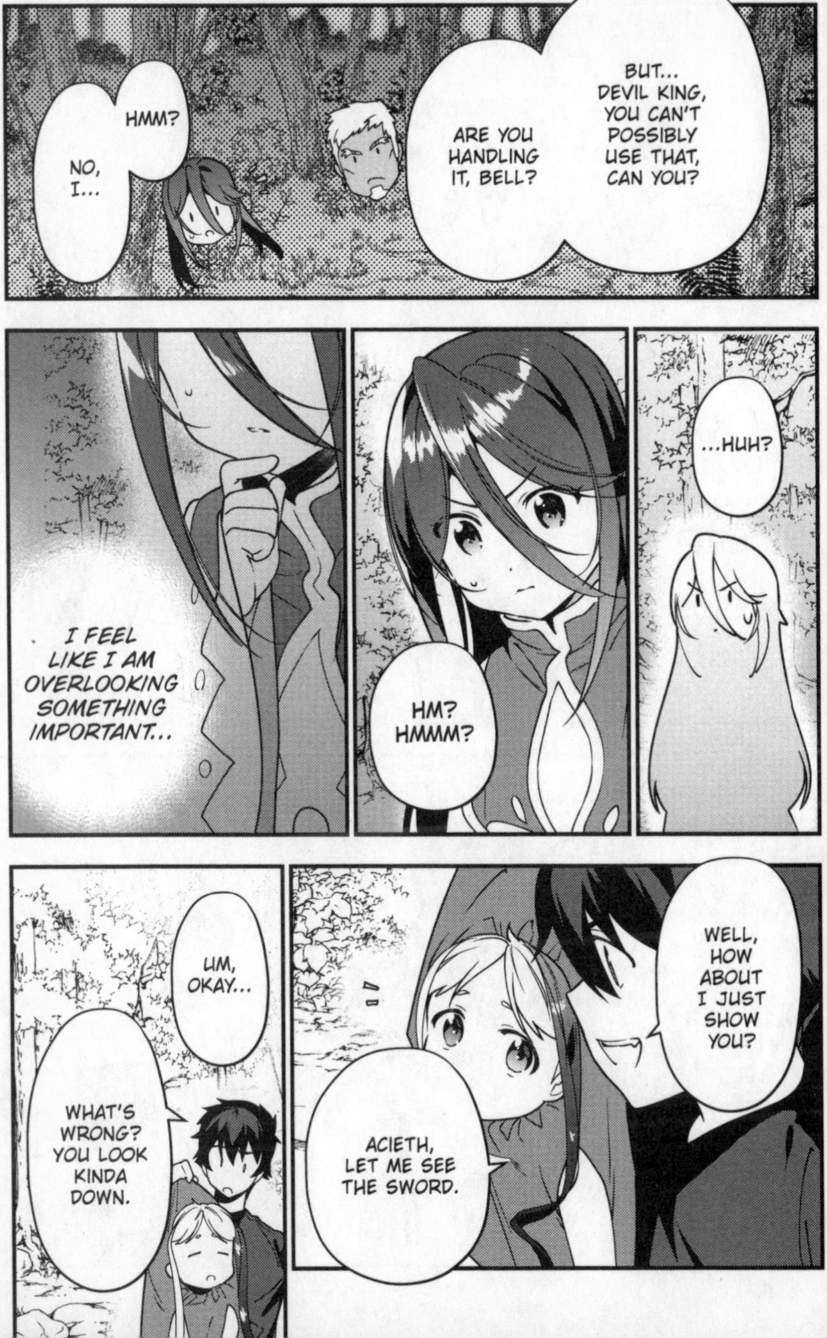
BUT... DEVIL KING, YOU CAN'T POSSIBLY USE THAT, CAN YOU?
ARE YOU HANDLING IT, BELL?
HMM? NO, I...
...HUH?
HM? HMMM?
I FEEL LIKE I AM OVERLOOKING SOMETHING IMPORTANT...
WELL, HOW ABOUT I JUST SHOW YOU?
ACIETH, LET ME SEE THE SWORD.
UM, OKAY...
WHAT'S WRONG? YOU LOOK KINDA DOWN.

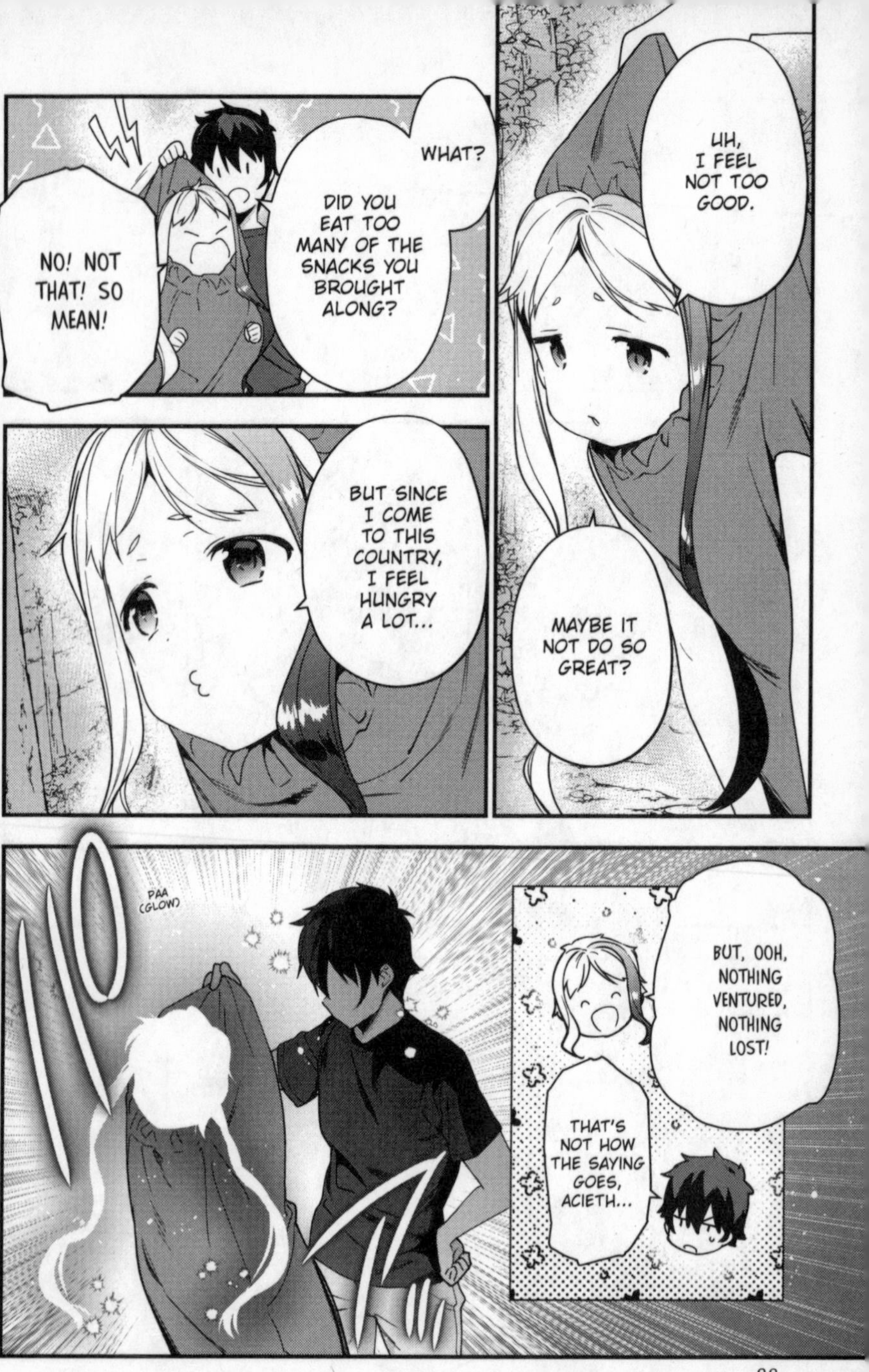
UH, I FEEL NOT TOO GOOD.
MAYBE IT NOT DO SO GREAT?
WHAT?
DID YOU EAT TOO MANY OF THE SNACKS YOU BROUGHT ALONG?
NO! NOT THAT! SO MEAN!
BUT SINCE I COME TO THIS COUNTRY, I FEEL HUNGRY A LOT...
BUT, OOH, NOTHING VENTURED, NOTHING LOST!
THAT'S NOT HOW THE SAYING GOES, ACIETH...
PAA (GLOW)

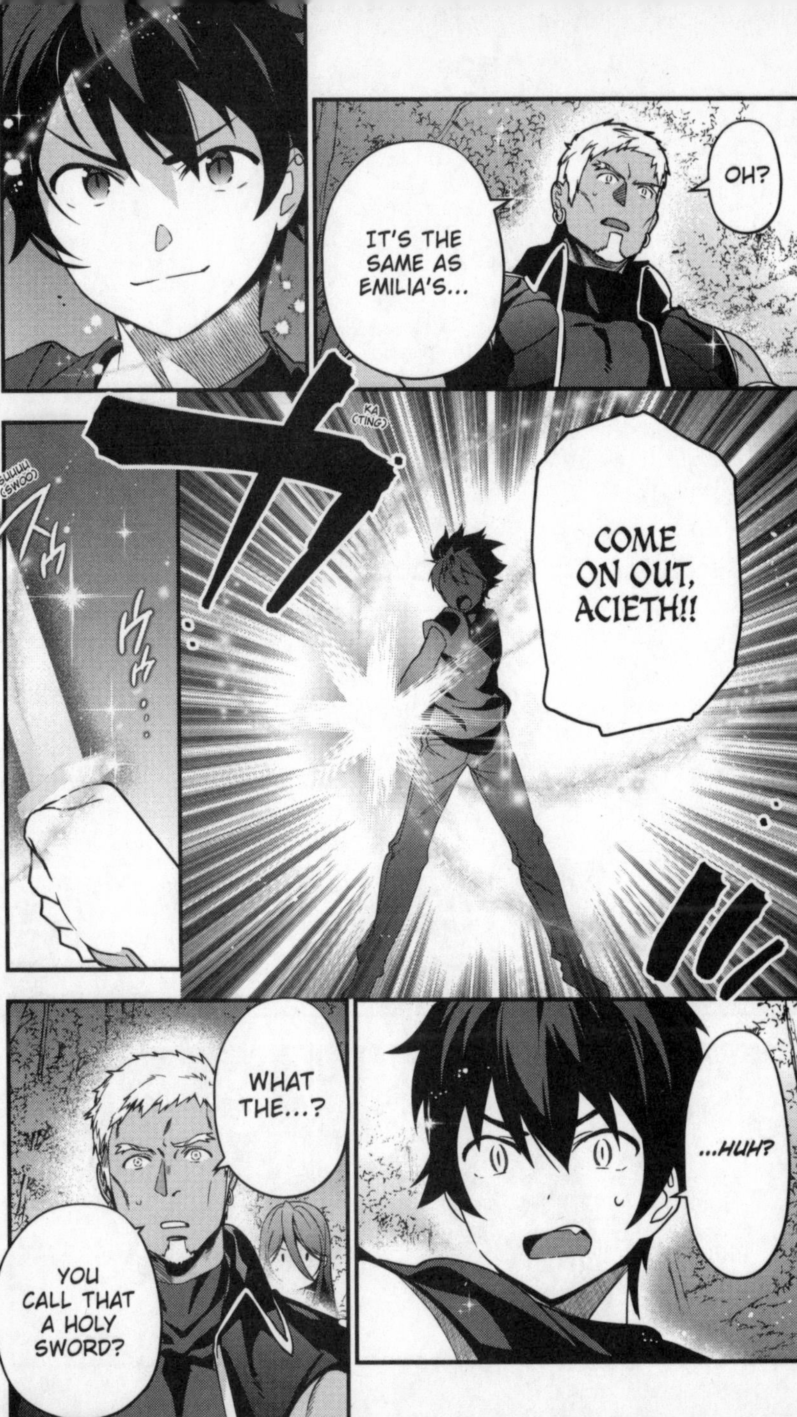
OH?
IT'S THE SAME AS EMILIA'S...
KA (TING)
COME ON OUT, ACIETH!!
SUUUN (SWOO)
...HUH?
WHAT THE...?
YOU CALL THAT A HOLY SWORD?

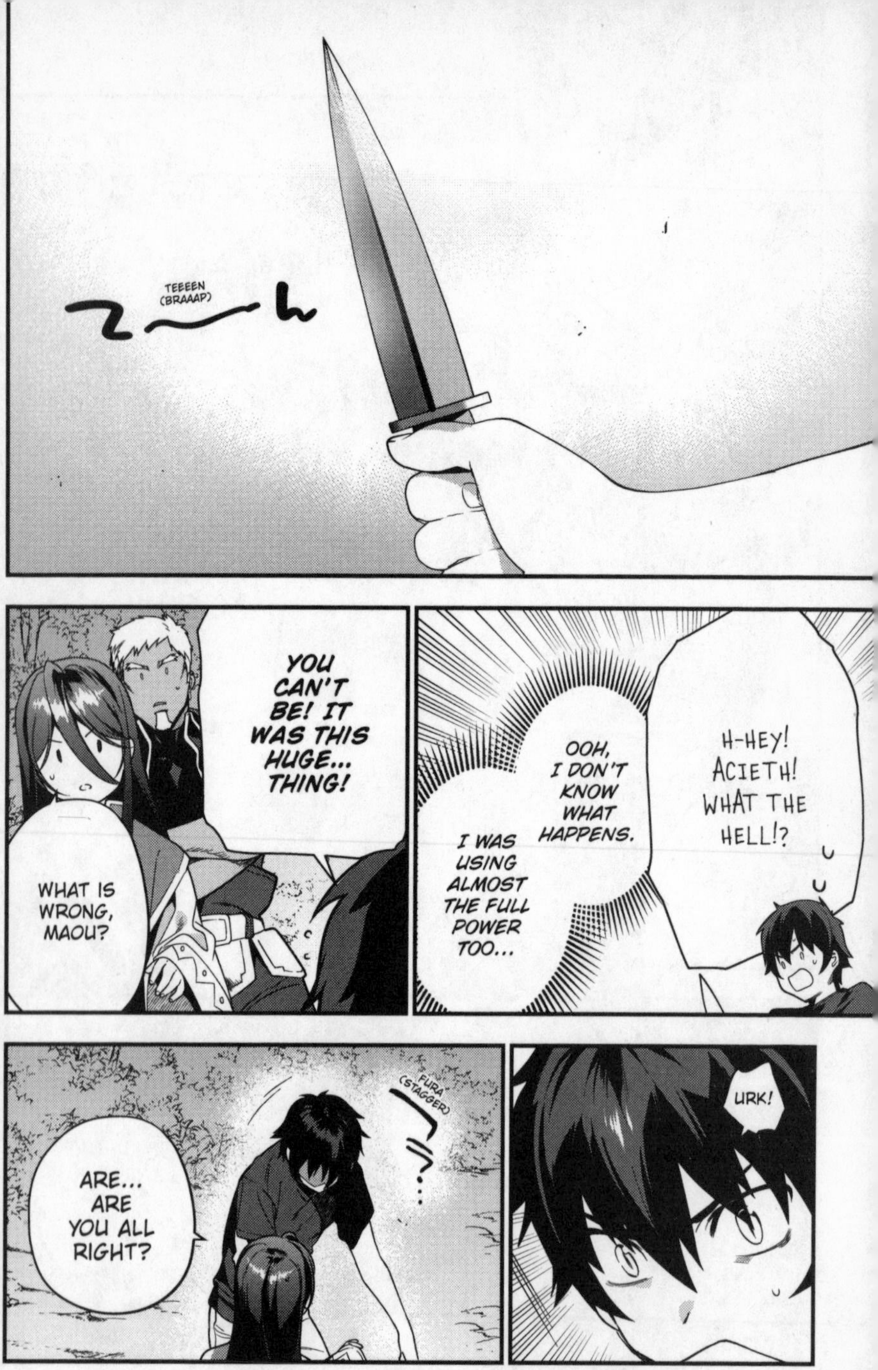
TEEEEN (BRAAAP)
H-HEY! ACIETH! WHAT THE HELL!?
OOH, I DON'T KNOW WHAT HAPPENS.
I WAS USING ALMOST THE FULL POWER TOO...
YOU CAN'T BE! IT WAS THIS HUGE... THING!
WHAT IS WRONG, MAOU?
URK!
FURA (STAGGER)
ARE... ARE YOU ALL RIGHT?

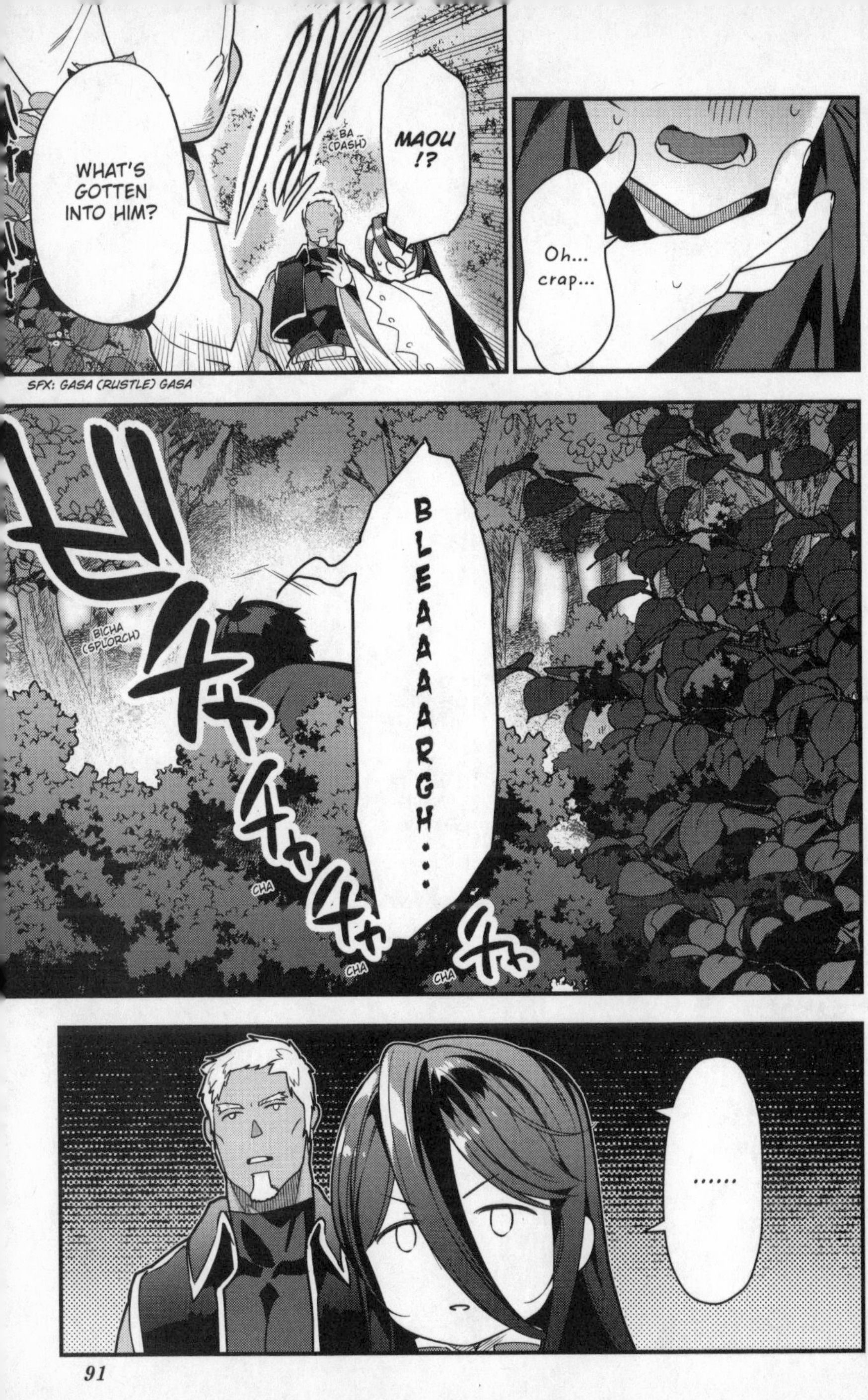
Oh... crap...
MAOU!?
BA (DASH)
WHAT'S GOTTEN INTO HIM?
SFX: GASA (RUSTLE) GASA
BLEAAAAARGH...
BICHA (SPLORCH)
CHA
CHA
CHA
......

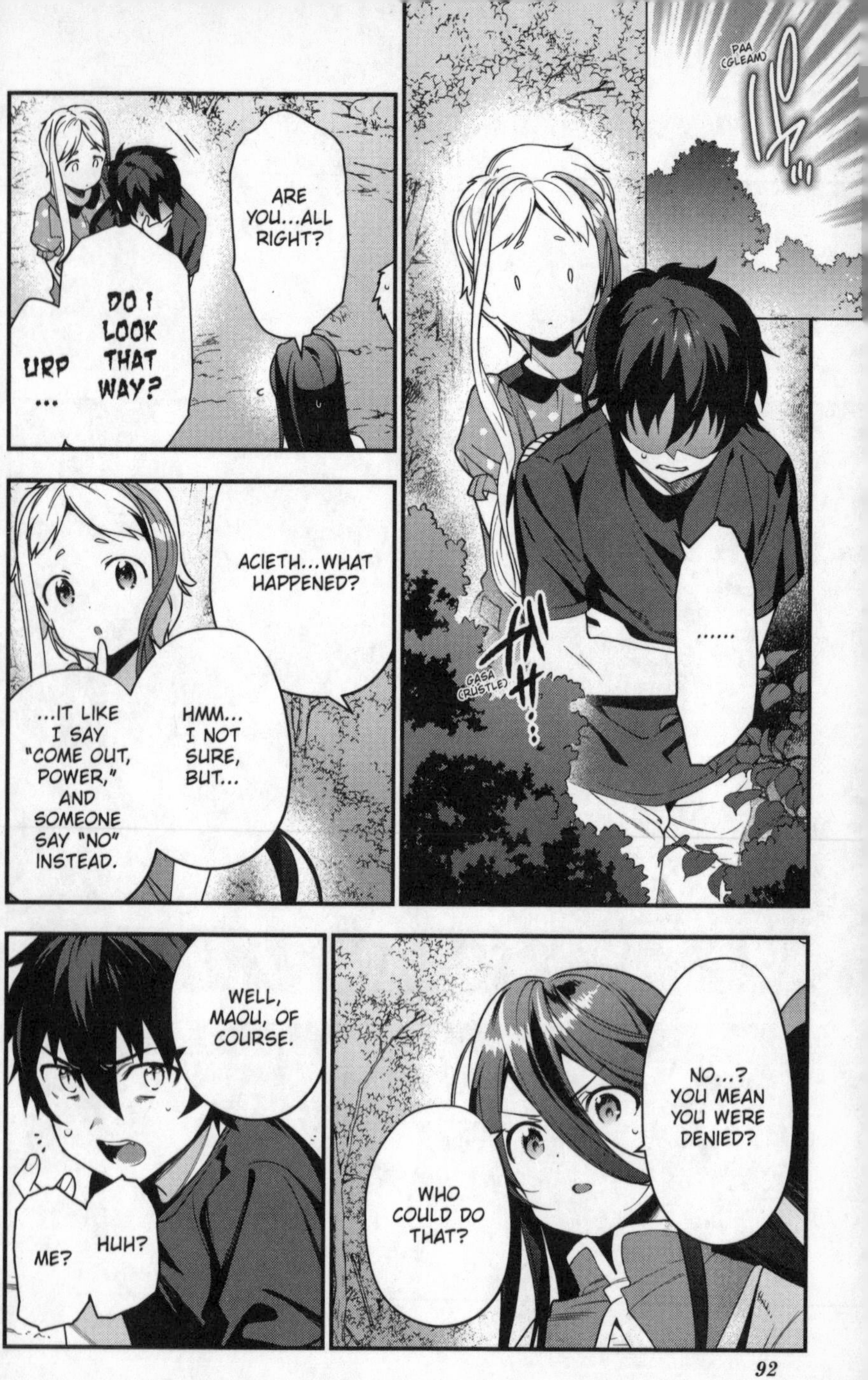
PAA (GLEAM)
GASA (RUSTLE)
......
ARE YOU...ALL RIGHT?
DO I LOOK THAT WAY?
URP...
ACIETH...WHAT HAPPENED?
HMM... I NOT SURE, BUT...
...IT LIKE I SAY "COME OUT, POWER," AND SOMEONE SAY "NO" INSTEAD.
NO...? YOU MEAN YOU WERE DENIED?
WHO COULD DO THAT?
WELL, MAOU, OF COURSE.
HUH?
ME?

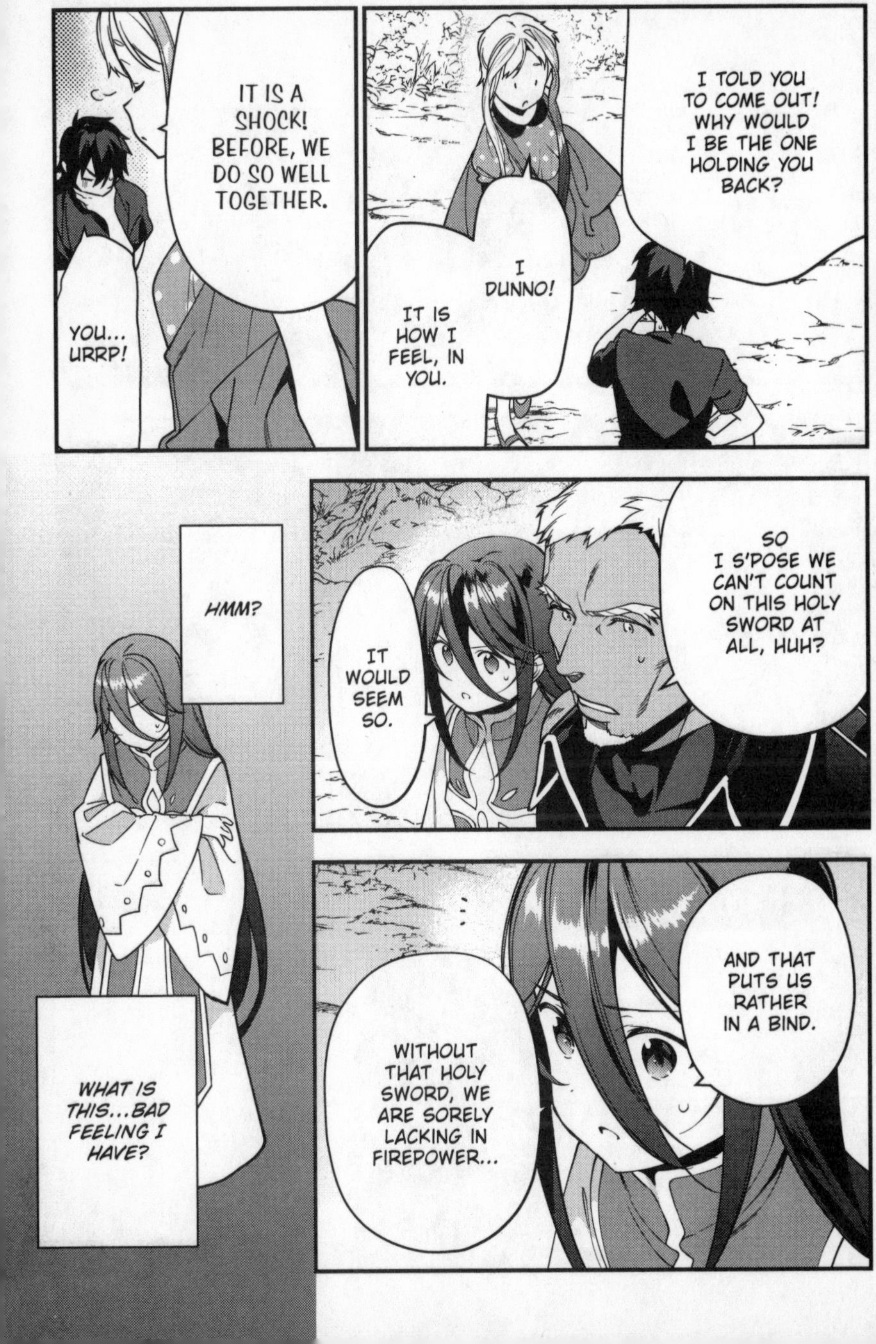
I TOLD YOU TO COME OUT! WHY WOULD I BE THE ONE HOLDING YOU BACK?
I DUNNO!
IT IS HOW I FEEL, IN YOU.
IT IS A SHOCK! BEFORE, WE DO SO WELL TOGETHER.
YOU... URRP!
SO I S'POSE WE CAN'T COUNT ON THIS HOLY SWORD AT ALL, HUH?
IT WOULD SEEM SO.
AND THAT PUTS US RATHER IN A BIND.
...
WITHOUT THAT HOLY SWORD, WE ARE SORELY LACKING IN FIREPOWER...
HMM?
WHAT IS THIS...BAD FEELING I HAVE?

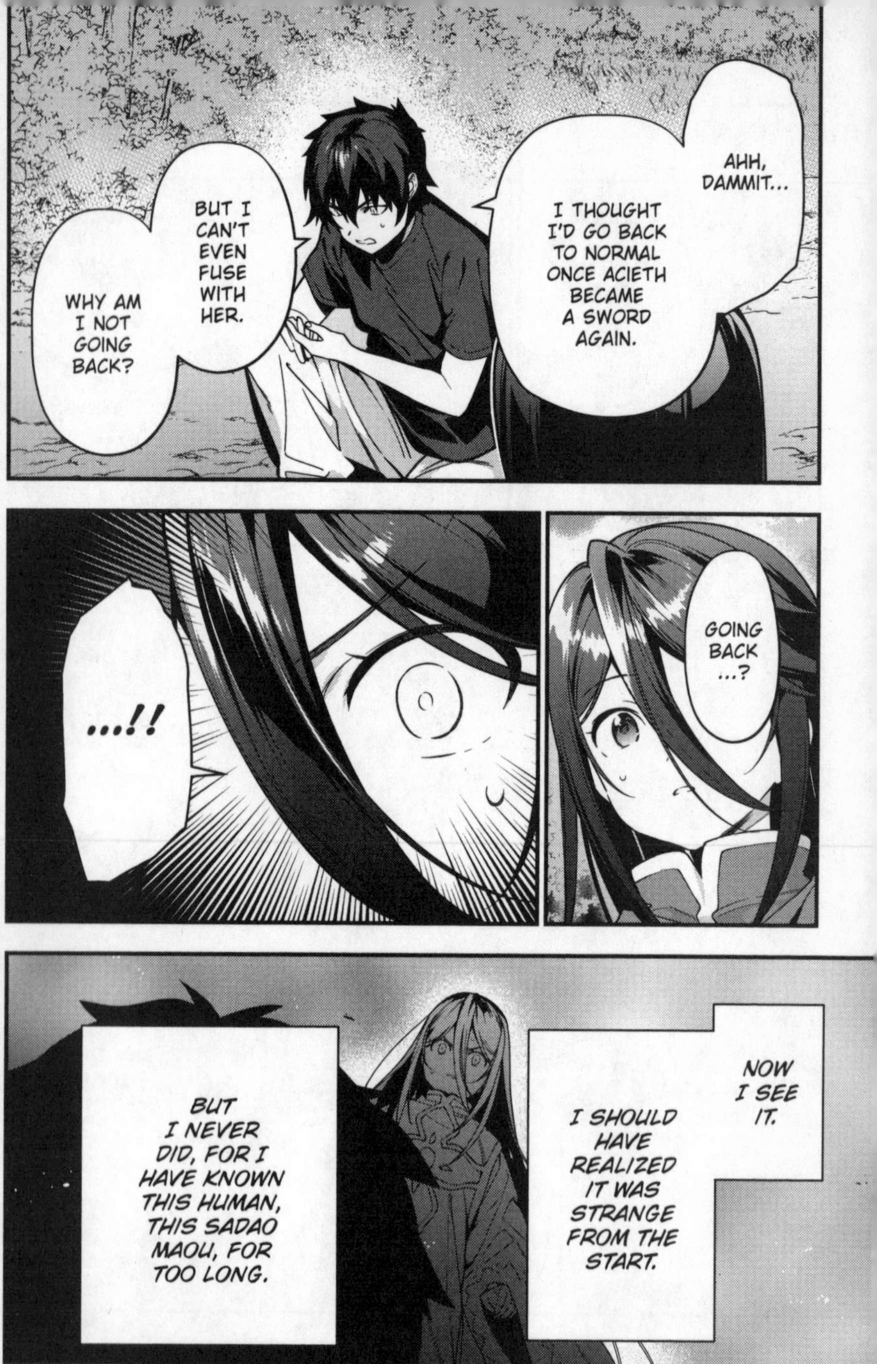
AHH, DAMMIT...
I THOUGHT I'D GO BACK TO NORMAL ONCE ACIETH BECAME A SWORD AGAIN.
BUT I CAN'T EVEN FUSE WITH HER.
WHY AM I NOT GOING BACK?
GOING BACK ...?
...!!
NOW I SEE IT.
I SHOULD HAVE REALIZED IT WAS STRANGE FROM THE START.
BUT I NEVER DID, FOR I HAVE KNOWN THIS HUMAN, THIS SADAO MAOU, FOR TOO LONG.

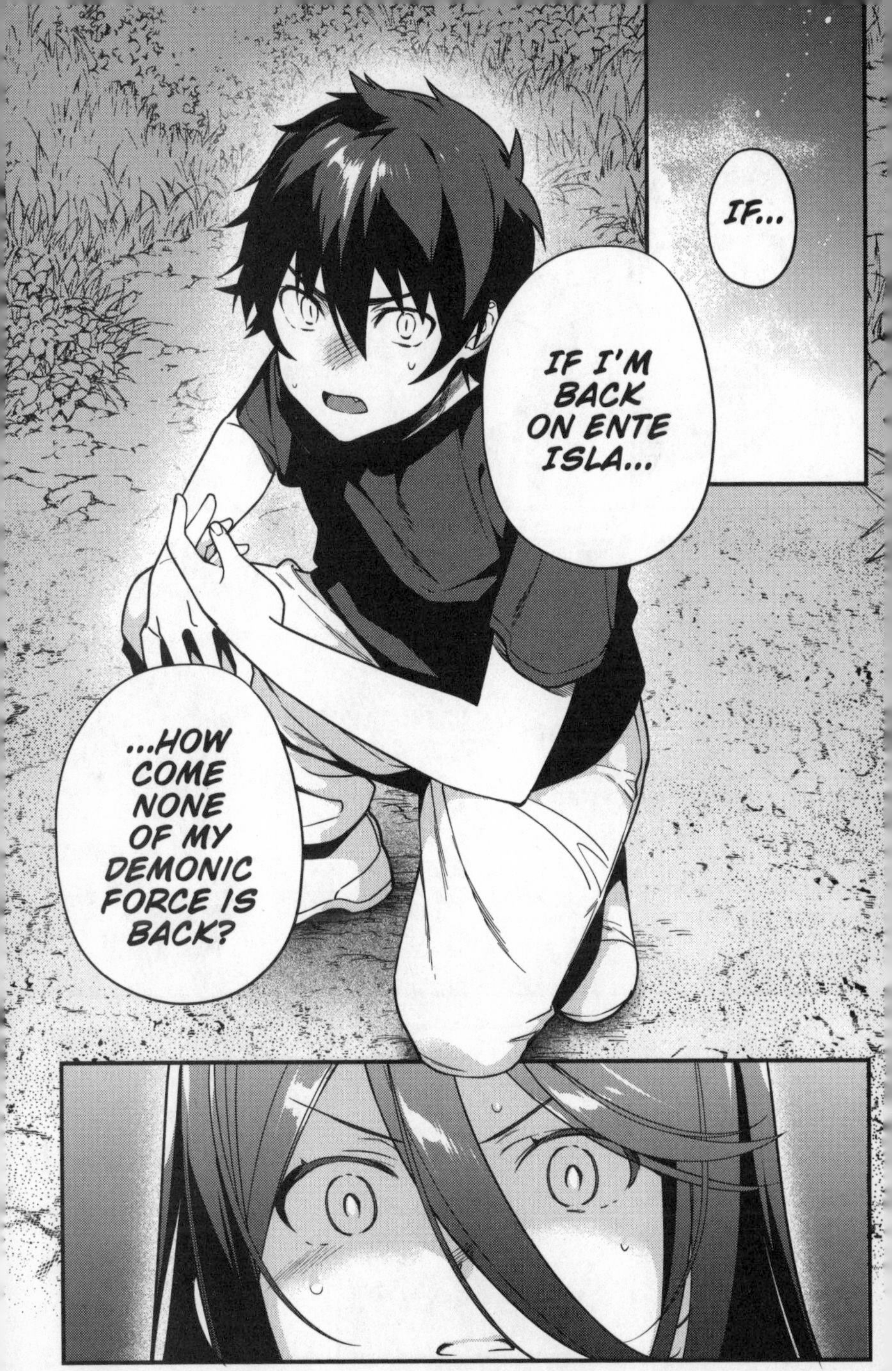
IF...
IF I'M BACK ON ENTE ISLA...
...HOW COME NONE OF MY DEMONIC FORCE IS BACK?

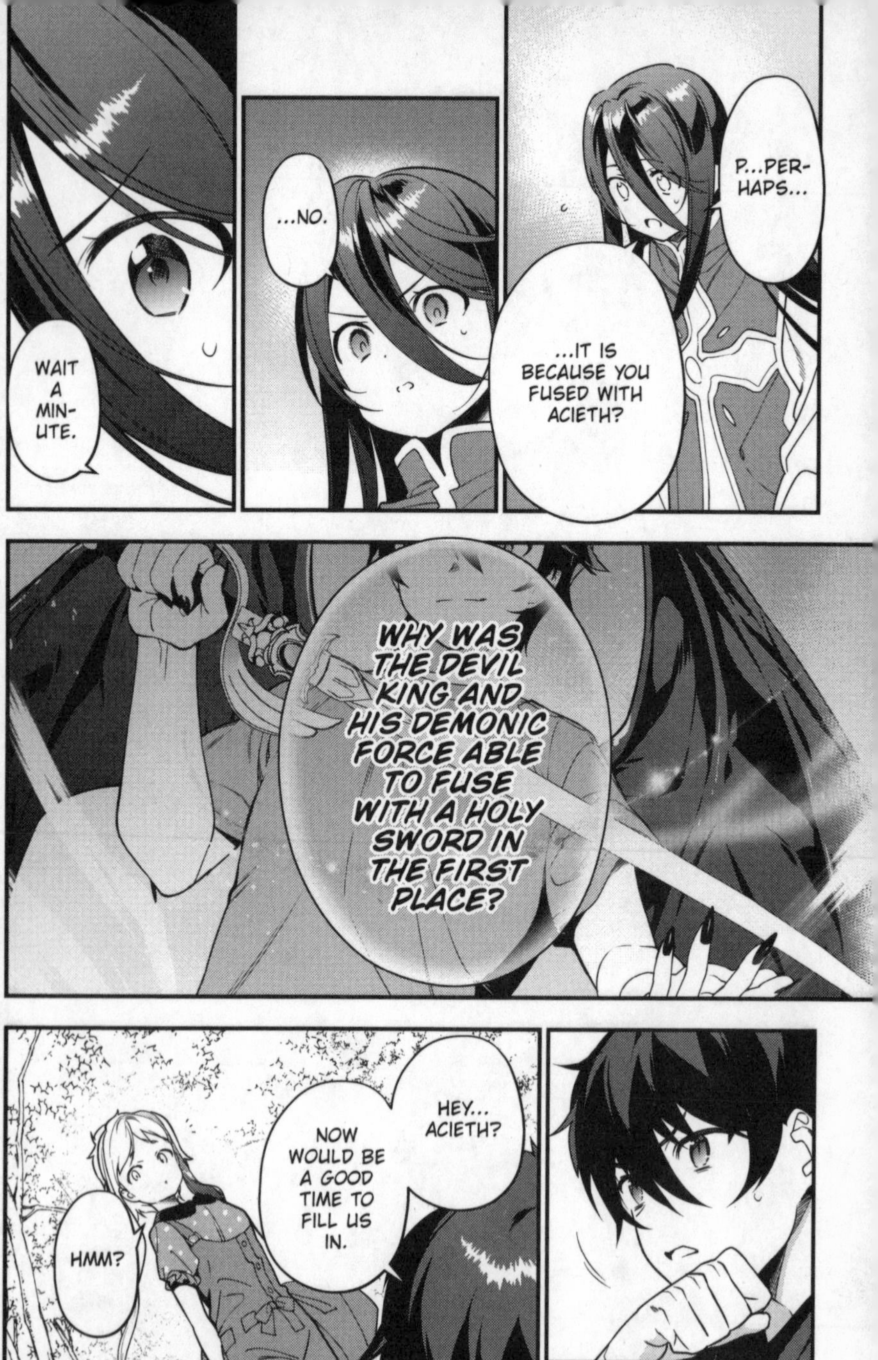
P...PER-HAPS...
...IT IS BECAUSE YOU FUSED WITH ACIETH?
...NO.
WAIT A MIN-UTE.
WHY WAS THE DEVIL KING AND HIS DEMONIC FORCE ABLE TO FUSE WITH A HOLY SWORD IN THE FIRST PLACE?
HEY... ACIETH?
NOW WOULD BE A GOOD TIME TO FILL US IN.
HMM?

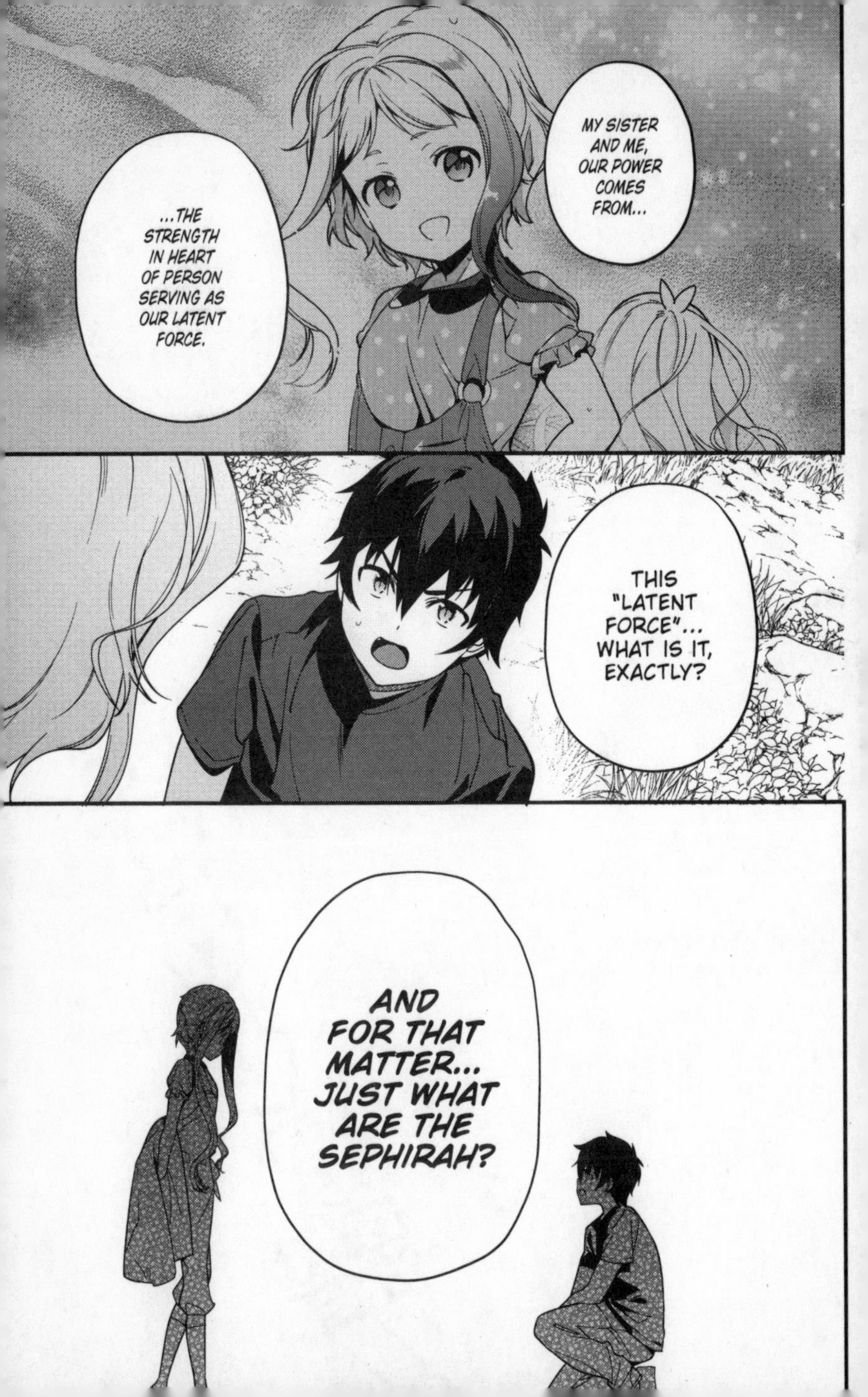
MY SISTER AND ME, OUR POWER COMES FROM...
...THE STRENGTH IN HEART OF PERSON SERVING AS OUR LATENT FORCE.
THIS "LATENT FORCE"... WHAT IS IT, EXACTLY?
AND FOR THAT MATTER... JUST WHAT ARE THE SEPHIRAH?

THE DEVIL IS A PART-TIMER!

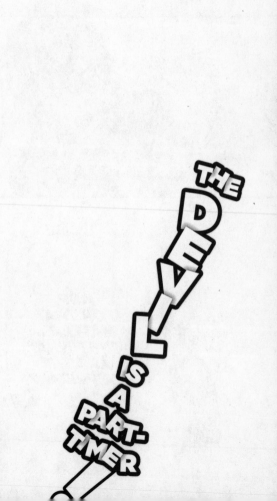

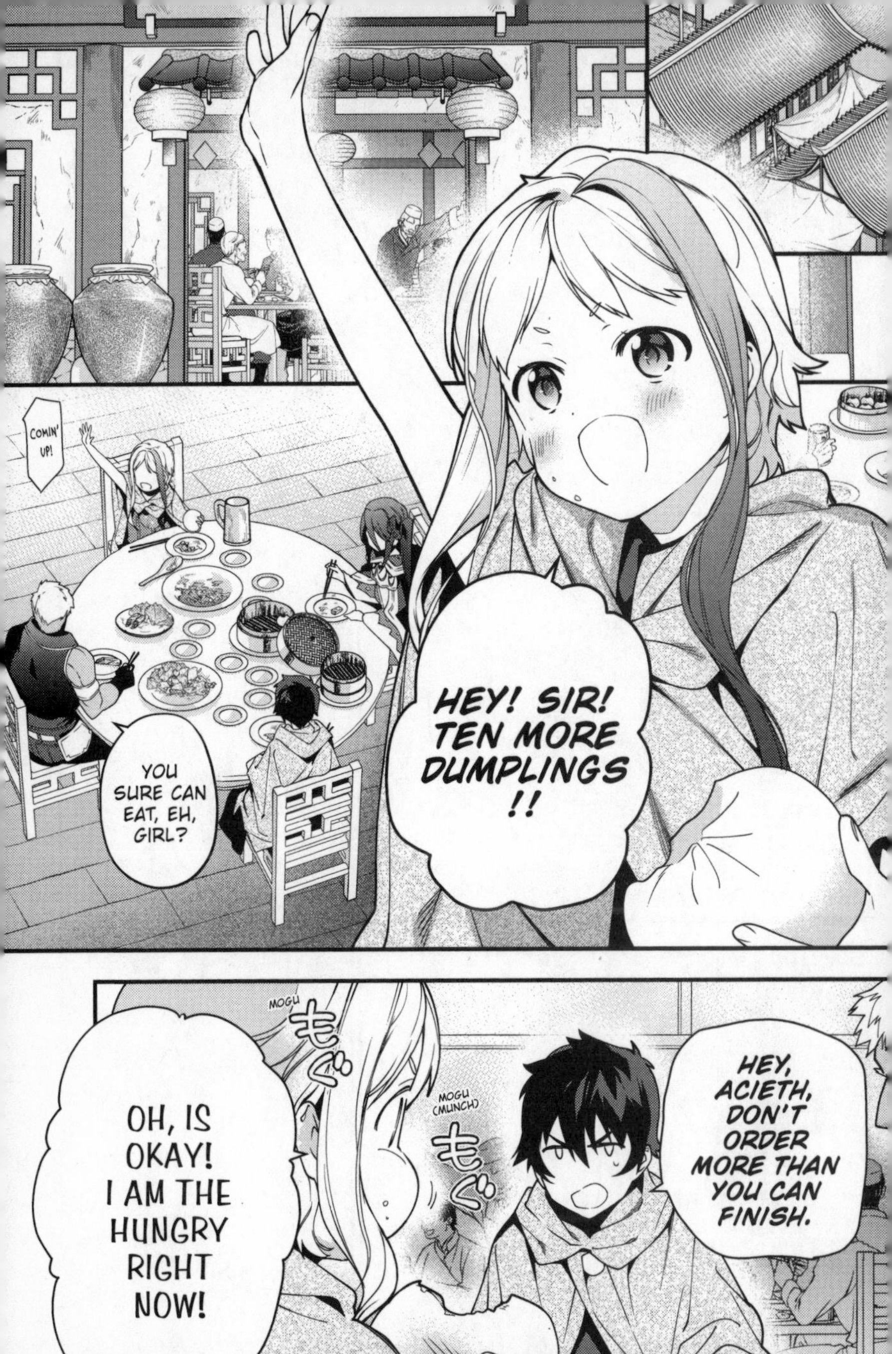
HEY! SIR! TEN MORE DUMPLINGS !!
COMIN' UP!
YOU SURE CAN EAT, EH, GIRL?
HEY, ACIETH, DON'T ORDER MORE THAN YOU CAN FINISH.
MOGU (MUNCH)
もぐ
MOGU
もぐ
OH, IS OKAY! I AM THE HUNGRY RIGHT NOW!

CHAPTER 87: THE DEVIL LOSES HIS SOCIAL STANDING

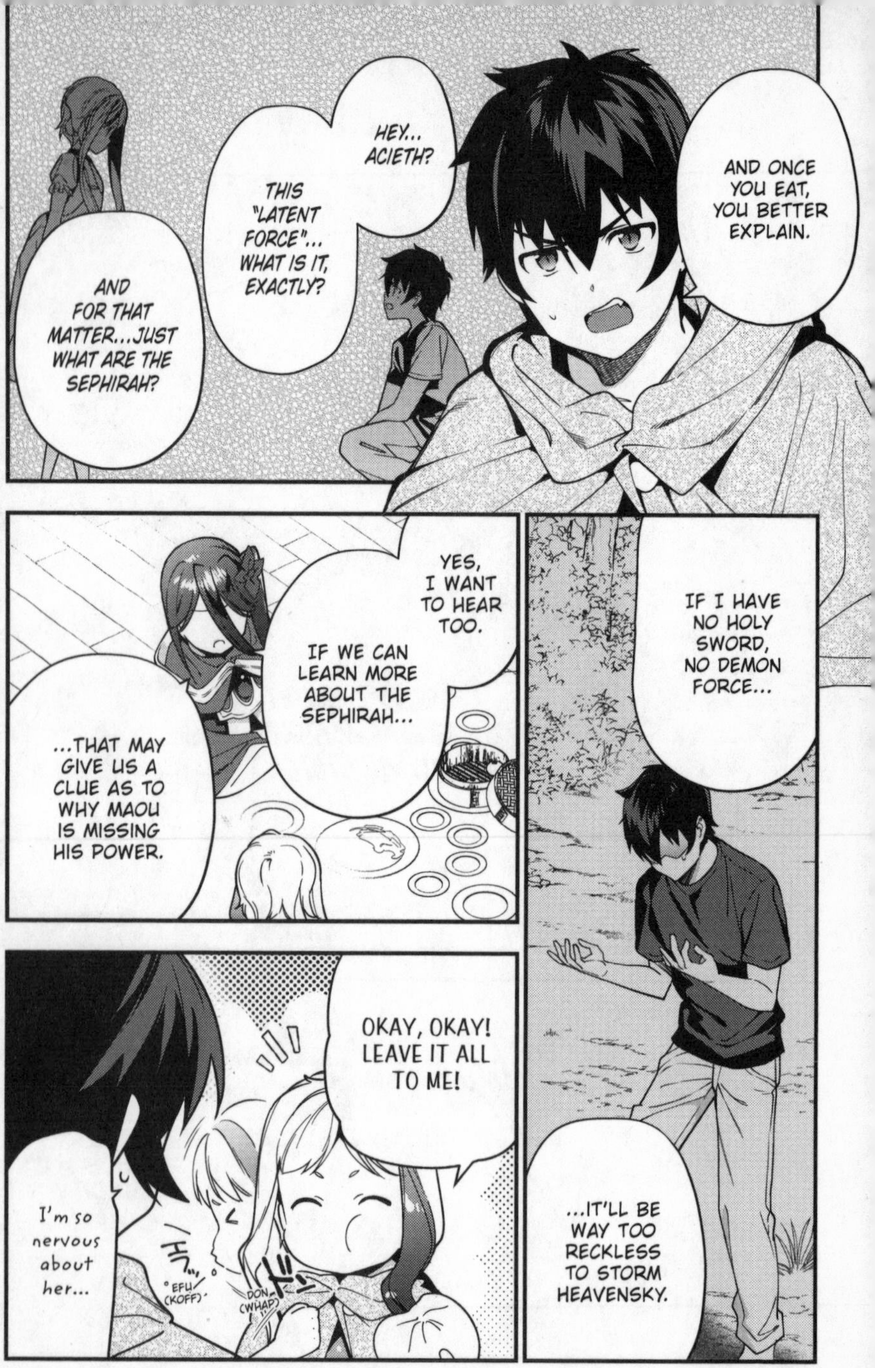
AND ONCE YOU EAT, YOU BETTER EXPLAIN.
HEY... ACIETH?
THIS "LATENT FORCE"... WHAT IS IT, EXACTLY?
AND FOR THAT MATTER...JUST WHAT ARE THE SEPHIRAH?
IF I HAVE NO HOLY SWORD, NO DEMON FORCE...
...IT'LL BE WAY TOO RECKLESS TO STORM HEAVENSKY.
YES, I WANT TO HEAR TOO.
IF WE CAN LEARN MORE ABOUT THE SEPHIRAH...
...THAT MAY GIVE US A CLUE AS TO WHY MAOU IS MISSING HIS POWER.
OKAY, OKAY! LEAVE IT ALL TO ME!
DON (WHAP)
EFU (KOFF)
I'm so nervous about her...

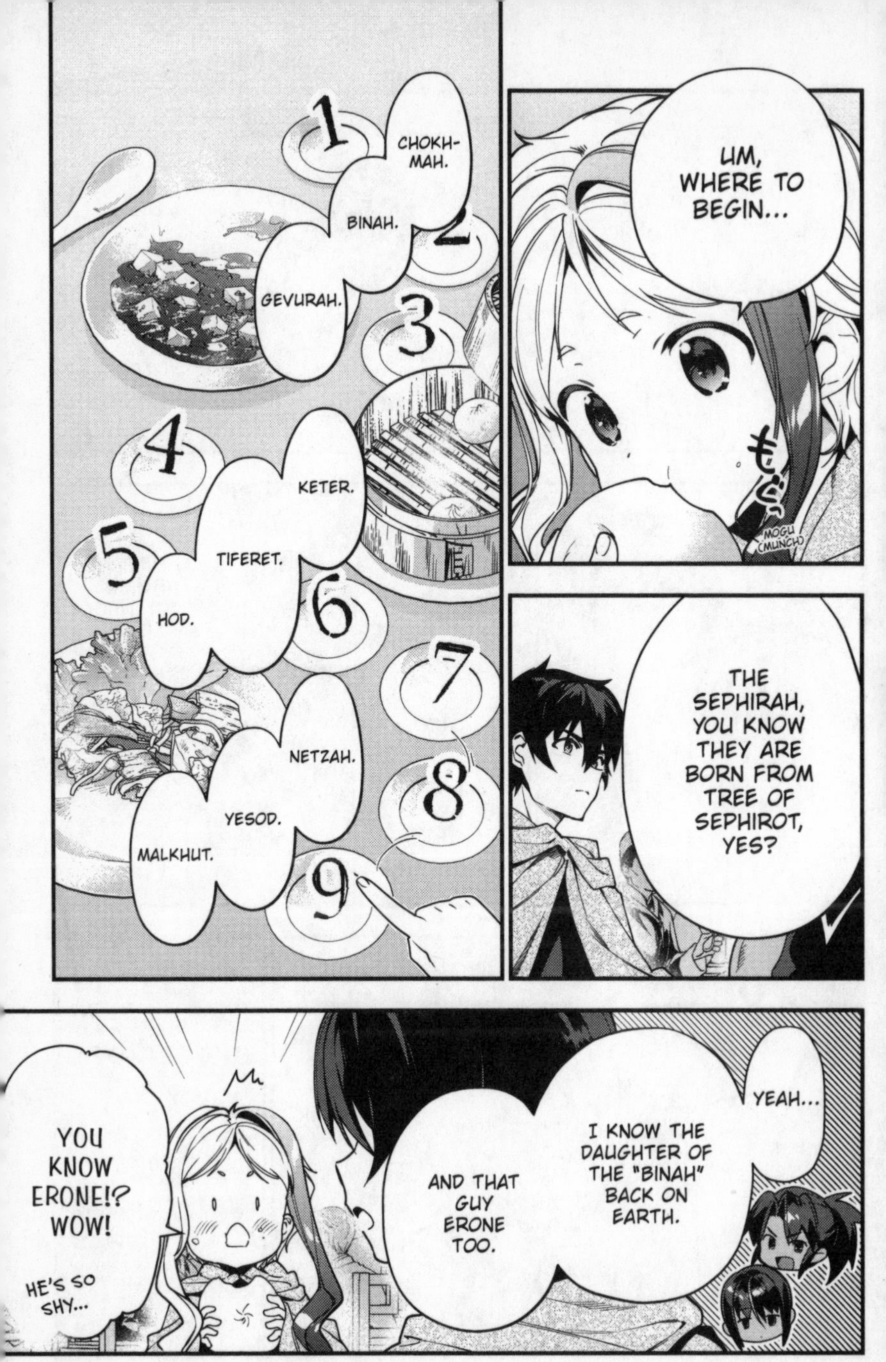
UM, WHERE TO BEGIN...
MOGU (MUNCH)
THE SEPHIRAH, YOU KNOW THEY ARE BORN FROM TREE OF SEPHIROT, YES?
CHOKH-MAH.
BINAH.
GEVURAH.
KETER.
TIFERET.
HOD.
NETZAH.
YESOD.
MALKHUT.
YEAH...
I KNOW THE DAUGHTER OF THE "BINAH" BACK ON EARTH.
AND THAT GUY ERONE TOO.
YOU KNOW ERONE!? WOW!
HE'S SO SHY...

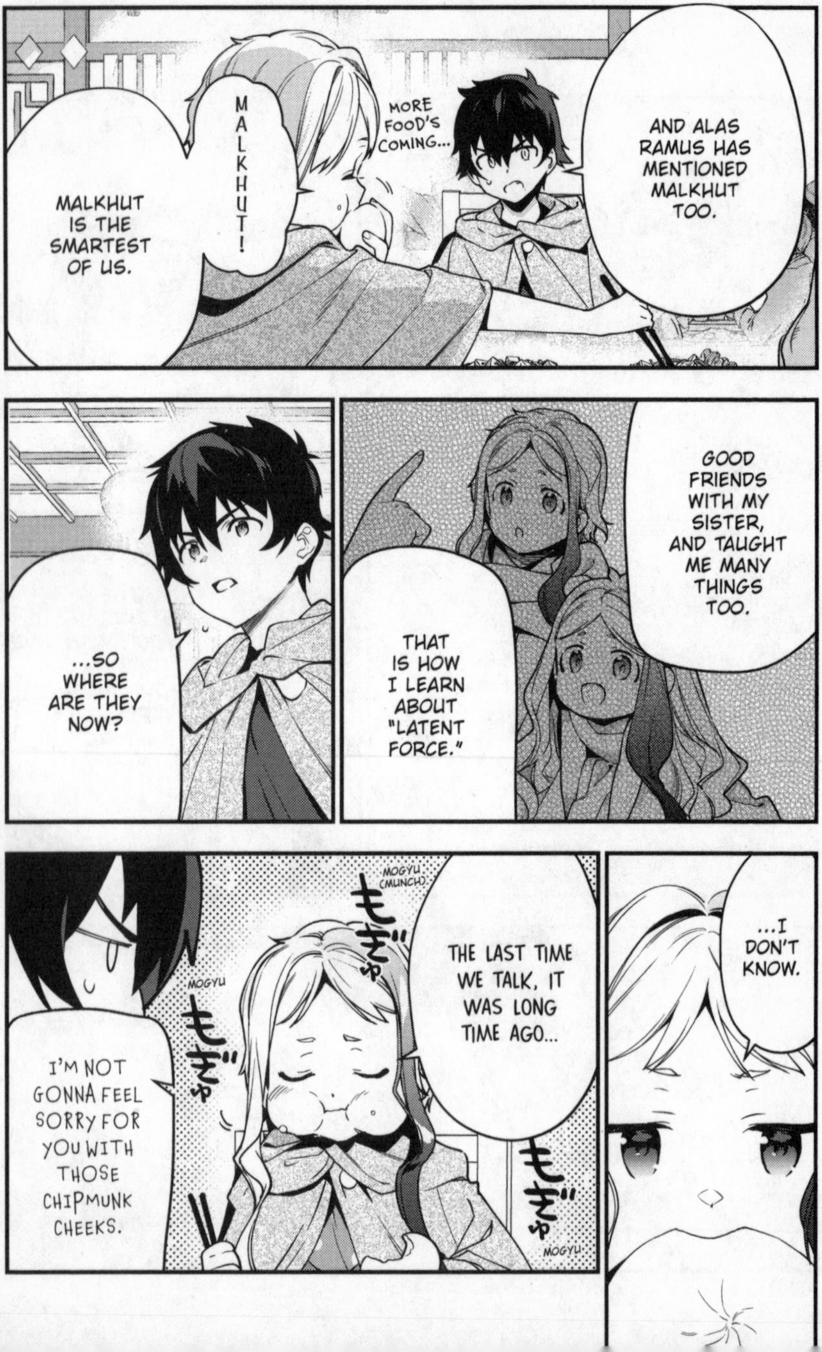
AND ALAS RAMUS HAS MENTIONED MALKHUT TOO.
MORE FOOD'S COMING...
MALKHUT!
MALKHUT IS THE SMARTEST OF US.
GOOD FRIENDS WITH MY SISTER, AND TAUGHT ME MANY THINGS TOO.
THAT IS HOW I LEARN ABOUT "LATENT FORCE."
...SO WHERE ARE THEY NOW?
...I DON'T KNOW.
THE LAST TIME WE TALK, IT WAS LONG TIME AGO...
もぎゅ
MOGYU (MUNCH)
もぎゅ
MOGYU
もぎゅ
MOGYU
I'M NOT GONNA FEEL SORRY FOR YOU WITH THOSE CHIPMUNK CHEEKS.

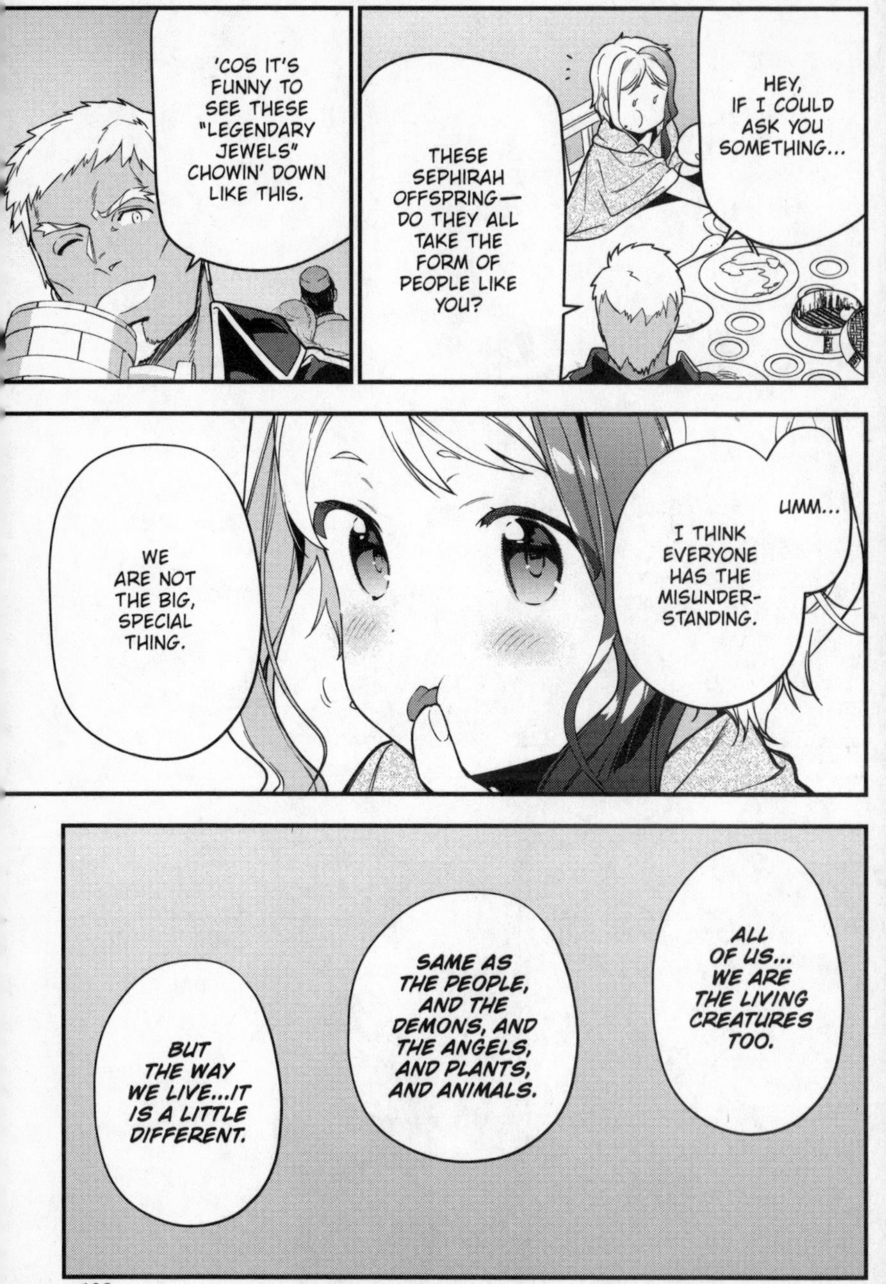
HEY, IF I COULD ASK YOU SOMETHING...
THESE SEPHIRAH OFFSPRING—DO THEY ALL TAKE THE FORM OF PEOPLE LIKE YOU?
'COS IT'S FUNNY TO SEE THESE "LEGENDARY JEWELS" CHOWIN' DOWN LIKE THIS.
UMM...
I THINK EVERYONE HAS THE MISUNDER-STANDING.
WE ARE NOT THE BIG, SPECIAL THING.
ALL OF US... WE ARE THE LIVING CREATURES TOO.
SAME AS THE PEOPLE, AND THE DEMONS, AND THE ANGELS, AND PLANTS, AND ANIMALS.
BUT THE WAY WE LIVE...IT IS A LITTLE DIFFERENT.

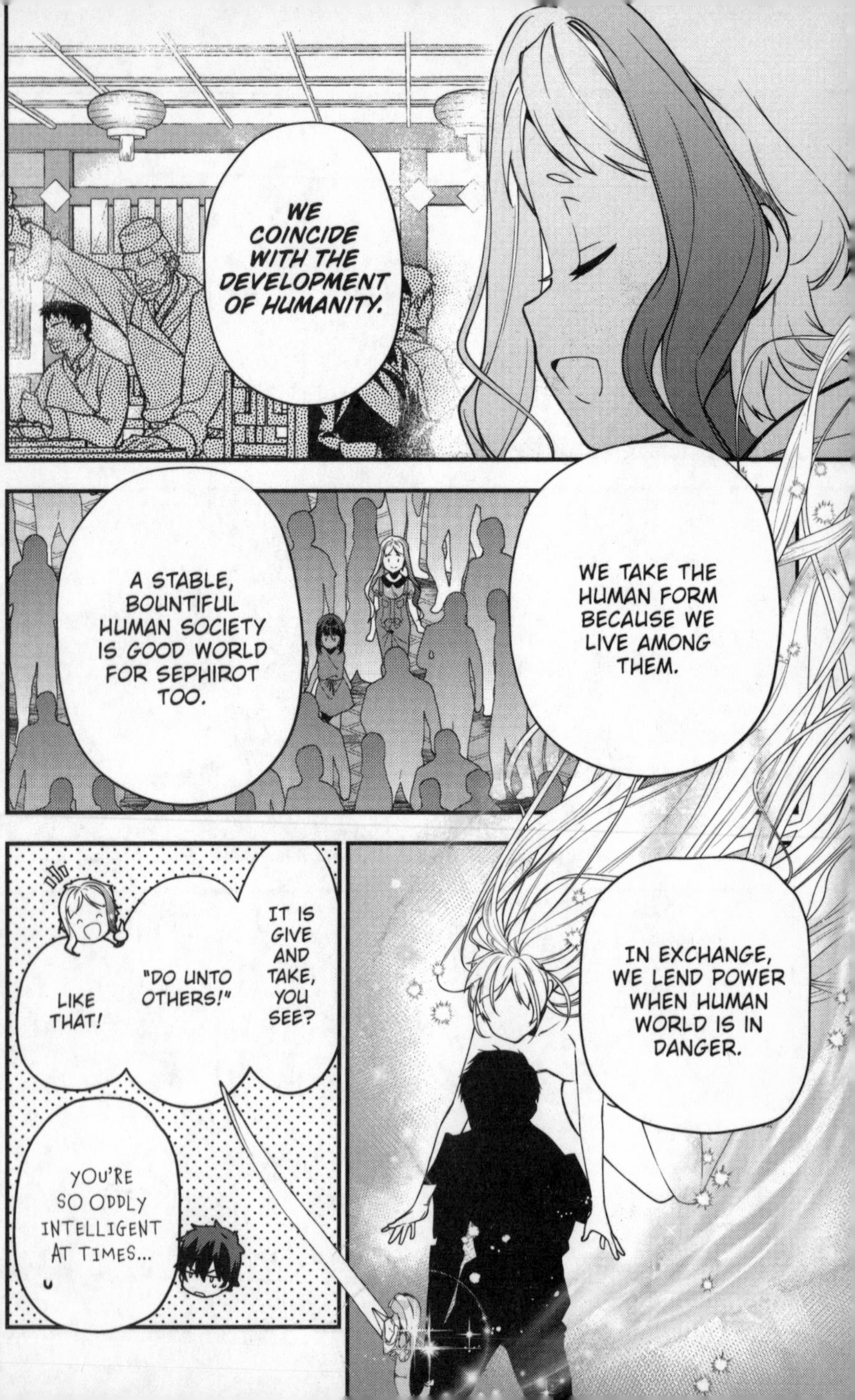
WE COINCIDE WITH THE DEVELOPMENT OF HUMANITY.
WE TAKE THE HUMAN FORM BECAUSE WE LIVE AMONG THEM.
A STABLE, BOUNTIFUL HUMAN SOCIETY IS GOOD WORLD FOR SEPHIROT TOO.
IN EXCHANGE, WE LEND POWER WHEN HUMAN WORLD IS IN DANGER.
IT IS GIVE AND TAKE, YOU SEE? "DO UNTO OTHERS!" LIKE THAT!
YOU'RE SO ODDLY INTELLIGENT AT TIMES...

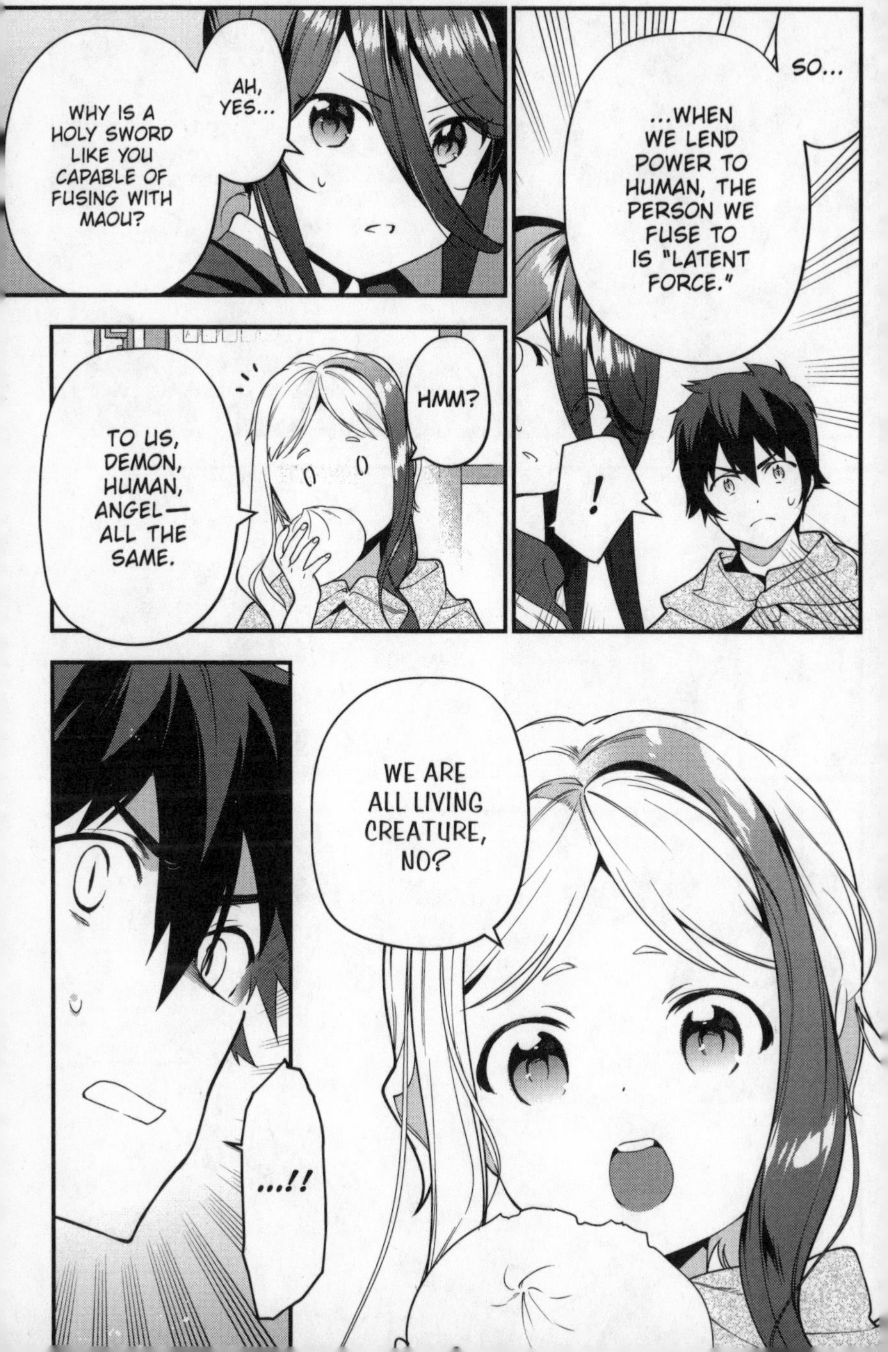
AH, YES...
WHY IS A HOLY SWORD LIKE YOU CAPABLE OF FUSING WITH MAOU?
HMM?
TO US, DEMON, HUMAN, ANGEL— ALL THE SAME.
SO...
...WHEN WE LEND POWER TO HUMAN, THE PERSON WE FUSE TO IS "LATENT FORCE."
!
WE ARE ALL LIVING CREATURE, NO?
...!!

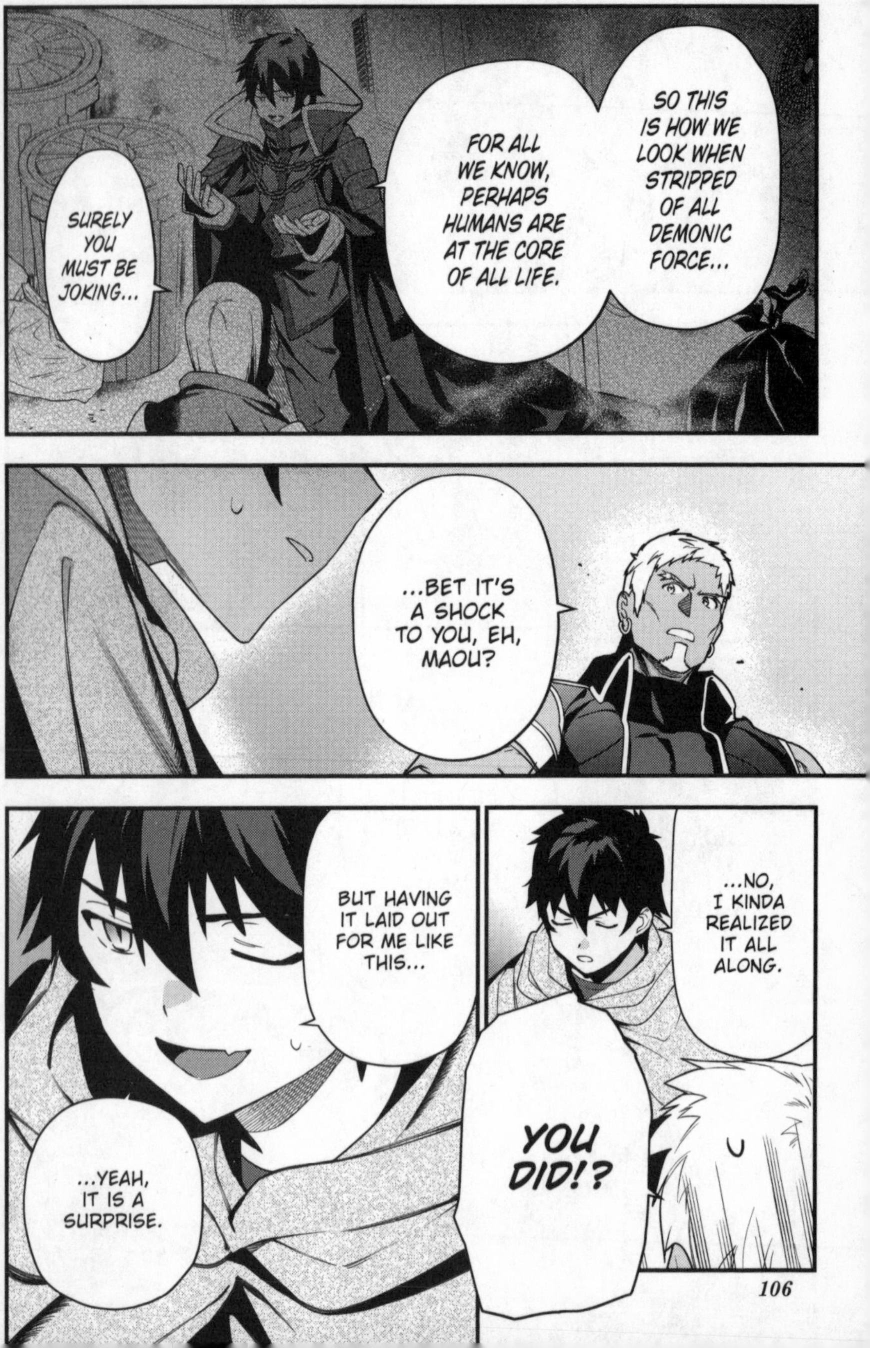
SO THIS IS HOW WE LOOK WHEN STRIPPED OF ALL DEMONIC FORCE...
FOR ALL WE KNOW, PERHAPS HUMANS ARE AT THE CORE OF ALL LIFE.
SURELY YOU MUST BE JOKING...
...BET IT'S A SHOCK TO YOU, EH, MAOU?
...NO, I KINDA REALIZED IT ALL ALONG.
YOU DID!?
BUT HAVING IT LAID OUT FOR ME LIKE THIS...
...YEAH, IT IS A SURPRISE.

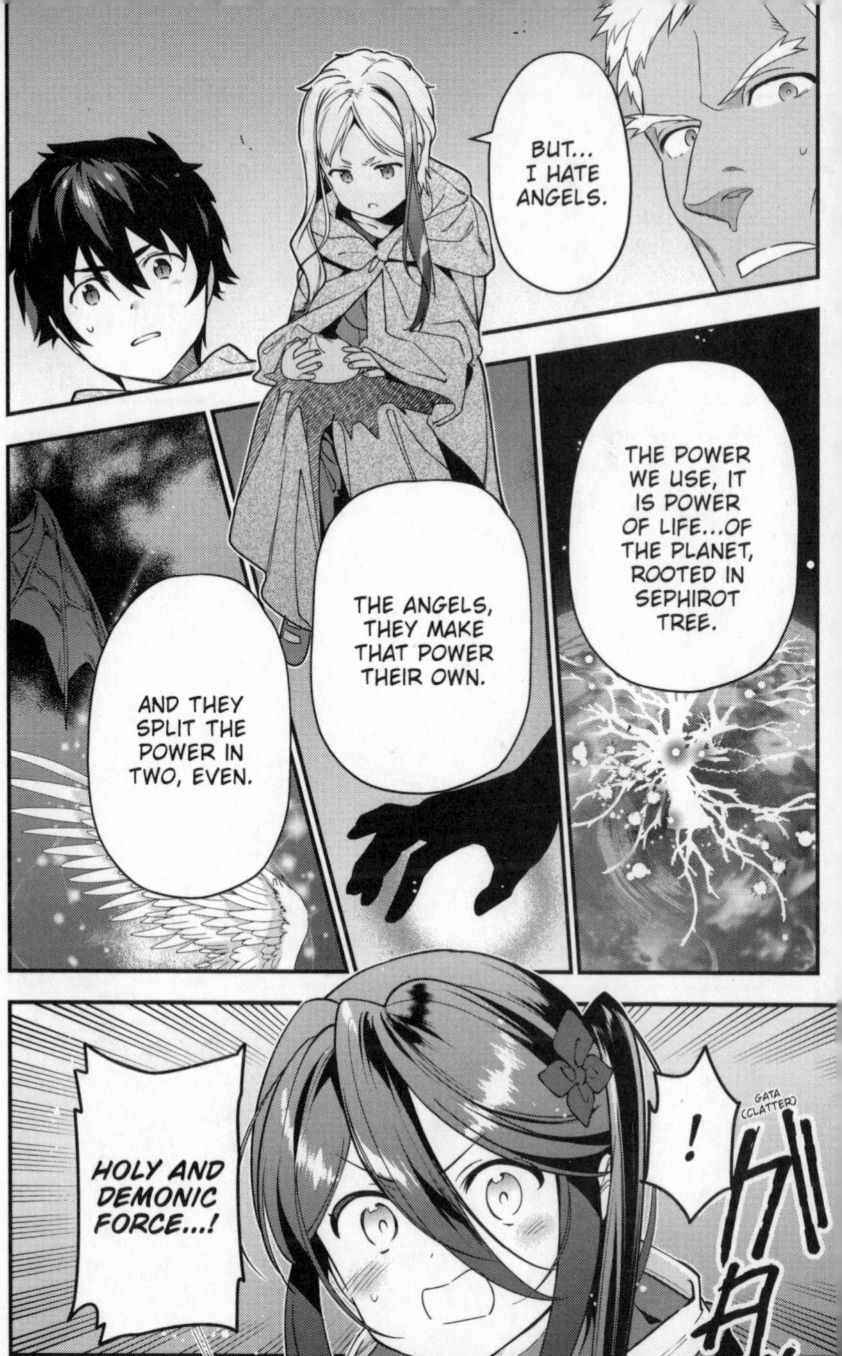
BUT... I HATE ANGELS.
THE POWER WE USE, IT IS POWER OF LIFE...OF THE PLANET, ROOTED IN SEPHIROT TREE.
THE ANGELS, THEY MAKE THAT POWER THEIR OWN.
AND THEY SPLIT THE POWER IN TWO, EVEN.
GATA (CLATTER)
!
HOLY AND DEMONIC FORCE...!

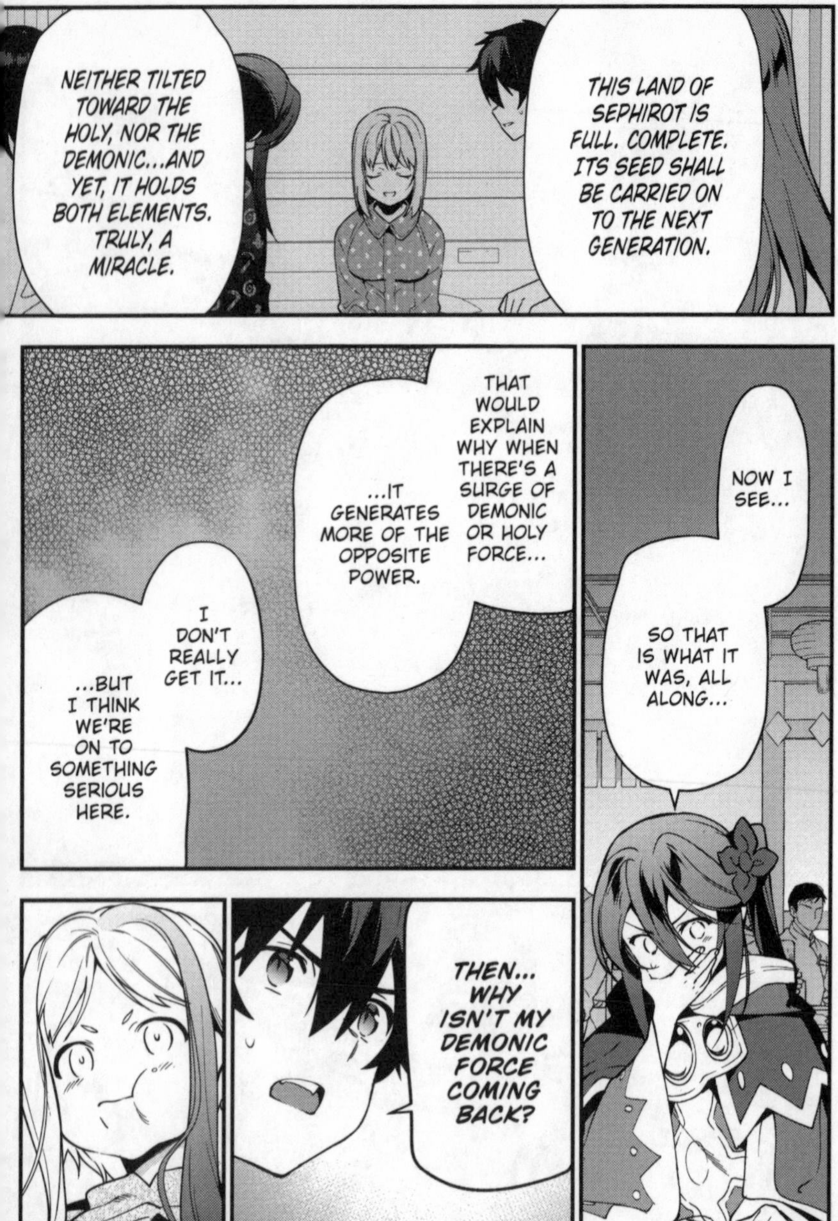
THIS LAND OF SEPHIROT IS FULL. COMPLETE. ITS SEED SHALL BE CARRIED ON TO THE NEXT GENERATION.
NEITHER TILTED TOWARD THE HOLY, NOR THE DEMONIC...AND YET, IT HOLDS BOTH ELEMENTS. TRULY, A MIRACLE.
NOW I SEE...
SO THAT IS WHAT IT WAS, ALL ALONG...
THAT WOULD EXPLAIN WHY WHEN THERE'S A SURGE OF DEMONIC OR HOLY FORCE...
...IT GENERATES MORE OF THE OPPOSITE POWER.
I DON'T REALLY GET IT...
...BUT I THINK WE'RE ON TO SOMETHING SERIOUS HERE.
THEN... WHY ISN'T MY DEMONIC FORCE COMING BACK?

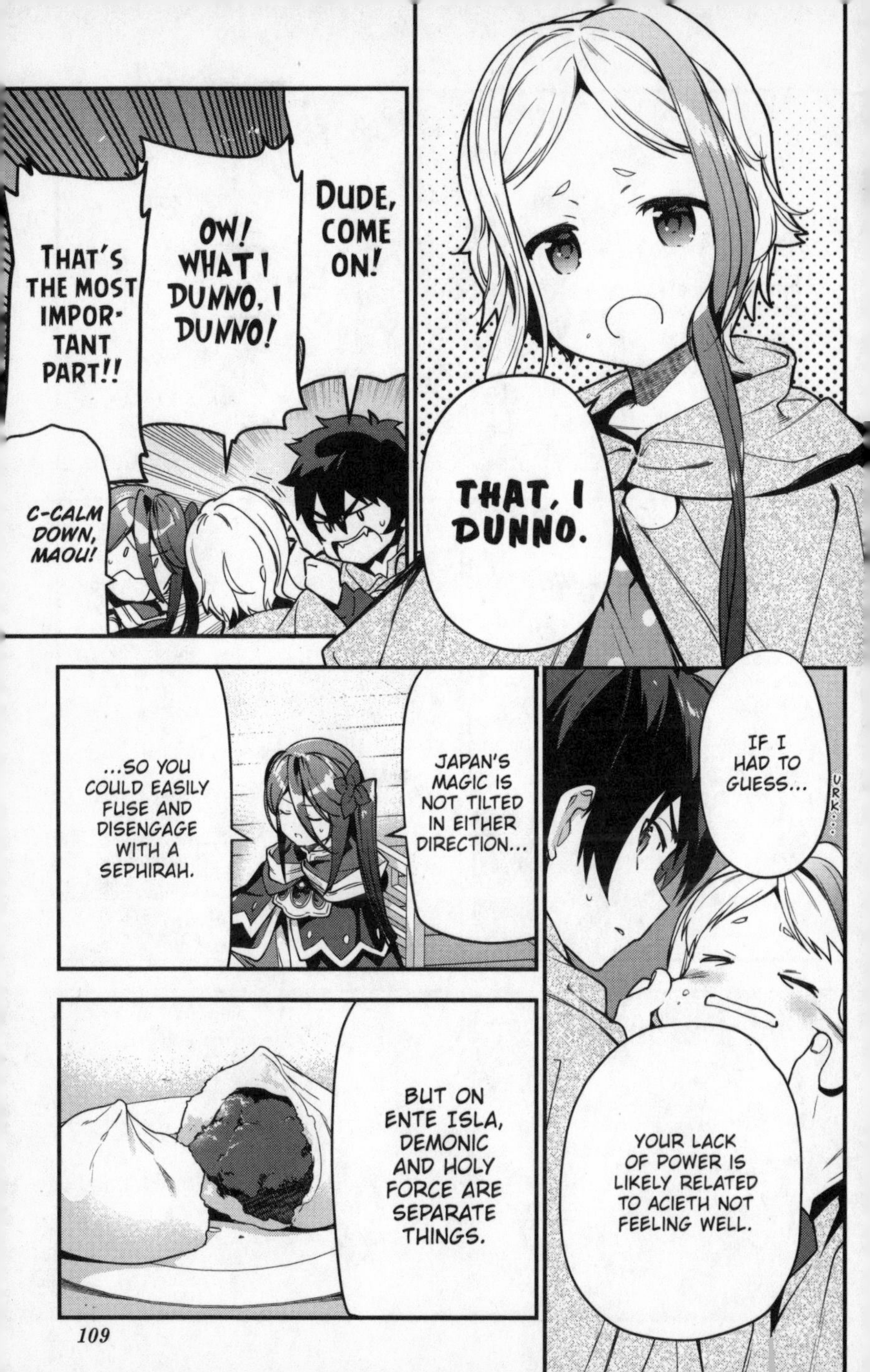
THAT, I DUNNO.
DUDE, COME ON!
OW! WHAT I DUNNO, I DUNNO!
THAT'S THE MOST IMPOR-TANT PART!!
C-CALM DOWN, MAOU!
IF I HAD TO GUESS...
URK...
YOUR LACK OF POWER IS LIKELY RELATED TO ACIETH NOT FEELING WELL.
JAPAN'S MAGIC IS NOT TILTED IN EITHER DIRECTION...
...SO YOU COULD EASILY FUSE AND DISENGAGE WITH A SEPHIRAH.
BUT ON ENTE ISLA, DEMONIC AND HOLY FORCE ARE SEPARATE THINGS.

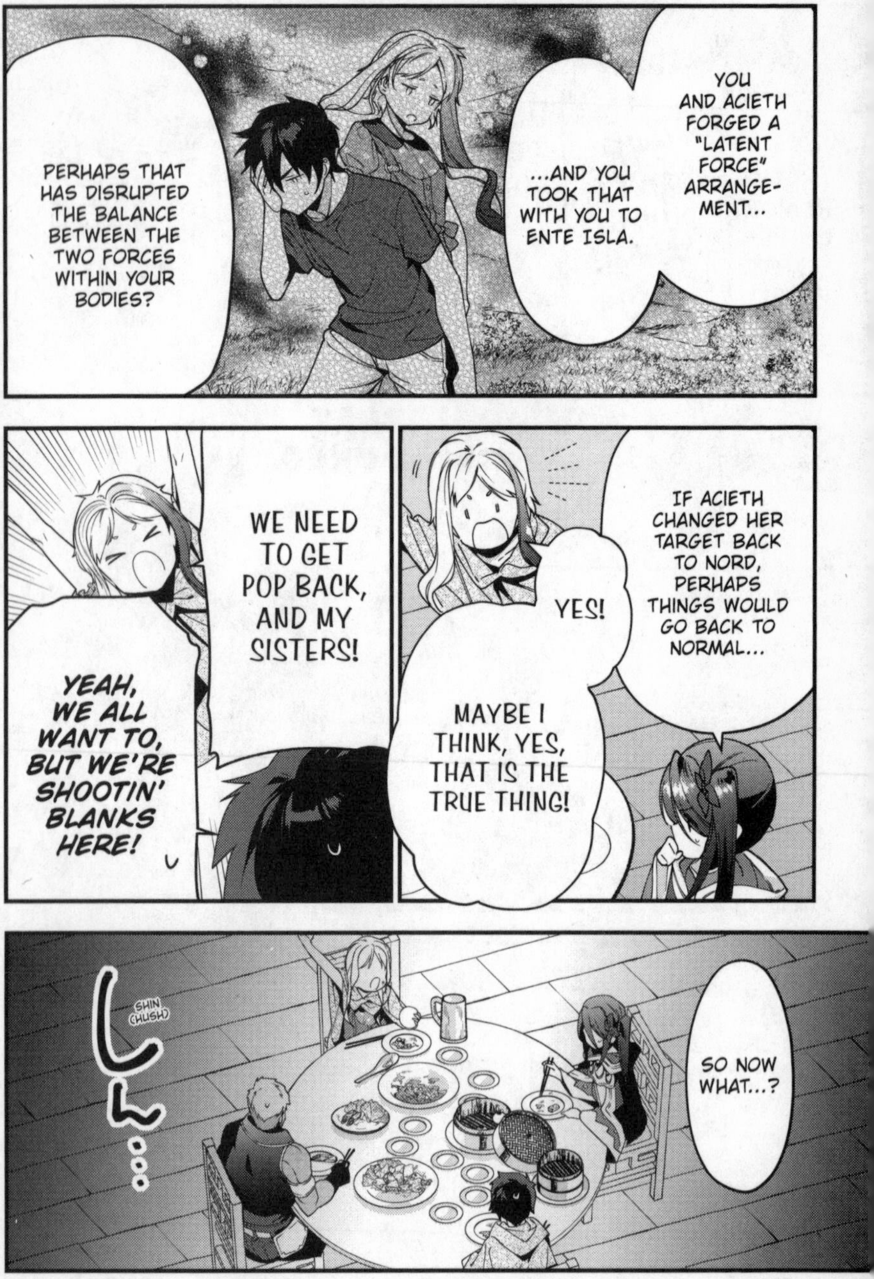
YOU AND ACIETH FORGED A "LATENT FORCE" ARRANGEMENT...
...AND YOU TOOK THAT WITH YOU TO ENTE ISLA.
PERHAPS THAT HAS DISRUPTED THE BALANCE BETWEEN THE TWO FORCES WITHIN YOUR BODIES?
IF ACIETH CHANGED HER TARGET BACK TO NORD, PERHAPS THINGS WOULD GO BACK TO NORMAL...
YES!
MAYBE I THINK, YES, THAT IS THE TRUE THING!
WE NEED TO GET POP BACK, AND MY SISTERS!
YEAH, WE ALL WANT TO, BUT WE'RE SHOOTIN' BLANKS HERE!
SO NOW WHAT...?
SHIN (HUSH)

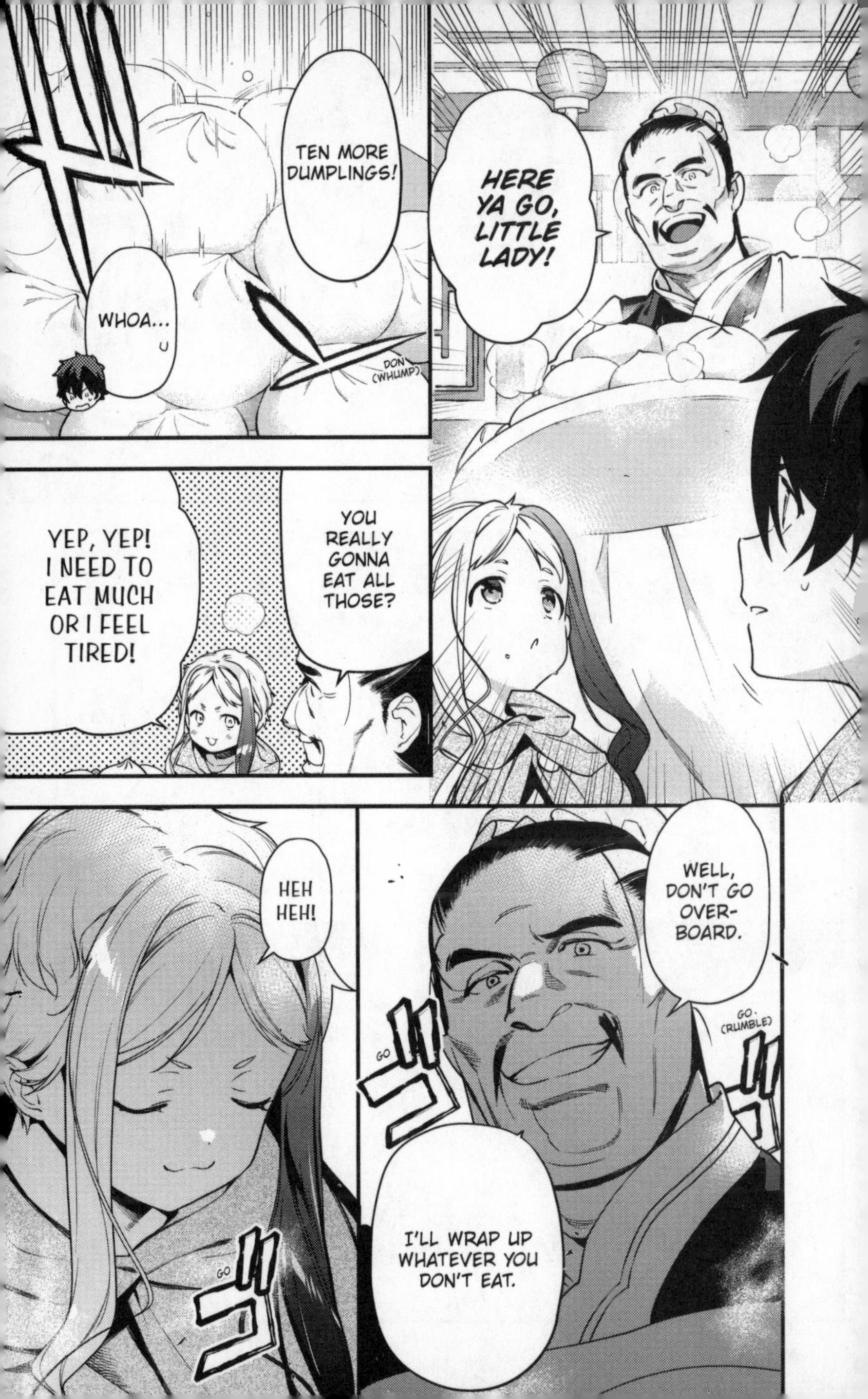
HERE YA GO, LITTLE LADY!
TEN MORE DUMPLINGS!
DON (WHUMP)
WHOA...
YOU REALLY GONNA EAT ALL THOSE?
YEP, YEP! I NEED TO EAT MUCH OR I FEEL TIRED!
WELL, DON'T GO OVER-BOARD.
GO (RUMBLE)
GO
I'LL WRAP UP WHATEVER YOU DON'T EAT.
HEH HEH!
GO

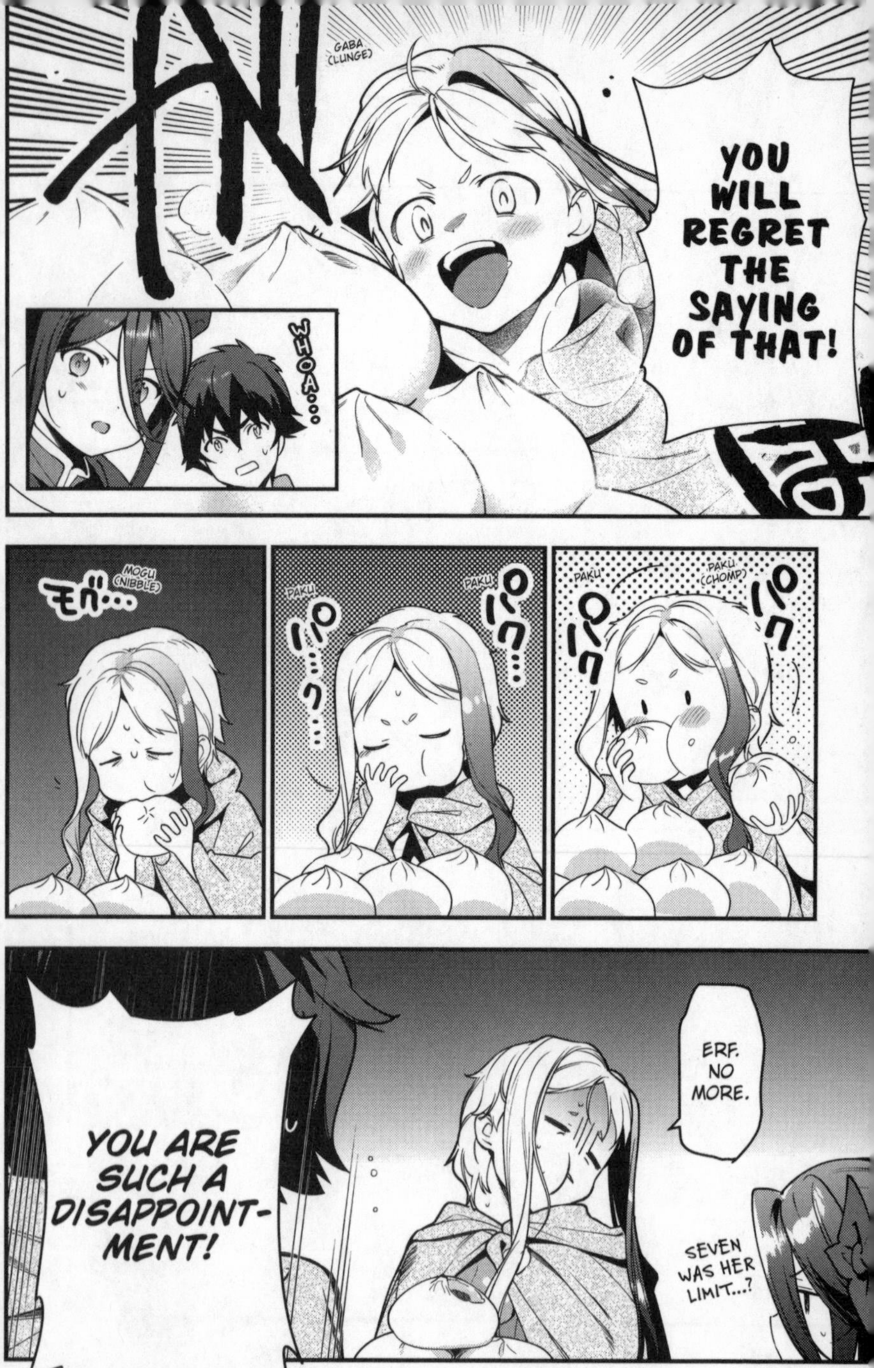
YOU WILL REGRET THE SAYING OF THAT!
GABA (LUNGE)
WHOA...
PAKU (CHOMP)
PAKU
PAKU
PAKU
MOGU (NIBBLE)
ERF. NO MORE.
SEVEN WAS HER LIMIT...?
YOU ARE SUCH A DISAPPOINT-MENT!

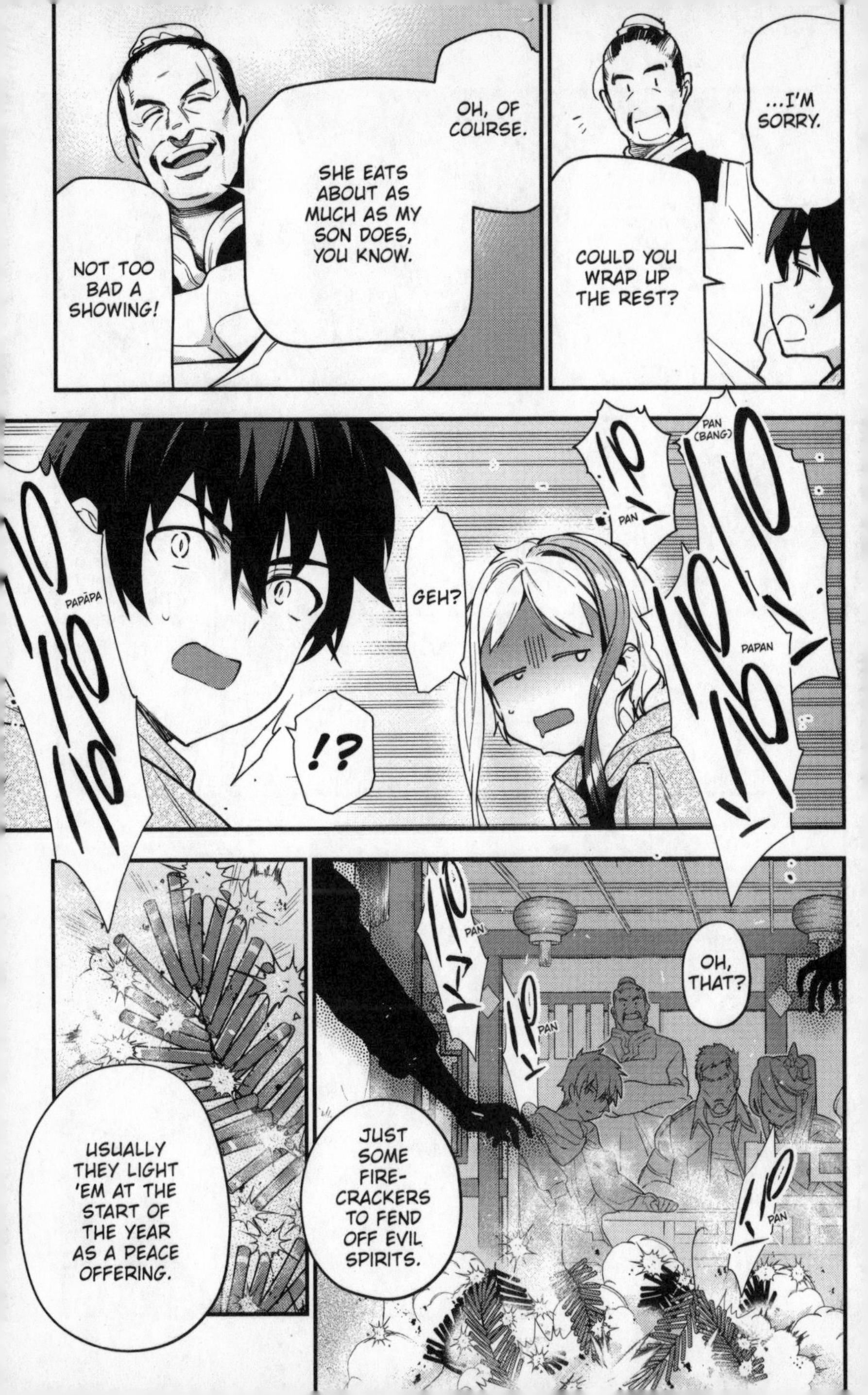
...I'M SORRY.
COULD YOU WRAP UP THE REST?
OH, OF COURSE.
SHE EATS ABOUT AS MUCH AS MY SON DOES, YOU KNOW.
NOT TOO BAD A SHOWING!
PAN (BANG)
PAN
PAPAN
GEH?
!?
PAPĀPA
OH, THAT?
PAN
PAN
JUST SOME FIRE-CRACKERS TO FEND OFF EVIL SPIRITS.
PAN
USUALLY THEY LIGHT 'EM AT THE START OF THE YEAR AS A PEACE OFFERING.

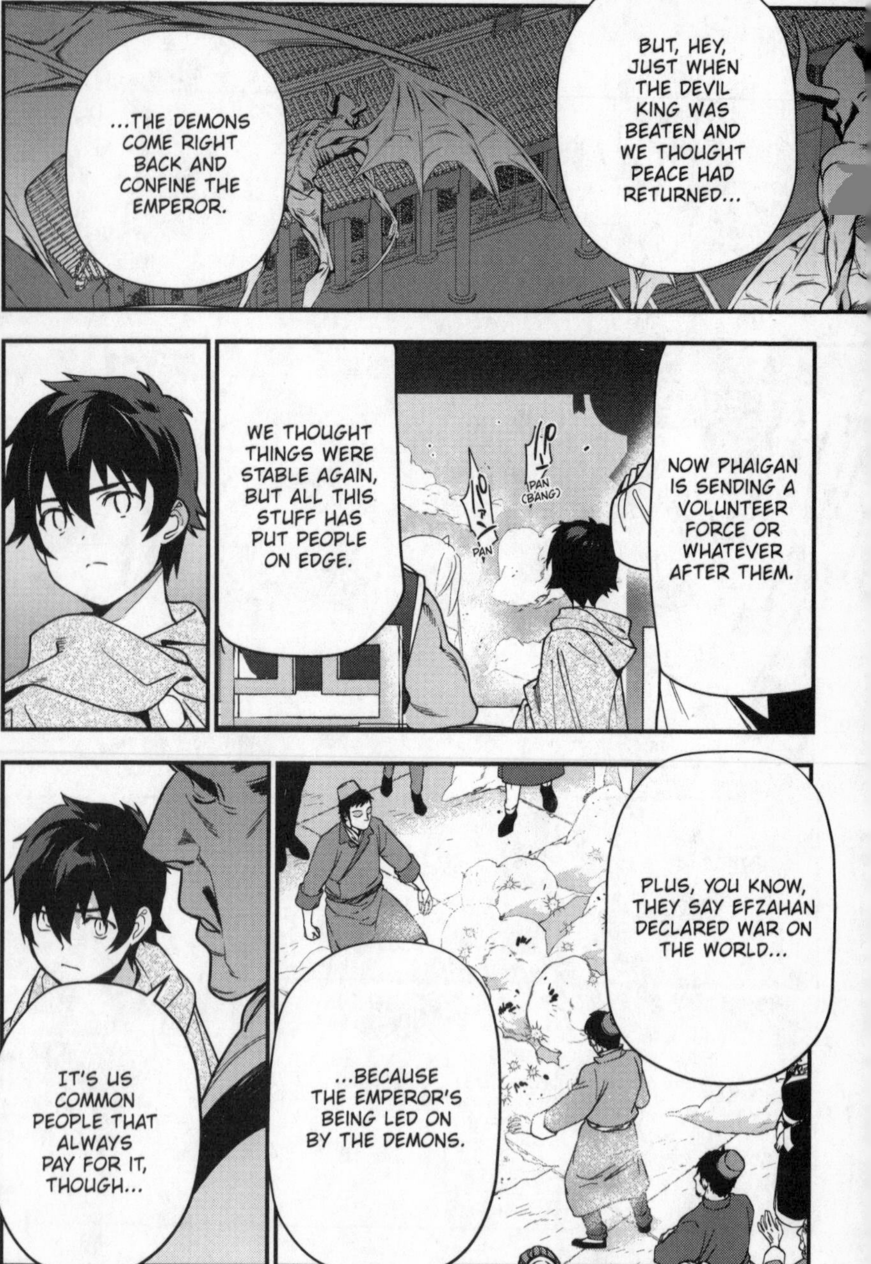
BUT, HEY, JUST WHEN THE DEVIL KING WAS BEATEN AND WE THOUGHT PEACE HAD RETURNED...
...THE DEMONS COME RIGHT BACK AND CONFINE THE EMPEROR.
NOW PHAIGAN IS SENDING A VOLUNTEER FORCE OR WHATEVER AFTER THEM.
PAN (BANG)
PAN
WE THOUGHT THINGS WERE STABLE AGAIN, BUT ALL THIS STUFF HAS PUT PEOPLE ON EDGE.
PLUS, YOU KNOW, THEY SAY EFZAHAN DECLARED WAR ON THE WORLD...
...BECAUSE THE EMPEROR'S BEING LED ON BY THE DEMONS.
IT'S US COMMON PEOPLE THAT ALWAYS PAY FOR IT, THOUGH...

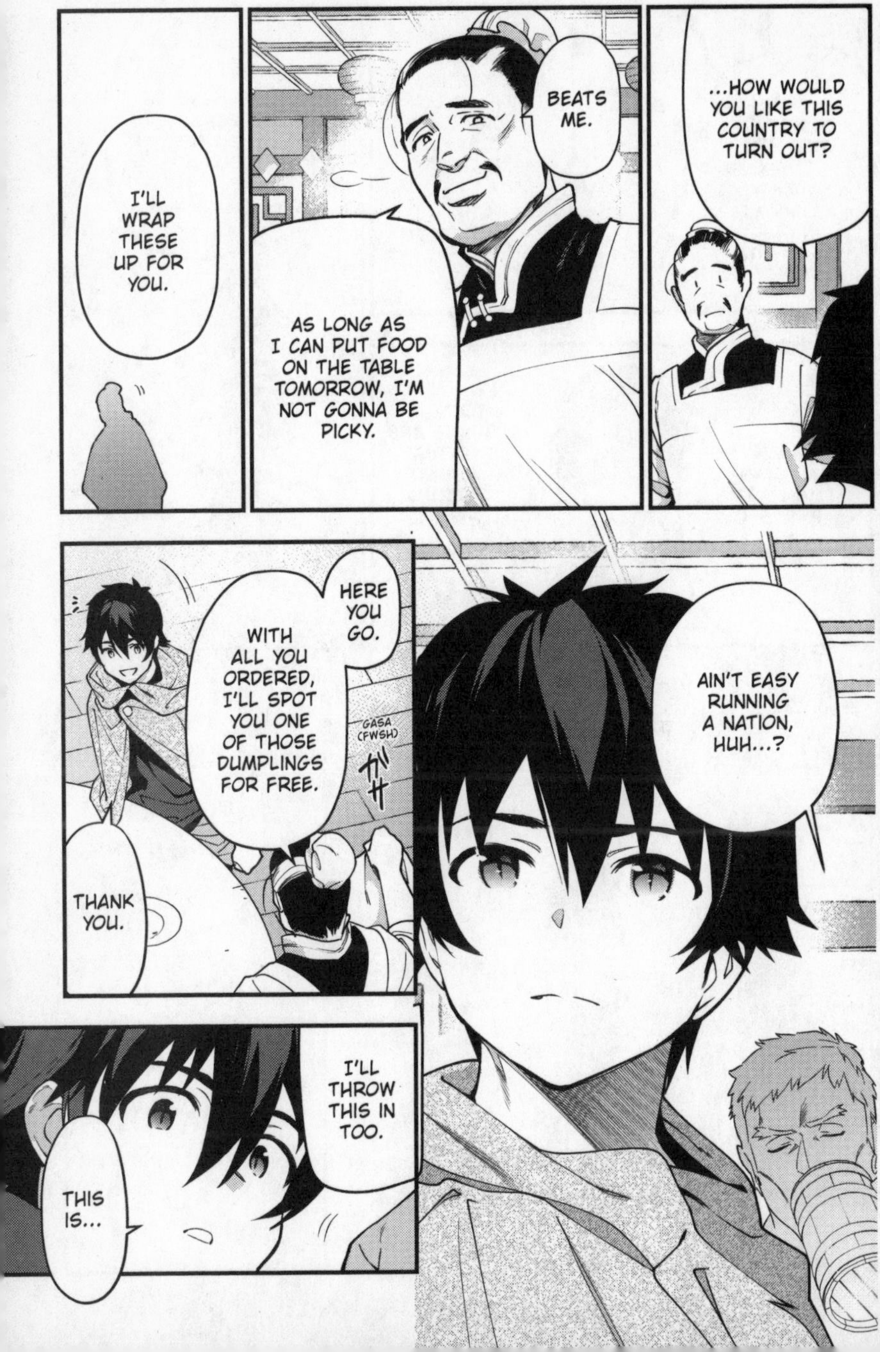
...HOW WOULD YOU LIKE THIS COUNTRY TO TURN OUT?
BEATS ME.
AS LONG AS I CAN PUT FOOD ON THE TABLE TOMORROW, I'M NOT GONNA BE PICKY.
I'LL WRAP THESE UP FOR YOU.
AIN'T EASY RUNNING A NATION, HUH...?
HERE YOU GO.
WITH ALL YOU ORDERED, I'LL SPOT YOU ONE OF THOSE DUMPLINGS FOR FREE.
GASA (FWSH)
ガサ
THANK YOU.
I'LL THROW THIS IN TOO.
THIS IS...

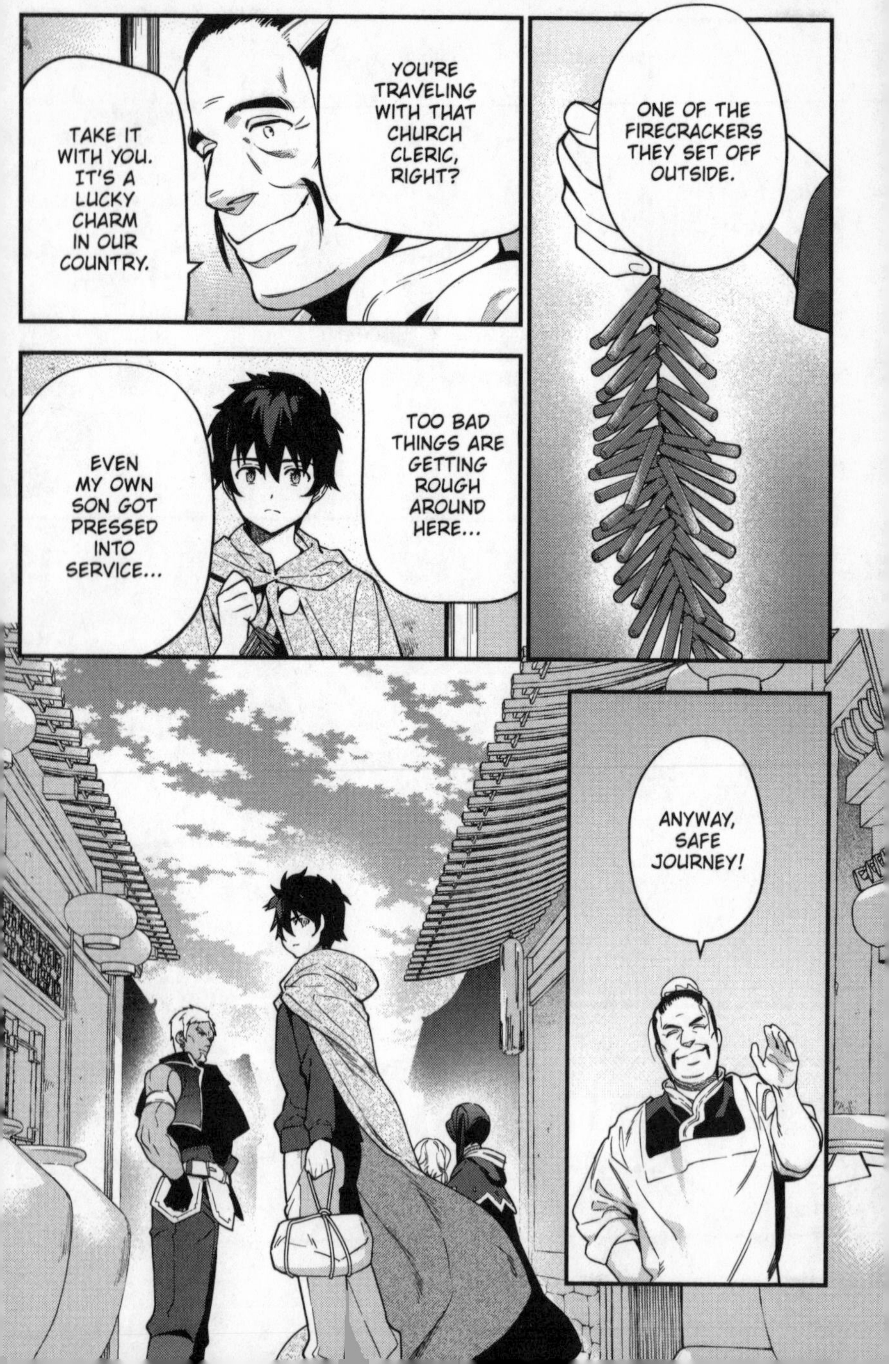

ONE OF THE FIRECRACKERS THEY SET OFF OUTSIDE.
YOU'RE TRAVELING WITH THAT CHURCH CLERIC, RIGHT?
TAKE IT WITH YOU. IT'S A LUCKY CHARM IN OUR COUNTRY.
TOO BAD THINGS ARE GETTING ROUGH AROUND HERE...
EVEN MY OWN SON GOT PRESSED INTO SERVICE...
ANYWAY, SAFE JOURNEY!

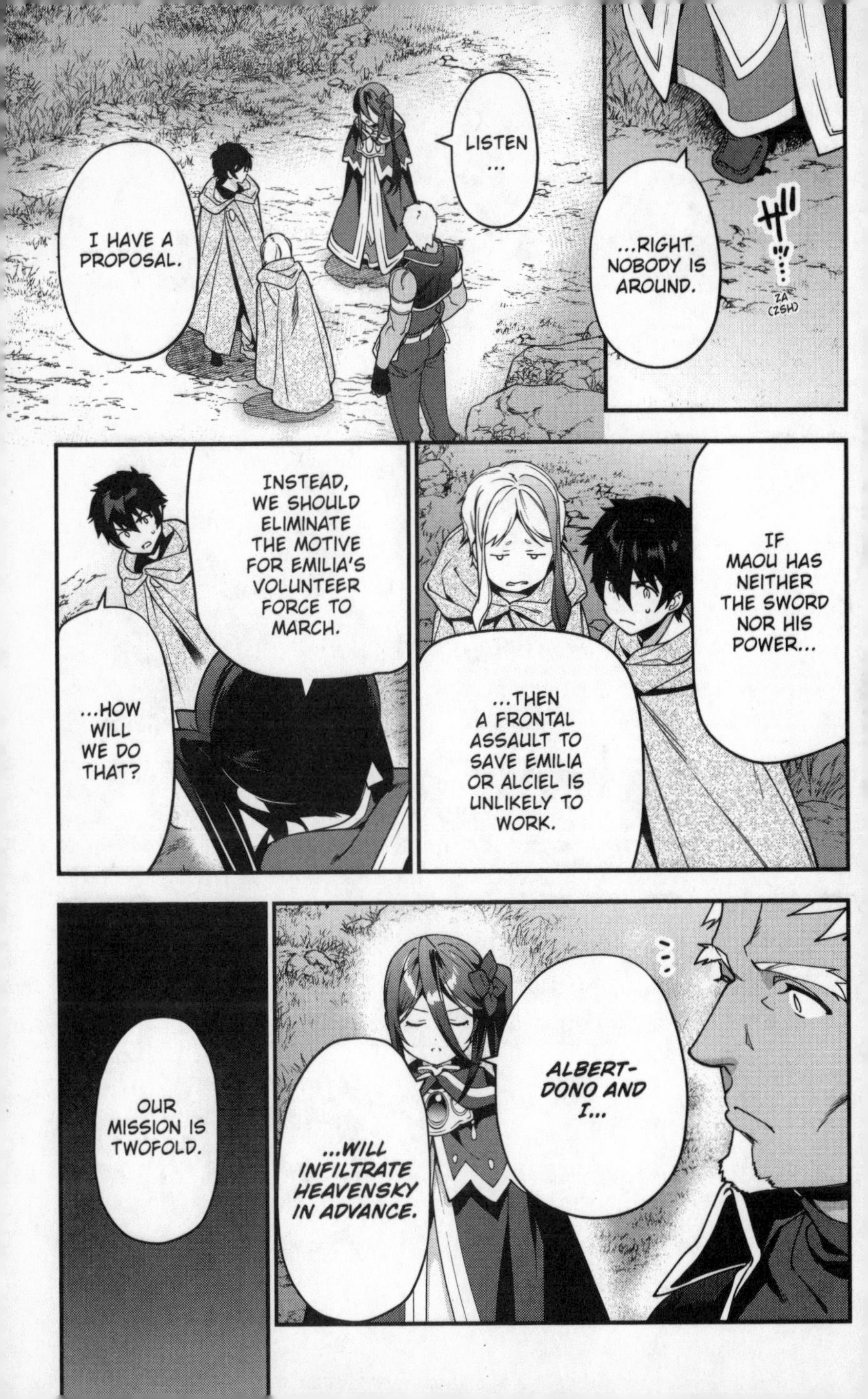
...RIGHT. NOBODY IS AROUND.
ZA (ZSH)
LISTEN...
I HAVE A PROPOSAL.
IF MAOU HAS NEITHER THE SWORD NOR HIS POWER...
...THEN A FRONTAL ASSAULT TO SAVE EMILIA OR ALCIEL IS UNLIKELY TO WORK.
INSTEAD, WE SHOULD ELIMINATE THE MOTIVE FOR EMILIA'S VOLUNTEER FORCE TO MARCH.
...HOW WILL WE DO THAT?
ALBERT-DONO AND I...
...WILL INFILTRATE HEAVENSKY IN ADVANCE.
OUR MISSION IS TWOFOLD.

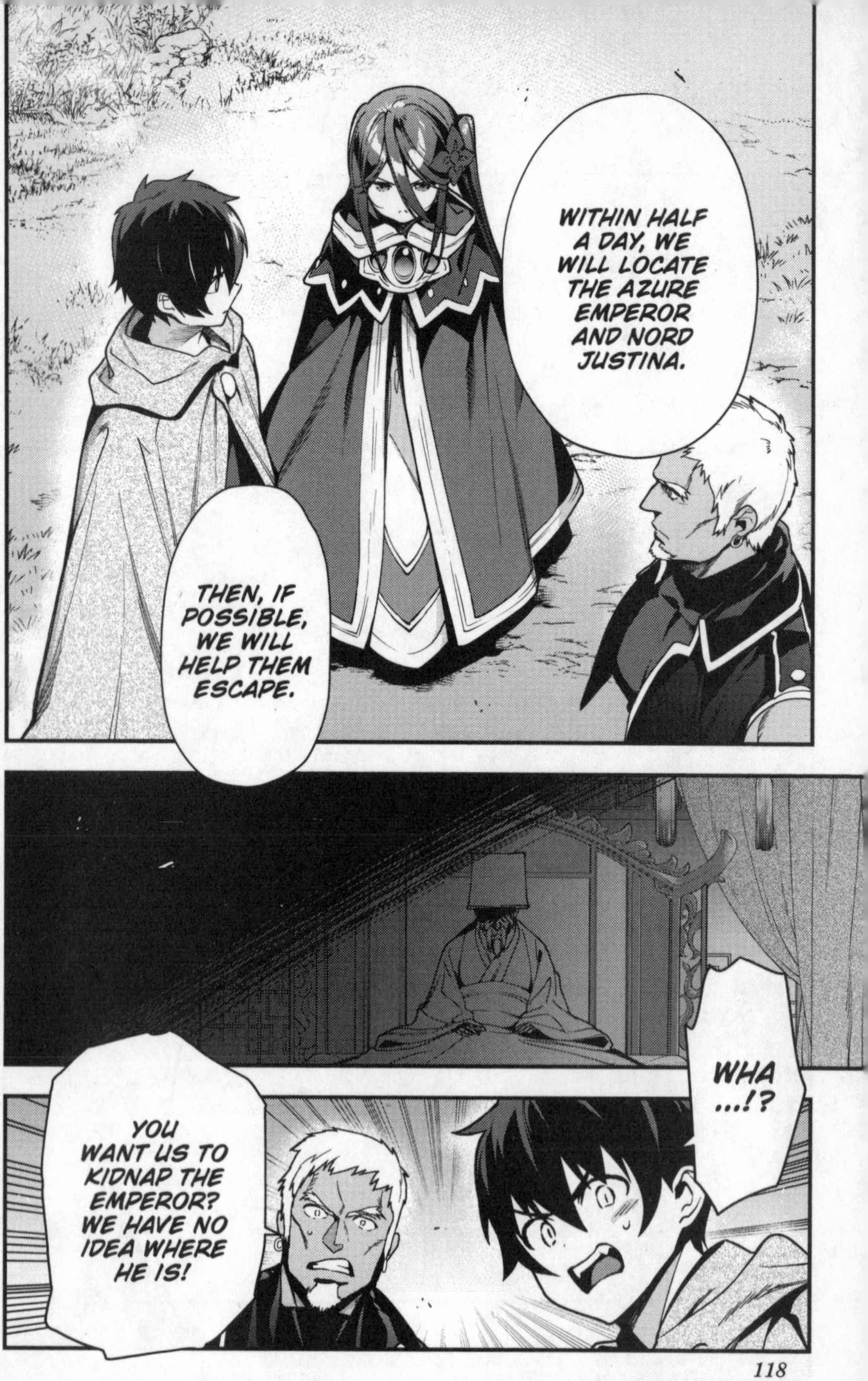
WITHIN HALF A DAY, WE WILL LOCATE THE AZURE EMPEROR AND NORD JUSTINA.
THEN, IF POSSIBLE, WE WILL HELP THEM ESCAPE.
WHA ...!?
YOU WANT US TO KIDNAP THE EMPEROR? WE HAVE NO IDEA WHERE HE IS!

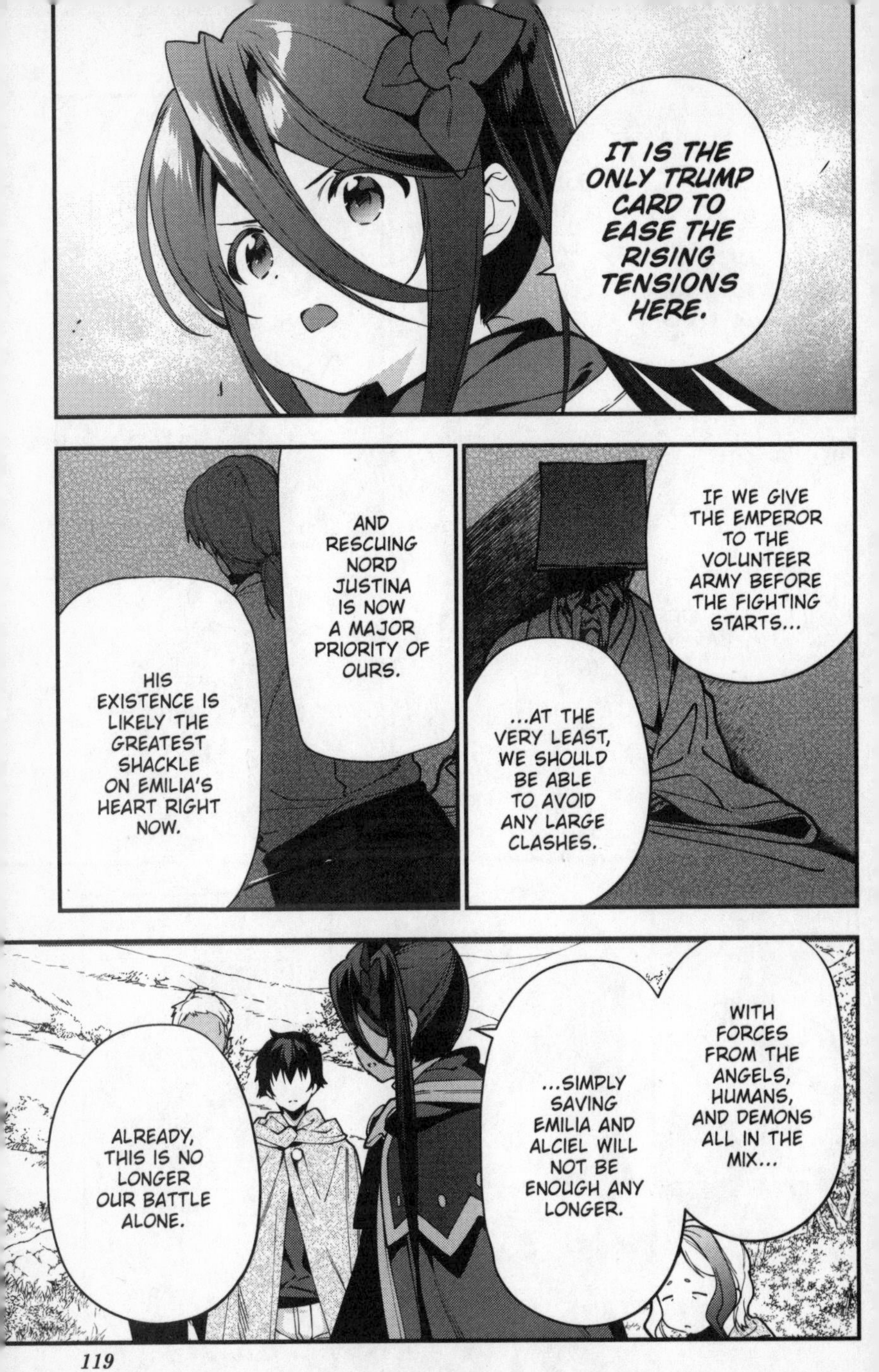
IT IS THE ONLY TRUMP CARD TO EASE THE RISING TENSIONS HERE.
IF WE GIVE THE EMPEROR TO THE VOLUNTEER ARMY BEFORE THE FIGHTING STARTS...
...AT THE VERY LEAST, WE SHOULD BE ABLE TO AVOID ANY LARGE CLASHES.
AND RESCUING NORD JUSTINA IS NOW A MAJOR PRIORITY OF OURS.
HIS EXISTENCE IS LIKELY THE GREATEST SHACKLE ON EMILIA'S HEART RIGHT NOW.
WITH FORCES FROM THE ANGELS, HUMANS, AND DEMONS ALL IN THE MIX...
...SIMPLY SAVING EMILIA AND ALCIEL WILL NOT BE ENOUGH ANY LONGER.
ALREADY, THIS IS NO LONGER OUR BATTLE ALONE.

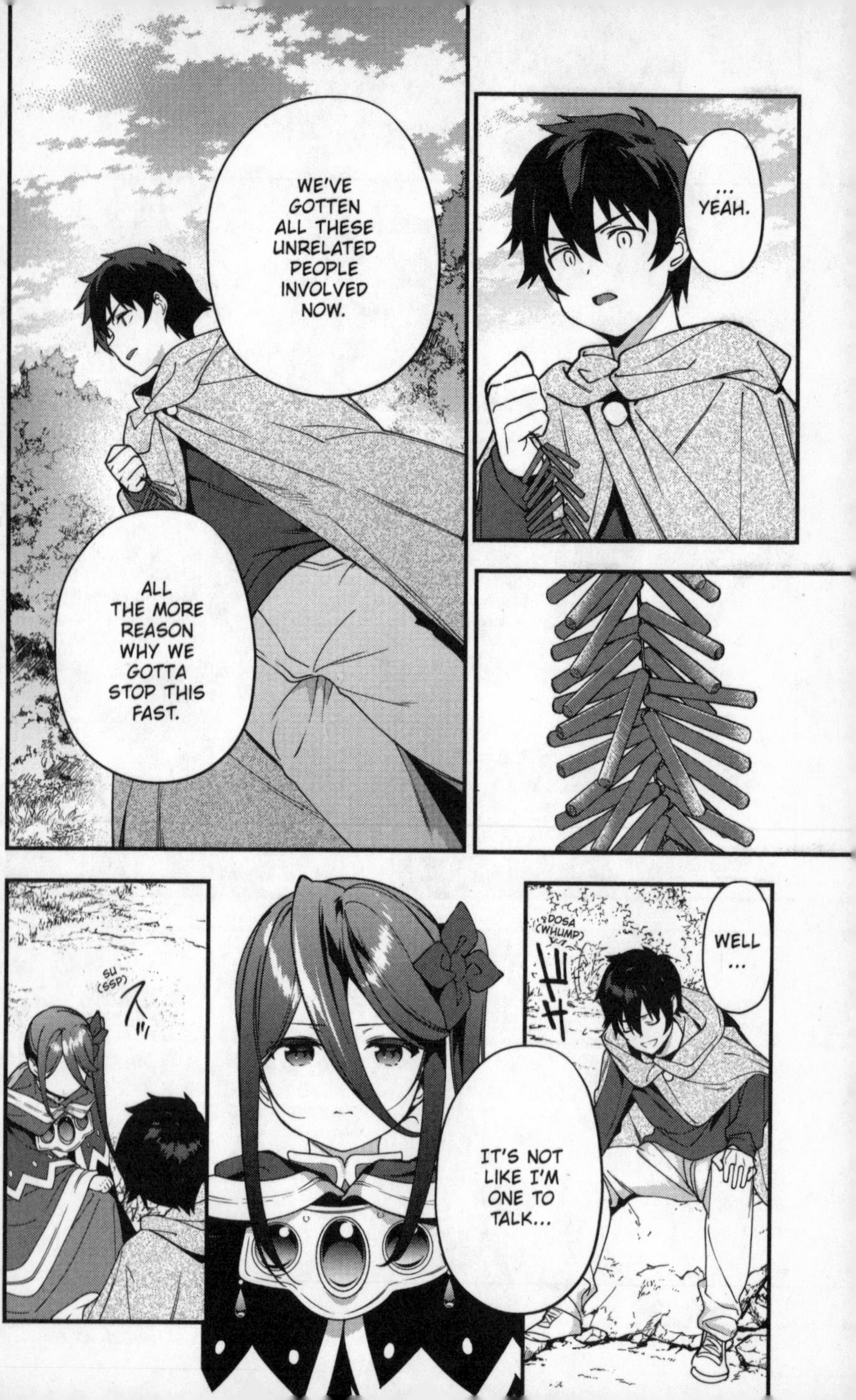
... YEAH.
WE'VE GOTTEN ALL THESE UNRELATED PEOPLE INVOLVED NOW.
ALL THE MORE REASON WHY WE GOTTA STOP THIS FAST.
WELL ...
DOSA (WHUMP)
IT'S NOT LIKE I'M ONE TO TALK...
SU (SSP)

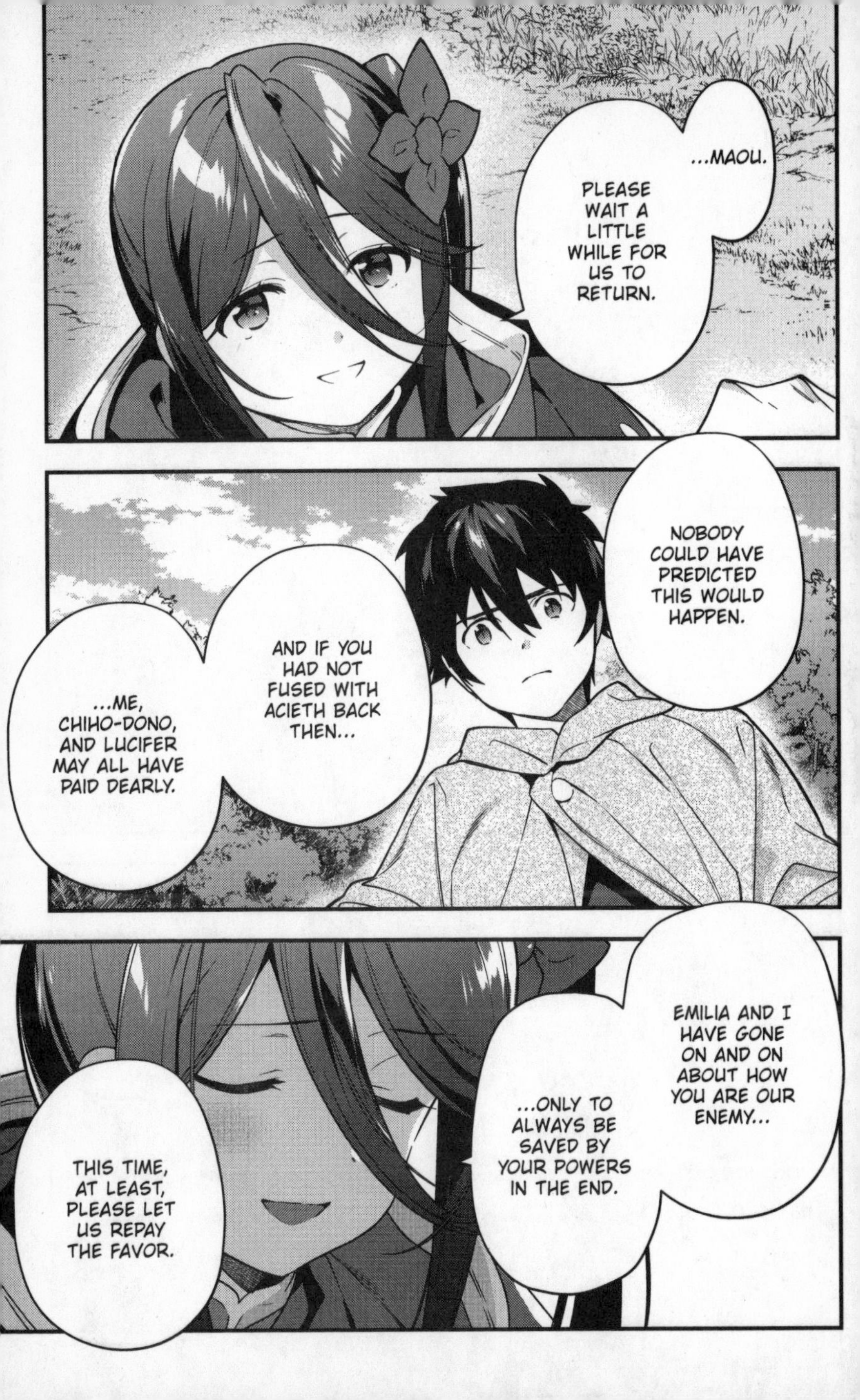
...MAOU. PLEASE WAIT A LITTLE WHILE FOR US TO RETURN.
NOBODY COULD HAVE PREDICTED THIS WOULD HAPPEN.
AND IF YOU HAD NOT FUSED WITH ACIETH BACK THEN...
...ME, CHIHO-DONO, AND LUCIFER MAY ALL HAVE PAID DEARLY.
EMILIA AND I HAVE GONE ON AND ON ABOUT HOW YOU ARE OUR ENEMY...
...ONLY TO ALWAYS BE SAVED BY YOUR POWERS IN THE END.
THIS TIME, AT LEAST, PLEASE LET US REPAY THE FAVOR.

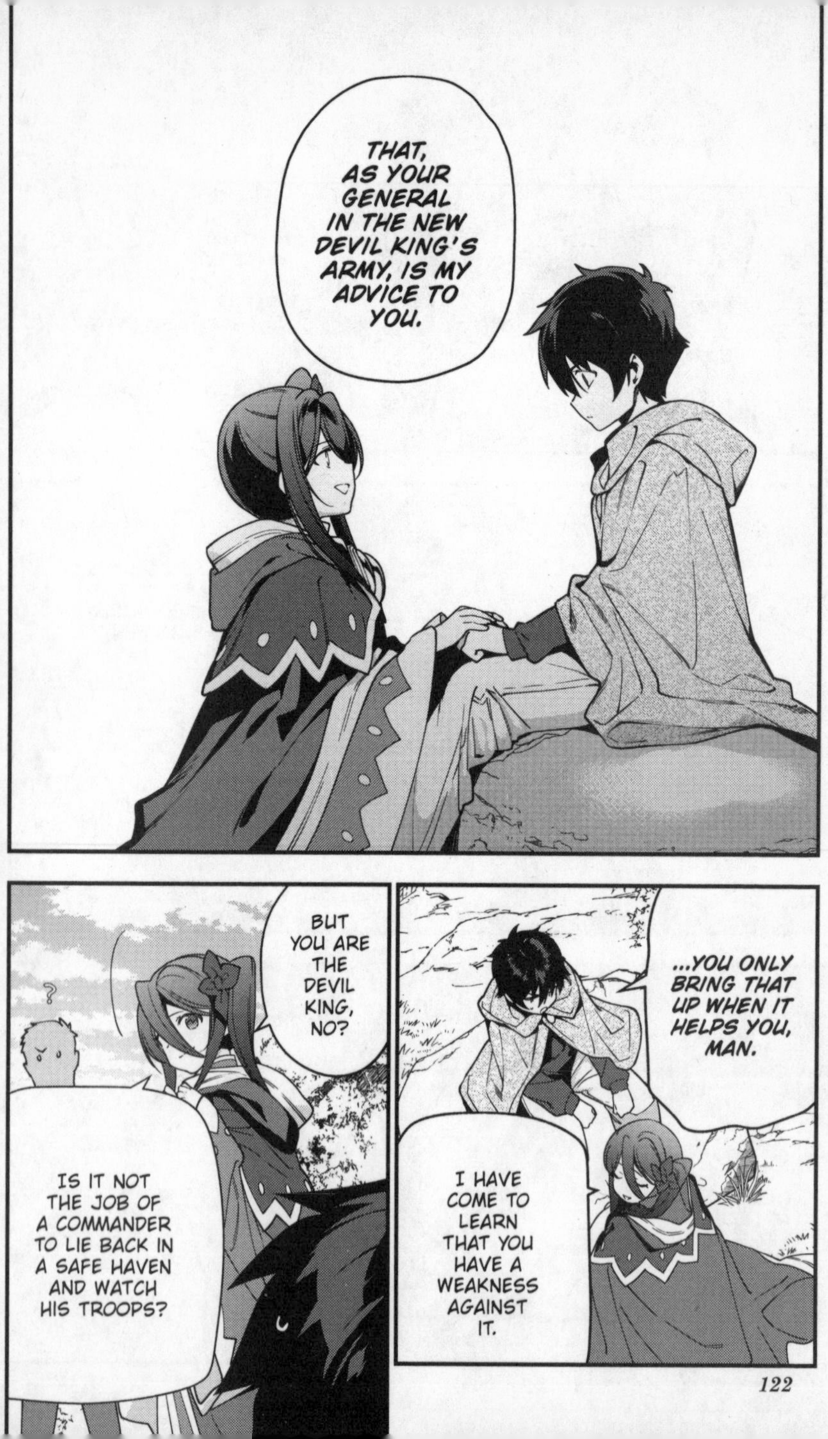
THAT, AS YOUR GENERAL IN THE NEW DEVIL KING'S ARMY, IS MY ADVICE TO YOU.
...YOU ONLY BRING THAT UP WHEN IT HELPS YOU, MAN.
I HAVE COME TO LEARN THAT YOU HAVE A WEAKNESS AGAINST IT.
BUT YOU ARE THE DEVIL KING, NO?
IS IT NOT THE JOB OF A COMMANDER TO LIE BACK IN A SAFE HAVEN AND WATCH HIS TROOPS?

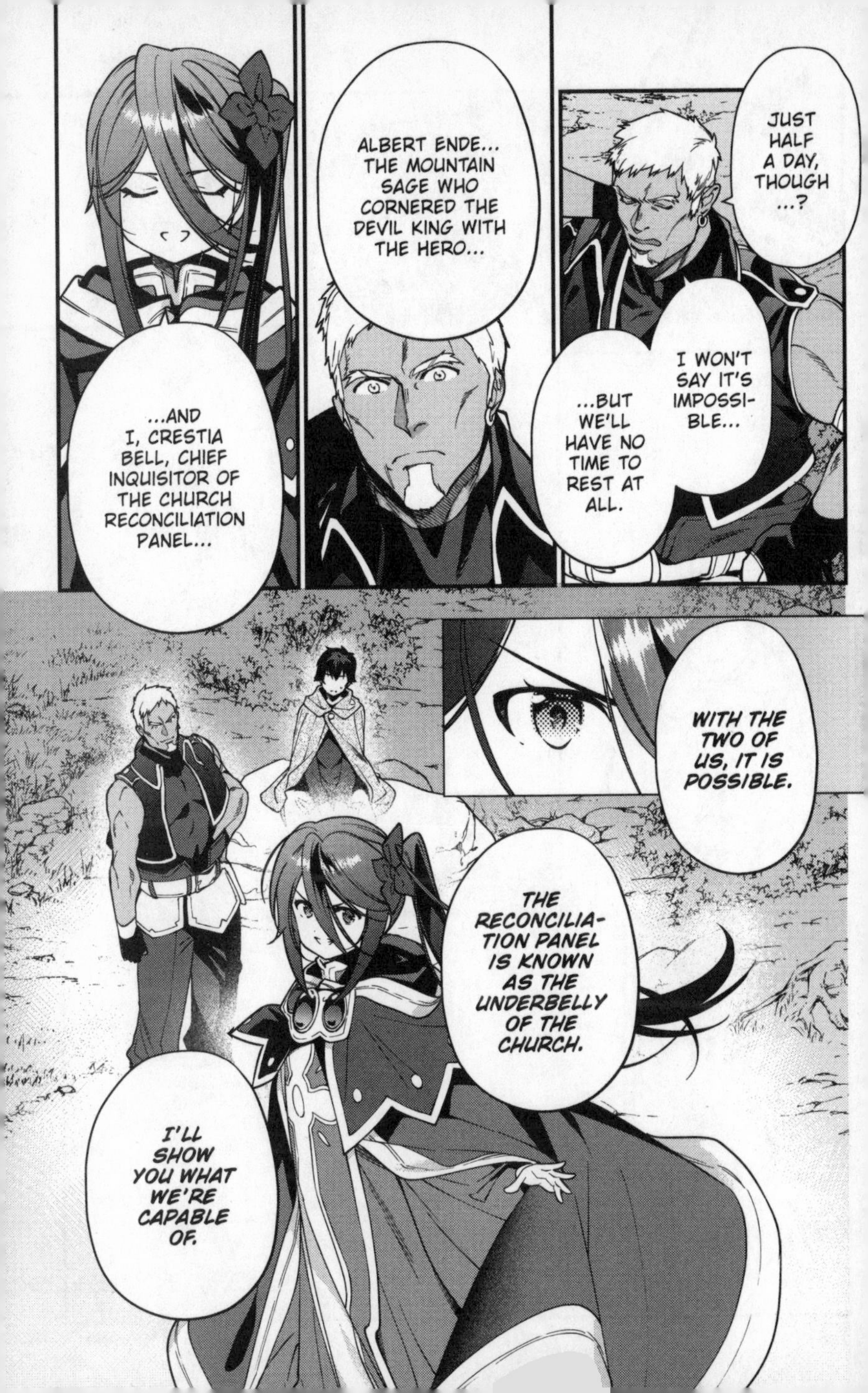
JUST HALF A DAY, THOUGH ...?
I WON'T SAY IT'S IMPOSSIBLE...
...BUT WE'LL HAVE NO TIME TO REST AT ALL.
ALBERT ENDE... THE MOUNTAIN SAGE WHO CORNERED THE DEVIL KING WITH THE HERO...
...AND I, CRESTIA BELL, CHIEF INQUISITOR OF THE CHURCH RECONCILIATION PANEL...
WITH THE TWO OF US, IT IS POSSIBLE.
THE RECONCILIATION PANEL IS KNOWN AS THE UNDERBELLY OF THE CHURCH.
I'LL SHOW YOU WHAT WE'RE CAPABLE OF.

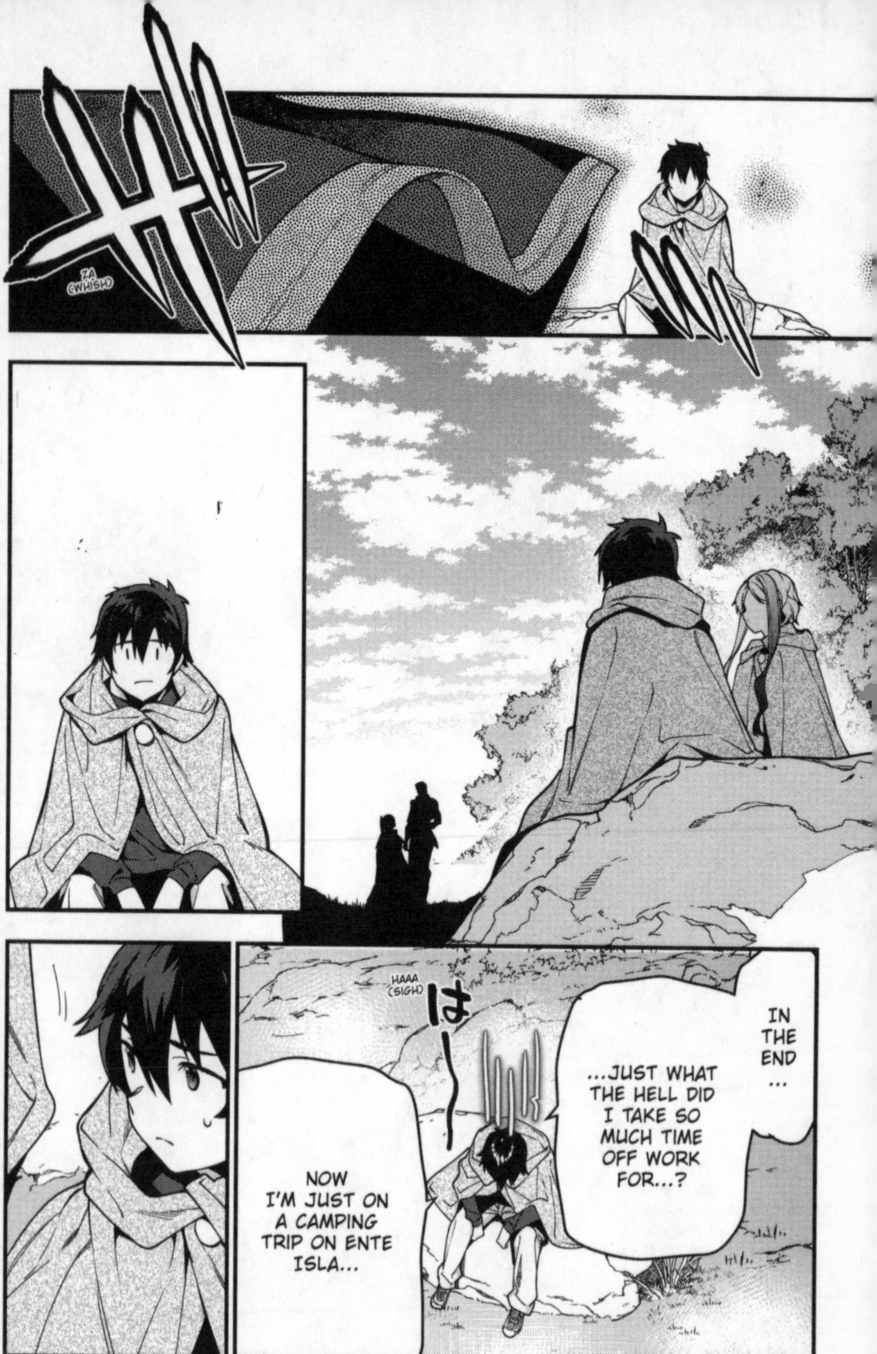
ZA (WHISH)
HAAA (SIGH)
は ー
IN THE END...
...JUST WHAT THE HELL DID I TAKE SO MUCH TIME OFF WORK FOR...?
NOW I'M JUST ON A CAMPING TRIP ON ENTE ISLA...

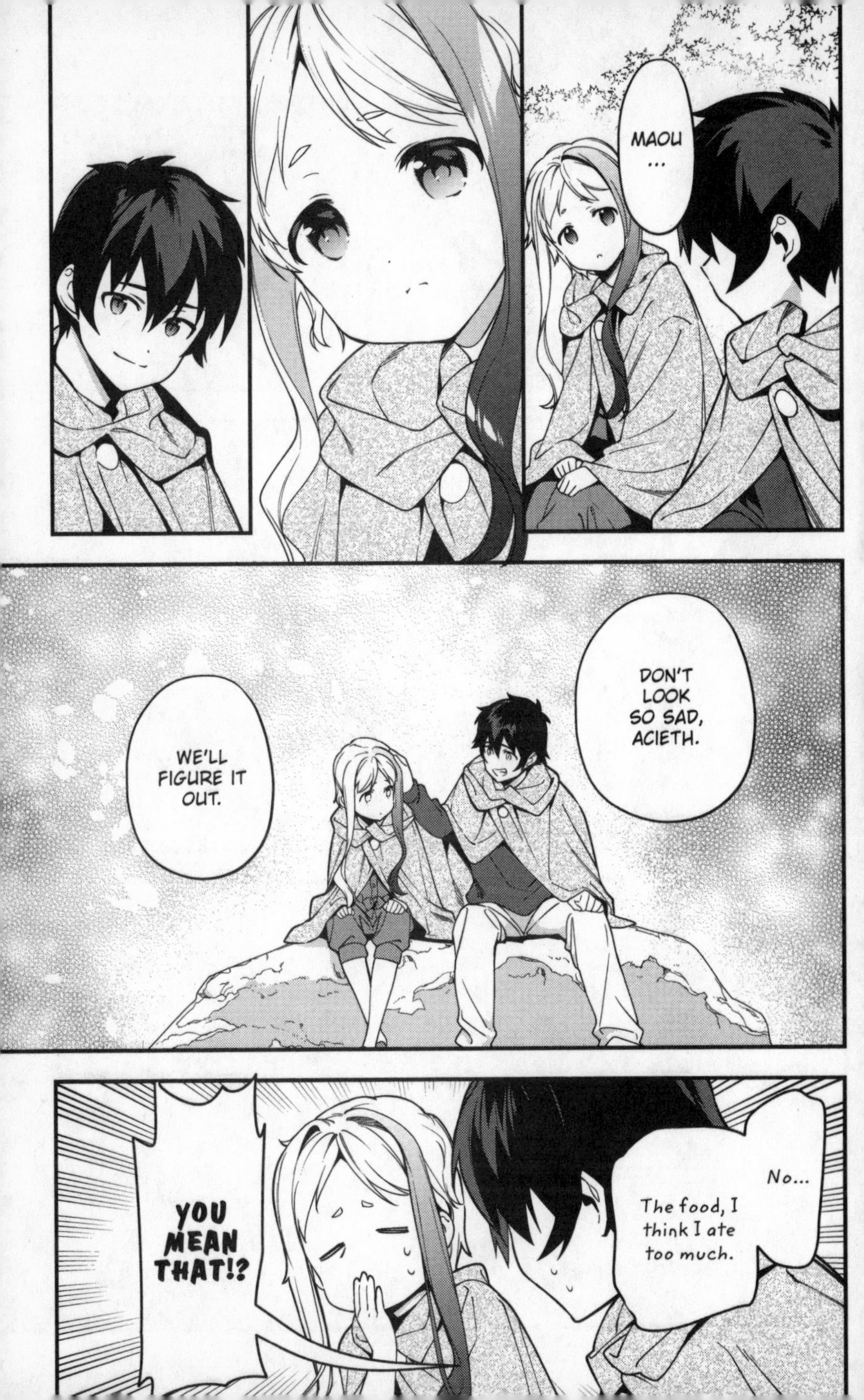
MAOU ...
DON'T LOOK SO SAD, ACIETH.
WE'LL FIGURE IT OUT.
No...
The food, I think I ate too much.
YOU MEAN THAT!?

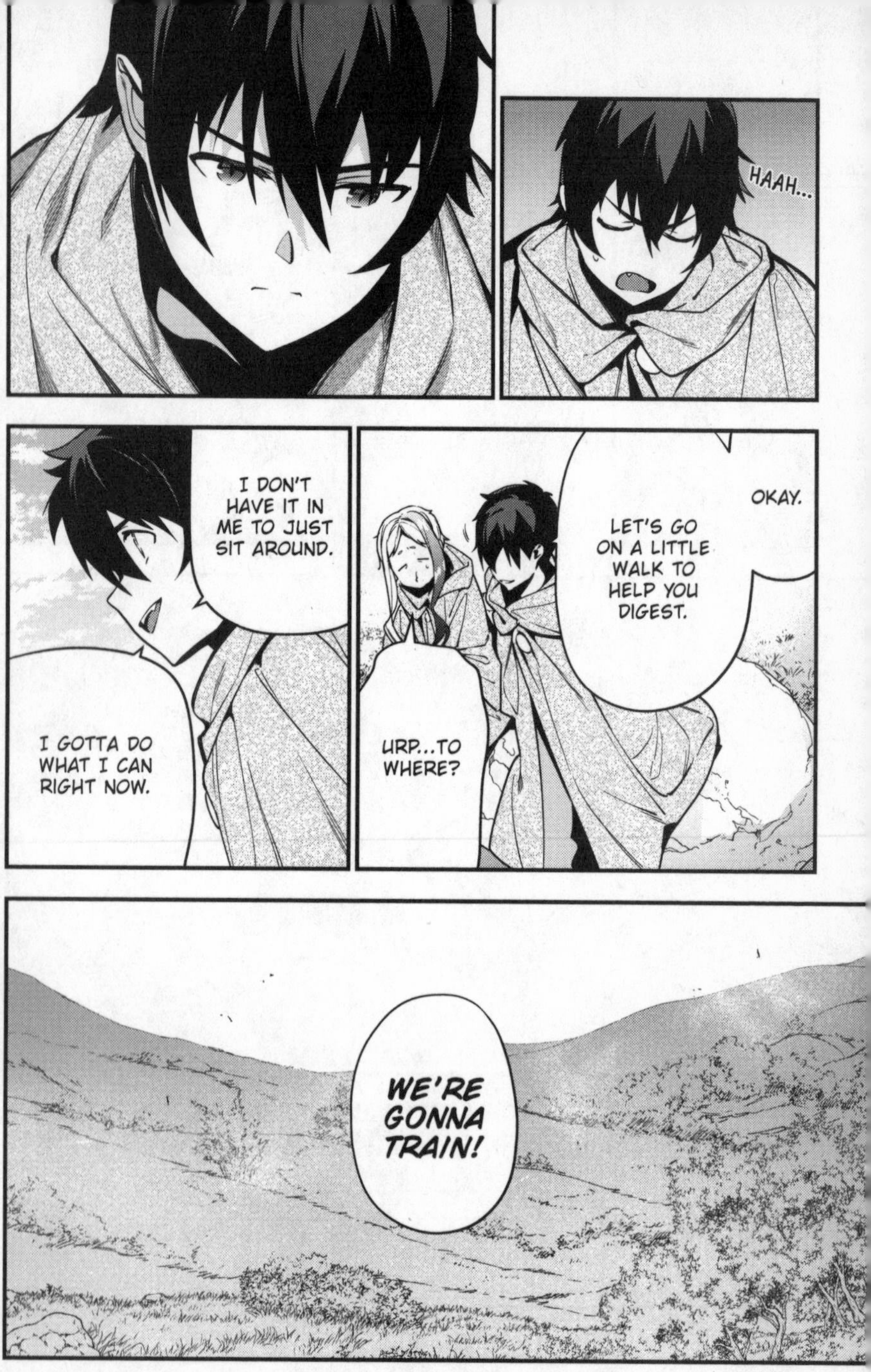
HAAH...
OKAY.
LET'S GO ON A LITTLE WALK TO HELP YOU DIGEST.
URP...TO WHERE?
I DON'T HAVE IT IN ME TO JUST SIT AROUND.
I GOTTA DO WHAT I CAN RIGHT NOW.
WE'RE GONNA TRAIN!

Acieth
Alla

THE DEVIL IS A PART-TIMER!

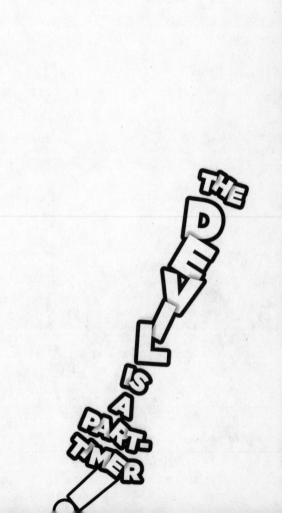

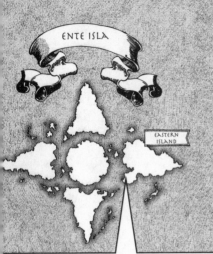

ENTE ISLA

EASTERN
ISLAND

CHAPTER 88:
THE HERO HAS THE TRUTH
PREACHED TO HER

EFZAHAN

PHAIGAN
A FORTRESS CITY AND
MILITARY PORT WHERE
EMI WAS HELD.

GWENVAN

HONFA
A VILLAGE NORTH OF
HEAVENSKY, NEAR THE
FOREST MAOU'S GROUP
LANDED IN.

HEAVENSKY
THE CAPITAL OF EFZAHAN,
WHOSE LANDS SPREAD
ACROSS THE ENTIRE
EASTERN ISLAND CONTINENT.
HEAVENSKY KEEP IS WHERE
ASHIYA IS BEING HELD.

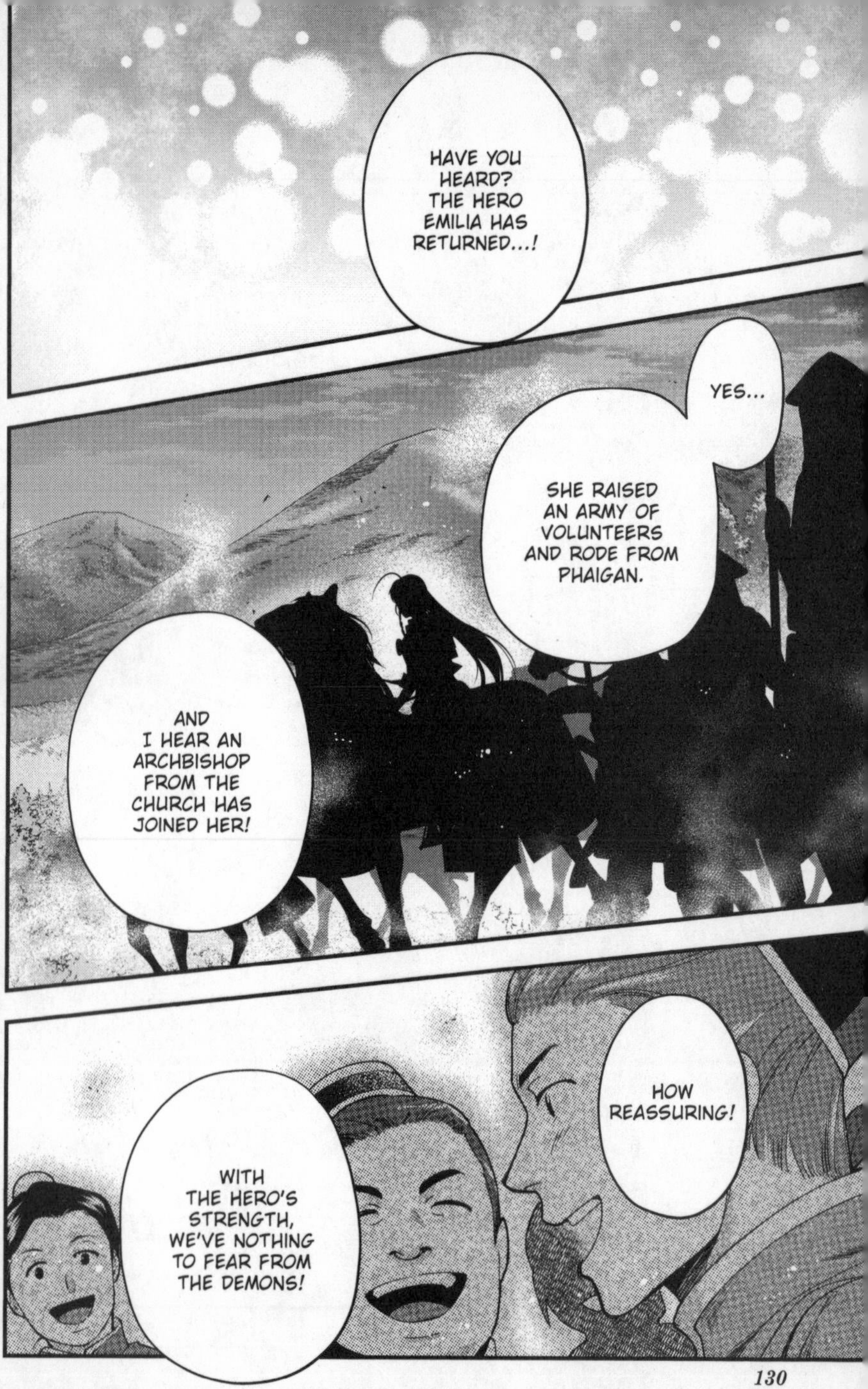
HAVE YOU HEARD? THE HERO EMILIA HAS RETURNED...!
YES...
SHE RAISED AN ARMY OF VOLUNTEERS AND RODE FROM PHAIGAN.
AND I HEAR AN ARCHBISHOP FROM THE CHURCH HAS JOINED HER!
HOW REASSURING!
WITH THE HERO'S STRENGTH, WE'VE NOTHING TO FEAR FROM THE DEMONS!

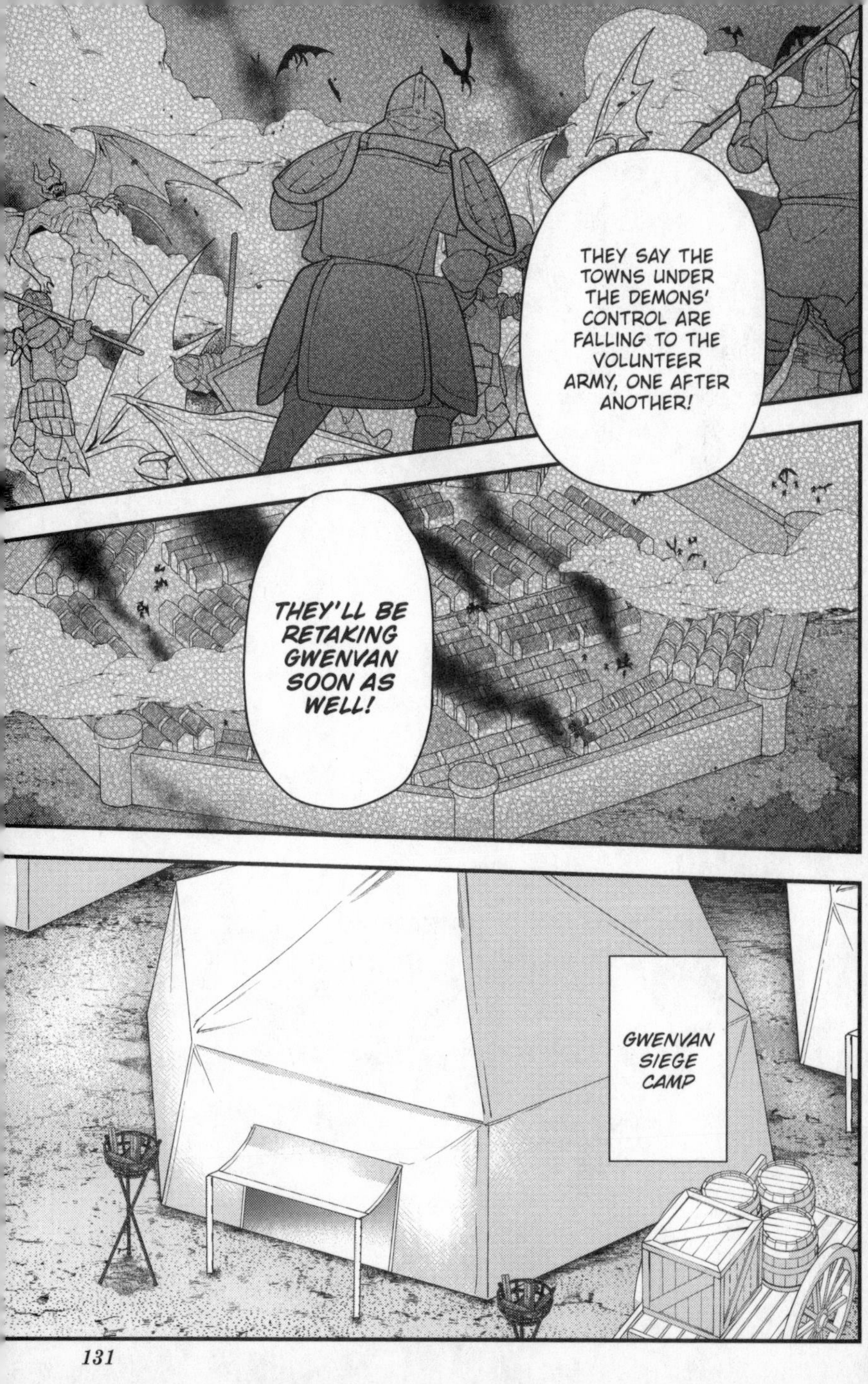
THEY SAY THE TOWNS UNDER THE DEMONS' CONTROL ARE FALLING TO THE VOLUNTEER ARMY, ONE AFTER ANOTHER!
THEY'LL BE RETAKING GWENVAN SOON AS WELL!
GWENVAN SIEGE CAMP

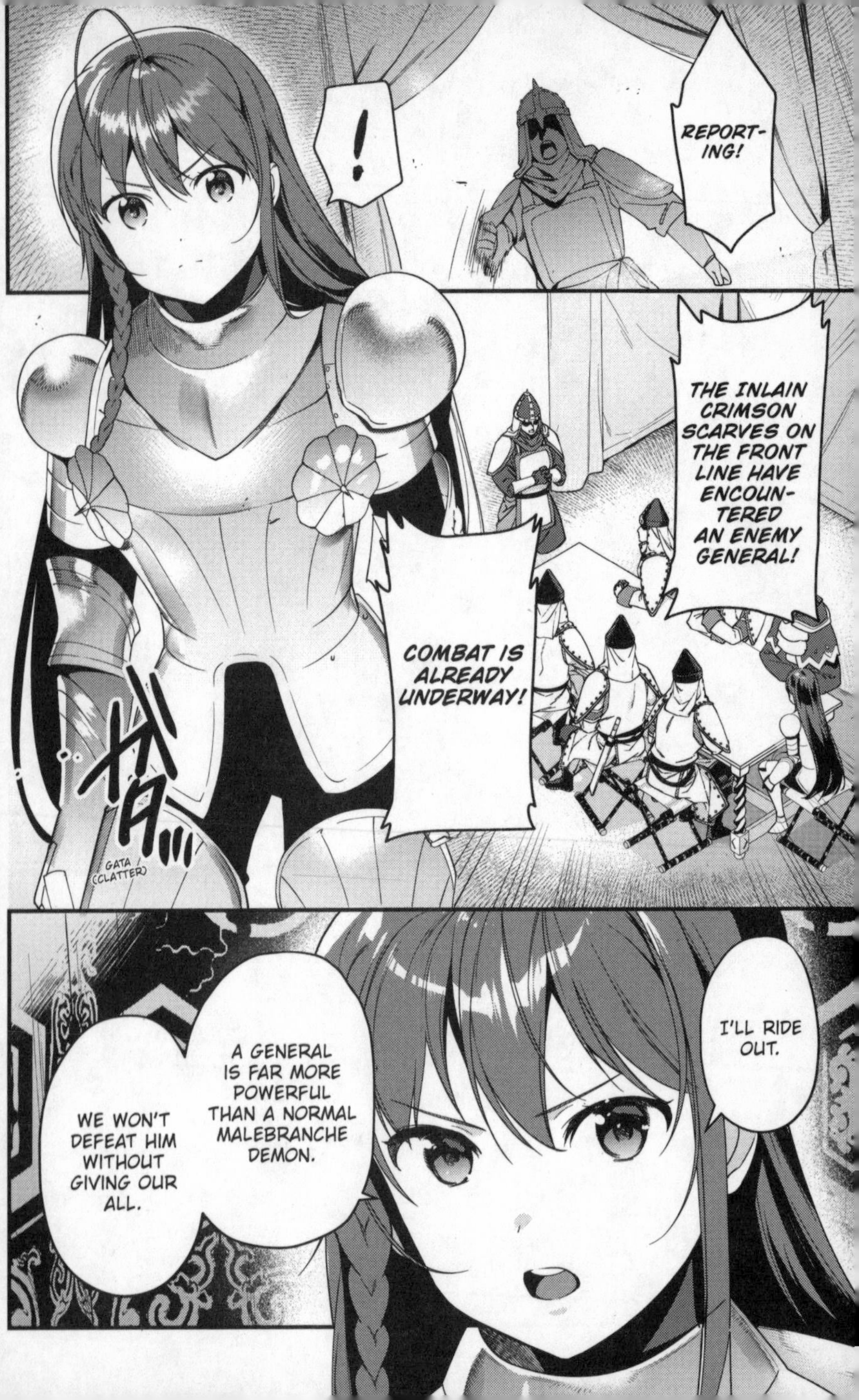
REPORT-
ING!
!
THE INLAIN CRIMSON SCARVES ON THE FRONT LINE HAVE ENCOUN-TERED AN ENEMY GENERAL!
COMBAT IS ALREADY UNDERWAY!
GATA (CLATTER)
I'LL RIDE OUT.
A GENERAL IS FAR MORE POWERFUL THAN A NORMAL MALEBRANCHE DEMON.
WE WON'T DEFEAT HIM WITHOUT GIVING OUR ALL.

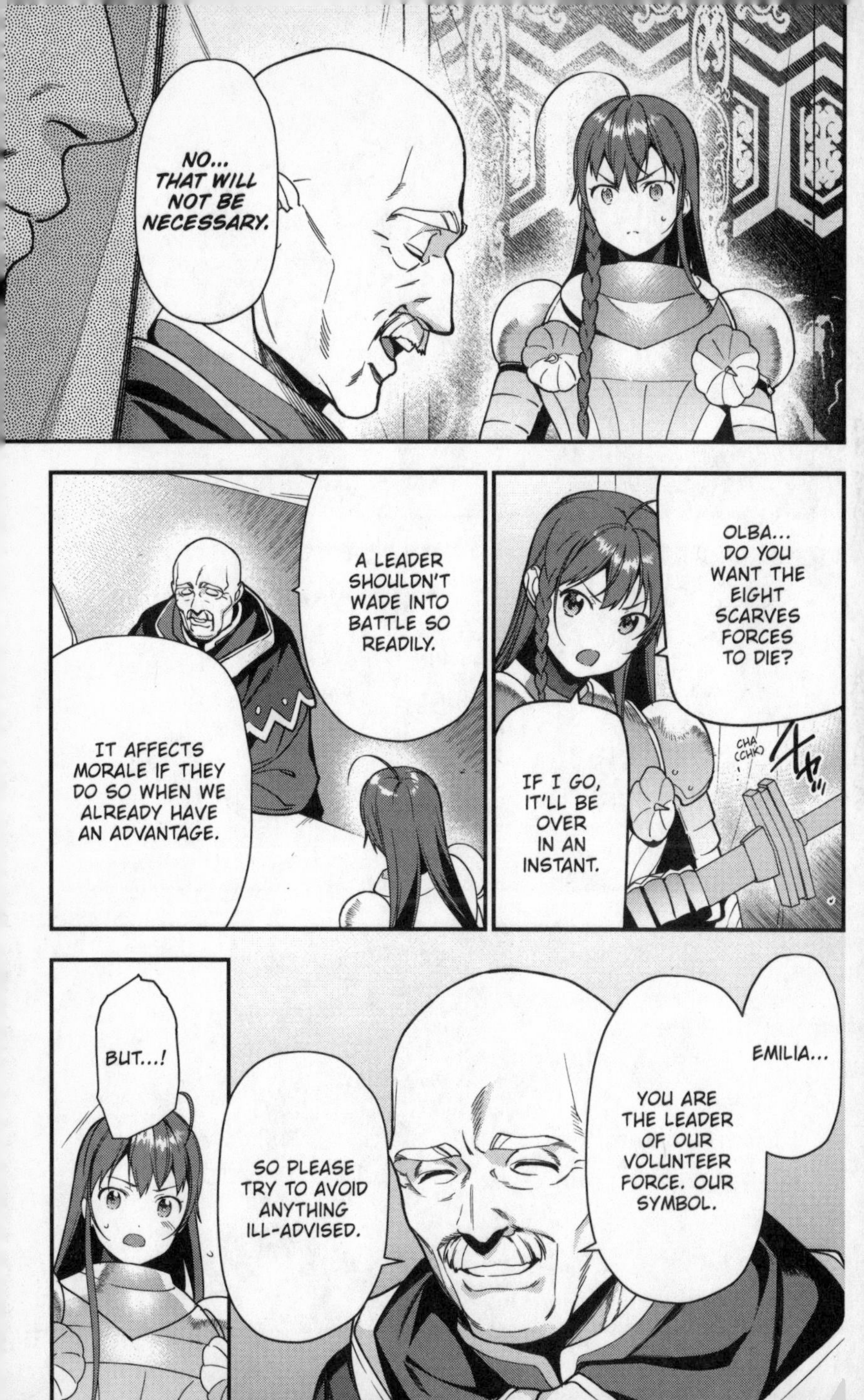
NO... THAT WILL NOT BE NECESSARY.
OLBA... DO YOU WANT THE EIGHT SCARVES FORCES TO DIE?
CHA (CHK)
IF I GO, IT'LL BE OVER IN AN INSTANT.
A LEADER SHOULDN'T WADE INTO BATTLE SO READILY.
IT AFFECTS MORALE IF THEY DO SO WHEN WE ALREADY HAVE AN ADVANTAGE.
EMILIA...
YOU ARE THE LEADER OF OUR VOLUNTEER FORCE. OUR SYMBOL.
SO PLEASE TRY TO AVOID ANYTHING ILL-ADVISED.
BUT...!

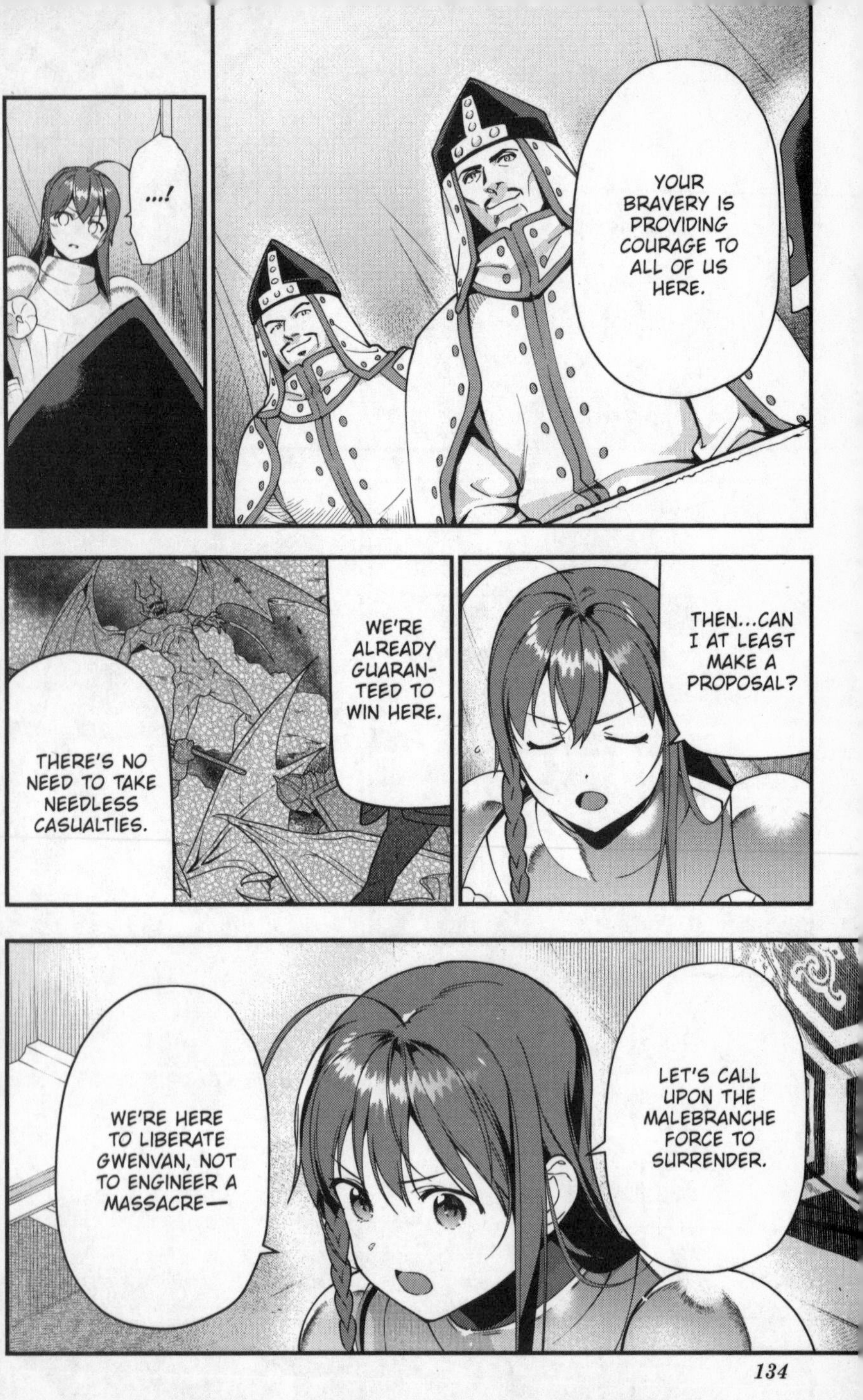
YOUR BRAVERY IS PROVIDING COURAGE TO ALL OF US HERE.
...!
THEN...CAN I AT LEAST MAKE A PROPOSAL?
WE'RE ALREADY GUARAN-TEED TO WIN HERE.
THERE'S NO NEED TO TAKE NEEDLESS CASUALTIES.
LET'S CALL UPON THE MALEBRANCHE FORCE TO SURRENDER.
WE'RE HERE TO LIBERATE GWENVAN, NOT TO ENGINEER A MASSACRE—

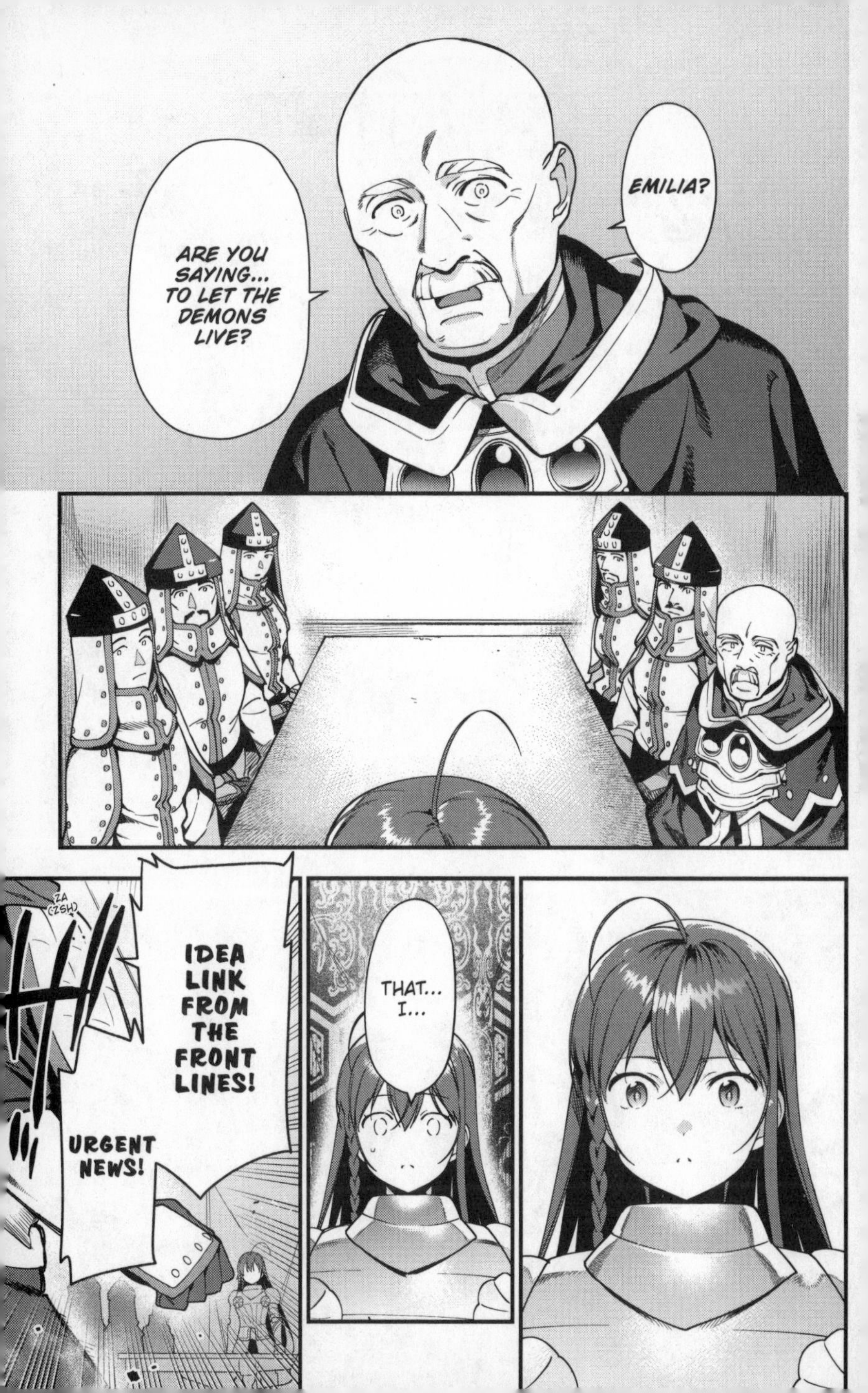
EMILIA?
ARE YOU SAYING... TO LET THE DEMONS LIVE?
THAT... I...
IDEA LINK FROM THE FRONT LINES!
URGENT NEWS!
ZA (ZSH)

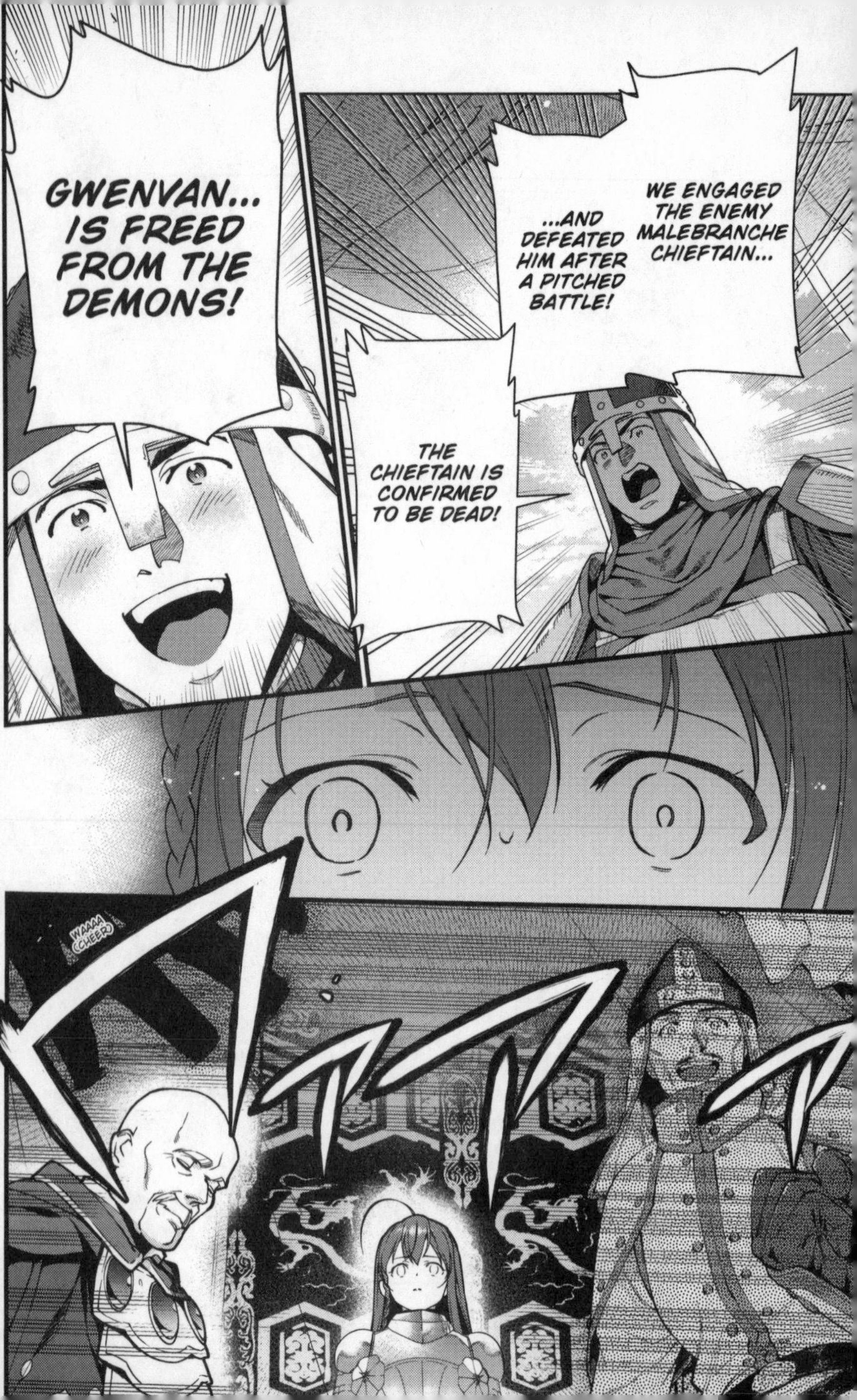
WE ENGAGED THE ENEMY MALEBRANCHE CHIEFTAIN...
...AND DEFEATED HIM AFTER A PITCHED BATTLE!
THE CHIEFTAIN IS CONFIRMED TO BE DEAD!
GWENVAN... IS FREED FROM THE DEMONS!
WAAAA (CHEER)

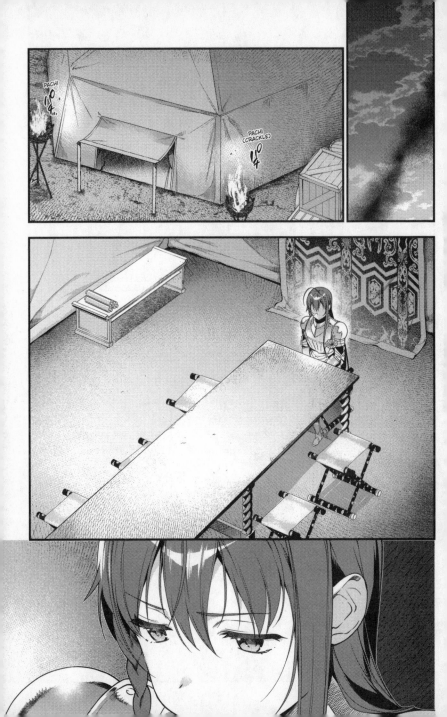

PACHI

PACHI
(CRACKLE)

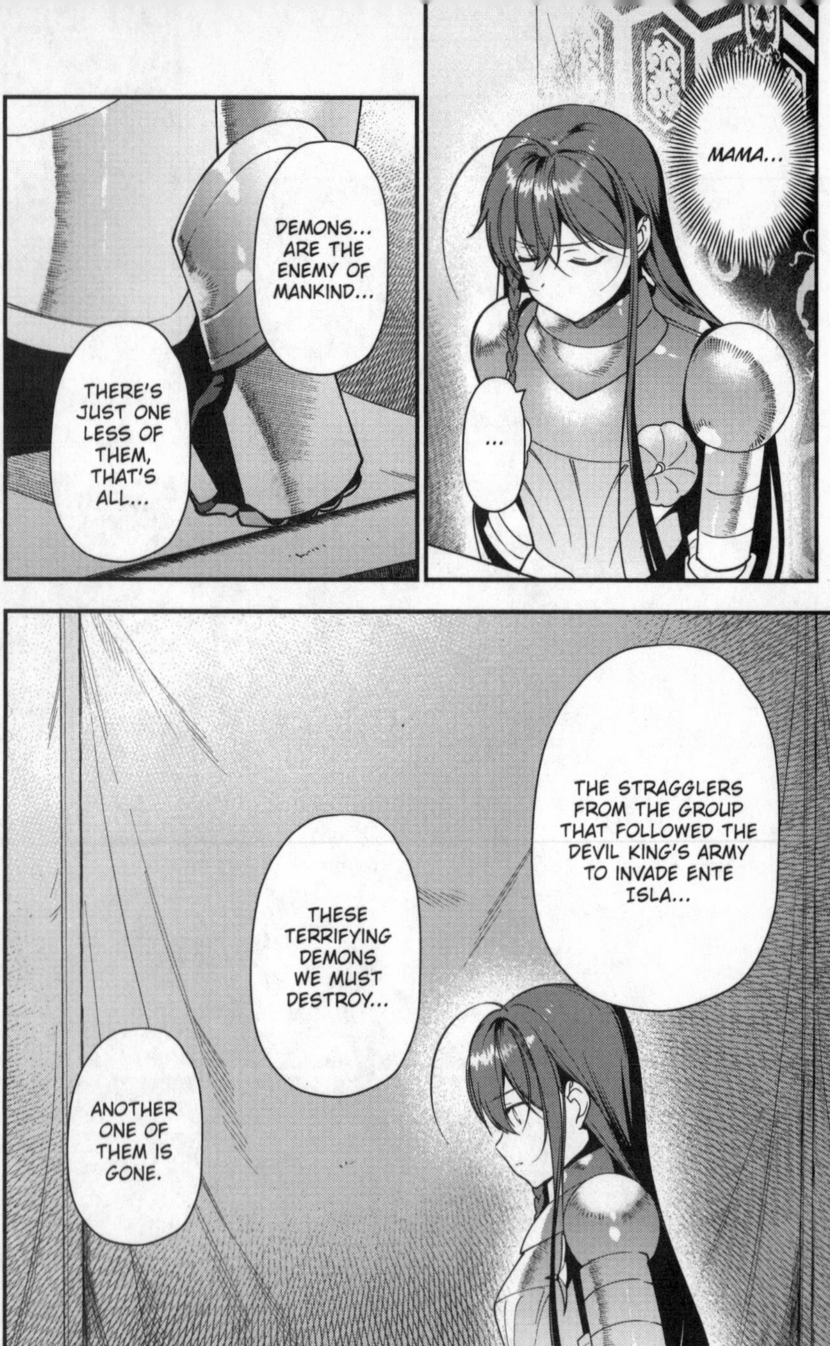
MAMA…
…
DEMONS… ARE THE ENEMY OF MANKIND…
THERE'S JUST ONE LESS OF THEM, THAT'S ALL…
THE STRAGGLERS FROM THE GROUP THAT FOLLOWED THE DEVIL KING'S ARMY TO INVADE ENTE ISLA…
THESE TERRIFYING DEMONS WE MUST DESTROY…
ANOTHER ONE OF THEM IS GONE.

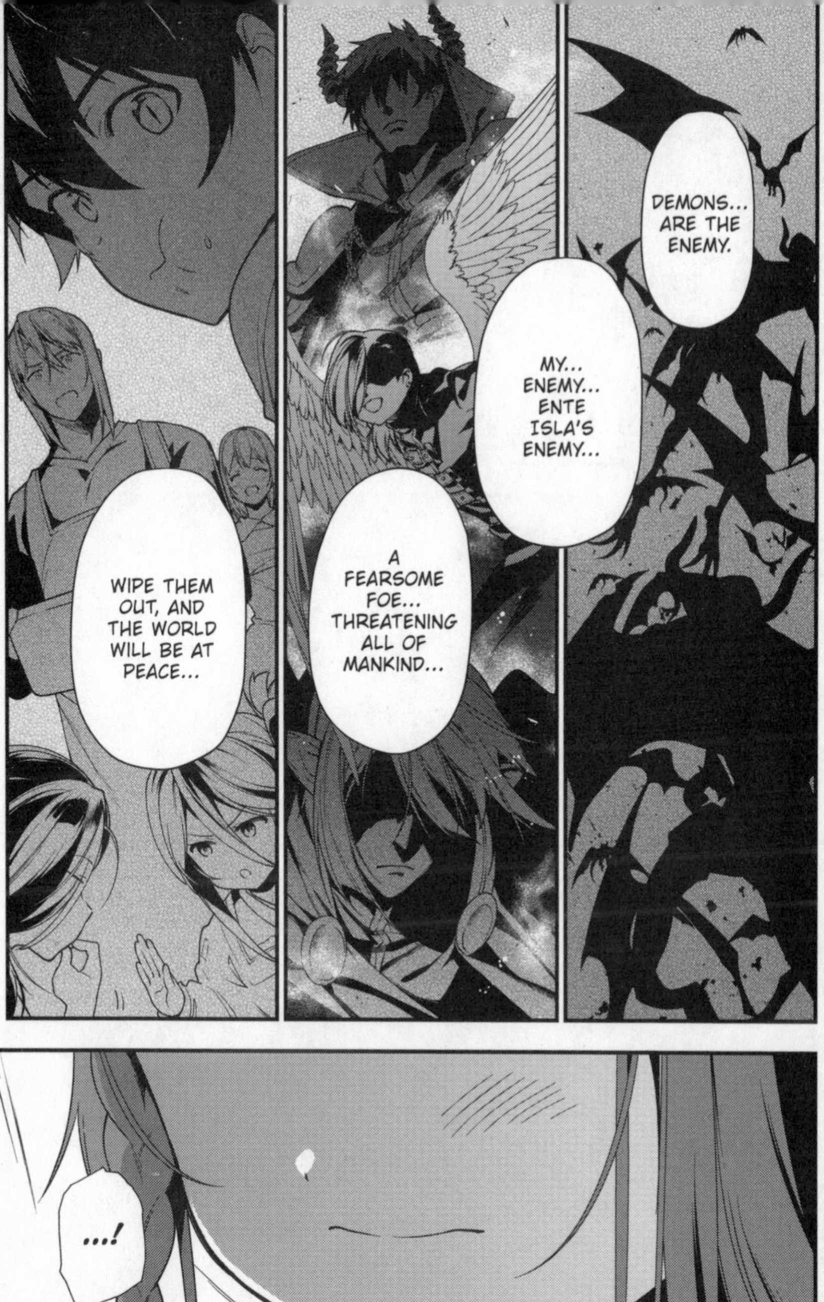
DEMONS... ARE THE ENEMY.
MY... ENEMY... ENTE ISLA'S ENEMY...
A FEARSOME FOE... THREATENING ALL OF MANKIND...
WIPE THEM OUT, AND THE WORLD WILL BE AT PEACE...
...!

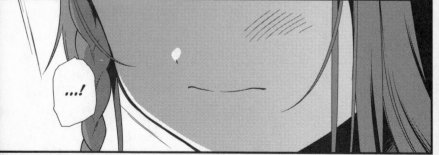

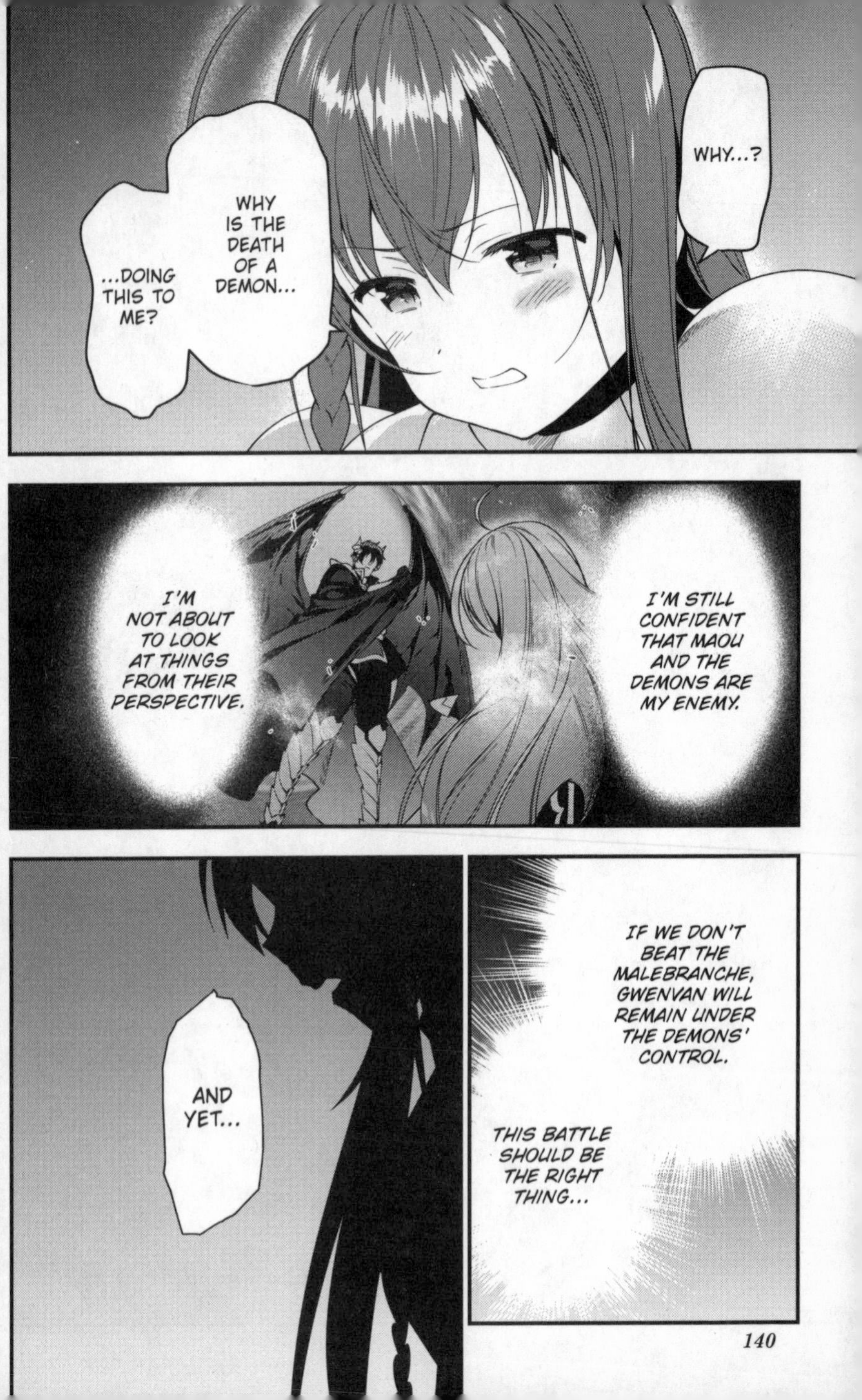
WHY...?
WHY IS THE DEATH OF A DEMON...
...DOING THIS TO ME?
I'M STILL CONFIDENT THAT MAOU AND THE DEMONS ARE MY ENEMY.
I'M NOT ABOUT TO LOOK AT THINGS FROM THEIR PERSPECTIVE.
IF WE DON'T BEAT THE MALEBRANCHE, GWENVAN WILL REMAIN UNDER THE DEMONS' CONTROL.
THIS BATTLE SHOULD BE THE RIGHT THING...
AND YET...

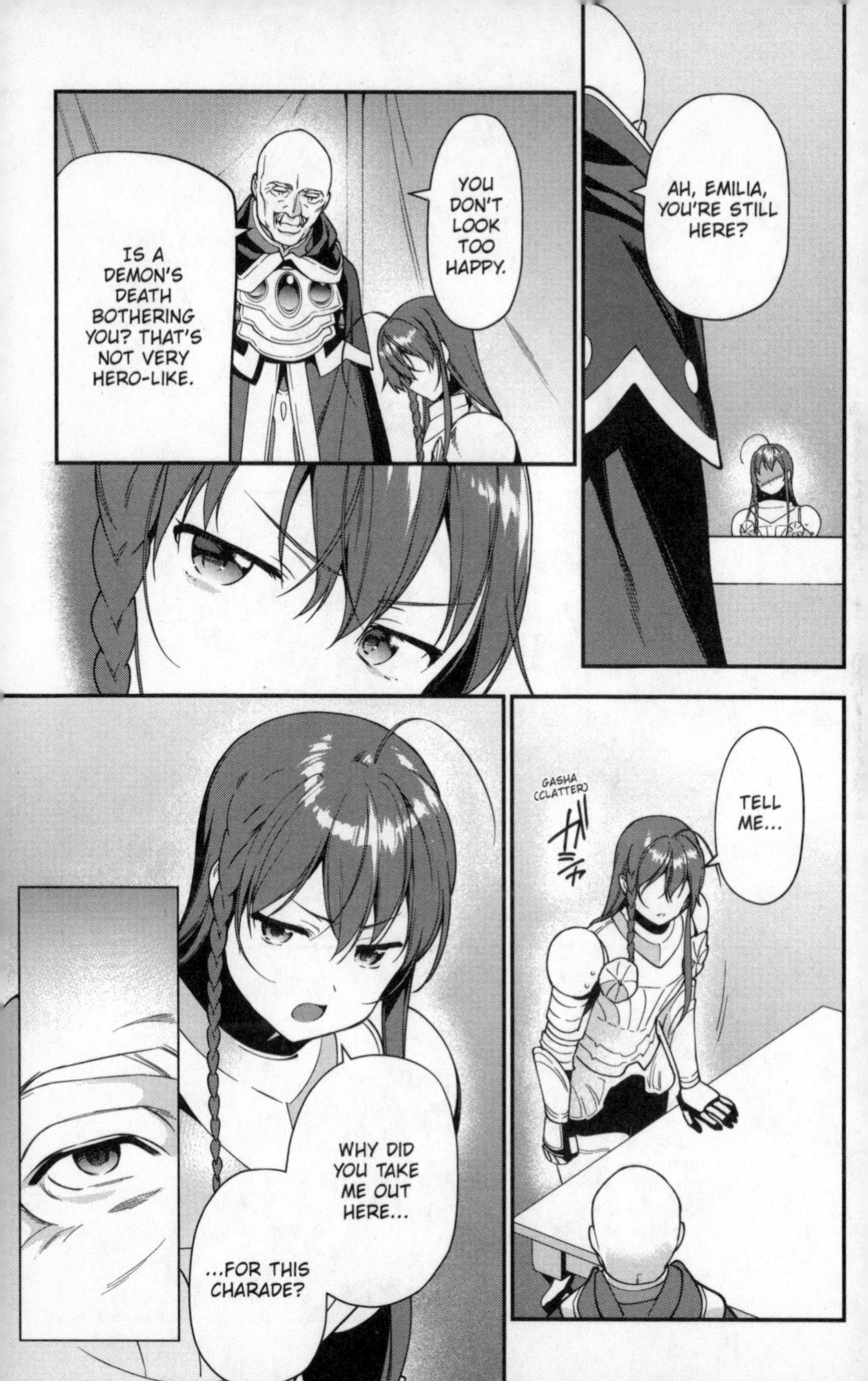
AH, EMILIA, YOU'RE STILL HERE?
YOU DON'T LOOK TOO HAPPY.
IS A DEMON'S DEATH BOTHERING YOU? THAT'S NOT VERY HERO-LIKE.
GASHA (CLATTER)
TELL ME...
WHY DID YOU TAKE ME OUT HERE...
...FOR THIS CHARADE?

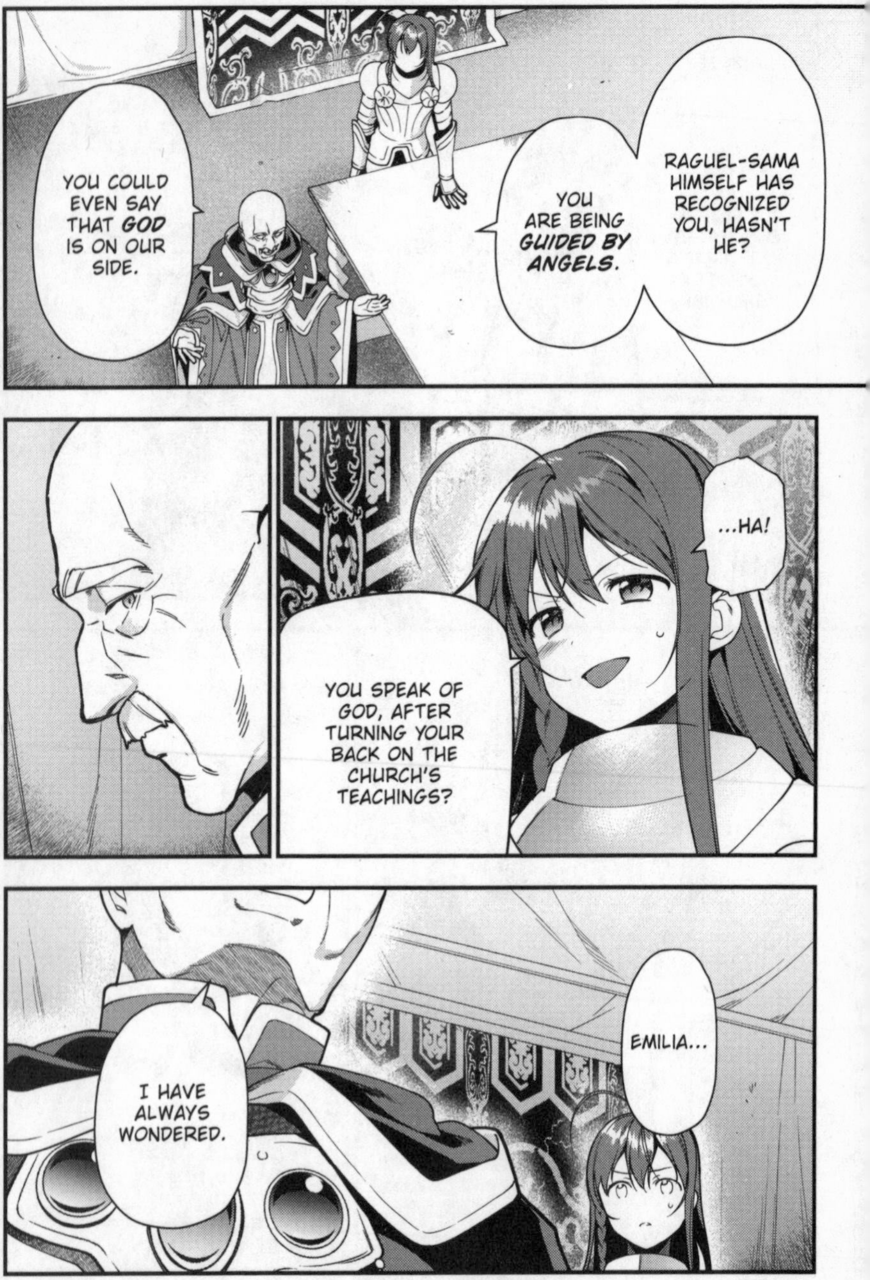
RAGUEL-SAMA HIMSELF HAS RECOGNIZED YOU, HASN'T HE?
YOU ARE BEING GUIDED BY ANGELS.
YOU COULD EVEN SAY THAT GOD IS ON OUR SIDE.
...HA!
YOU SPEAK OF GOD, AFTER TURNING YOUR BACK ON THE CHURCH'S TEACHINGS?
EMILIA...
I HAVE ALWAYS WONDERED.

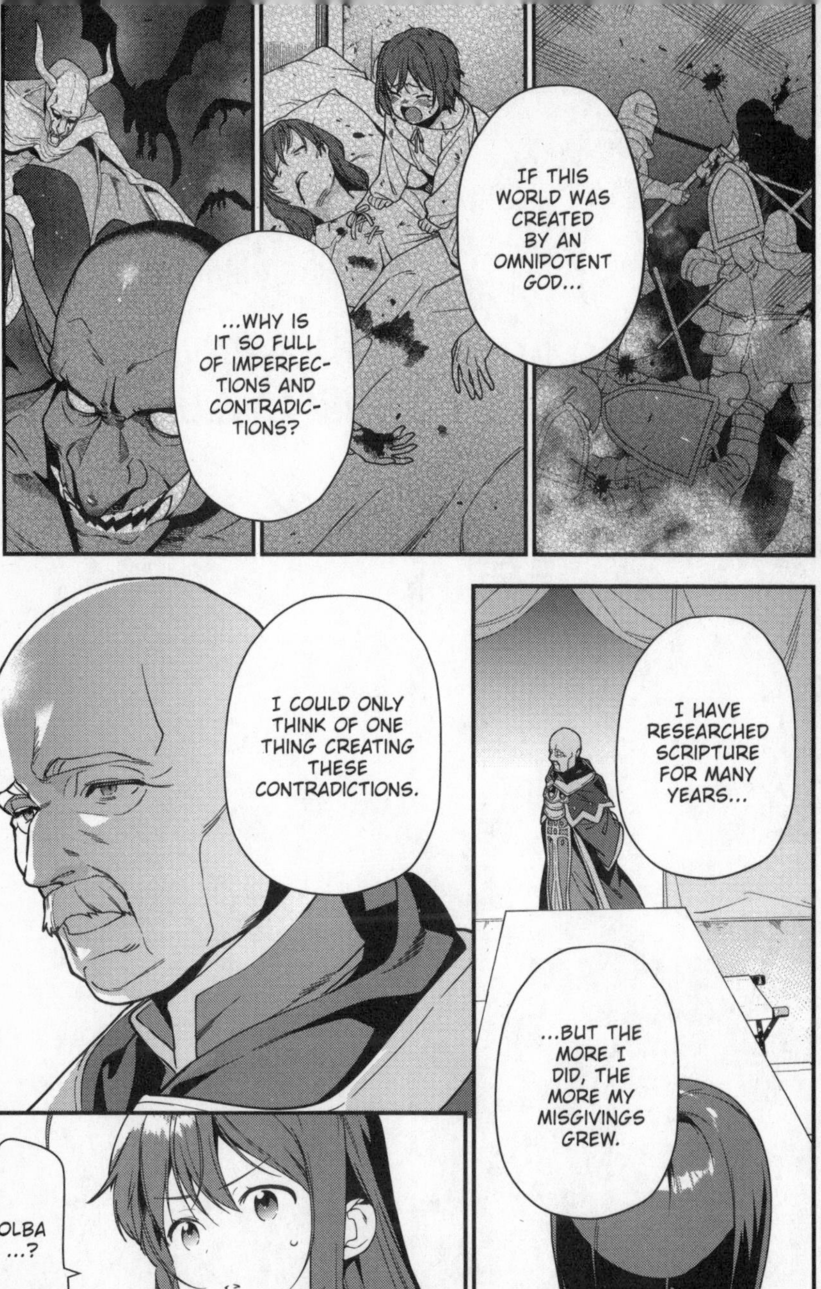
IF THIS WORLD WAS CREATED BY AN OMNIPOTENT GOD...
...WHY IS IT SO FULL OF IMPERFECTIONS AND CONTRADICTIONS?
I HAVE RESEARCHED SCRIPTURE FOR MANY YEARS...
...BUT THE MORE I DID, THE MORE MY MISGIVINGS GREW.
I COULD ONLY THINK OF ONE THING CREATING THESE CONTRADICTIONS.
OLBA ...?

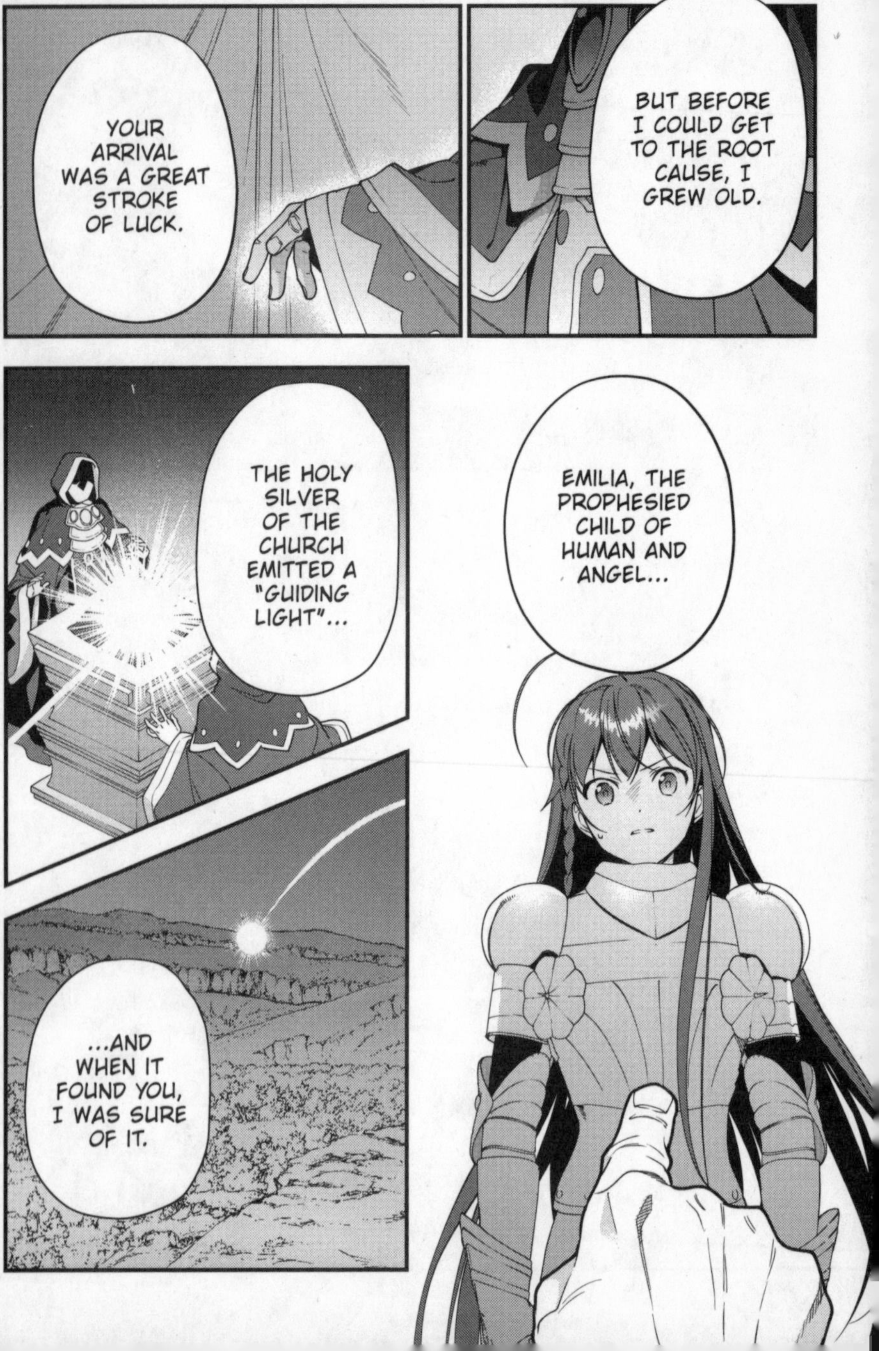
BUT BEFORE I COULD GET TO THE ROOT CAUSE, I GREW OLD.
YOUR ARRIVAL WAS A GREAT STROKE OF LUCK.
EMILIA, THE PROPHESIED CHILD OF HUMAN AND ANGEL...
THE HOLY SILVER OF THE CHURCH EMITTED A "GUIDING LIGHT"...
...AND WHEN IT FOUND YOU, I WAS SURE OF IT.

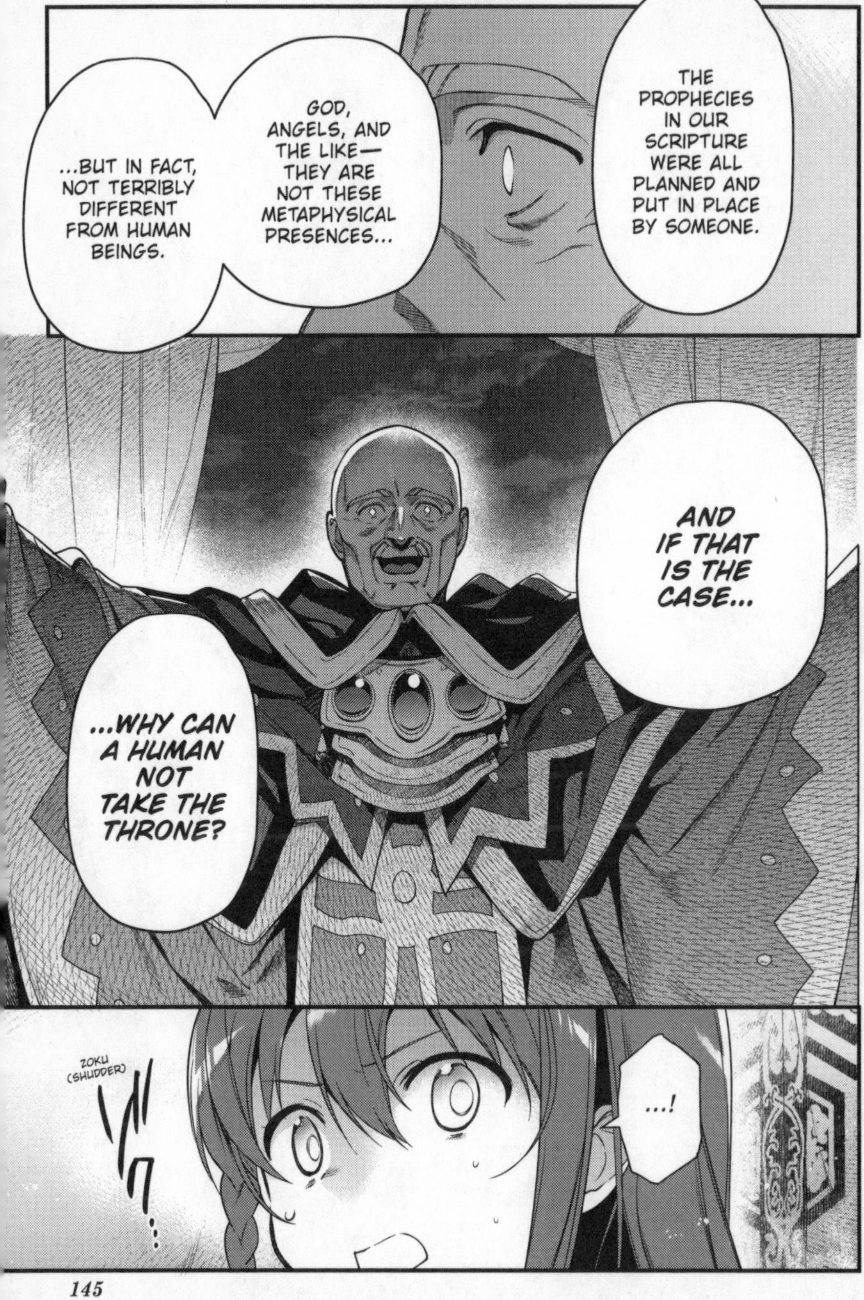
THE PROPHECIES IN OUR SCRIPTURE WERE ALL PLANNED AND PUT IN PLACE BY SOMEONE.
GOD, ANGELS, AND THE LIKE—THEY ARE NOT THESE METAPHYSICAL PRESENCES...
...BUT IN FACT, NOT TERRIBLY DIFFERENT FROM HUMAN BEINGS.
AND IF THAT IS THE CASE...
...WHY CAN A HUMAN NOT TAKE THE THRONE?
...!
ZOKU (SHUDDER)

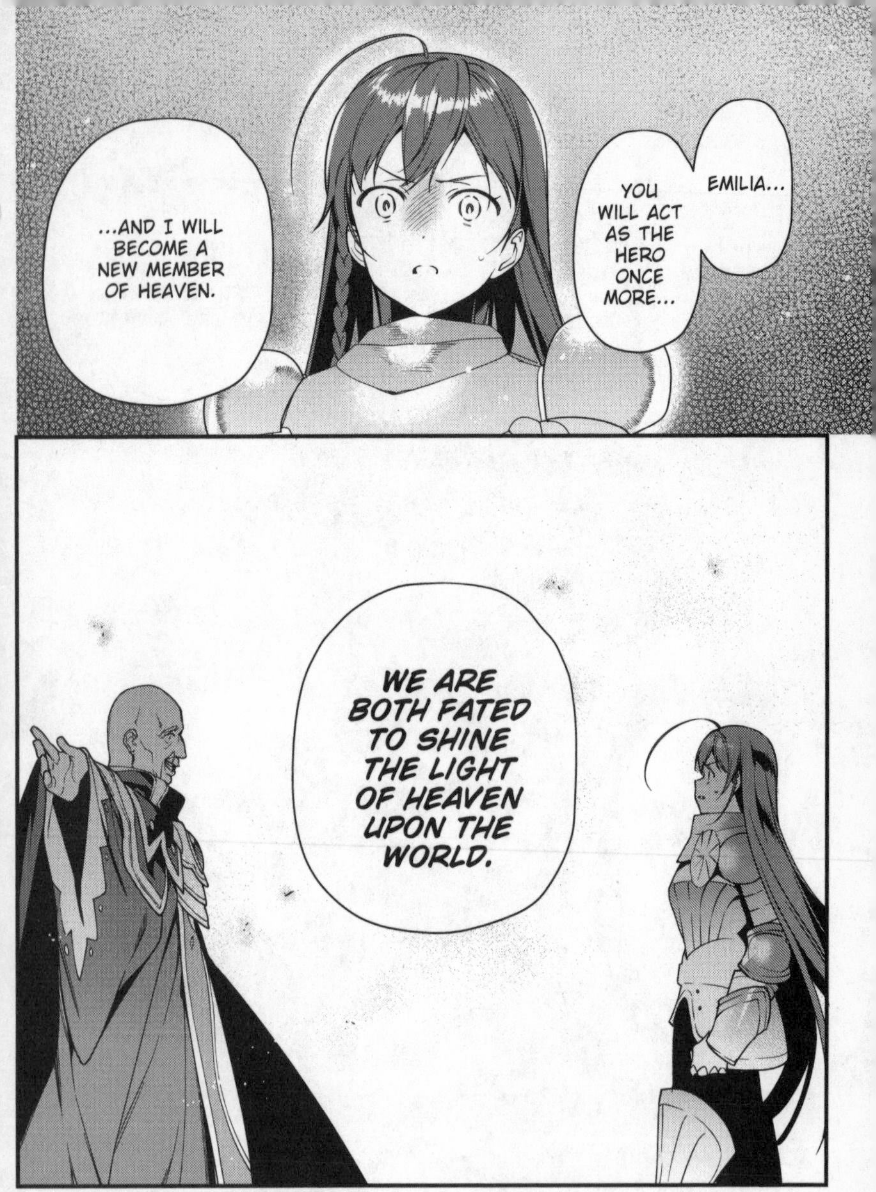
EMILIA...
YOU WILL ACT AS THE HERO ONCE MORE...
...AND I WILL BECOME A NEW MEMBER OF HEAVEN.
WE ARE BOTH FATED TO SHINE THE LIGHT OF HEAVEN UPON THE WORLD.

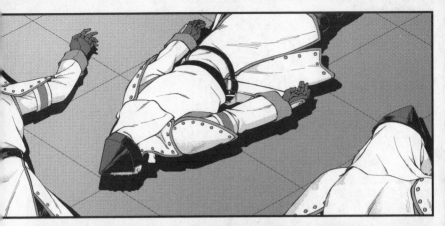

OH MAN, WHAT A MESS.

HEY...

...

YOU HEARD ME, DIDN'T YOU? I TRIED TO STOP 'EM.

CAN WE KINDA TRY TO MAKE THIS AN ACTUAL CONVERSATION?

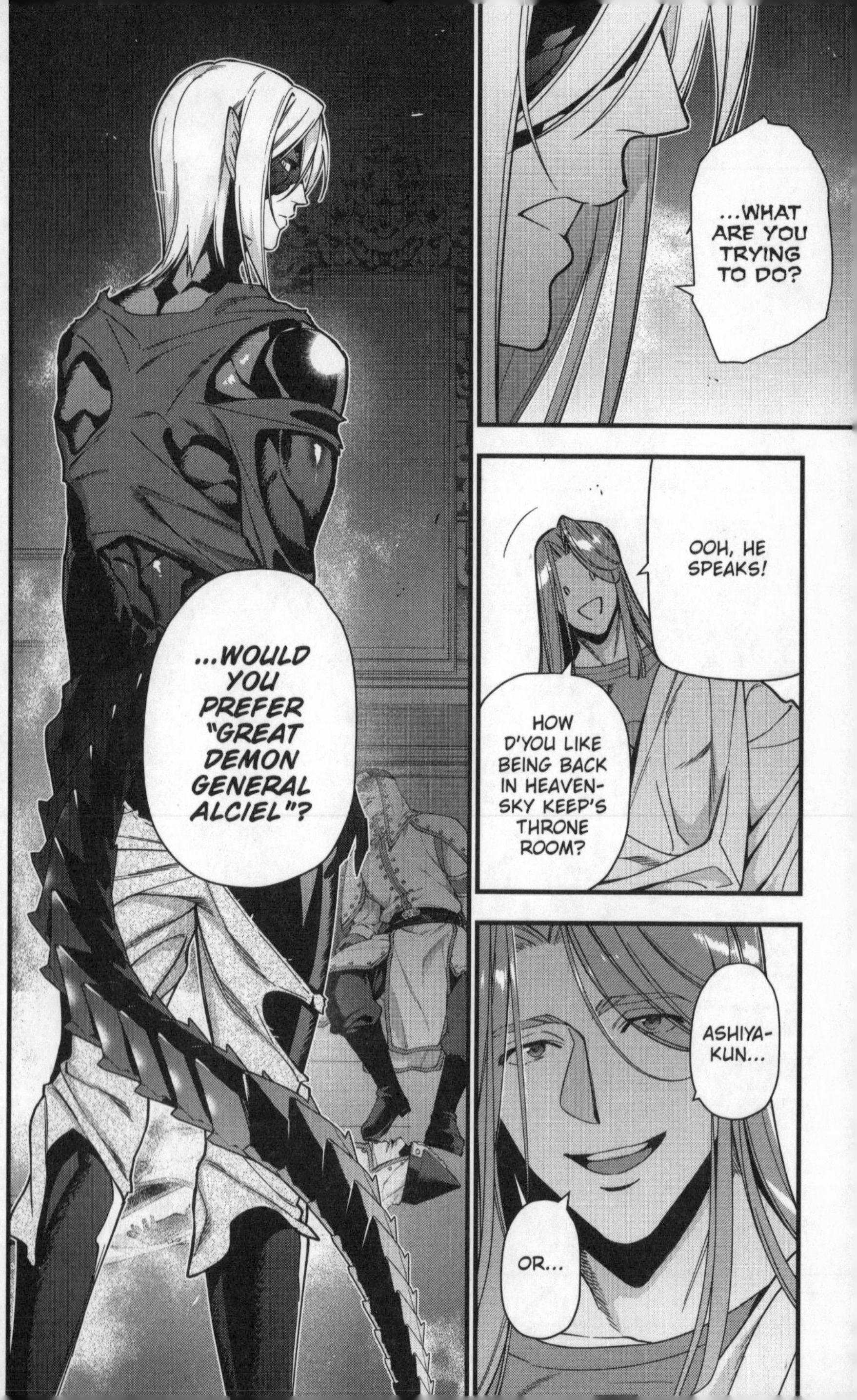
...WHAT ARE YOU TRYING TO DO?
OOH, HE SPEAKS!
HOW D'YOU LIKE BEING BACK IN HEAVEN-SKY KEEP'S THRONE ROOM?
ASHIYA-KUN...
OR...
...WOULD YOU PREFER "GREAT DEMON GENERAL ALCIEL"?

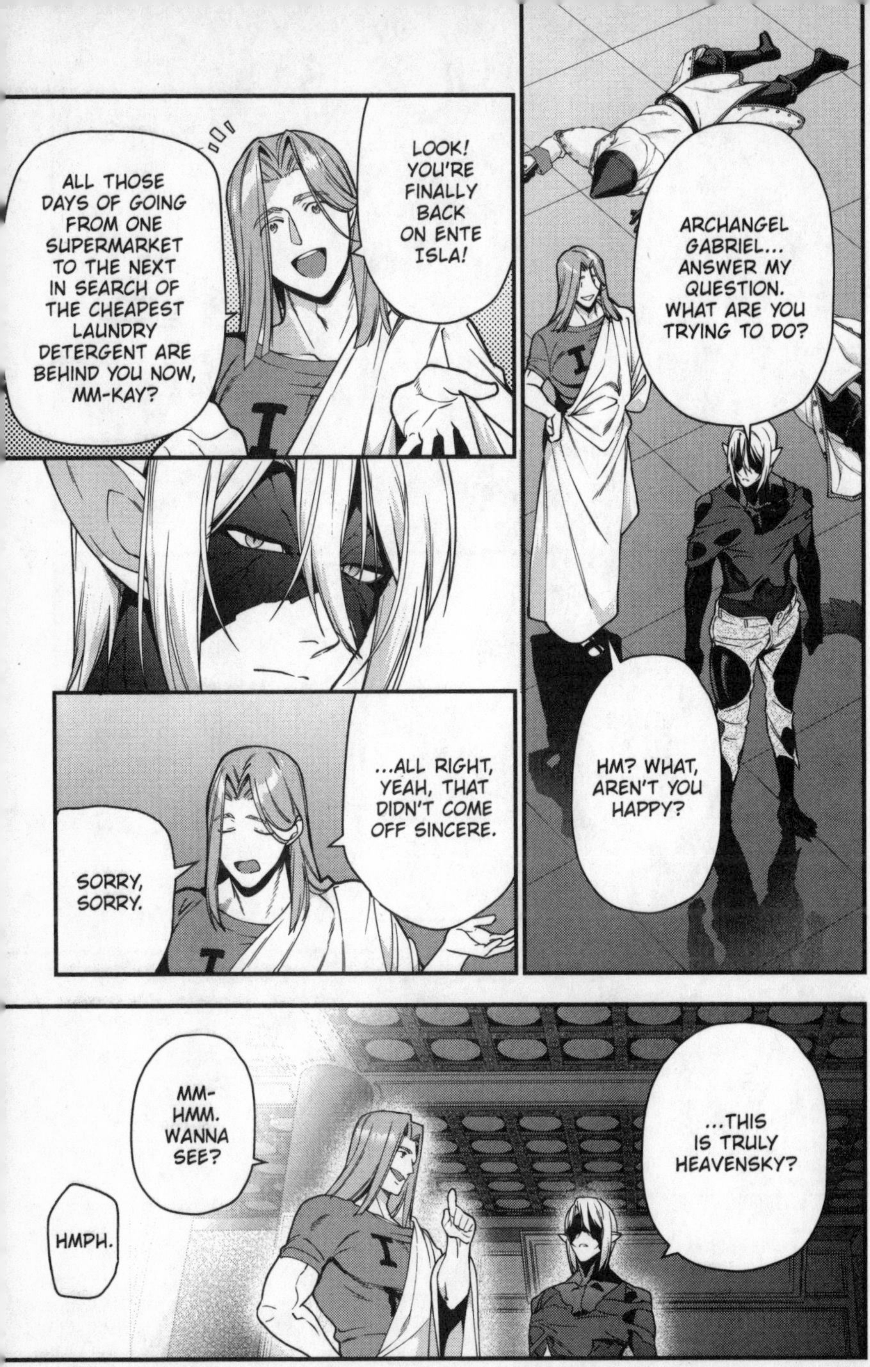
ARCHANGEL GABRIEL... ANSWER MY QUESTION. WHAT ARE YOU TRYING TO DO?
HM? WHAT, AREN'T YOU HAPPY?
LOOK! YOU'RE FINALLY BACK ON ENTE ISLA!
ALL THOSE DAYS OF GOING FROM ONE SUPERMARKET TO THE NEXT IN SEARCH OF THE CHEAPEST LAUNDRY DETERGENT ARE BEHIND YOU NOW, MM-KAY?
...ALL RIGHT, YEAH, THAT DIDN'T COME OFF SINCERE.
SORRY, SORRY.
...THIS IS TRULY HEAVENSKY?
MM-HMM. WANNA SEE?
HMPH.

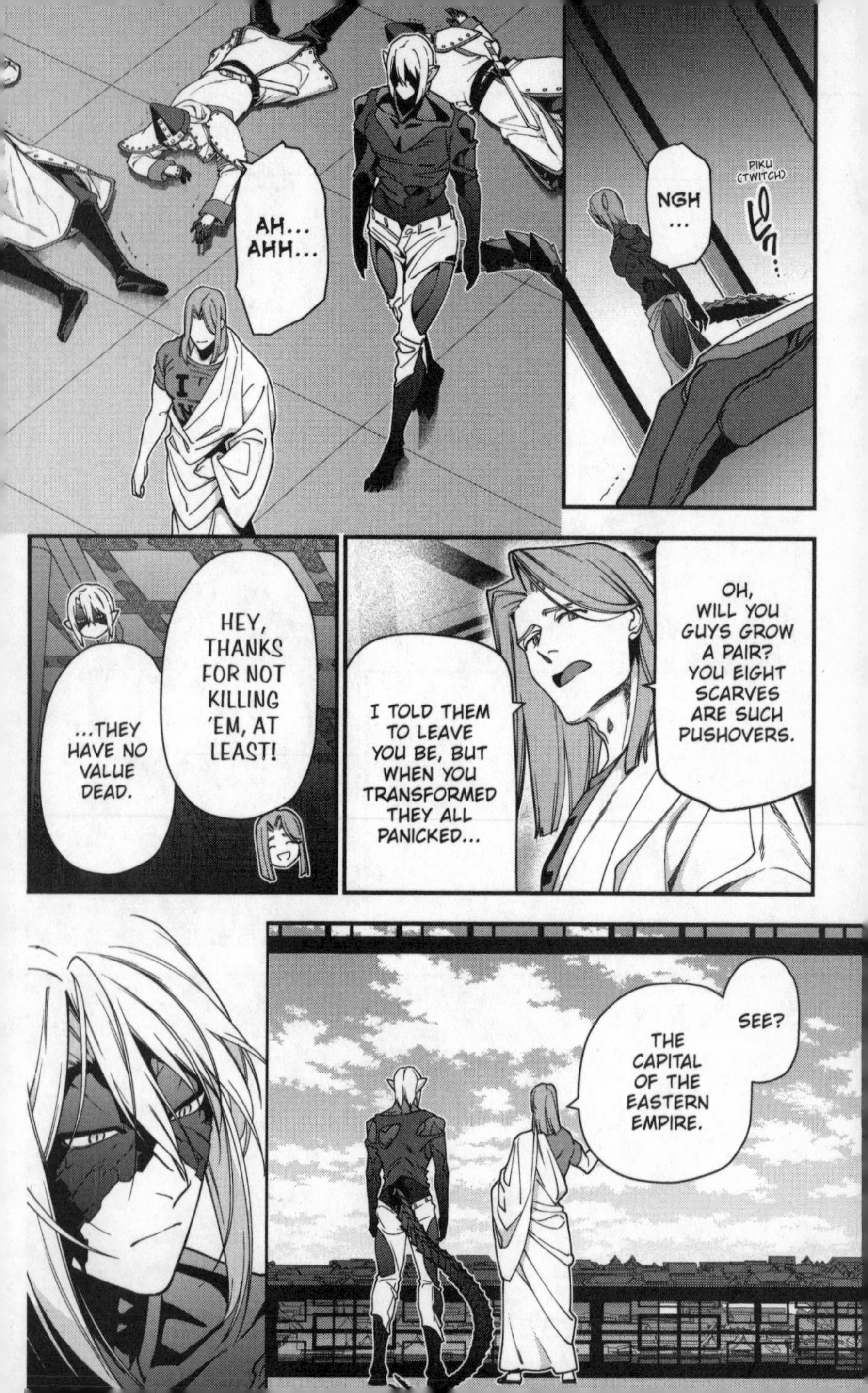
PIKU (TWITCH)
NGH ...
AH... AHH...
OH, WILL YOU GUYS GROW A PAIR? YOU EIGHT SCARVES ARE SUCH PUSHOVERS.
I TOLD THEM TO LEAVE YOU BE, BUT WHEN YOU TRANSFORMED THEY ALL PANICKED...
HEY, THANKS FOR NOT KILLING 'EM, AT LEAST!
...THEY HAVE NO VALUE DEAD.
SEE?
THE CAPITAL OF THE EASTERN EMPIRE.

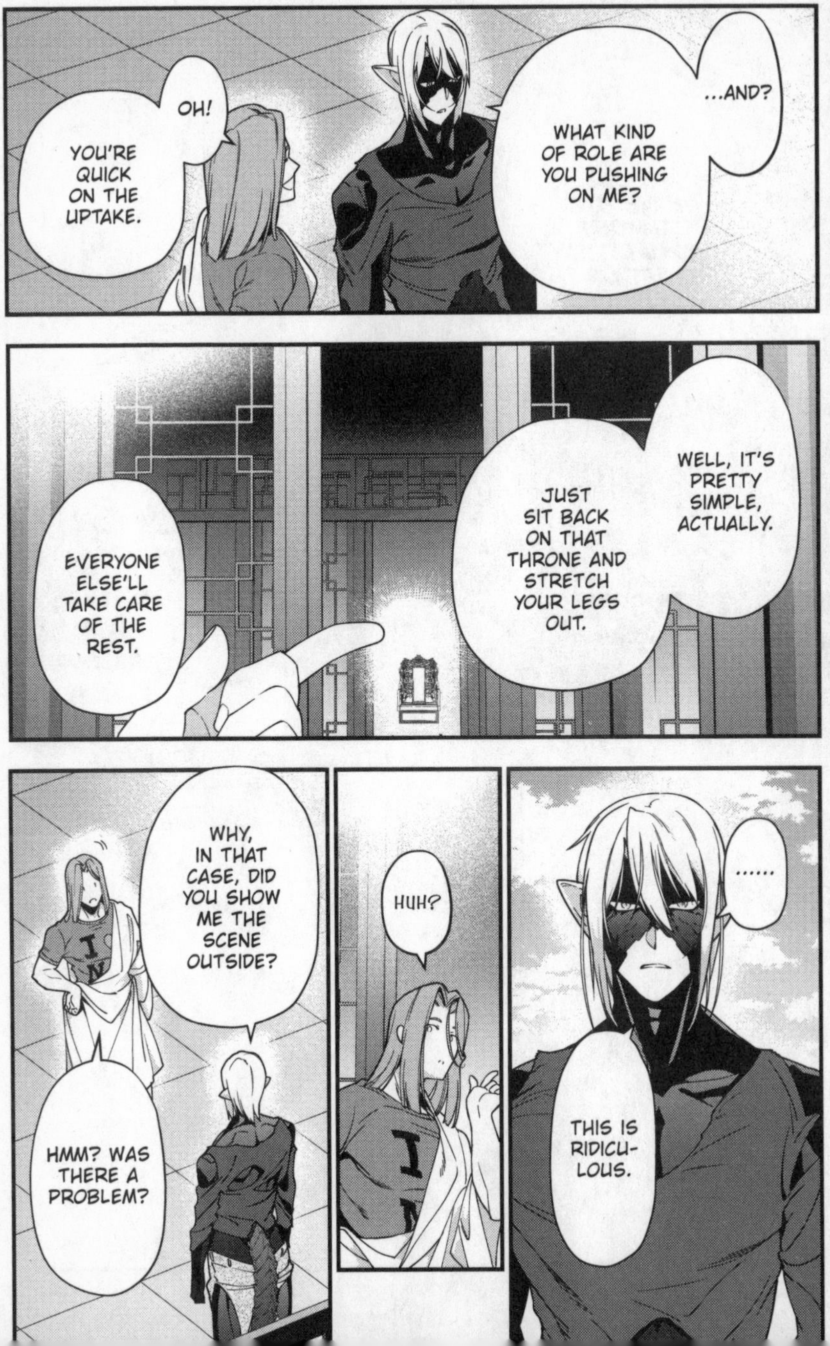
...AND?
WHAT KIND OF ROLE ARE YOU PUSHING ON ME?
OH!
YOU'RE QUICK ON THE UPTAKE.
WELL, IT'S PRETTY SIMPLE, ACTUALLY.
JUST SIT BACK ON THAT THRONE AND STRETCH YOUR LEGS OUT.
EVERYONE ELSE'LL TAKE CARE OF THE REST.
......
THIS IS RIDICU-LOUS.
HUH?
WHY, IN THAT CASE, DID YOU SHOW ME THE SCENE OUTSIDE?
HMM? WAS THERE A PROBLEM?

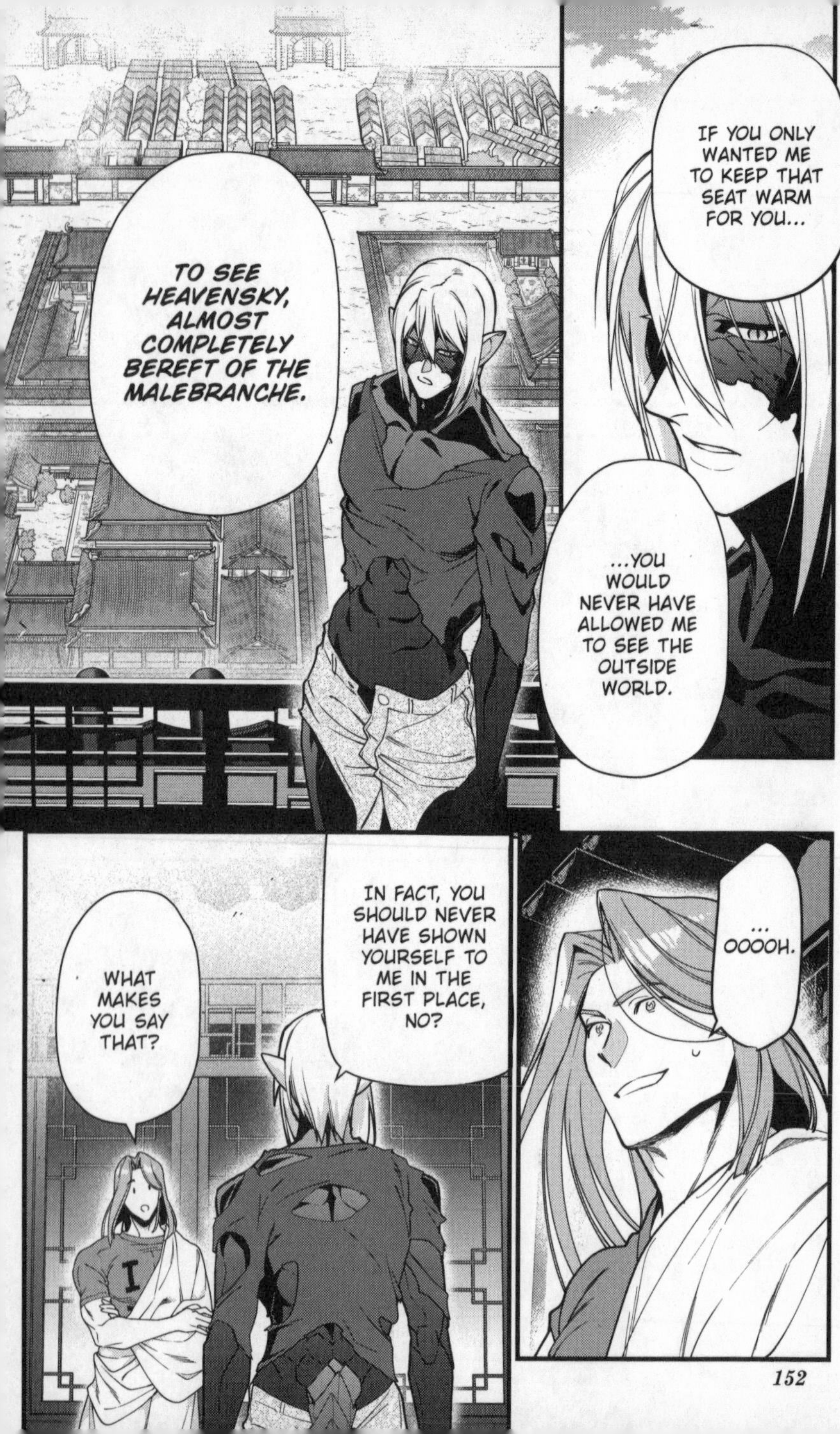
IF YOU ONLY WANTED ME TO KEEP THAT SEAT WARM FOR YOU...
...YOU WOULD NEVER HAVE ALLOWED ME TO SEE THE OUTSIDE WORLD.
TO SEE HEAVENSKY, ALMOST COMPLETELY BEREFT OF THE MALEBRANCHE.
...OOOOH.
IN FACT, YOU SHOULD NEVER HAVE SHOWN YOURSELF TO ME IN THE FIRST PLACE, NO?
WHAT MAKES YOU SAY THAT?

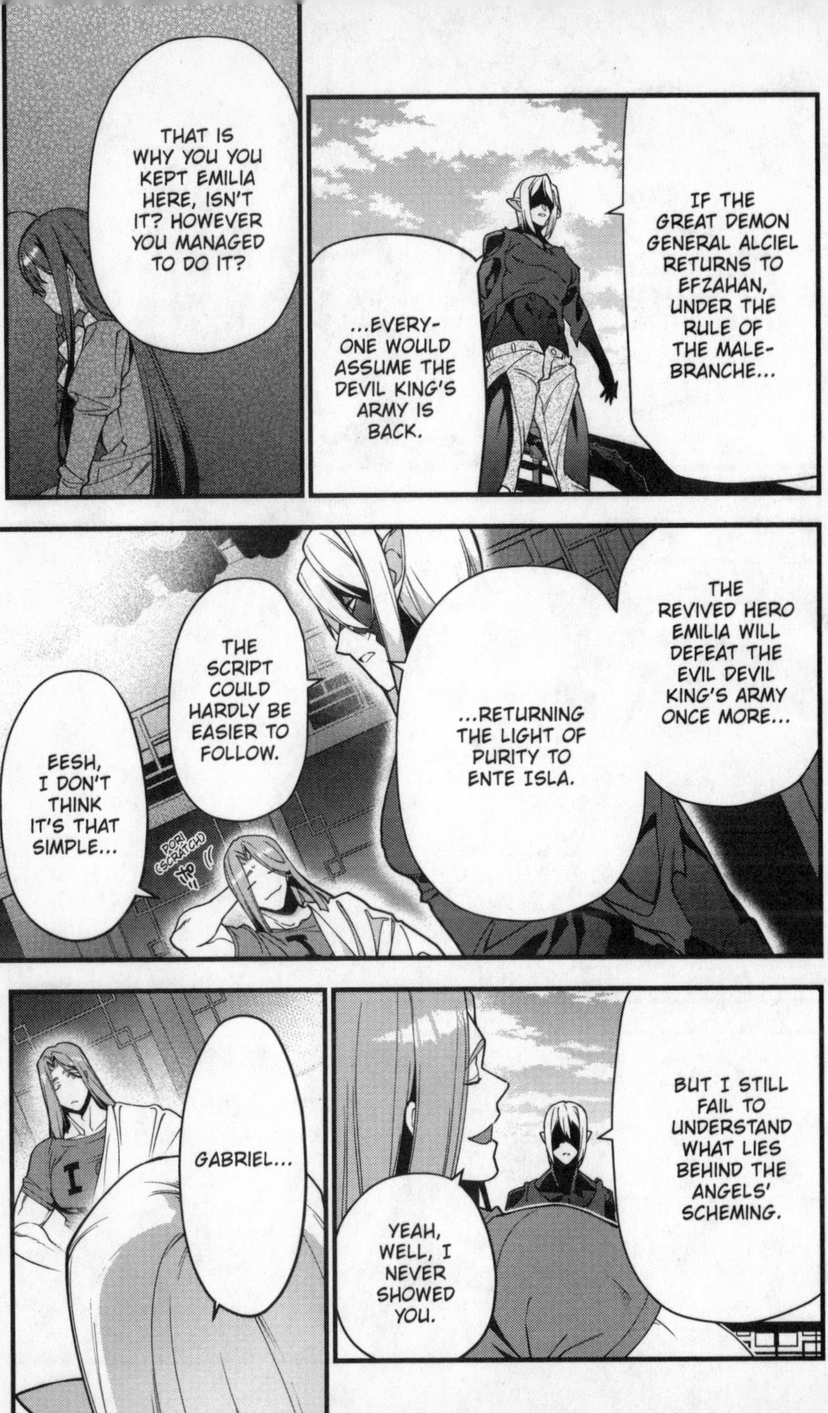
IF THE GREAT DEMON GENERAL ALCIEL RETURNS TO EFZAHAN, UNDER THE RULE OF THE MALE-BRANCHE...
...EVERY-ONE WOULD ASSUME THE DEVIL KING'S ARMY IS BACK.
THAT IS WHY YOU YOU KEPT EMILIA HERE, ISN'T IT? HOWEVER YOU MANAGED TO DO IT?
THE REVIVED HERO EMILIA WILL DEFEAT THE EVIL DEVIL KING'S ARMY ONCE MORE...
...RETURNING THE LIGHT OF PURITY TO ENTE ISLA.
THE SCRIPT COULD HARDLY BE EASIER TO FOLLOW.
PORI (SCRATCH)
EESH, I DON'T THINK IT'S THAT SIMPLE...
BUT I STILL FAIL TO UNDERSTAND WHAT LIES BEHIND THE ANGELS' SCHEMING.
YEAH, WELL, I NEVER SHOWED YOU.
GABRIEL...

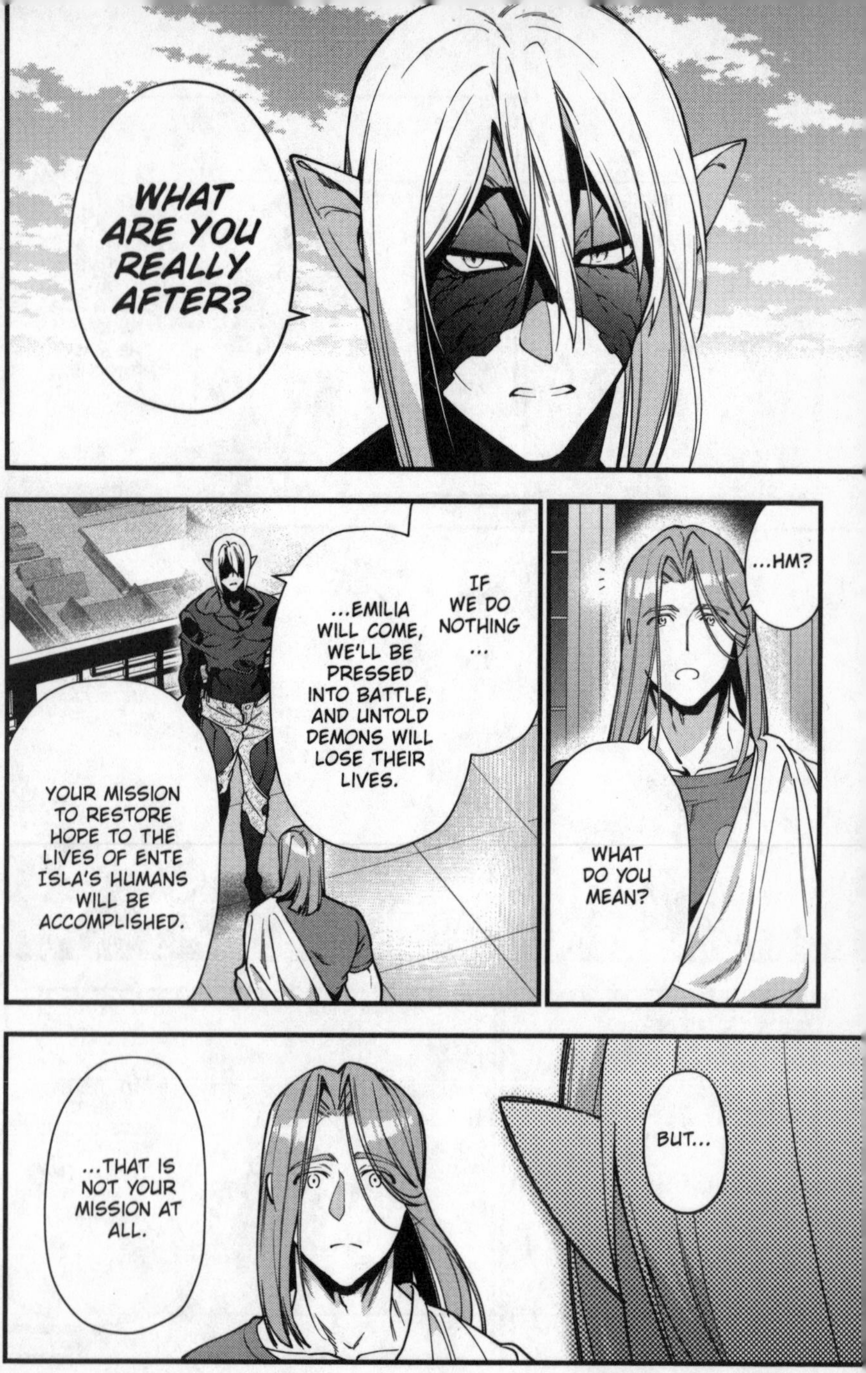
WHAT ARE YOU REALLY AFTER?
...HM?
WHAT DO YOU MEAN?
IF WE DO NOTHING ...
...EMILIA WILL COME, WE'LL BE PRESSED INTO BATTLE, AND UNTOLD DEMONS WILL LOSE THEIR LIVES.
YOUR MISSION TO RESTORE HOPE TO THE LIVES OF ENTE ISLA'S HUMANS WILL BE ACCOMPLISHED.
BUT...
...THAT IS NOT YOUR MISSION AT ALL.

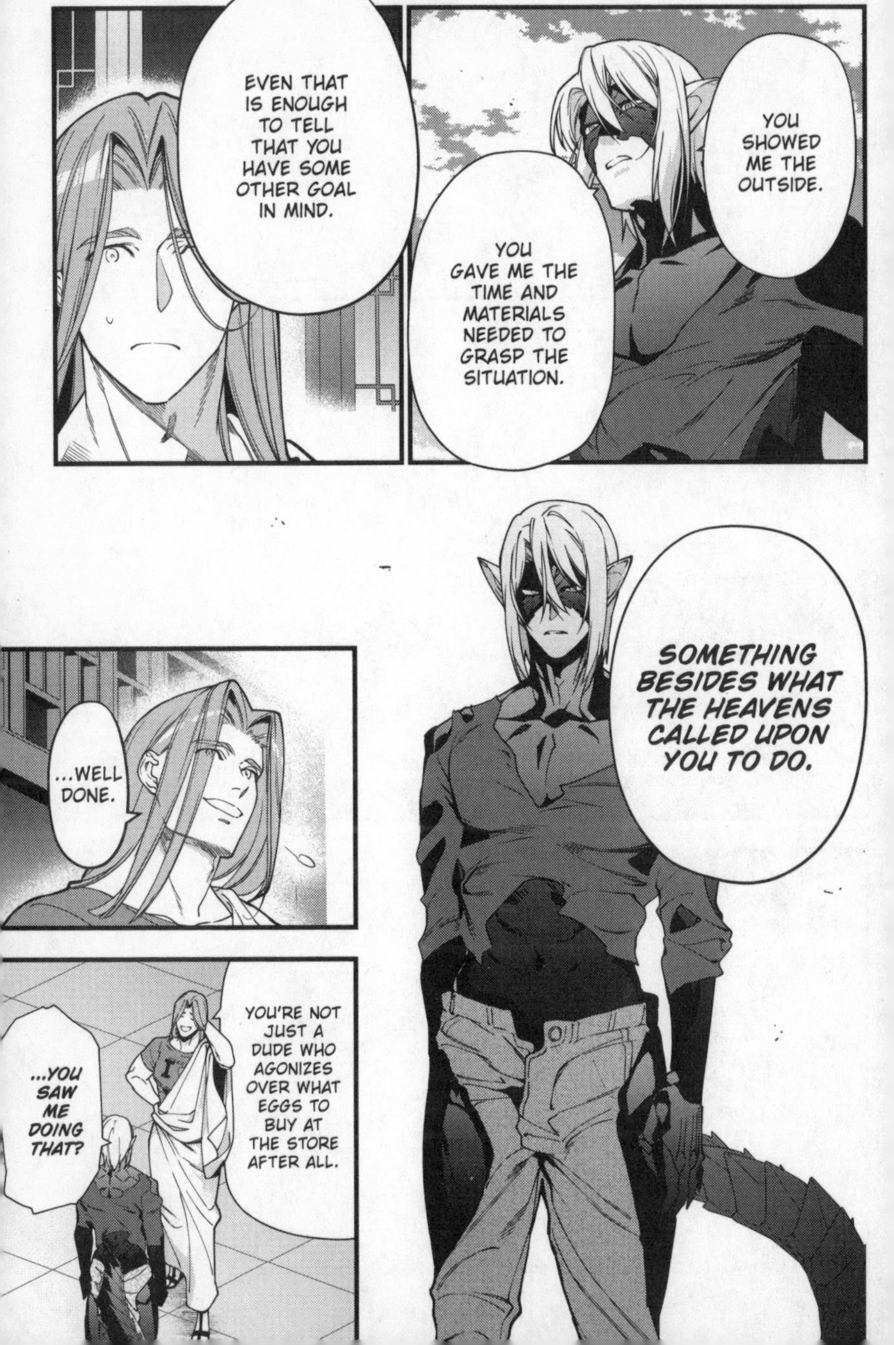
YOU SHOWED ME THE OUTSIDE.
YOU GAVE ME THE TIME AND MATERIALS NEEDED TO GRASP THE SITUATION.
EVEN THAT IS ENOUGH TO TELL THAT YOU HAVE SOME OTHER GOAL IN MIND.
SOMETHING BESIDES WHAT THE HEAVENS CALLED UPON YOU TO DO.
...WELL DONE.
YOU'RE NOT JUST A DUDE WHO AGONIZES OVER WHAT EGGS TO BUY AT THE STORE AFTER ALL.
...YOU SAW ME DOING THAT?

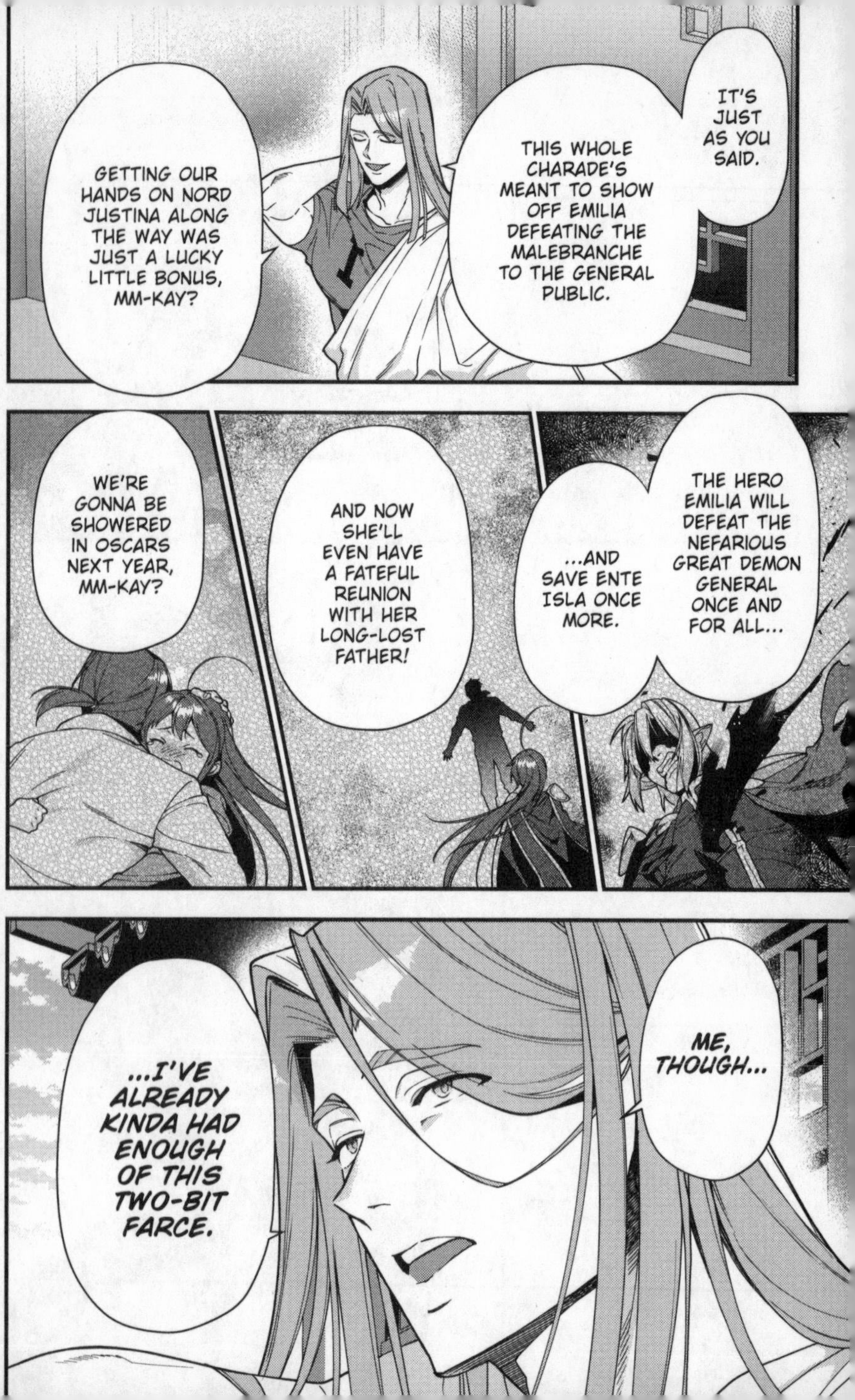
IT'S JUST AS YOU SAID.
THIS WHOLE CHARADE'S MEANT TO SHOW OFF EMILIA DEFEATING THE MALEBRANCHE TO THE GENERAL PUBLIC.
GETTING OUR HANDS ON NORD JUSTINA ALONG THE WAY WAS JUST A LUCKY LITTLE BONUS, MM-KAY?
THE HERO EMILIA WILL DEFEAT THE NEFARIOUS GREAT DEMON GENERAL ONCE AND FOR ALL...
...AND SAVE ENTE ISLA ONCE MORE.
AND NOW SHE'LL EVEN HAVE A FATEFUL REUNION WITH HER LONG-LOST FATHER!
WE'RE GONNA BE SHOWERED IN OSCARS NEXT YEAR, MM-KAY?
ME, THOUGH...
...I'VE ALREADY KINDA HAD ENOUGH OF THIS TWO-BIT FARCE.

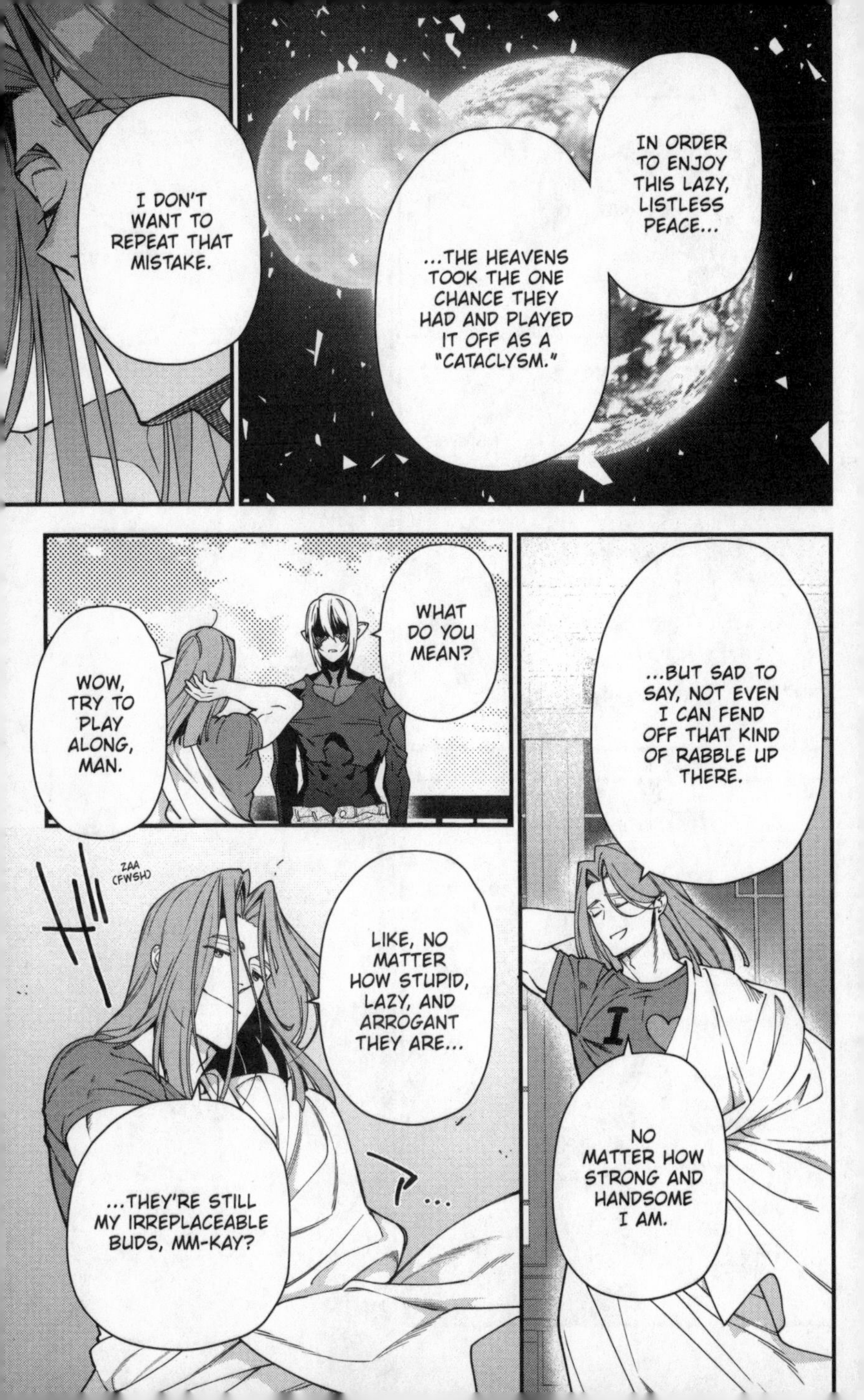
IN ORDER TO ENJOY THIS LAZY, LISTLESS PEACE...
...THE HEAVENS TOOK THE ONE CHANCE THEY HAD AND PLAYED IT OFF AS A "CATACLYSM."
I DON'T WANT TO REPEAT THAT MISTAKE.
...BUT SAD TO SAY, NOT EVEN I CAN FEND OFF THAT KIND OF RABBLE UP THERE.
NO MATTER HOW STRONG AND HANDSOME I AM.
WHAT DO YOU MEAN?
WOW, TRY TO PLAY ALONG, MAN.
ZAA (FWSH)
LIKE, NO MATTER HOW STUPID, LAZY, AND ARROGANT THEY ARE...
...THEY'RE STILL MY IRREPLACEABLE BUDS, MM-KAY?

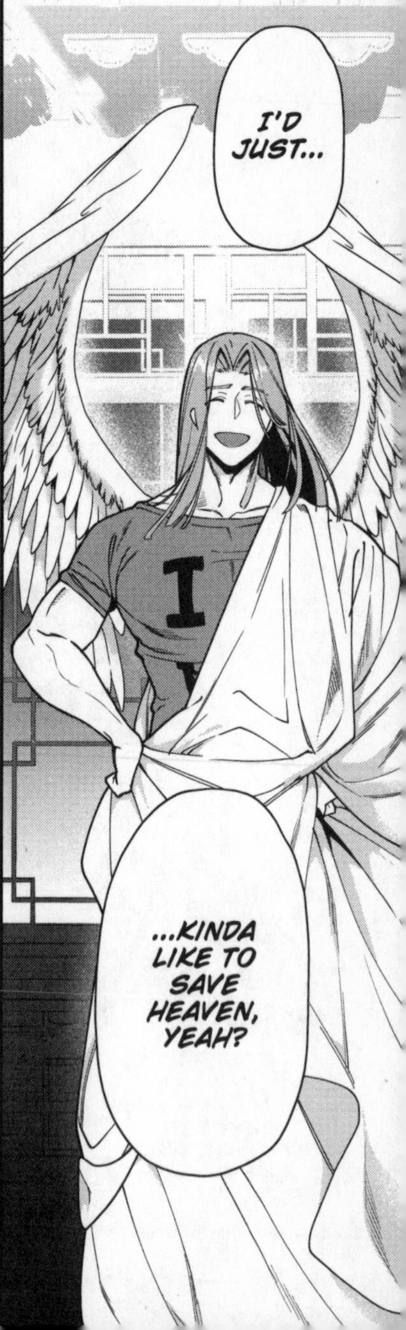
I'D JUST...
...KINDA LIKE TO SAVE HEAVEN, YEAH?

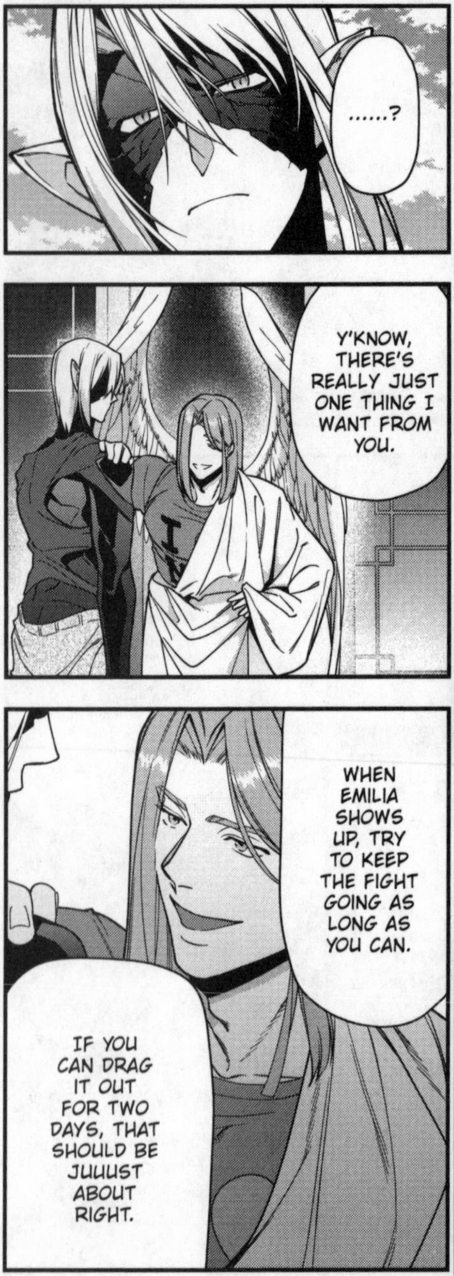
......?
Y'KNOW, THERE'S REALLY JUST ONE THING I WANT FROM YOU.
WHEN EMILIA SHOWS UP, TRY TO KEEP THE FIGHT GOING AS LONG AS YOU CAN.
IF YOU CAN DRAG IT OUT FOR TWO DAYS, THAT SHOULD BE JUUUST ABOUT RIGHT.

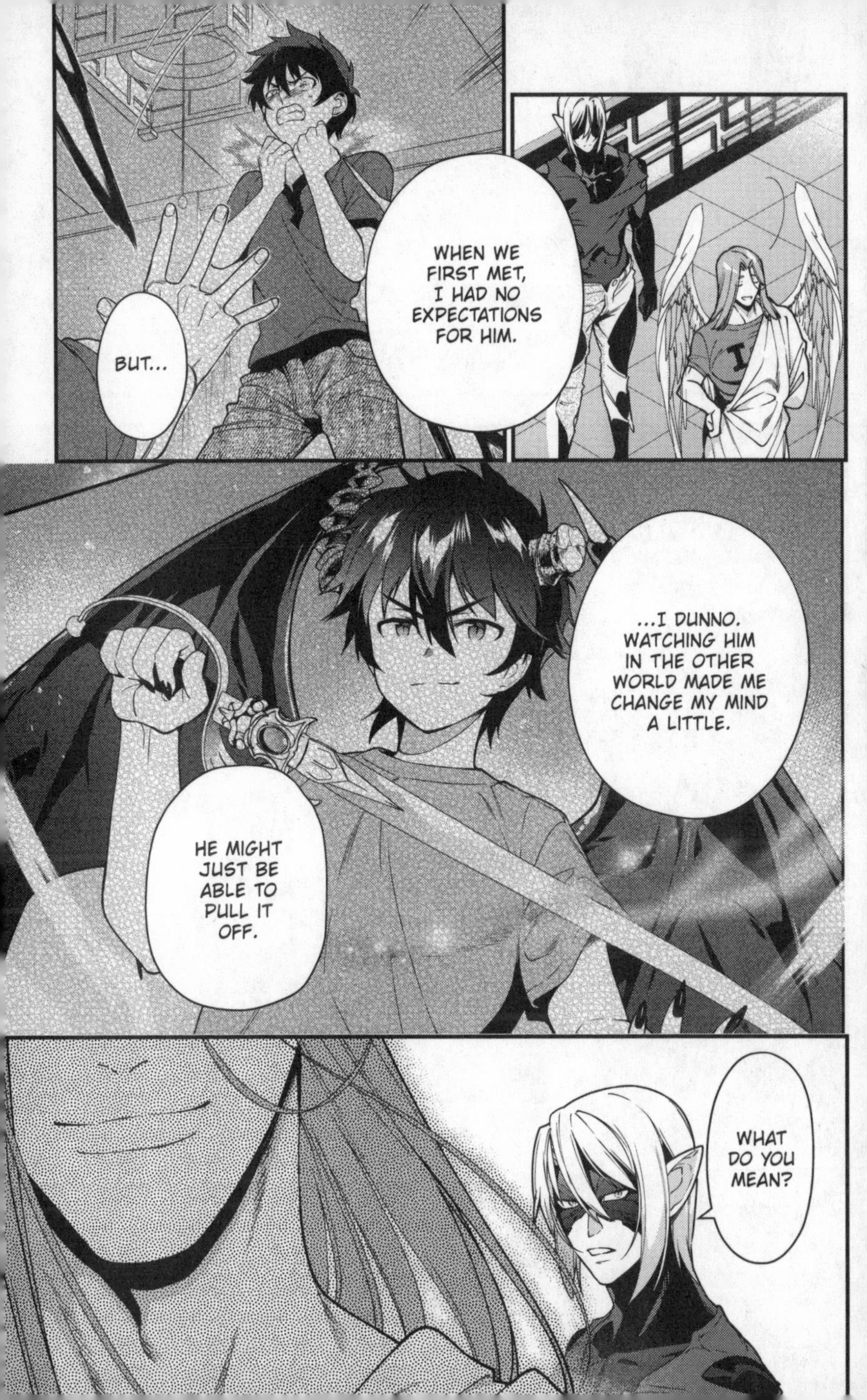
WHEN WE FIRST MET, I HAD NO EXPECTATIONS FOR HIM.
BUT...
...I DUNNO. WATCHING HIM IN THE OTHER WORLD MADE ME CHANGE MY MIND A LITTLE.
HE MIGHT JUST BE ABLE TO PULL IT OFF.
WHAT DO YOU MEAN?

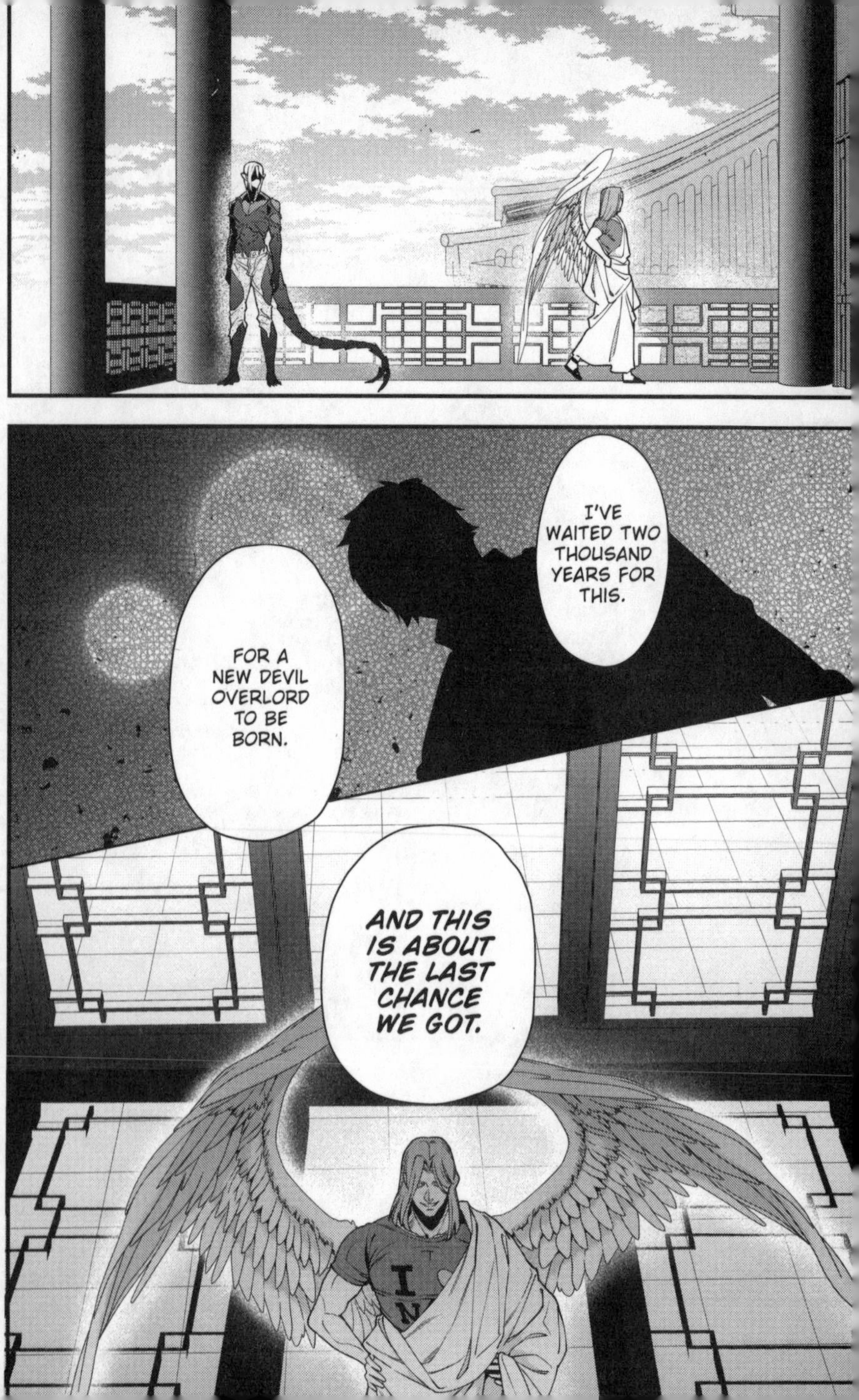
I'VE WAITED TWO THOUSAND YEARS FOR THIS.
FOR A NEW DEVIL OVERLORD TO BE BORN.
AND THIS IS ABOUT THE LAST CHANCE WE GOT.

Emilia
Justina

THE DEVIL IS A PART-TIMER!

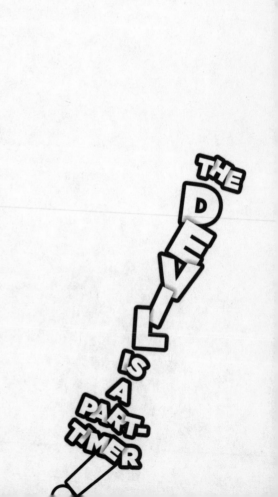

CHAPTER 89: THE DEVIL'S LIKE AN OPEN BOOK

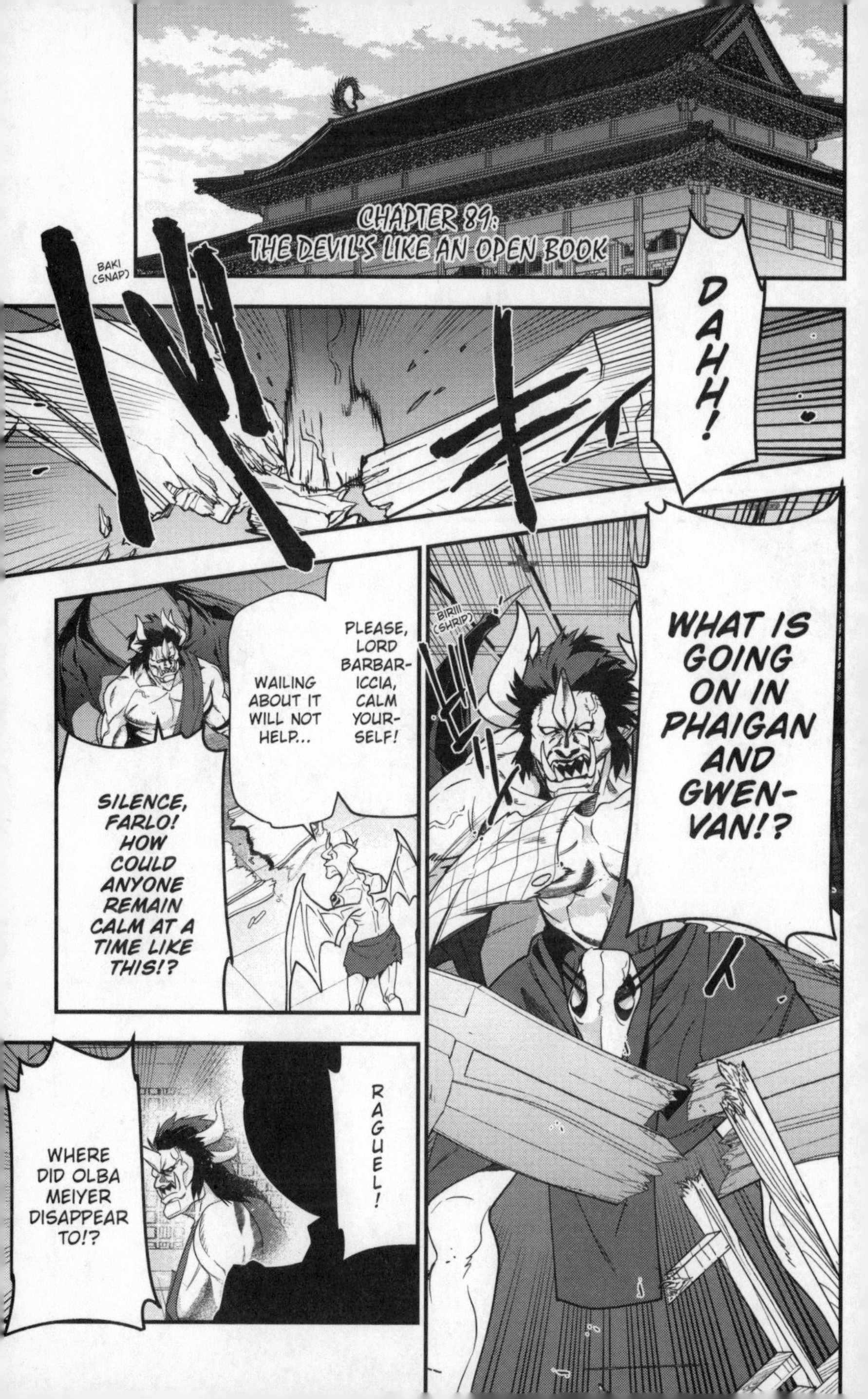
DAHH!
BAKI (SNAP)
WHAT IS GOING ON IN PHAIGAN AND GWEN-VAN!?
BIRIII (SHRIP)
PLEASE, LORD BARBAR-ICCIA, CALM YOUR-SELF!
WAILING ABOUT IT WILL NOT HELP...
SILENCE, FARLO! HOW COULD ANYONE REMAIN CALM AT A TIME LIKE THIS!?
RAGUEL!
WHERE DID OLBA MEIYER DISAPPEAR TO!?

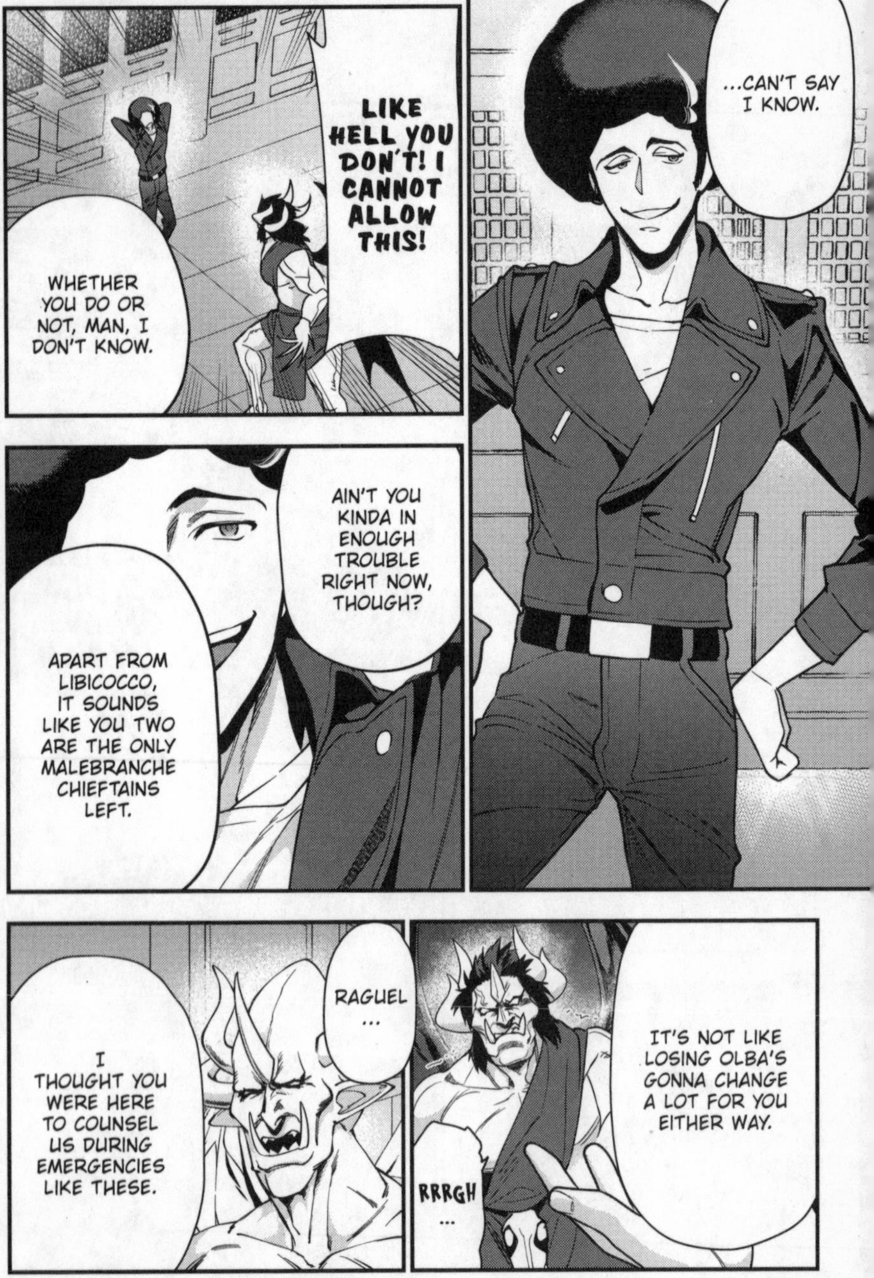
...CAN'T SAY I KNOW.
LIKE HELL YOU DON'T! I CANNOT ALLOW THIS!
WHETHER YOU DO OR NOT, MAN, I DON'T KNOW.
AIN'T YOU KINDA IN ENOUGH TROUBLE RIGHT NOW, THOUGH?
APART FROM LIBICOCCO, IT SOUNDS LIKE YOU TWO ARE THE ONLY MALEBRANCHE CHIEFTAINS LEFT.
IT'S NOT LIKE LOSING OLBA'S GONNA CHANGE A LOT FOR YOU EITHER WAY.
RRRGH ...
RAGUEL ...
I THOUGHT YOU WERE HERE TO COUNSEL US DURING EMERGENCIES LIKE THESE.

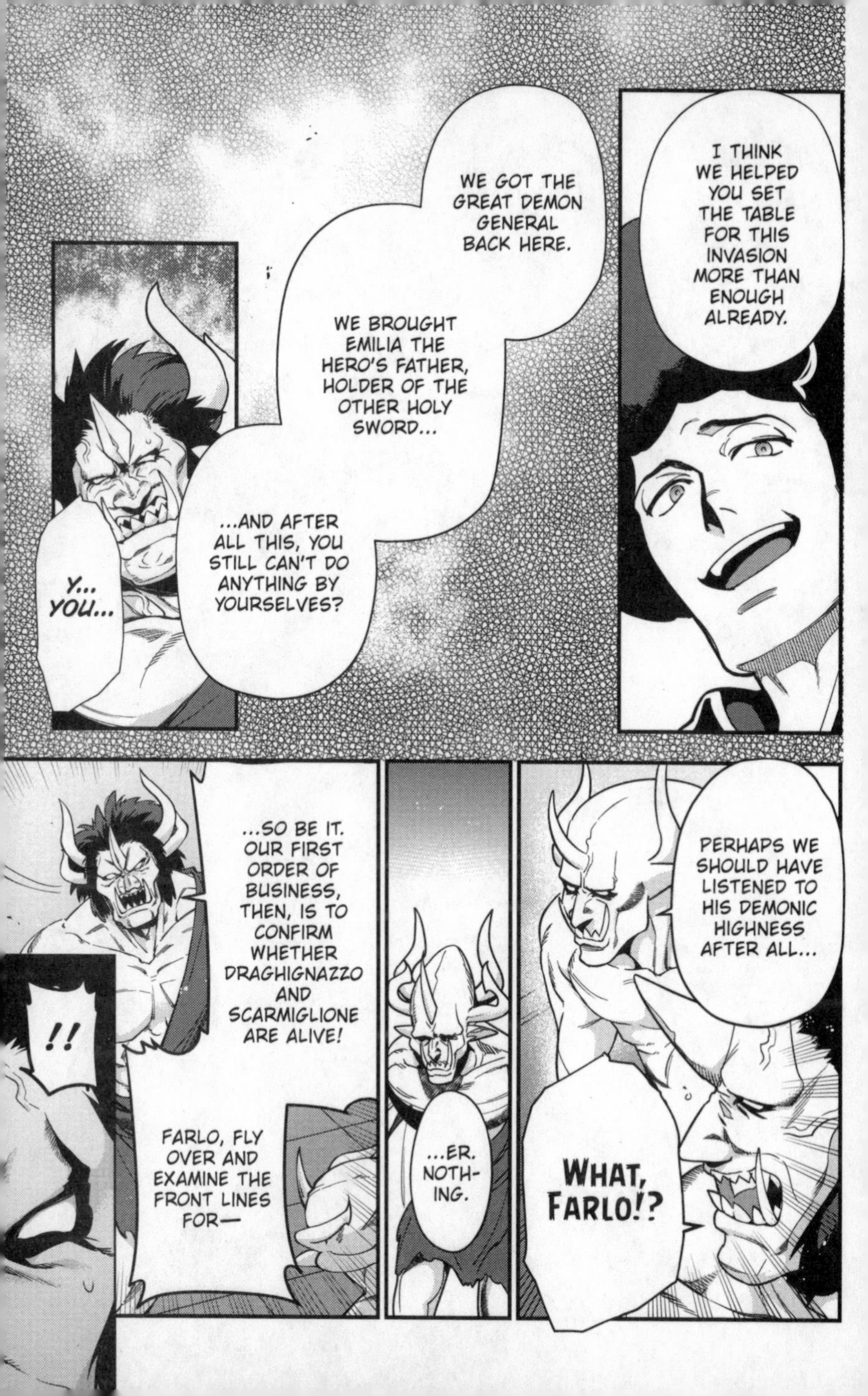
I THINK WE HELPED YOU SET THE TABLE FOR THIS INVASION MORE THAN ENOUGH ALREADY.
WE GOT THE GREAT DEMON GENERAL BACK HERE.
WE BROUGHT EMILIA THE HERO'S FATHER, HOLDER OF THE OTHER HOLY SWORD...
...AND AFTER ALL THIS, YOU STILL CAN'T DO ANYTHING BY YOURSELVES?
Y... YOU...
PERHAPS WE SHOULD HAVE LISTENED TO HIS DEMONIC HIGHNESS AFTER ALL...
WHAT, FARLO!?
...ER. NOTH-ING.
...SO BE IT. OUR FIRST ORDER OF BUSINESS, THEN, IS TO CONFIRM WHETHER DRAGHIGNAZZO AND SCARMIGLIONE ARE ALIVE!
!!
FARLO, FLY OVER AND EXAMINE THE FRONT LINES FOR—

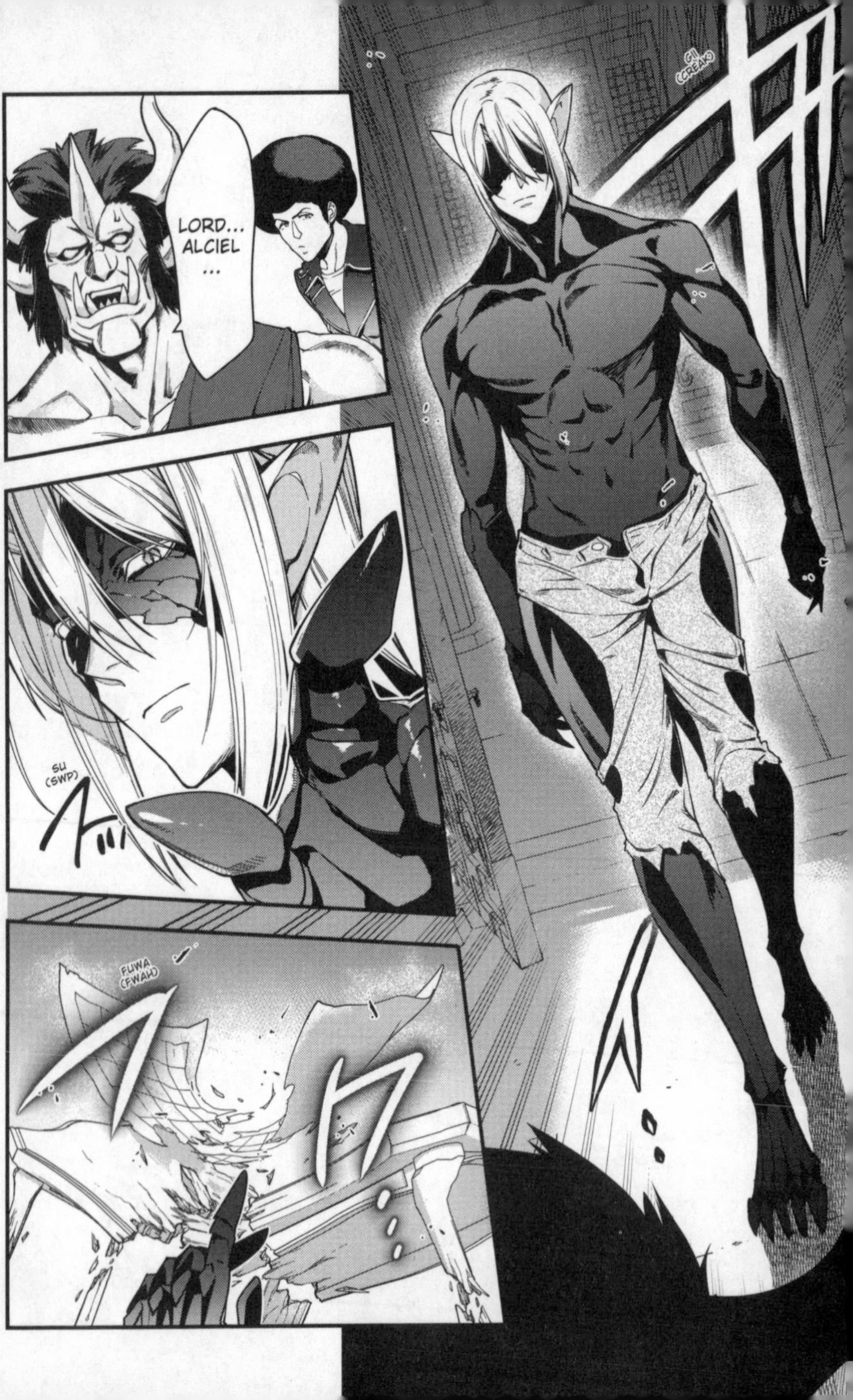
GII
(CREAK)
LORD... ALCIEL ...
SU
(SWP)
FUWA
(FWAH)

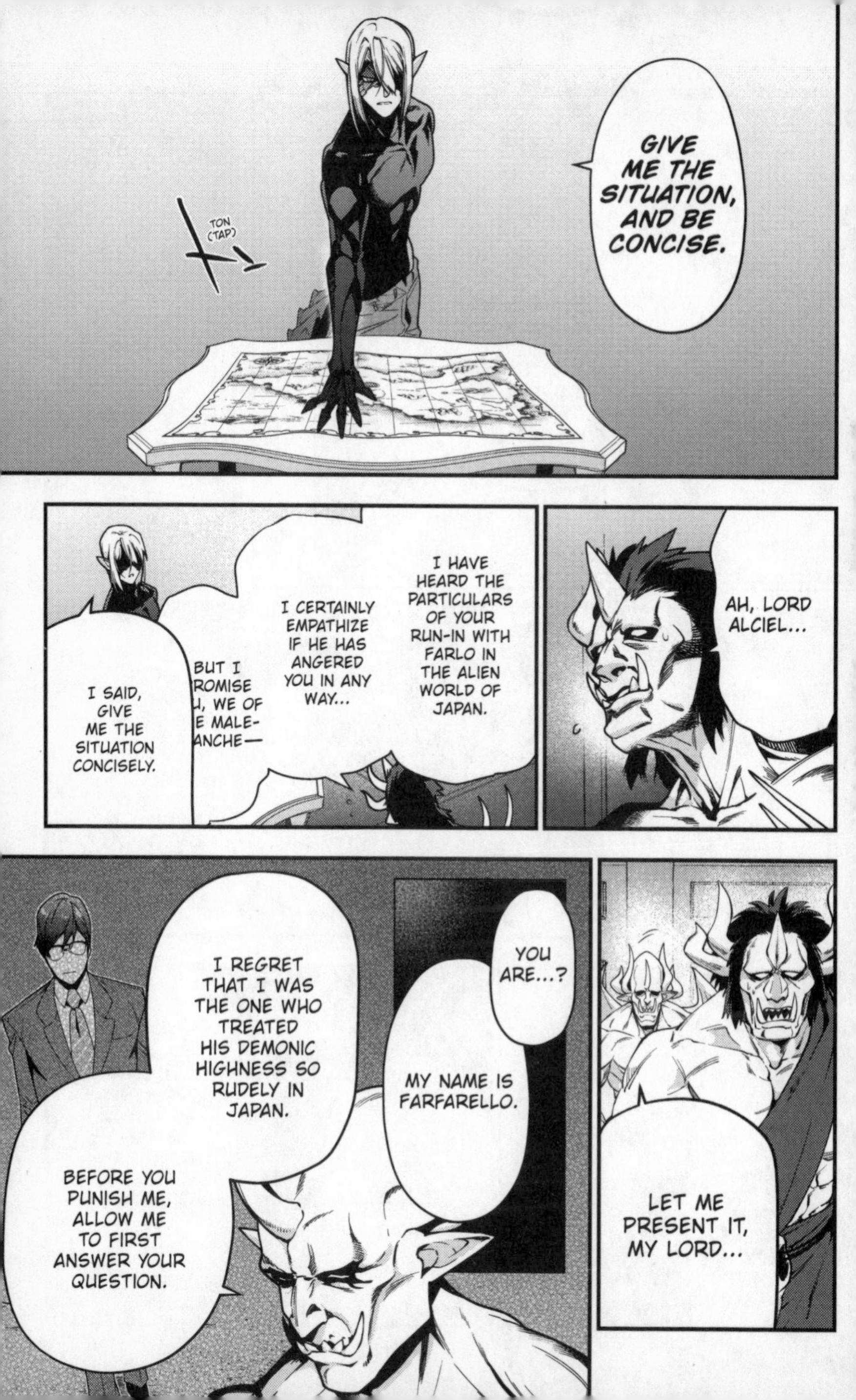
GIVE ME THE SITUATION, AND BE CONCISE.
TON (TAP)
AH, LORD ALCIEL...
I HAVE HEARD THE PARTICULARS OF YOUR RUN-IN WITH FARLO IN THE ALIEN WORLD OF JAPAN.
I CERTAINLY EMPATHIZE IF HE HAS ANGERED YOU IN ANY WAY...
BUT I ROMISE U, WE OF E MALE- ANCHE—
I SAID, GIVE ME THE SITUATION CONCISELY.
LET ME PRESENT IT, MY LORD...
YOU ARE...?
MY NAME IS FARFARELLO.
I REGRET THAT I WAS THE ONE WHO TREATED HIS DEMONIC HIGHNESS SO RUDELY IN JAPAN.
BEFORE YOU PUNISH ME, ALLOW ME TO FIRST ANSWER YOUR QUESTION.

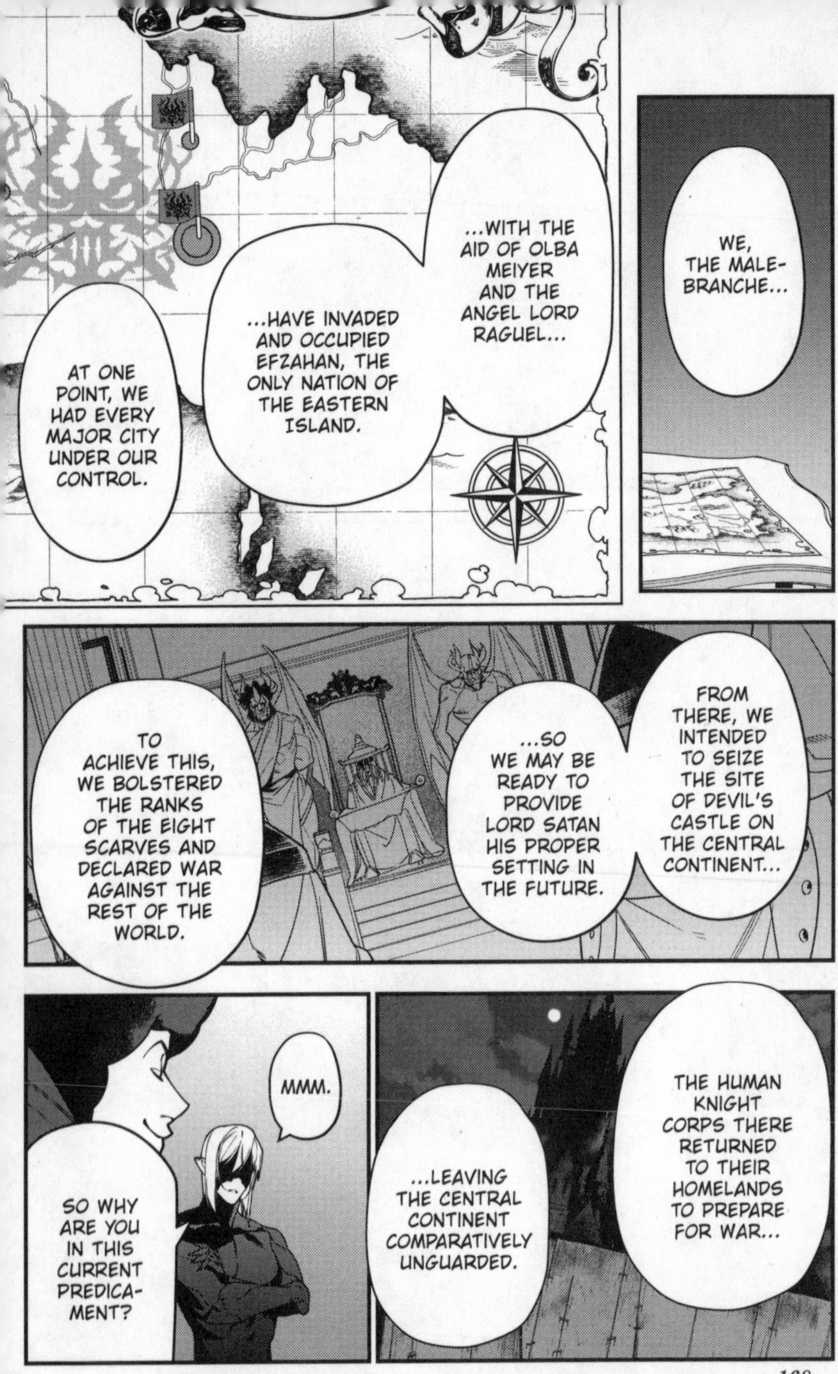
WE, THE MALE-BRANCHE...
...WITH THE AID OF OLBA MEIYER AND THE ANGEL LORD RAGUEL...
...HAVE INVADED AND OCCUPIED EFZAHAN, THE ONLY NATION OF THE EASTERN ISLAND.
AT ONE POINT, WE HAD EVERY MAJOR CITY UNDER OUR CONTROL.
FROM THERE, WE INTENDED TO SEIZE THE SITE OF DEVIL'S CASTLE ON THE CENTRAL CONTINENT...
...SO WE MAY BE READY TO PROVIDE LORD SATAN HIS PROPER SETTING IN THE FUTURE.
TO ACHIEVE THIS, WE BOLSTERED THE RANKS OF THE EIGHT SCARVES AND DECLARED WAR AGAINST THE REST OF THE WORLD.
THE HUMAN KNIGHT CORPS THERE RETURNED TO THEIR HOMELANDS TO PREPARE FOR WAR...
...LEAVING THE CENTRAL CONTINENT COMPARATIVELY UNGUARDED.
MMM.
SO WHY ARE YOU IN THIS CURRENT PREDICA-MENT?

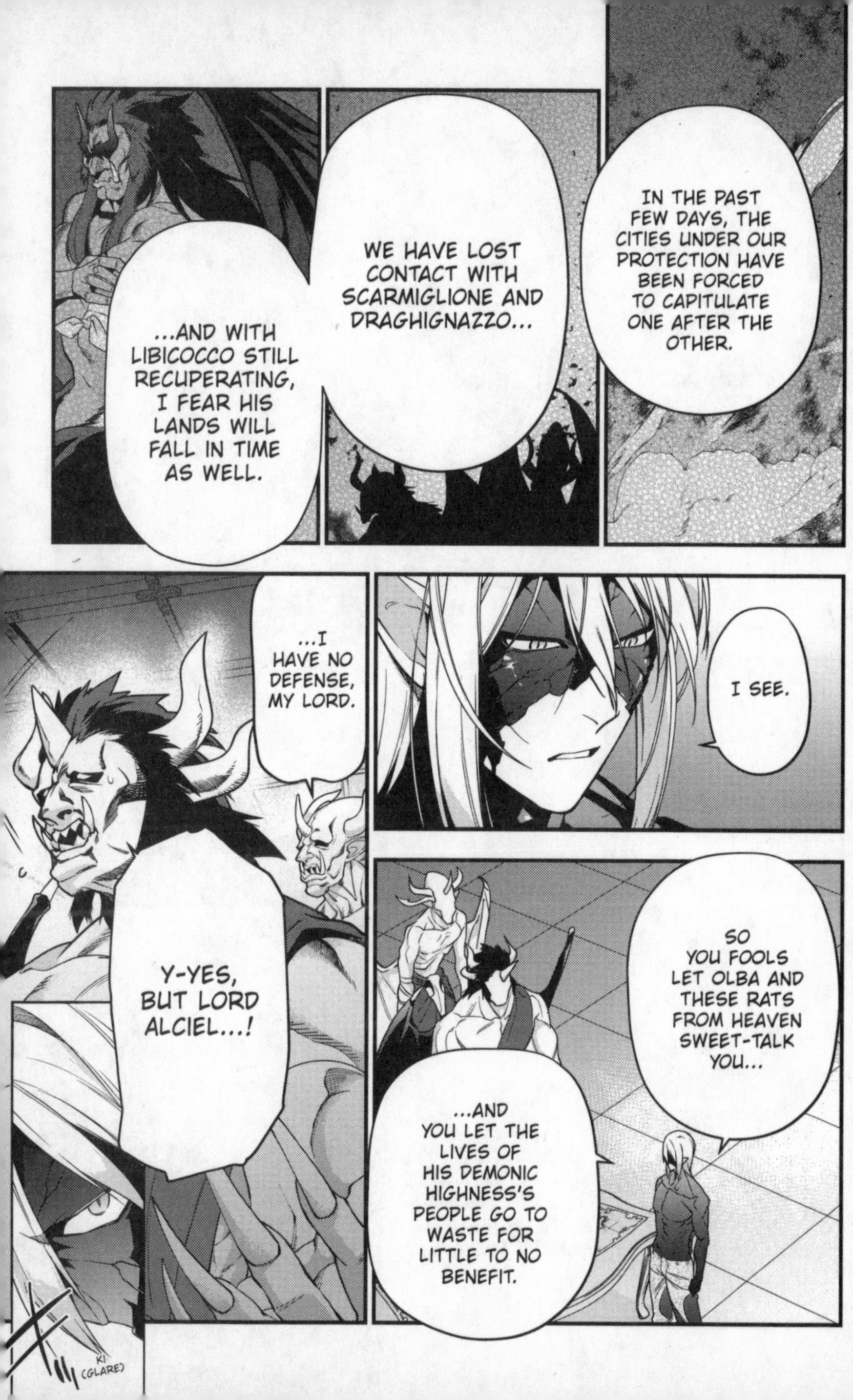
IN THE PAST FEW DAYS, THE CITIES UNDER OUR PROTECTION HAVE BEEN FORCED TO CAPITULATE ONE AFTER THE OTHER.
WE HAVE LOST CONTACT WITH SCARMIGLIONE AND DRAGHIGNAZZO...
...AND WITH LIBICOCCO STILL RECUPERATING, I FEAR HIS LANDS WILL FALL IN TIME AS WELL.
I SEE.
SO YOU FOOLS LET OLBA AND THESE RATS FROM HEAVEN SWEET-TALK YOU...
...AND YOU LET THE LIVES OF HIS DEMONIC HIGHNESS'S PEOPLE GO TO WASTE FOR LITTLE TO NO BENEFIT.
...I HAVE NO DEFENSE, MY LORD.
Y-YES, BUT LORD ALCIEL...!
KI (GLARE)

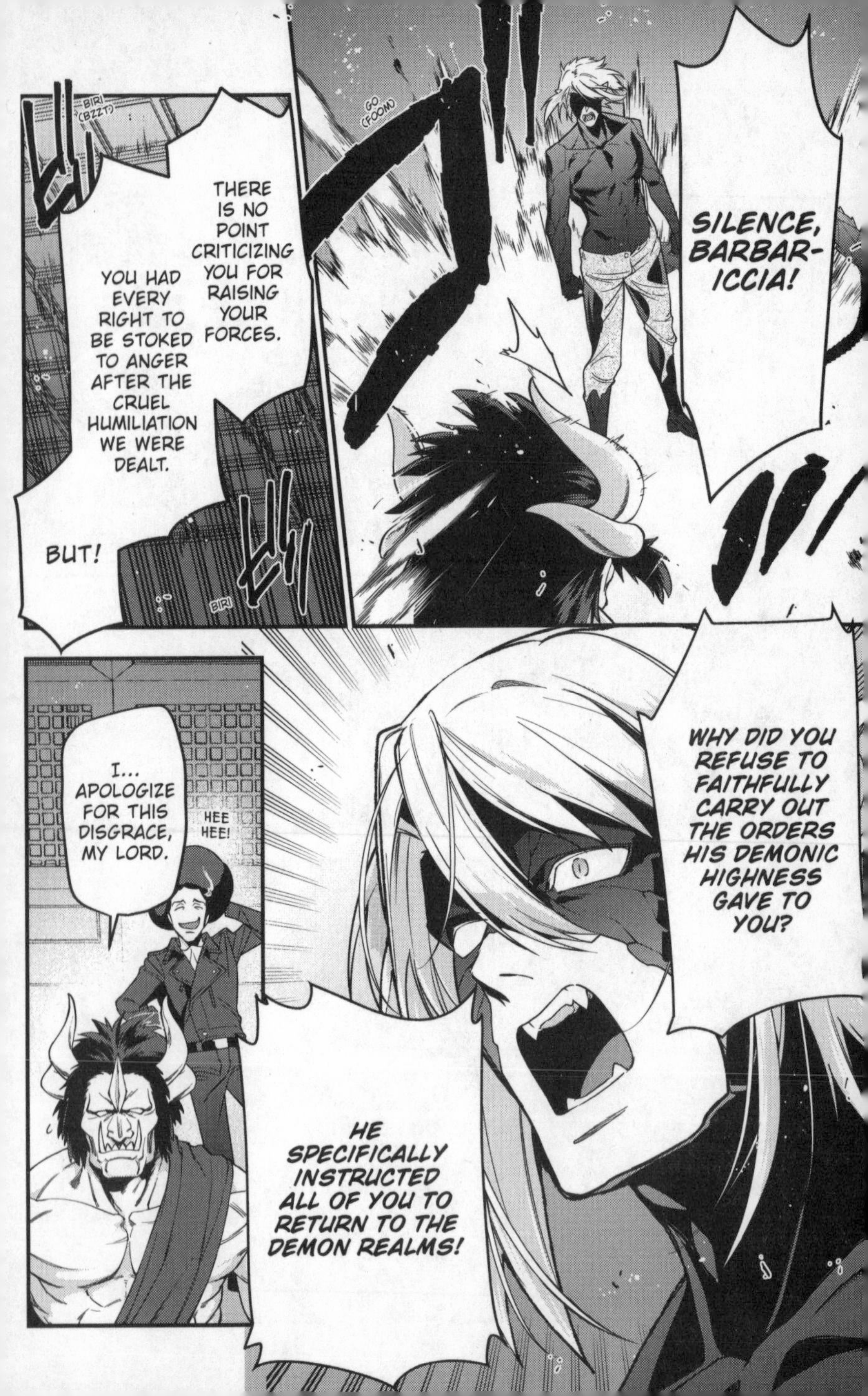
GO (FOOM)
SILENCE, BARBAR-ICCIA!
BIRI (BZZT)
THERE IS NO POINT CRITICIZING YOU FOR RAISING YOUR FORCES.
YOU HAD EVERY RIGHT TO BE STOKED TO ANGER AFTER THE CRUEL HUMILIATION WE WERE DEALT.
BUT!
BIRI
WHY DID YOU REFUSE TO FAITHFULLY CARRY OUT THE ORDERS HIS DEMONIC HIGHNESS GAVE TO YOU?
HE SPECIFICALLY INSTRUCTED ALL OF YOU TO RETURN TO THE DEMON REALMS!
I... APOLOGIZE FOR THIS DISGRACE, MY LORD.
HEE HEE!

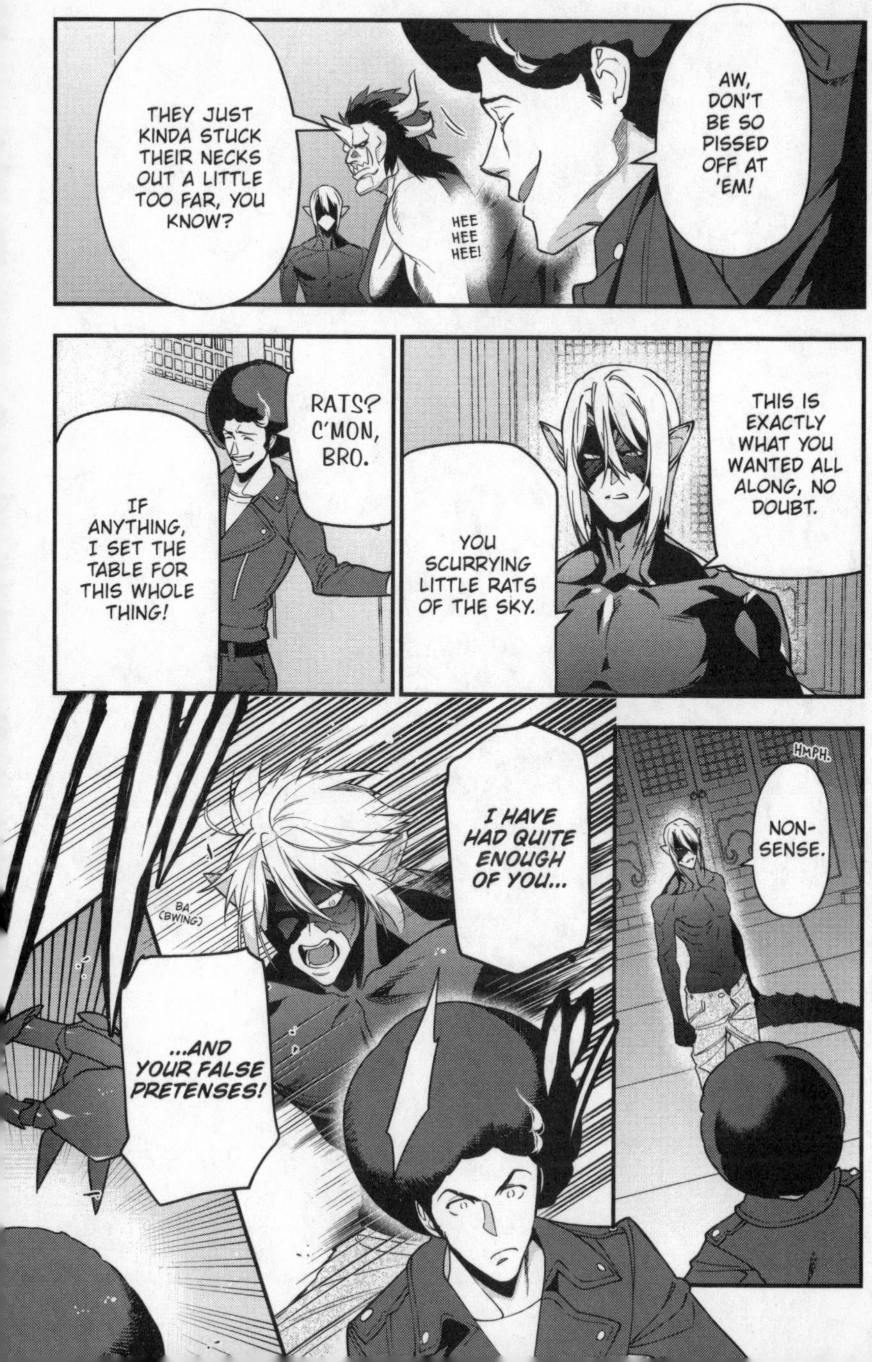
AW, DON'T BE SO PISSED OFF AT 'EM!
HEE HEE HEE!
THEY JUST KINDA STUCK THEIR NECKS OUT A LITTLE TOO FAR, YOU KNOW?
THIS IS EXACTLY WHAT YOU WANTED ALL ALONG, NO DOUBT.
YOU SCURRYING LITTLE RATS OF THE SKY.
RATS? C'MON, BRO.
IF ANYTHING, I SET THE TABLE FOR THIS WHOLE THING!
HMPH.
NON-SENSE.
I HAVE HAD QUITE ENOUGH OF YOU...
BA (BWING)
...AND YOUR FALSE PRETENSES!

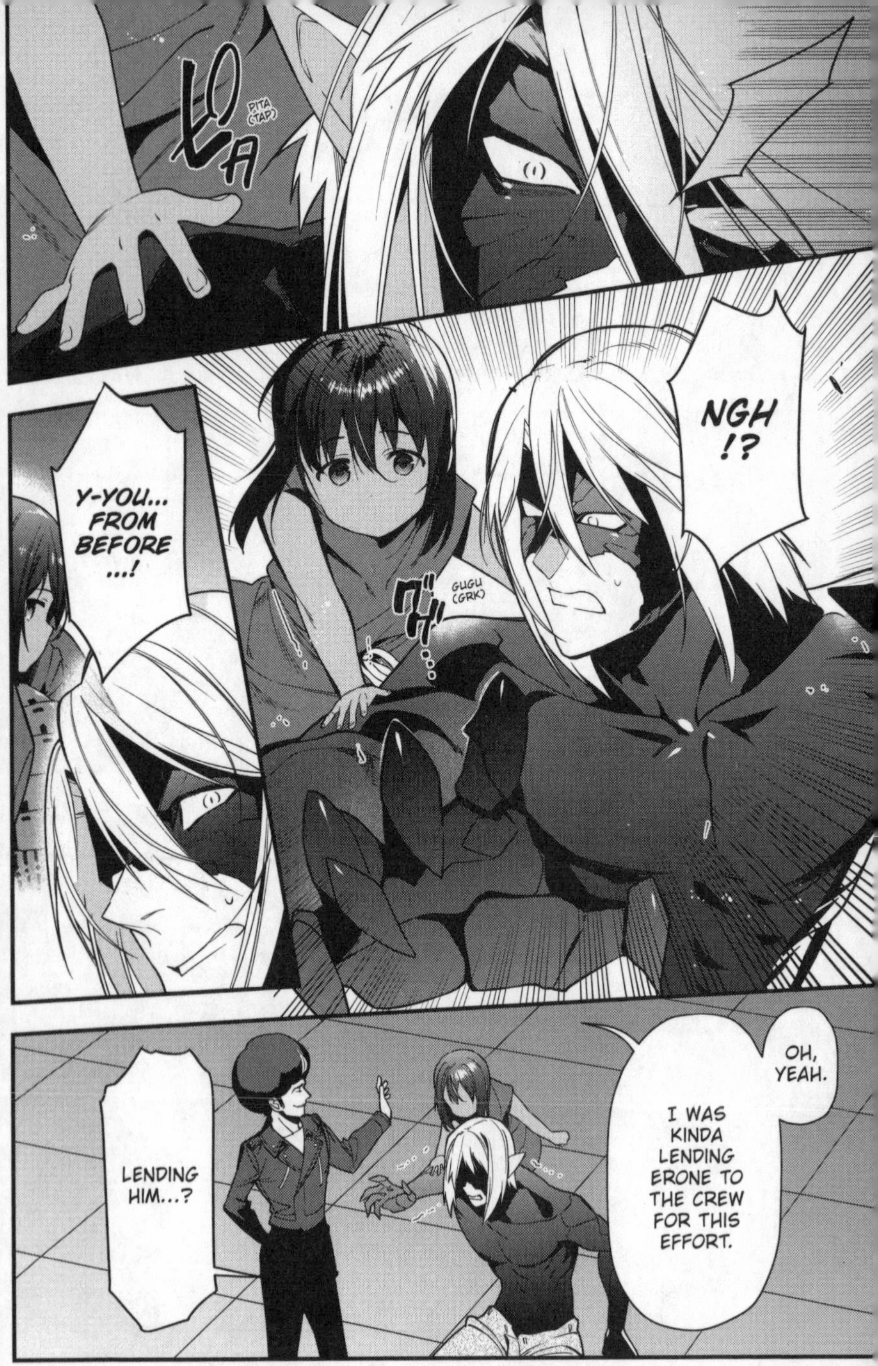
PITA (TAP)
NGH !?
GUGU (GRK)
Y-YOU... FROM BEFORE ...!
OH, YEAH.
I WAS KINDA LENDING ERONE TO THE CREW FOR THIS EFFORT.
LENDING HIM...?

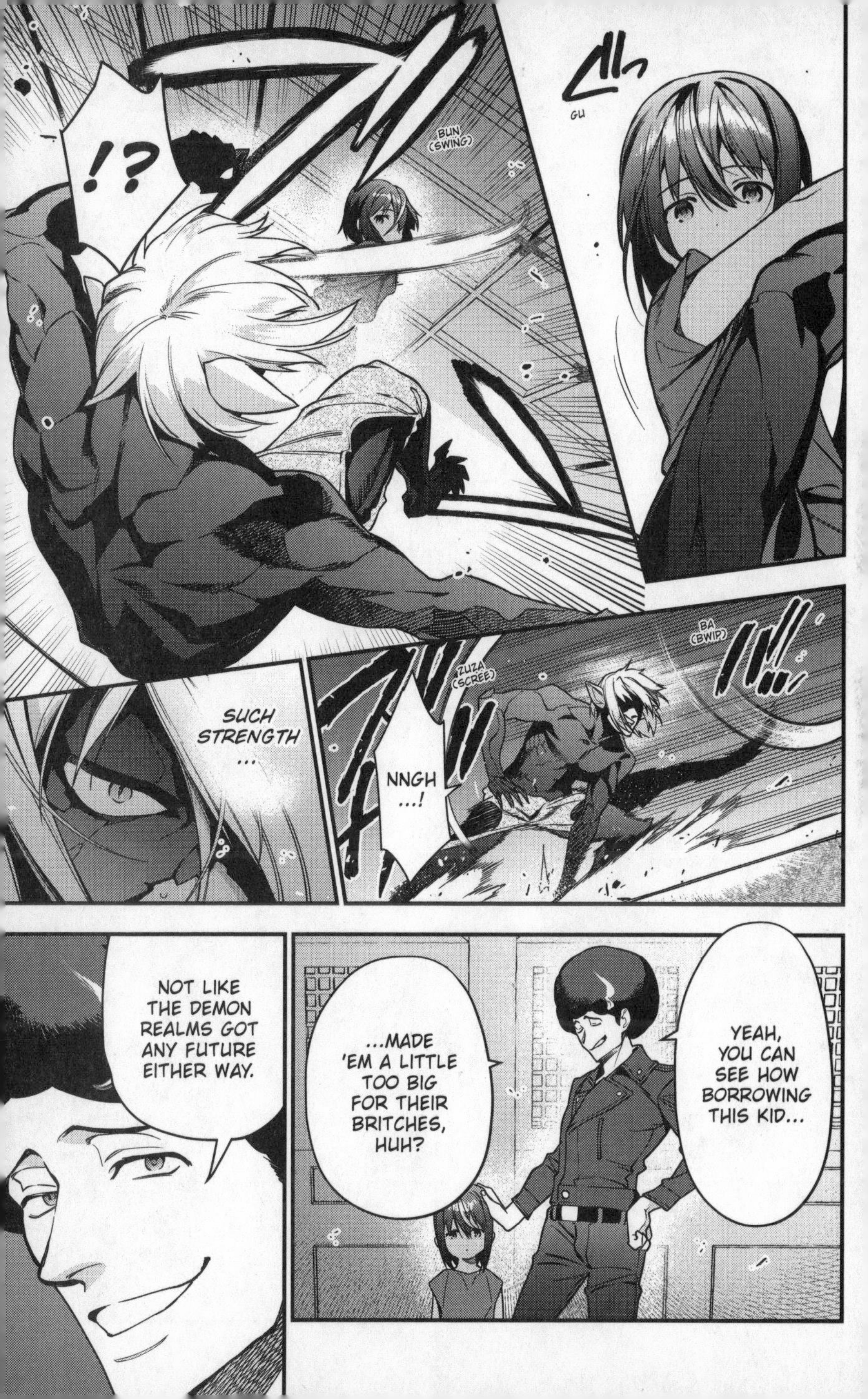
GU
BUN (SWING)
!?
BA (BWIP)
ZUZA (SCREE)
NNGH ...!
SUCH STRENGTH ...
YEAH, YOU CAN SEE HOW BORROWING THIS KID...
...MADE 'EM A LITTLE TOO BIG FOR THEIR BRITCHES, HUH?
NOT LIKE THE DEMON REALMS GOT ANY FUTURE EITHER WAY.

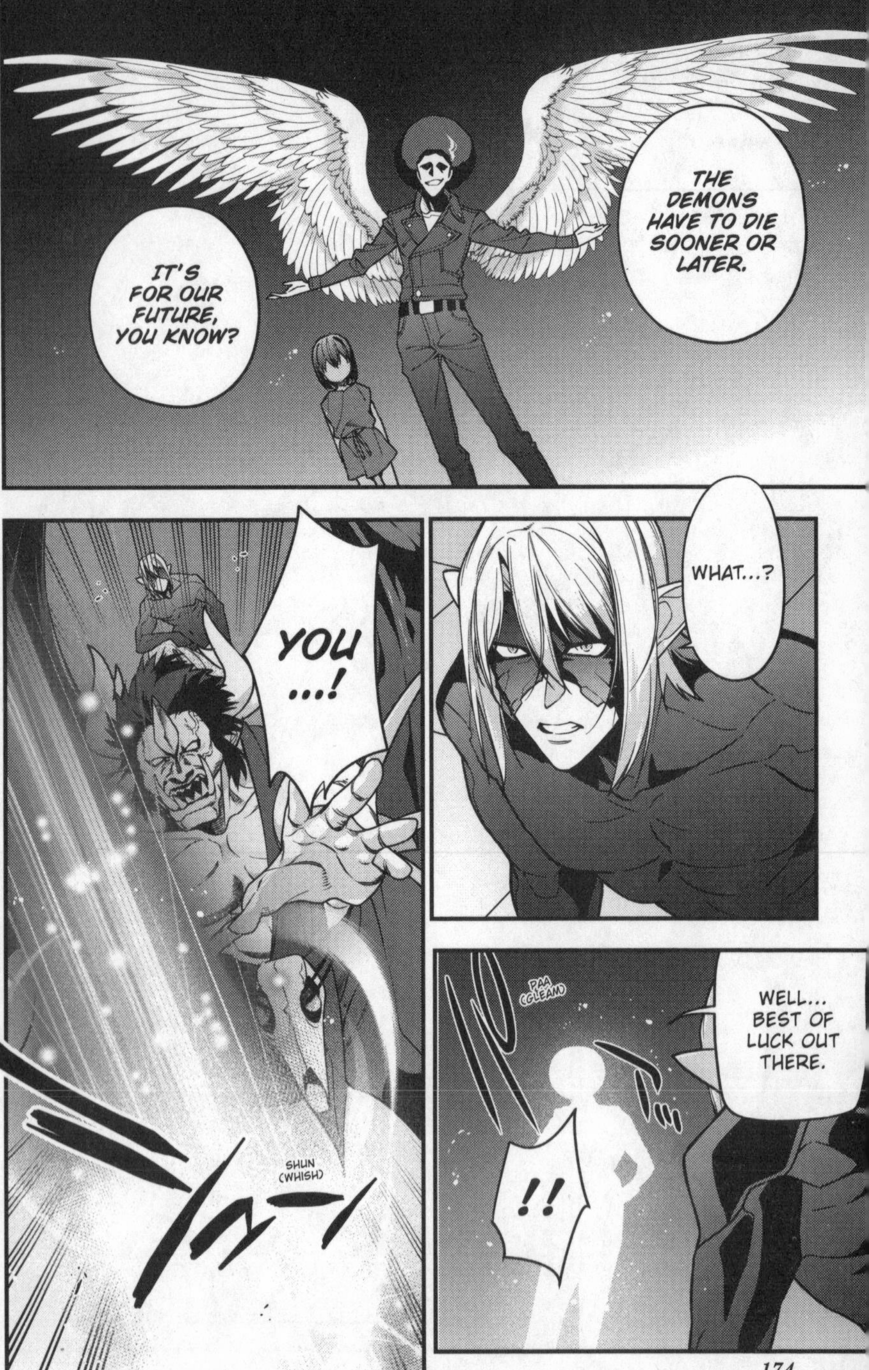
THE DEMONS HAVE TO DIE SOONER OR LATER.
IT'S FOR OUR FUTURE, YOU KNOW?
WHAT...?
WELL... BEST OF LUCK OUT THERE.
PAA (GLEAM)
!!
YOU...!
SHUN (WHISH)

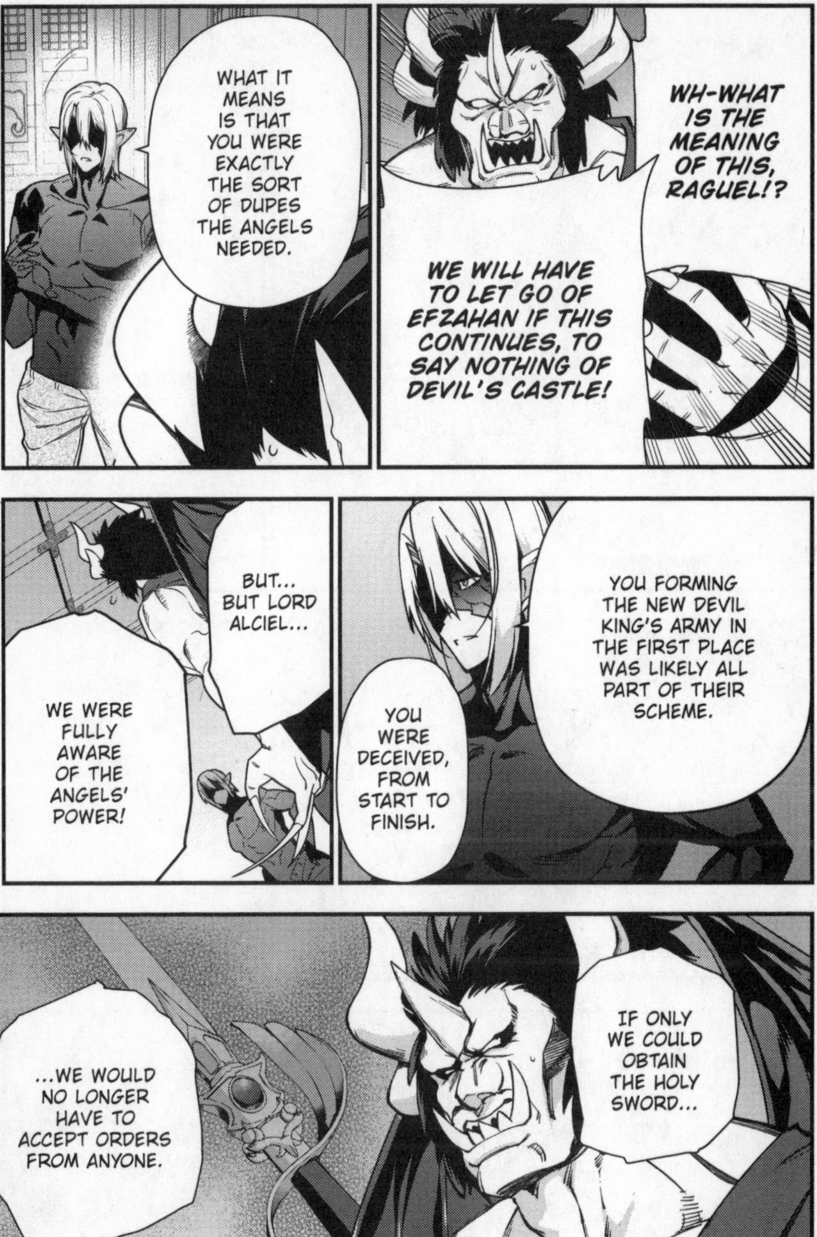
WH-WHAT IS THE MEANING OF THIS, RAGUEL!?
WE WILL HAVE TO LET GO OF EFZAHAN IF THIS CONTINUES, TO SAY NOTHING OF DEVIL'S CASTLE!
WHAT IT MEANS IS THAT YOU WERE EXACTLY THE SORT OF DUPES THE ANGELS NEEDED.
YOU FORMING THE NEW DEVIL KING'S ARMY IN THE FIRST PLACE WAS LIKELY ALL PART OF THEIR SCHEME.
YOU WERE DECEIVED, FROM START TO FINISH.
BUT... BUT LORD ALCIEL...
WE WERE FULLY AWARE OF THE ANGELS' POWER!
IF ONLY WE COULD OBTAIN THE HOLY SWORD...
...WE WOULD NO LONGER HAVE TO ACCEPT ORDERS FROM ANYONE.

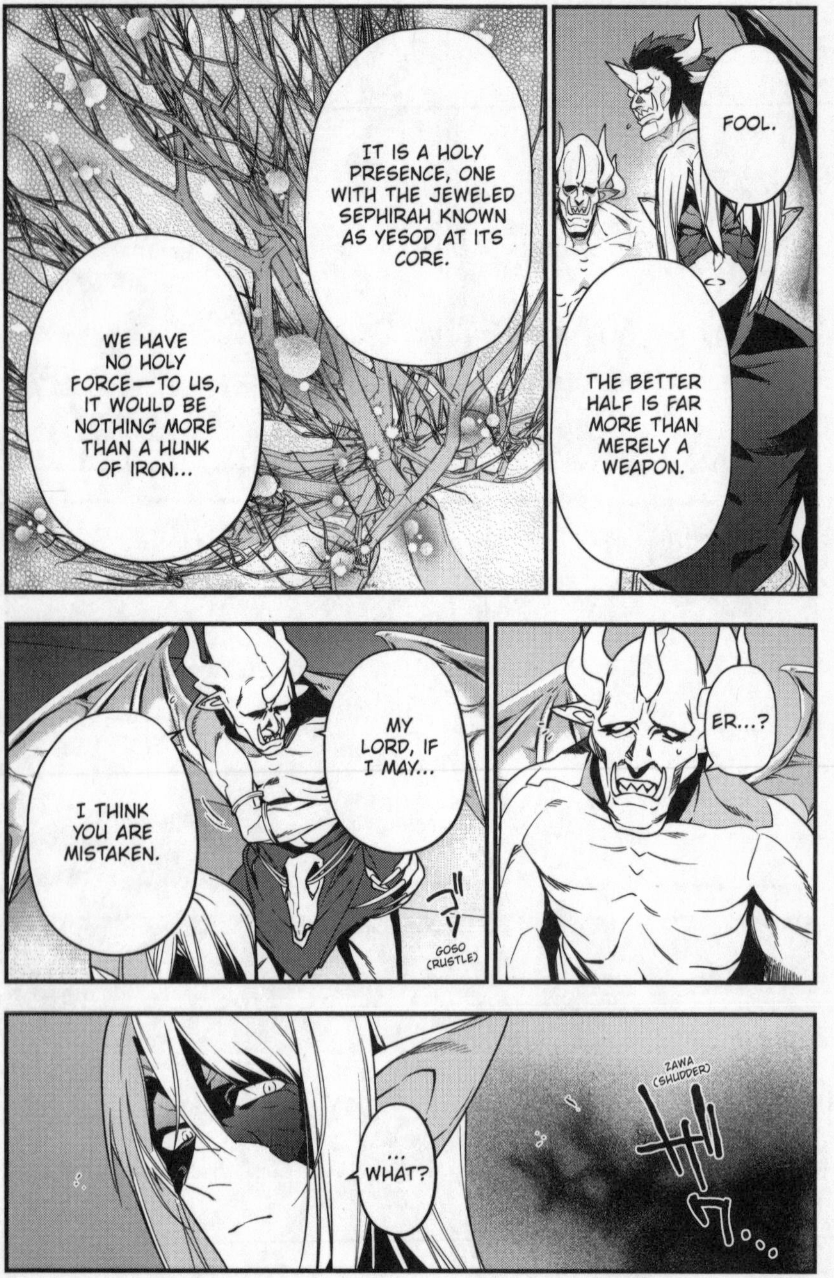
FOOL.
THE BETTER HALF IS FAR MORE THAN MERELY A WEAPON.
IT IS A HOLY PRESENCE, ONE WITH THE JEWELED SEPHIRAH KNOWN AS YESOD AT ITS CORE.
WE HAVE NO HOLY FORCE—TO US, IT WOULD BE NOTHING MORE THAN A HUNK OF IRON...
ER...?
MY LORD, IF I MAY...
I THINK YOU ARE MISTAKEN.
GOSO (RUSTLE)
ZAWA (SHUDDER)
... WHAT?

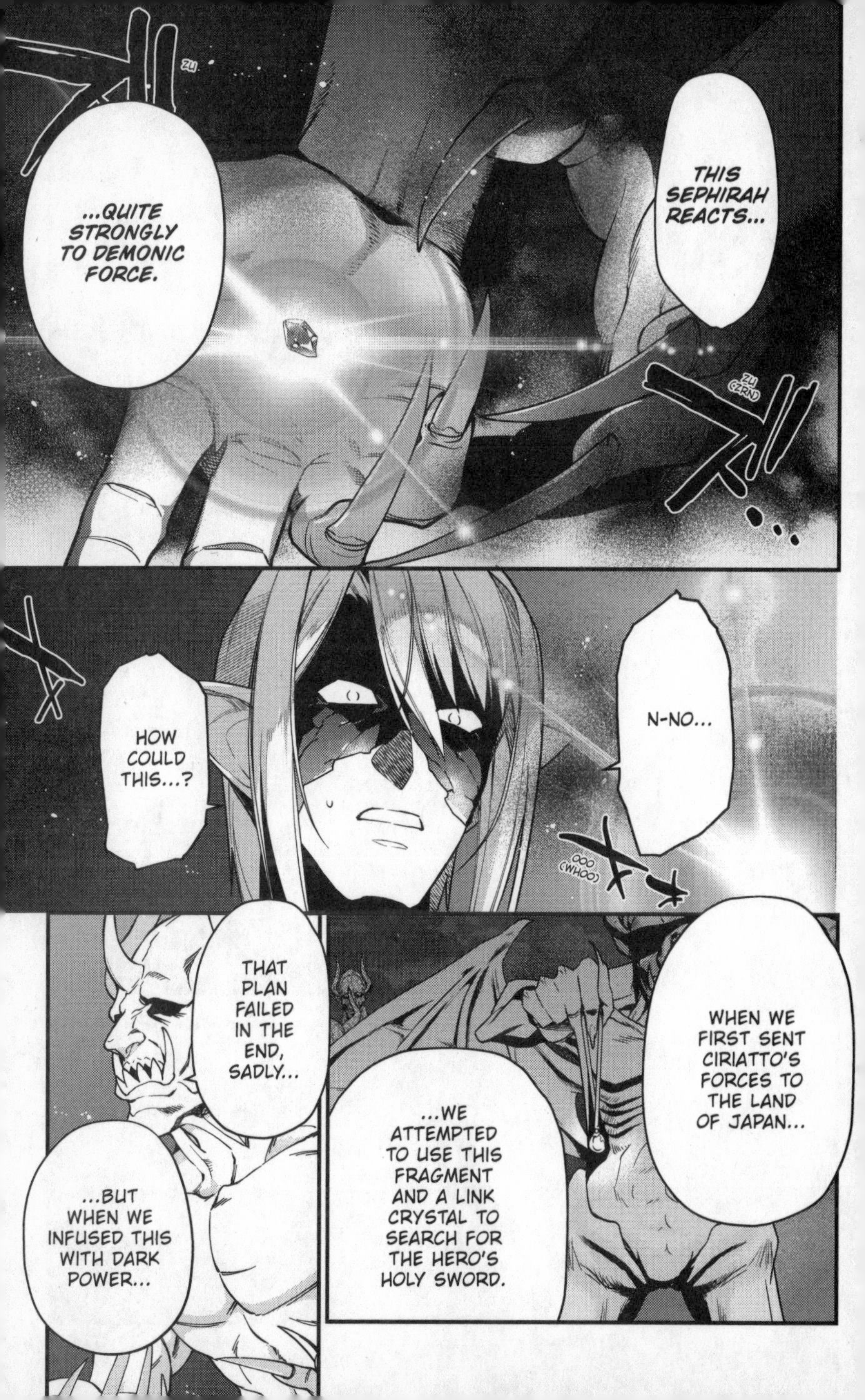
THIS SEPHIRAH REACTS...
ZU (ZRN)
ZU
...QUITE STRONGLY TO DEMONIC FORCE.
N-NO...
OOO (WHOO)
HOW COULD THIS...?
WHEN WE FIRST SENT CIRIATTO'S FORCES TO THE LAND OF JAPAN...
...WE ATTEMPTED TO USE THIS FRAGMENT AND A LINK CRYSTAL TO SEARCH FOR THE HERO'S HOLY SWORD.
THAT PLAN FAILED IN THE END, SADLY...
...BUT WHEN WE INFUSED THIS WITH DARK POWER...

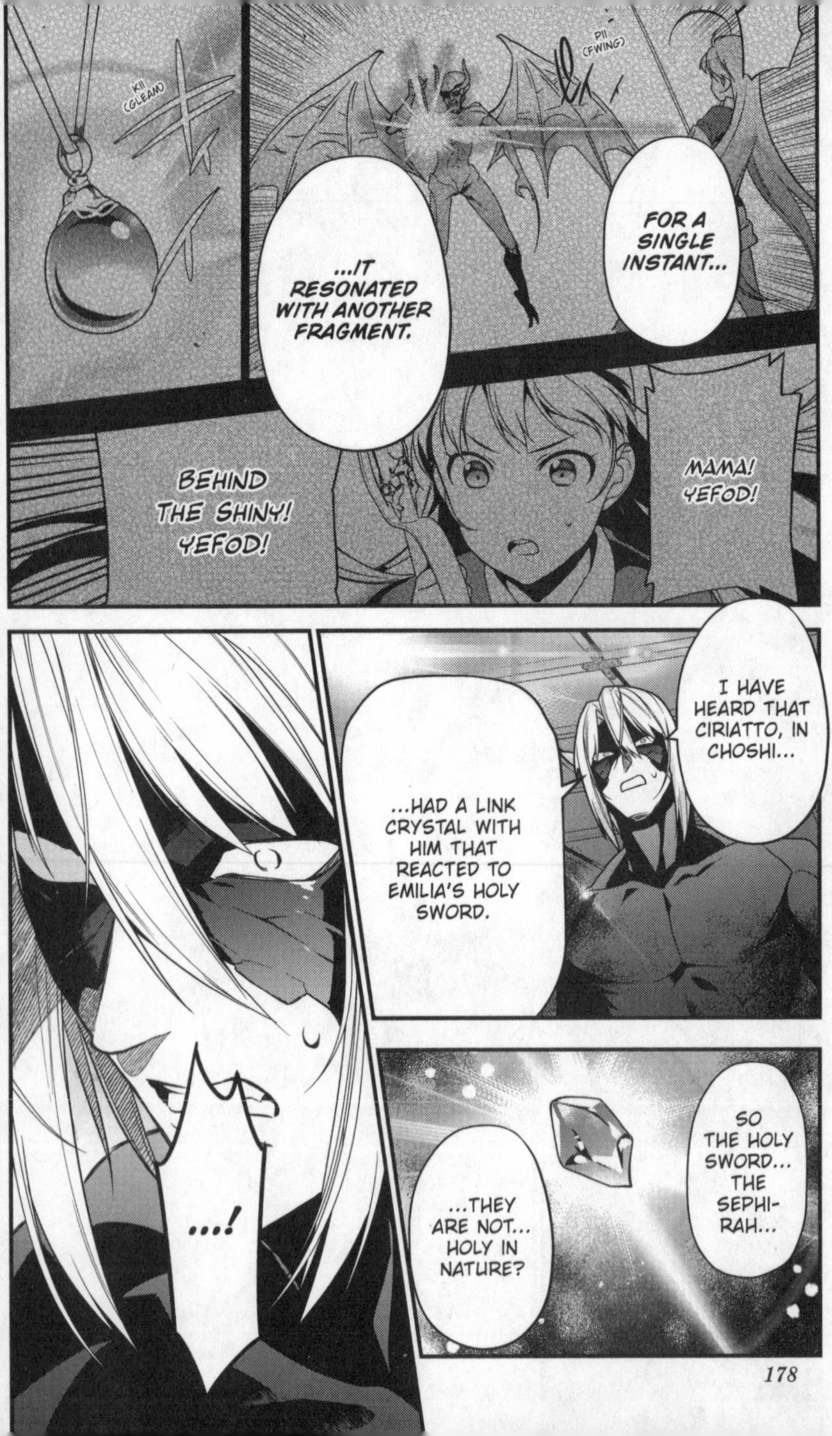
PII (FWING)
FOR A SINGLE INSTANT...
...IT RESONATED WITH ANOTHER FRAGMENT.
KII (GLEAM)
MAMA! YEFOD!
BEHIND THE SHINY! YEFOD!
I HAVE HEARD THAT CIRIATTO, IN CHOSHI...
...HAD A LINK CRYSTAL WITH HIM THAT REACTED TO EMILIA'S HOLY SWORD.
SO THE HOLY SWORD... THE SEPHIRAH...
...THEY ARE NOT... HOLY IN NATURE?
...!

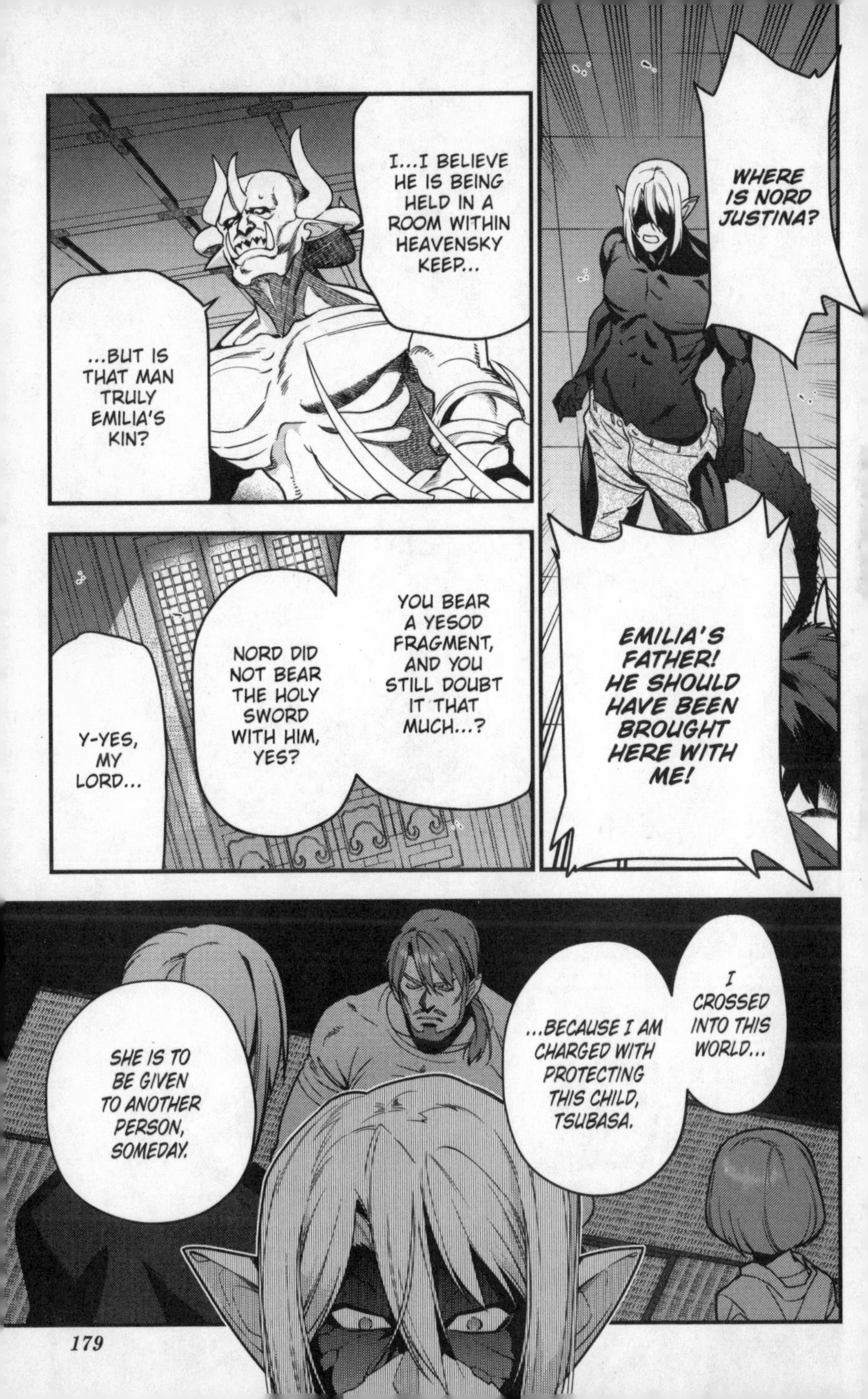
WHERE IS NORD JUSTINA?
EMILIA'S FATHER! HE SHOULD HAVE BEEN BROUGHT HERE WITH ME!
I...I BELIEVE HE IS BEING HELD IN A ROOM WITHIN HEAVENSKY KEEP...
...BUT IS THAT MAN TRULY EMILIA'S KIN?
YOU BEAR A YESOD FRAGMENT, AND YOU STILL DOUBT IT THAT MUCH...?
NORD DID NOT BEAR THE HOLY SWORD WITH HIM, YES?
Y-YES, MY LORD...
I CROSSED INTO THIS WORLD...
...BECAUSE I AM CHARGED WITH PROTECTING THIS CHILD, TSUBASA.
SHE IS TO BE GIVEN TO ANOTHER PERSON, SOMEDAY.

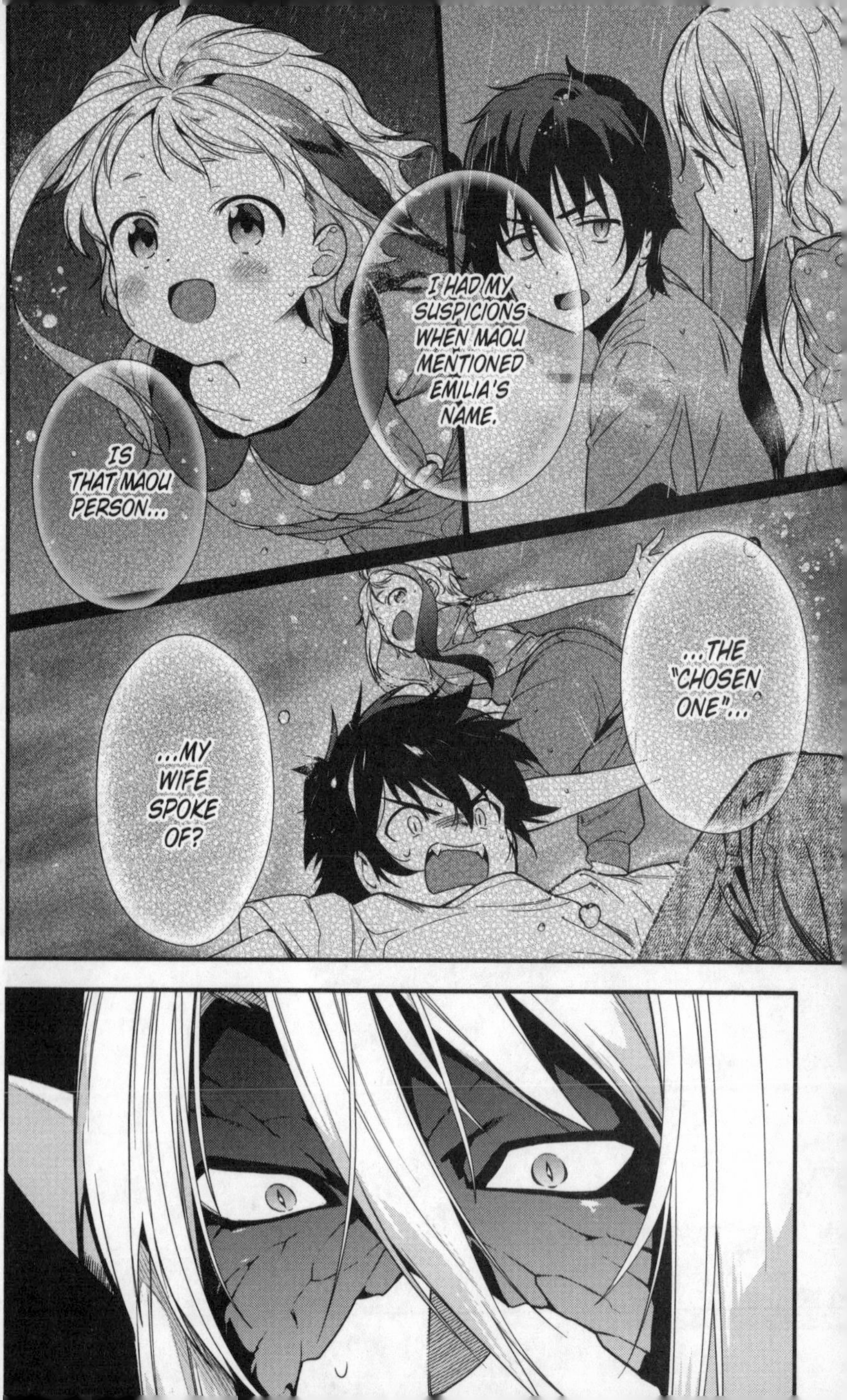
I HAD MY SUSPICIONS WHEN MAOU MENTIONED EMILIA'S NAME.
IS THAT MAOU PERSON...
..."THE "CHOSEN ONE"...
...MY WIFE SPOKE OF?

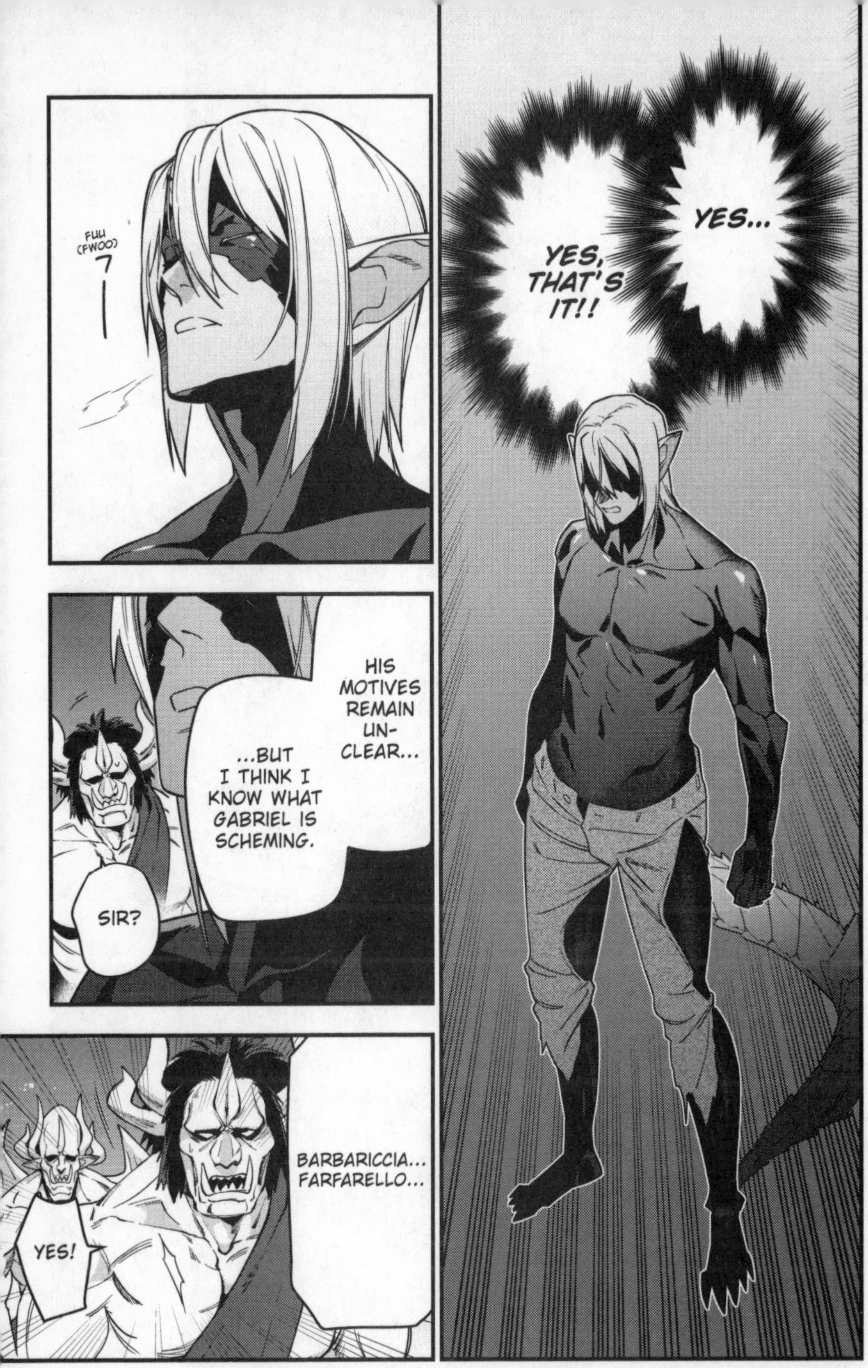
YES...
YES, THAT'S IT!!
FUU (FWOO)
HIS MOTIVES REMAIN UN-CLEAR...
...BUT I THINK I KNOW WHAT GABRIEL IS SCHEMING.
SIR?
BARBARICCIA... FARFARELLO...
YES!

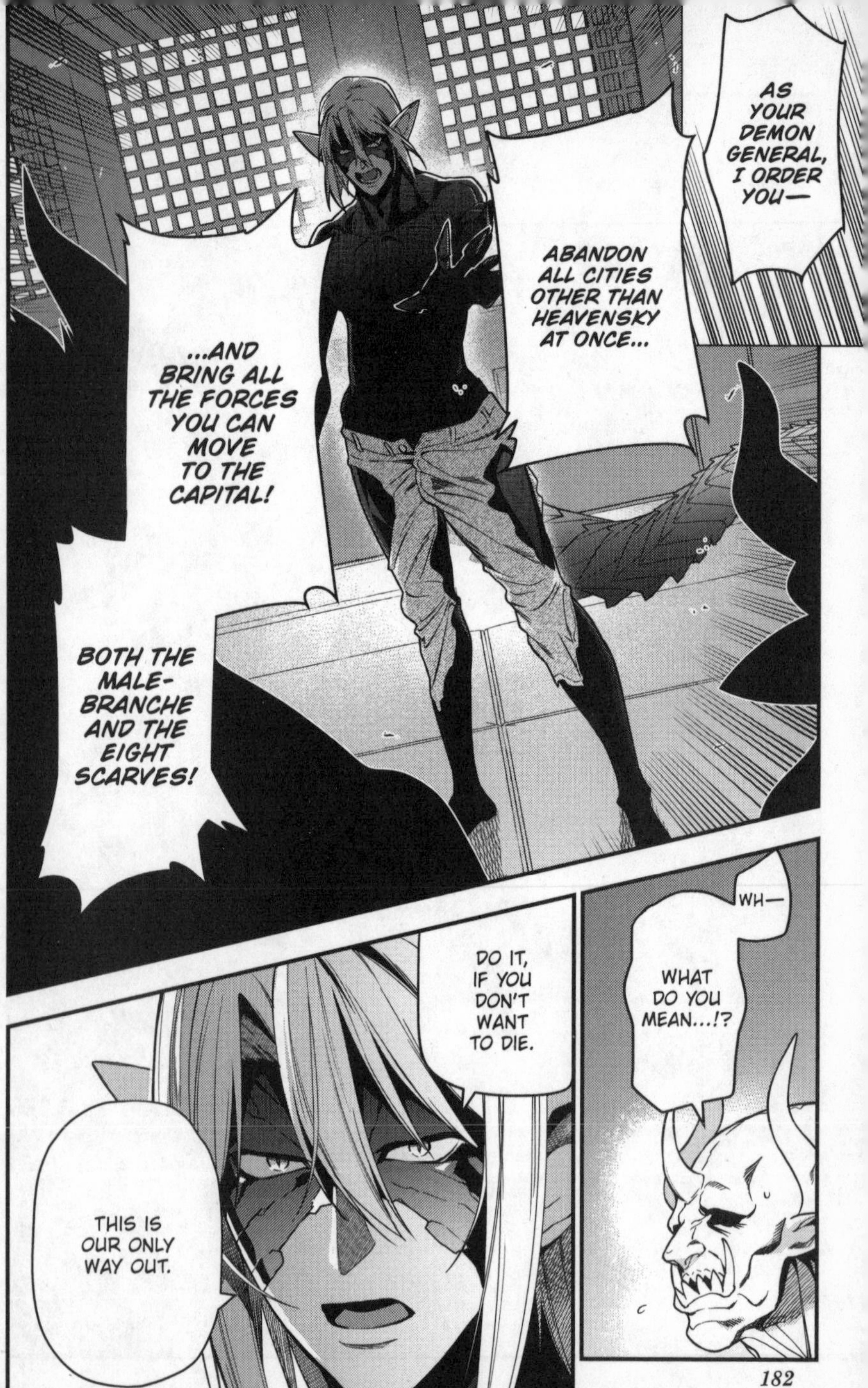
AS YOUR DEMON GENERAL, I ORDER YOU—
ABANDON ALL CITIES OTHER THAN HEAVENSKY AT ONCE...
...AND BRING ALL THE FORCES YOU CAN MOVE TO THE CAPITAL!
BOTH THE MALE-BRANCHE AND THE EIGHT SCARVES!
WH—
WHAT DO YOU MEAN...!?
DO IT, IF YOU DON'T WANT TO DIE.
THIS IS OUR ONLY WAY OUT.

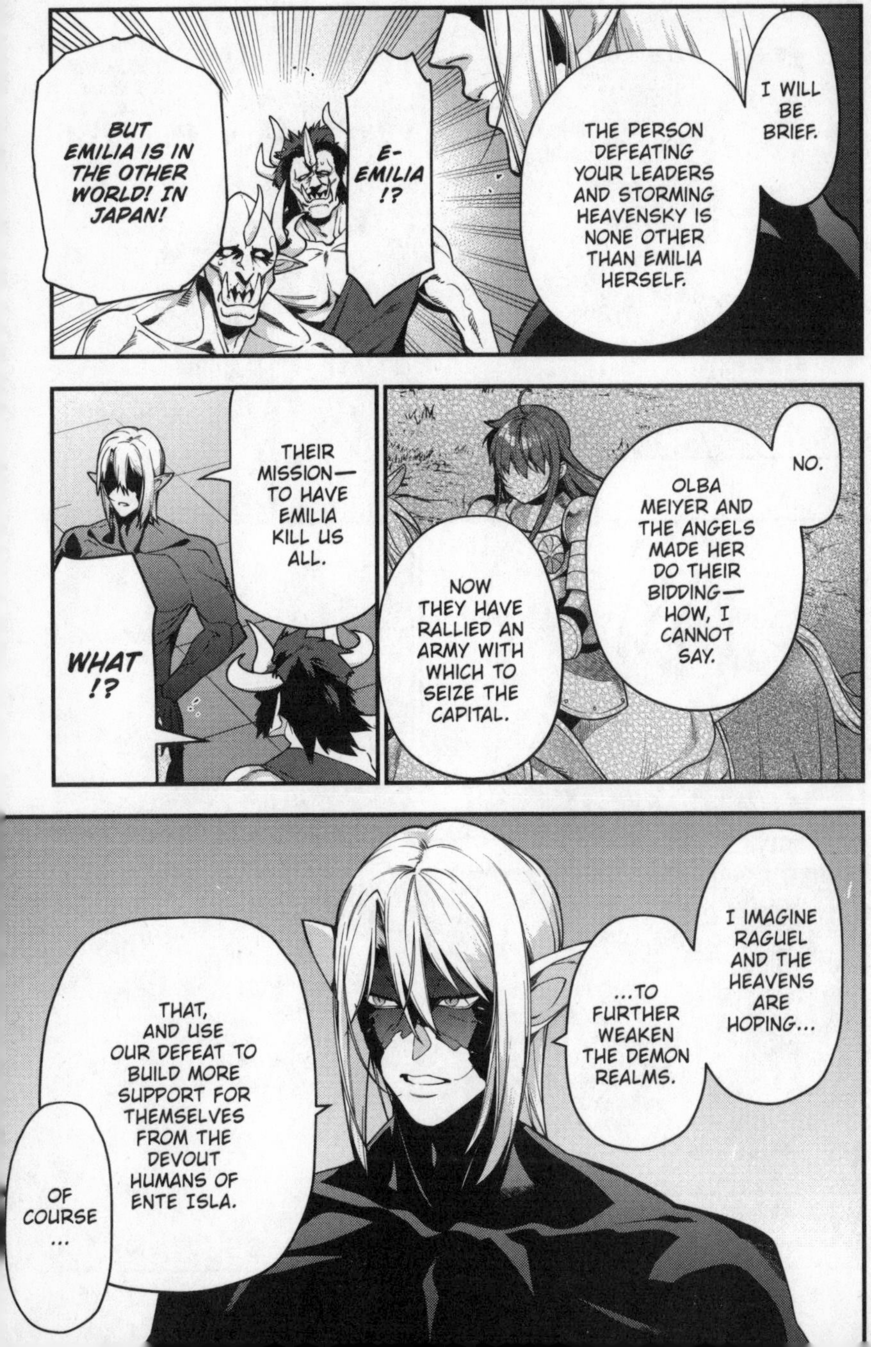
I WILL BE BRIEF.
THE PERSON DEFEATING YOUR LEADERS AND STORMING HEAVENSKY IS NONE OTHER THAN EMILIA HERSELF.
E-EMILIA!?
BUT EMILIA IS IN THE OTHER WORLD! IN JAPAN!
NO.
OLBA MEIYER AND THE ANGELS MADE HER DO THEIR BIDDING—HOW, I CANNOT SAY.
NOW THEY HAVE RALLIED AN ARMY WITH WHICH TO SEIZE THE CAPITAL.
THEIR MISSION—TO HAVE EMILIA KILL US ALL.
WHAT!?
I IMAGINE RAGUEL AND THE HEAVENS ARE HOPING...
...TO FURTHER WEAKEN THE DEMON REALMS.
THAT, AND USE OUR DEFEAT TO BUILD MORE SUPPORT FOR THEMSELVES FROM THE DEVOUT HUMANS OF ENTE ISLA.
OF COURSE...

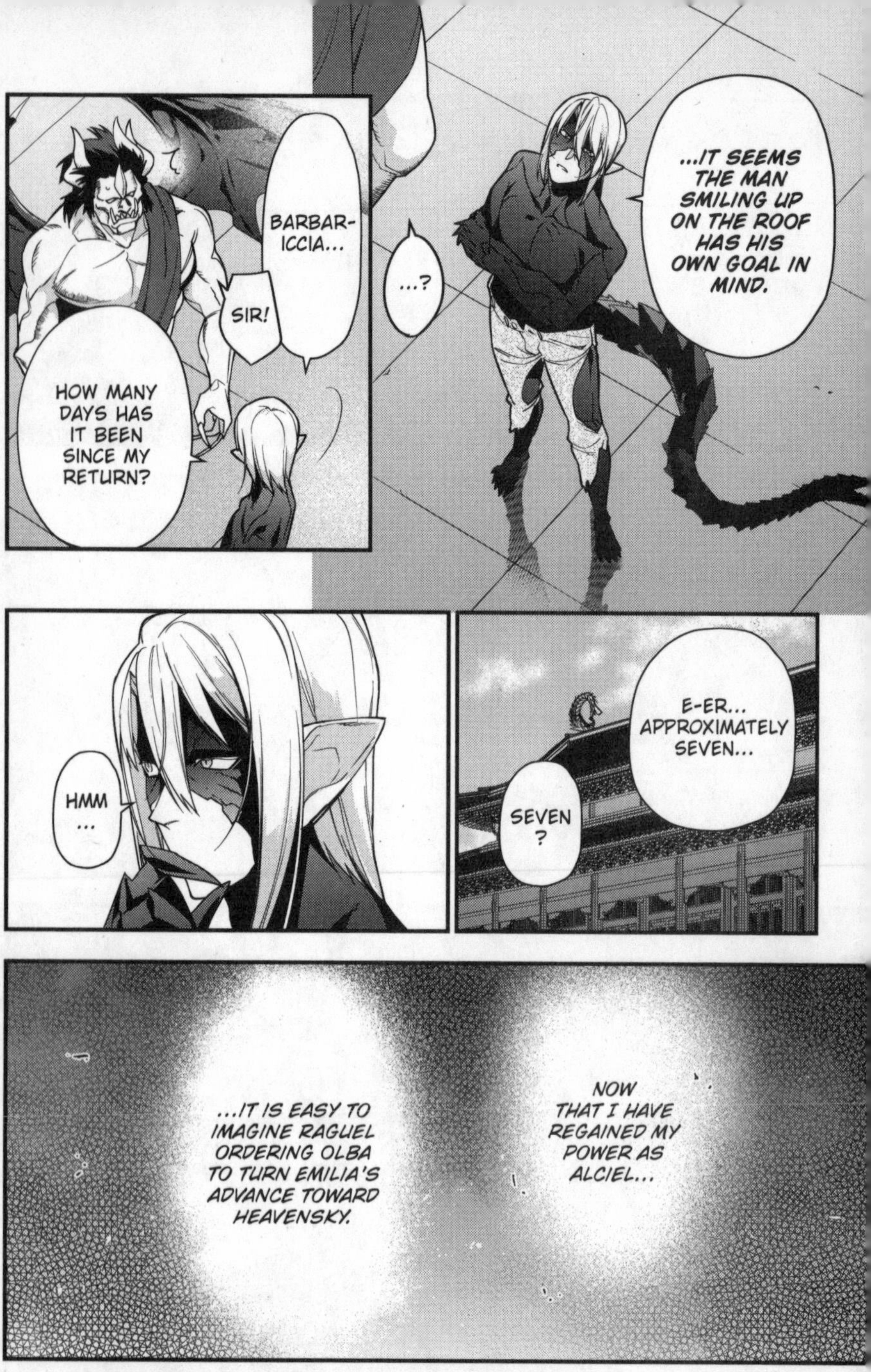
...IT SEEMS THE MAN SMILING UP ON THE ROOF HAS HIS OWN GOAL IN MIND.
...?
BARBAR-ICCIA...
SIR!
HOW MANY DAYS HAS IT BEEN SINCE MY RETURN?
E-ER... APPROXIMATELY SEVEN...
SEVEN ?
HMM ...
NOW THAT I HAVE REGAINED MY POWER AS ALCIEL...
...IT IS EASY TO IMAGINE RAGUEL ORDERING OLBA TO TURN EMILIA'S ADVANCE TOWARD HEAVENSKY.

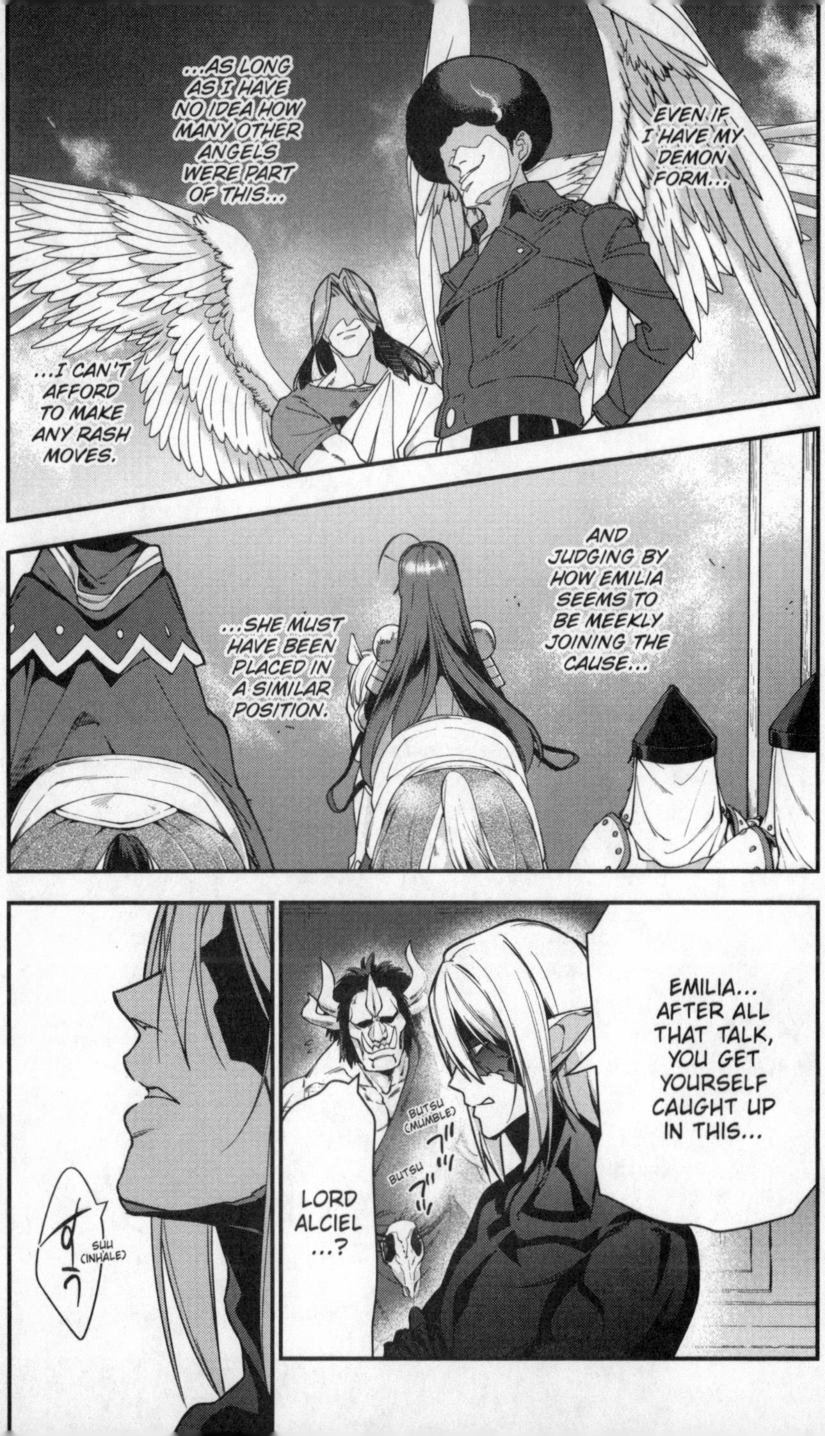
EVEN IF I HAVE MY DEMON FORM...
...AS LONG AS I HAVE NO IDEA HOW MANY OTHER ANGELS WERE PART OF THIS...
...I CAN'T AFFORD TO MAKE ANY RASH MOVES.
AND JUDGING BY HOW EMILIA SEEMS TO BE MEEKLY JOINING THE CAUSE...
...SHE MUST HAVE BEEN PLACED IN A SIMILAR POSITION.
EMILIA... AFTER ALL THAT TALK, YOU GET YOURSELF CAUGHT UP IN THIS...
BUTSU (MUMBLE)
BUTSU
LORD ALCIEL ...?
SUU (INHALE)

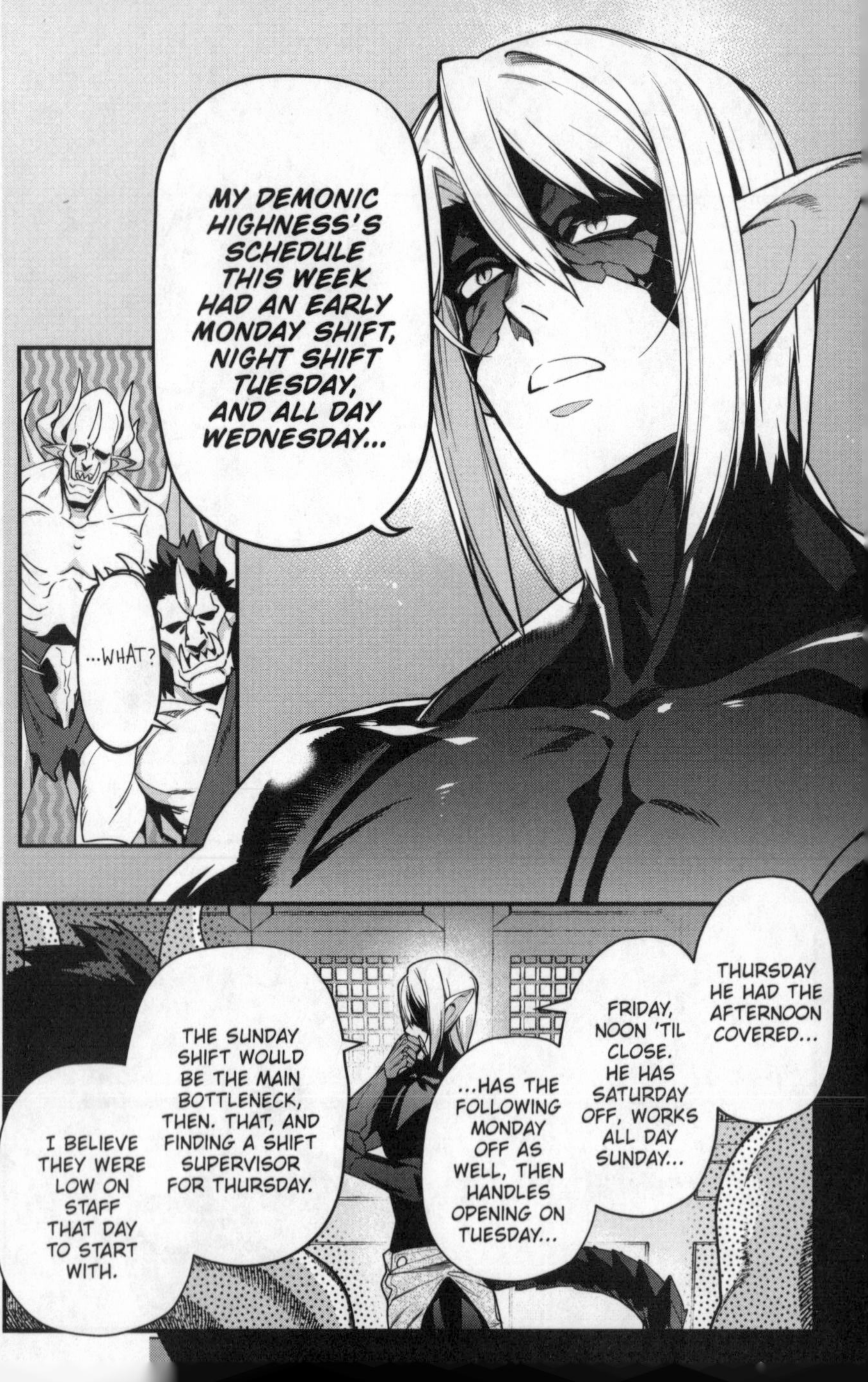
MY DEMONIC HIGHNESS'S SCHEDULE THIS WEEK HAD AN EARLY MONDAY SHIFT, NIGHT SHIFT TUESDAY, AND ALL DAY WEDNESDAY...
...WHAT?
THURSDAY HE HAD THE AFTERNOON COVERED...
FRIDAY, NOON 'TIL CLOSE. HE HAS SATURDAY OFF, WORKS ALL DAY SUNDAY...
...HAS THE FOLLOWING MONDAY OFF AS WELL, THEN HANDLES OPENING ON TUESDAY...
THE SUNDAY SHIFT WOULD BE THE MAIN BOTTLENECK, THEN. THAT, AND FINDING A SHIFT SUPERVISOR FOR THURSDAY.
I BELIEVE THEY WERE LOW ON STAFF THAT DAY TO START WITH.

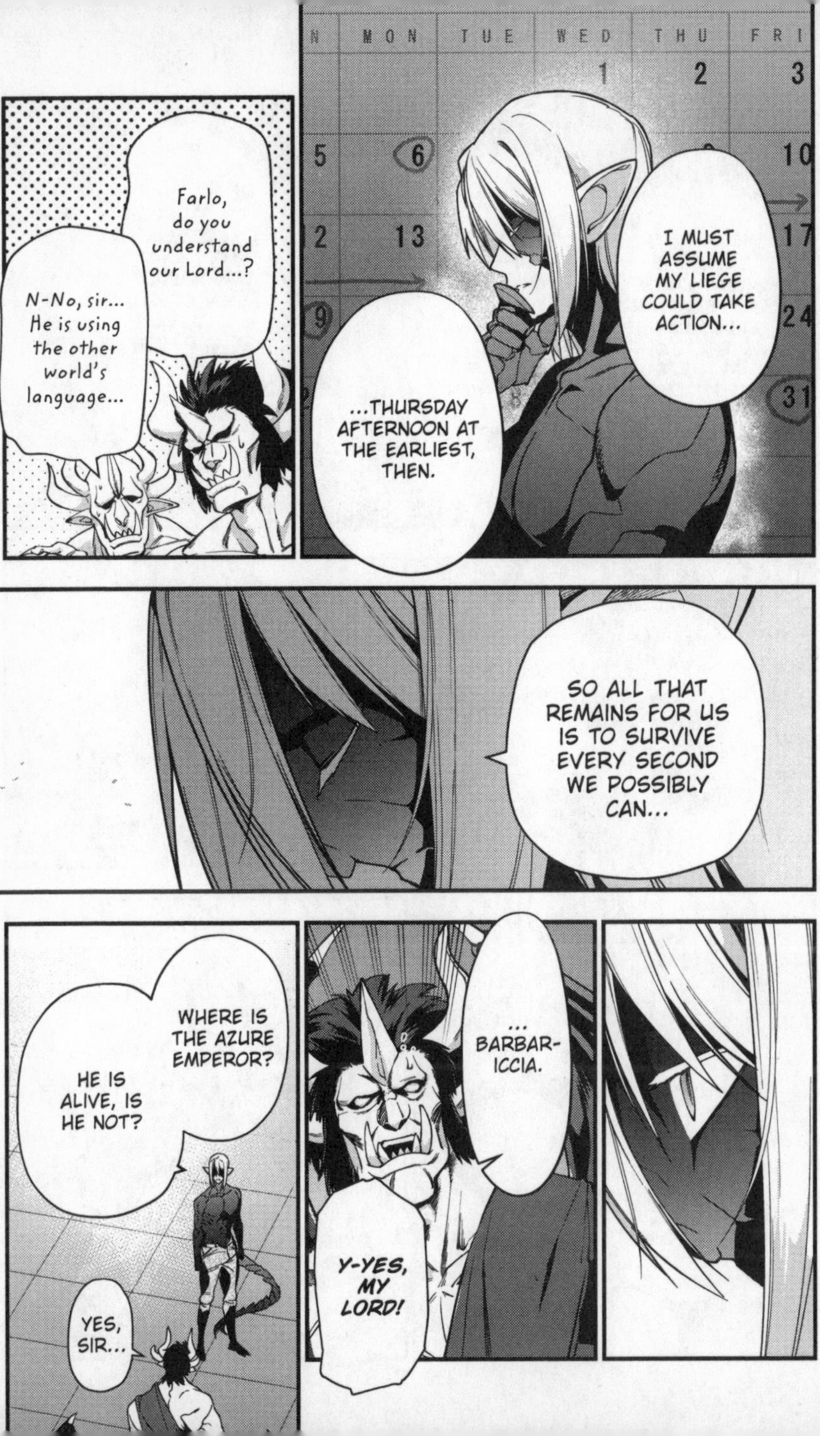
MON TUE WED THU FRI
1 2 3
5 6 10
13 17
9 24
31
I MUST ASSUME MY LIEGE COULD TAKE ACTION...
...THURSDAY AFTERNOON AT THE EARLIEST, THEN.
Farlo, do you understand our Lord...?
N-No, sir... He is using the other world's language...
SO ALL THAT REMAINS FOR US IS TO SURVIVE EVERY SECOND WE POSSIBLY CAN...
... BARBARICCIA.
Y-YES, MY LORD!
WHERE IS THE AZURE EMPEROR?
HE IS ALIVE, IS HE NOT?
YES, SIR...

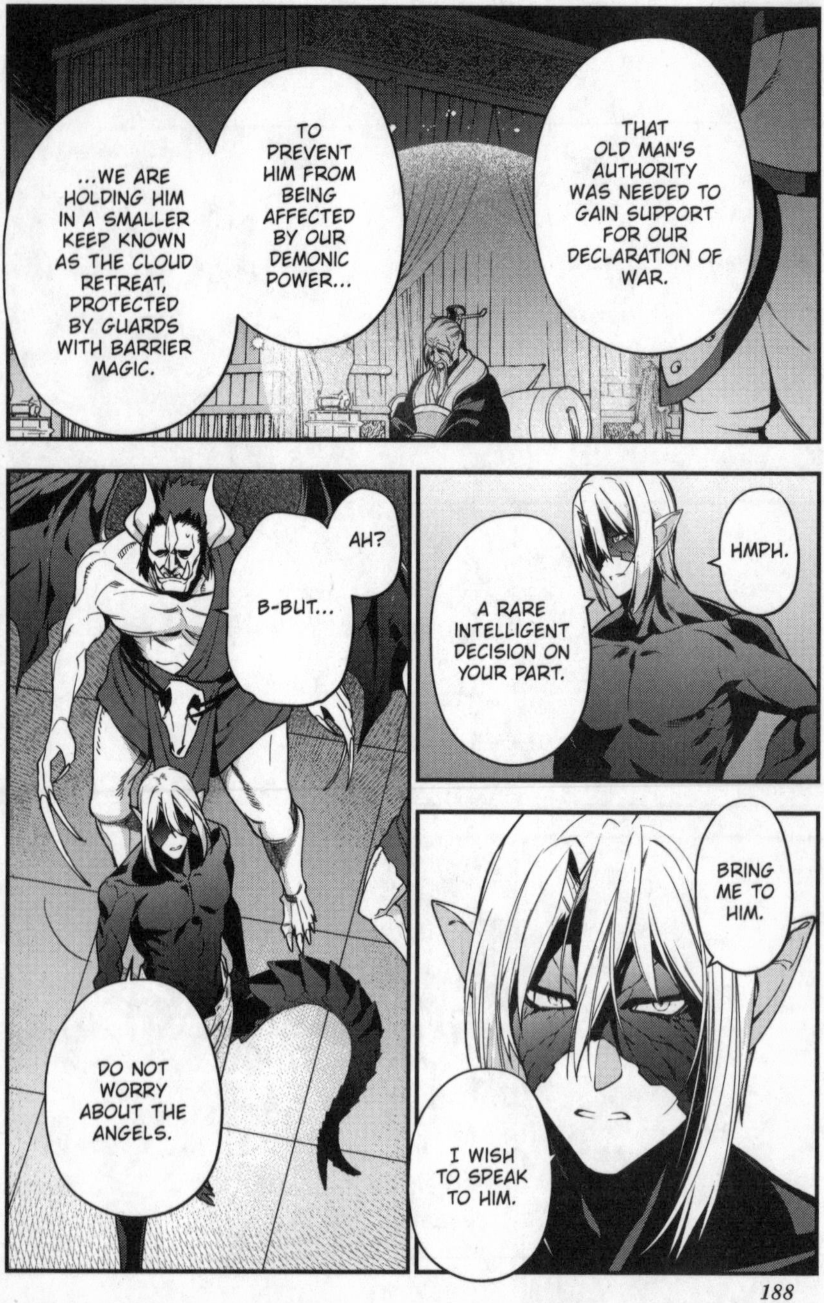
THAT OLD MAN'S AUTHORITY WAS NEEDED TO GAIN SUPPORT FOR OUR DECLARATION OF WAR.
TO PREVENT HIM FROM BEING AFFECTED BY OUR DEMONIC POWER...
...WE ARE HOLDING HIM IN A SMALLER KEEP KNOWN AS THE CLOUD RETREAT, PROTECTED BY GUARDS WITH BARRIER MAGIC.
HMPH.
A RARE INTELLIGENT DECISION ON YOUR PART.
BRING ME TO HIM.
I WISH TO SPEAK TO HIM.
AH?
B-BUT...
DO NOT WORRY ABOUT THE ANGELS.

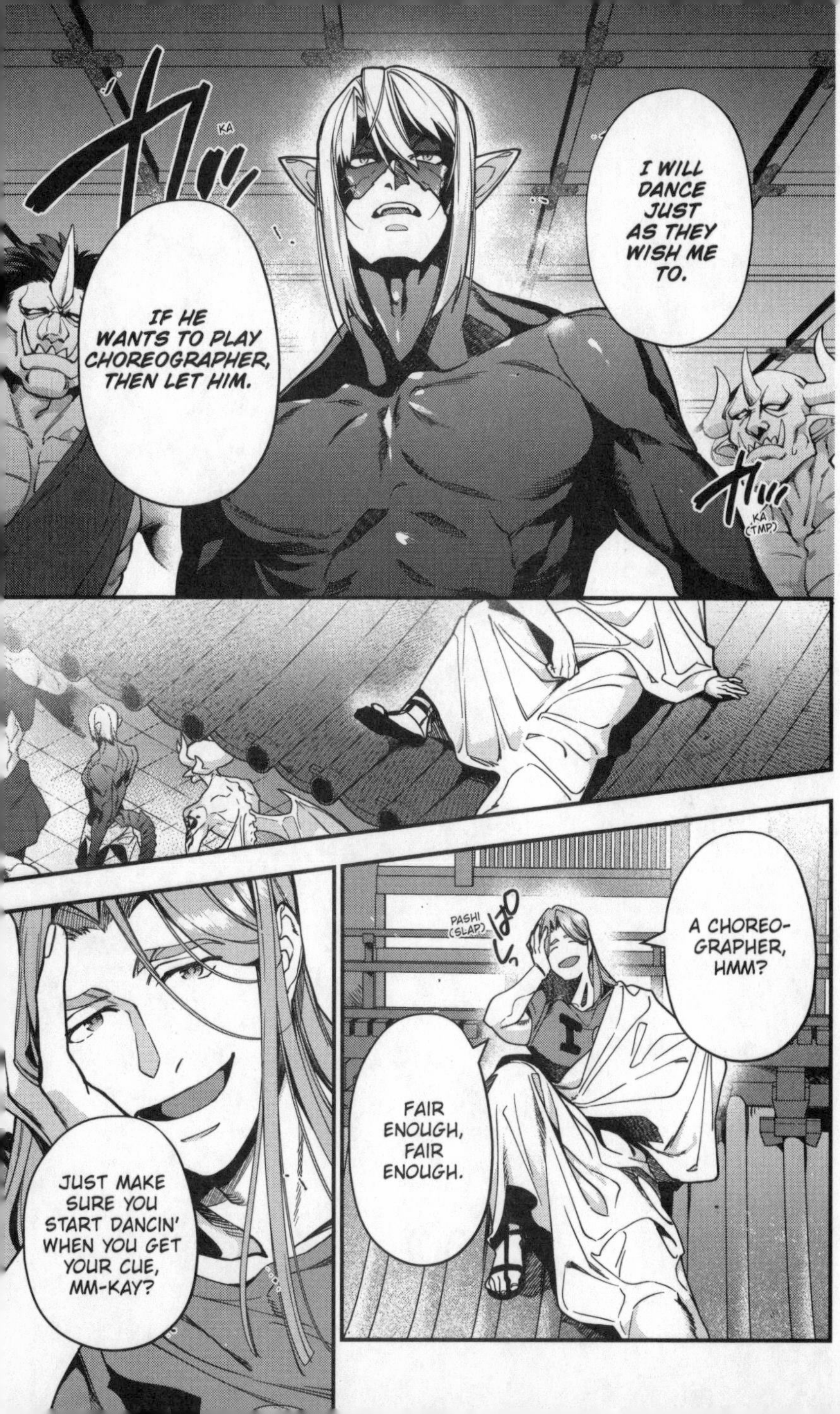
I WILL DANCE JUST AS THEY WISH ME TO.
KA
IF HE WANTS TO PLAY CHOREOGRAPHER, THEN LET HIM.
KA (TMP)
A CHOREO-GRAPHER, HMM?
PASHI (SLAP)
FAIR ENOUGH, FAIR ENOUGH.
JUST MAKE SURE YOU START DANCIN' WHEN YOU GET YOUR CUE, MM-KAY?

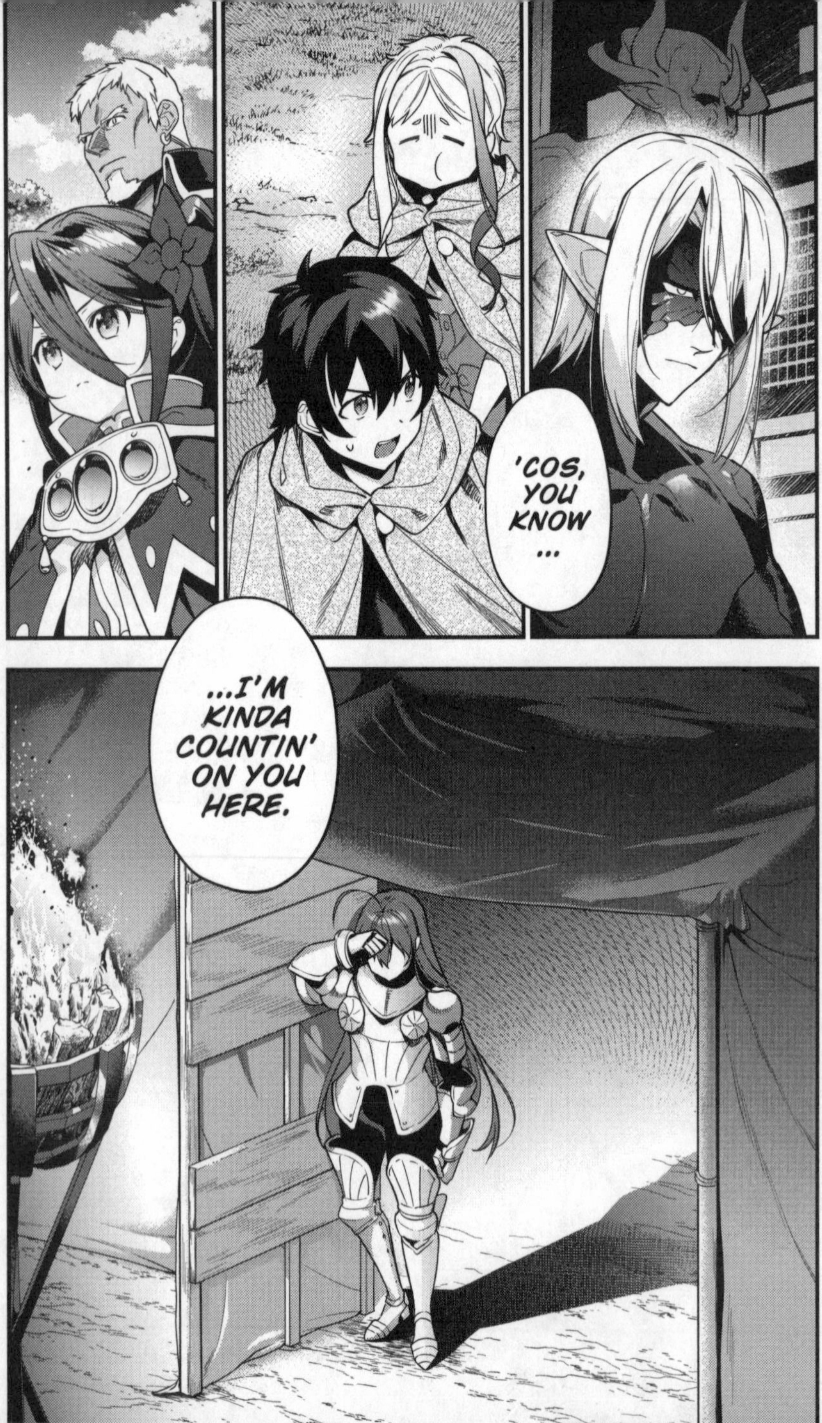
'COS, YOU KNOW ...
...I'M KINDA COUNTIN' ON YOU HERE.

Alciel

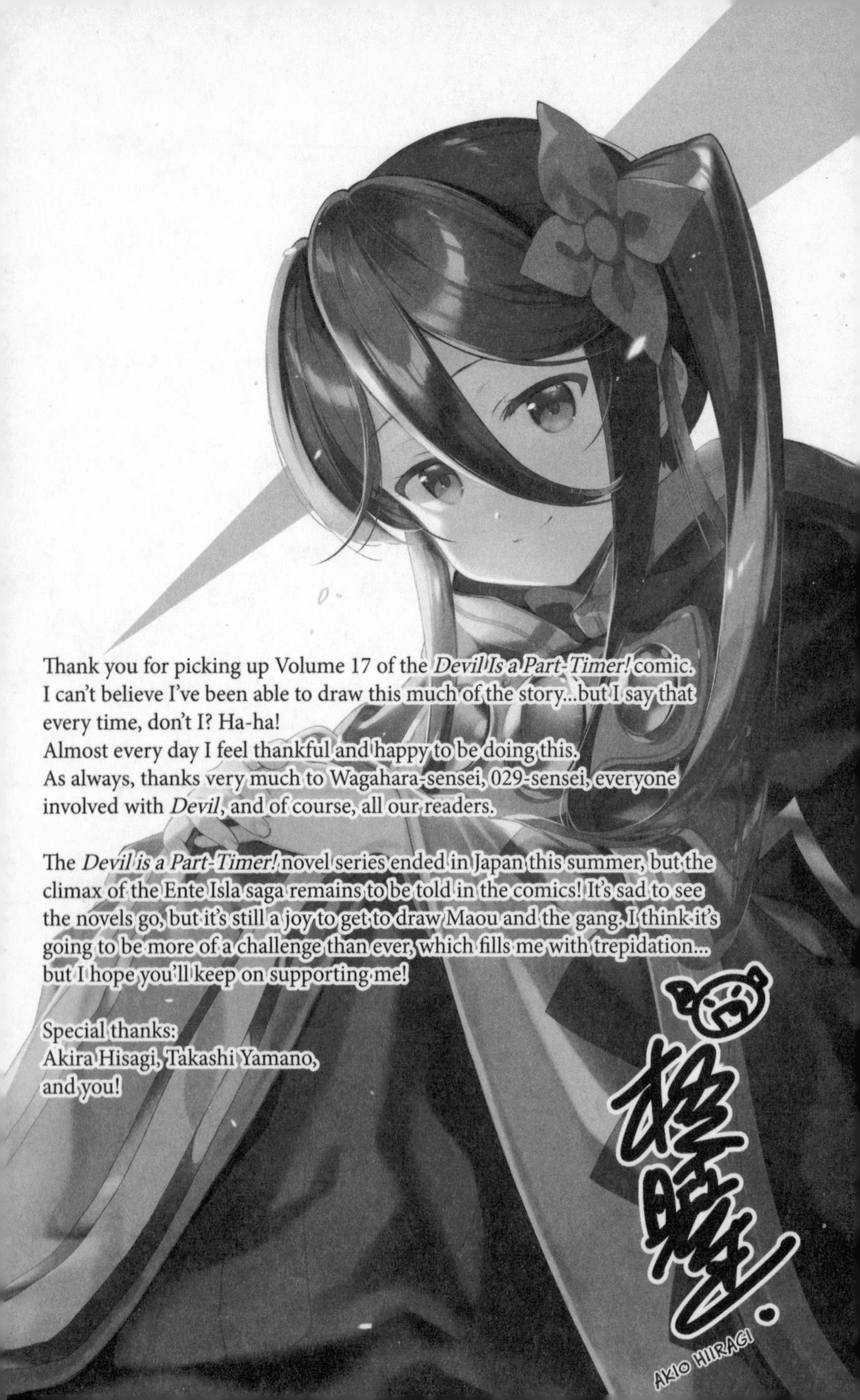
AKIO HIIRAGI

Thank you for picking up Volume 17 of the *Devil Is a Part-Timer!* comic.
I can't believe I've been able to draw this much of the story...but I say that every time, don't I? Ha-ha!
Almost every day I feel thankful and happy to be doing this.
As always, thanks very much to Wagahara-sensei, 029-sensei, everyone involved with *Devil*, and of course, all our readers.

The *Devil is a Part-Timer!* novel series ended in Japan this summer, but the climax of the Ente Isla saga remains to be told in the comics! It's sad to see the novels go, but it's still a joy to get to draw Maou and the gang. I think it's going to be more of a challenge than ever, which fills me with trepidation... but I hope you'll keep on supporting me!

Special thanks:
Akira Hisagi, Takashi Yamano,
and you!

The world of the Devil King isn't over with yet!
Have fun enjoying his wanderings through Ente Isla via
Hiiragi-san's dynamic art!

Satoshi

SATOSHI WAGAHARA

This is my first comment for the manga
in a while, but first off, congratulations on
Volume 17! Seeing the series make it this
far in comic form truly makes me happy
on an emotional level. Thanks to Hiiragi-
san's hard work, you'll continue to see
the Devil King and his cohorts cavorting
around, and I look forward to it as much
as you.

ONIKU

THE DEVIL IS A PART-TIMER! ⑰

ART: AKIO HIIRAGI
ORIGINAL STORY: SATOSHI WAGAHARA
CHARACTER DESIGN: 029 (ONIKU)

Translation: Kevin Gifford

Lettering: Brandon Bovia

HATARAKU MAOUSAMA! Vol. 17

First published in Japan in 2020 by KADOKAWA CORPORATION, Tokyo.
English translation rights arranged with KADOKAWA CORPORATION, Tokyo, through Tuttle-Mori Agency, Inc., Tokyo.

Yen Press
150 West 30th Street, 19th Floor
New York, NY 10001

Visit us at yenpress.com
facebook.com/yenpress
twitter.com/yenpress
yenpress.tumblr.com
instagram.com/yenpress

First Yen Press Edition: November 2021

Yen Press is an imprint of Yen Press, LLC.
The Yen Press name and logo are trademarks of Yen Press, LLC.

The publisher is not responsible for websites (or their content) that are not owned by the publisher.

Library of Congress Control Number: 2014504637

ISBNs: 978-1-9753-3607-3 (paperback)
978-1-9753-3608-0 (ebook)

10 9 8 7 6 5 4 3 2 1

WOR

Printed in the United States of America